W9-CEU-121

Butler Area Public Library
218 North McKean Street
Butler PA 16001

ALSO BY TY BURR

The Best Old Movies for Families

GODS LIKE US

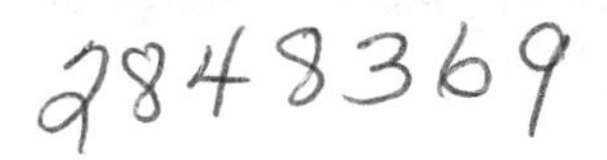

GODS LIKE US

On Movie Stardom and Modern Fame

Ty Burr

306.48
BUR

PANTHEON BOOKS, New York

Copyright © 2012 by Ty Burr

All rights reserved. Published in the United States by Pantheon Books, a division of Random House, Inc., New York, and in Canada by Random House of Canada Limited, Toronto.

Pantheon Books and colophon are registered trademarks of Random House, Inc.

Library of Congress Cataloging-in-Publication Data
Burr, Ty.
Gods like us : on movie stardom and modern fame / Ty Burr.
p. cm.
Includes bibliographical references and index.
ISBN 978-0-307-37766-1 (hardback)
1. Celebrities in mass media—History—20th century. 2. Celebrities in mass media—History—21st century. 3. Fame—Social aspects—United States—History—20th century. 4. Fame—Social aspects—United States—History—21st century. 5. Popular culture—United States—History—20th century. 6. Popular culture—United States—History—21st century. I. Title.
P96.C35B85 2012 306.4'8—dc23 2012000618

www.pantheonbooks.com

All photographs are courtesy of the Kobal Collection/Art Resource, New York.

Jacket photograph of Marlon Brando by John Kobal Foundation/Getty Images
Jacket design by Emily Mahon

Printed in the United States of America

First Edition

2 4 6 8 9 7 5 3 1

For Lori

"It's all—nothing! It's all a joke. It can all be explained, I tell you.
It's all—nothing."

—**CHARLIE CHAPLIN,** under assault from a mob of fans
outside the Cirque Medrano, Paris, 1925

Contents

Introduction: **The Faces in the Mirror**

What are the stars really like?

That question is not the subject of this book. The subject of this book is why we ask the question in the first place.

Still, people want to know. In my day job, I'm a professional film critic for a major metropolitan daily newspaper and throughout the 1990s I wrote reviews and articles for a national weekly entertainment magazine. Over the years, I've interviewed a number of actors and directors, ingénues and legends, and often the first question I'm asked by people is just that: What are they *really* like?

The answers always disappoint. Always. They range from "Pretty much what you see on the screen" to "Not all that interesting sometimes" to "Pleasantly professional" to an unspoken "Why do you care?" When pressed (and I'm usually pressed), I'll allow that Keira Knightley and I had a lovely chat once and Lauren Bacall was nastier than she needed to be to a young reporter just starting out. That Laura Linney seemed graciously guarded, Steve Carell centered and sincere,

Kevin Spacey cagey and smart. I once took the young Elijah Wood to a Hollywood burger joint while interviewing him for the magazine. He was a kid who really liked that burger, no more and no less.

They are, in short, working actors, life-sized and fallible. There is no mystery here. But this is not what you want to hear, is it? If there's nothing genuinely special about movie stars, why do we give them our money? Why do we pay for cheaper and cheaper substitutes—reality stars, hotel heiresses, the Kardashians? Are we interested in the actual person behind the star facade, or just desperate to believe the magic has a basis in reality?

In truth, the relationship between persona and person can be problematic. Of all the celebrity encounters I've experienced, the one that sticks with me is the briefest, most random, possibly the saddest. Early one morning, many years ago, I came out of my apartment building on the Upper West Side of Manhattan and got ready to go for a run. As I breathed the spring air, the door to the adjoining building opened and another jogger emerged. We started stretching our hamstrings side by side, and I glanced over and acknowledged the other man with a friendly nod.

Three almost invisible things happened in rapid succession. First, he nodded back with a pleasant smile. Second, I realized that he was Robin Williams. Third, *he* realized that I realized he was Robin Williams, and his eyes went dead. Not just dead: empty. It was as if the storefront to his face had been shuttered, cutting off any possibility of interaction. There wasn't anything rude about this, and I respected his privacy, honoring the code observed by all New Yorkers who know they can potentially cross paths with an A-list name at any corner deli. Or was it his celebrity I was respecting? Whichever, a very small moment of human connection between two people had been squelched by the appearance of a third, not-quite-real person: the movie star. The second I recognized who the other jogger was, his persona got in the way. I couldn't *not* see him as "Robin Williams." And he knew it.

This happens dozens of times in any well-known person's day. It's why Williams's eyes shut down so completely; it's why I left him alone and went for my run. I felt bad for the man, even if I hadn't actually done anything. Because people do, in fact, do things. Think of all those fans who meet movie stars and insist on being photographed with them, the snapshot serving as both proof and relic. Think, too, of the man who shot and killed John Lennon but made sure to get his autograph first.

Why a history of movie stardom? To celebrate, interrogate, and marvel over where we've been, and to weigh where we are now. As the twenty-first century settles into its second decade, we are more than ever a culture that worships images and shrinks from realities. Once those images were graven; now they are projected, broadcast, podcast, blogged, and streamed. There is not a public space that doesn't have a screen to distract us from our lives, nor is there a corner of our private existence that doesn't offer an interface, wireless or not, with the Omniverse, that roiling sea of infotainment we jack into from multiple access points a hundred times a day. The Omniverse isn't real, but it's never turned off. You can't touch it, but you can't escape from it. And its most common unit of exchange, the thing that attracts so many people in the hopes of becoming it, is celebrity. Famous people. Stars.

Or what we've traditionally called stars, which traditionally arose from a place called the movies. As originally conceived during the heyday of the Hollywood studio system, movie stars were bigger and more beautiful than they are now, domestic gods who looked like us but with our imperfections removed (or, in some cases, gorgeously heightened). Our feelings about them were mixed. We wanted to be these people, and we were jealous of them too. We paid to see them in the stories the movie factories packaged for us, but we were just as fascinated—more fascinated, really—with the stories we believed happened offscreen, to the people the stars seemed to be.

Not many of us remember those days. Moreover, few are interested in connecting the dots between what we want from movie stars now and what we wanted from them then—and the "then" before that, and the "then" before that, all the way back to the first flickering images in Thomas Edison's laboratory. The desires have changed, but so has the intensity. Mass media fame, a cultural concept that arose a century ago as a side effect of a new technology called moving pictures, now not only drives the popular culture of America (and, by extension, much of the world), but has become for many people a central goal and measure of self-worth.

When we were content to gaze up at movie stars on a screen that seemed bigger than life, the exchange was fairly simple. We paid money to watch our daily dilemmas acted out on a dreamlike stage, with ourselves recast as people who were prettier, smarter, tougher, or just not as scared. The stories illustrated the dangers of ambition, the ecstasies of falling in love, the sheer delight of song and dance. Because certain people embodied uniquely charismatic variations on how to react in certain situations—Bogart's street smarts, Kate Hepburn's gumption, Jimmy Stewart's bruised decency, Bette Davis's refusal ever to budge—we wanted to see them over and over again.

We wanted to *be* them. Why else would women have bought knockoffs of Joan Crawford's white organdy dress in 1932's *Letty Lynton* (half a million sold through Macy's) or men have chosen to go without an undershirt like Clark Gable in 1934's *It Happened One Night*? On an even deeper level, we also burned with resentment at the stars' presumption to set themselves up as gods when our egos told us *we* were the ones deserving of attention. Behind every adoring fan letter is the urge to murder and replace. An image that reoccurs time and again in the pages that follow is that of a star out in public, surrounded by a mob that grabs and tears, ripping off buttons, chunks of clothing, as if to simultaneously absorb and obliterate the object of affection. There is love there and also a powerful, inarticulate rage. We want the stars, but we want what they have even more.

The strange part is that we got it, and the book in your hands hopes to show how that happened. The history of modern stardom isn't just a roll call of icons but a narrative of how those icons affected the people and society that watched them, what psychic and cultural needs each star answered, and how that has changed over time. It's an ever-evolving story of industrial consolidation intertwined with technological advancement, each wondrous new machine bringing the dream tantalizingly closer to the control of the dreamers—to us.

The early cinema, for instance, allowed audiences to see actors close up, which rendered them both more specific and more archetypal than the players of the stage. The arrival of sound then let us hear the new stars' voices. Radio brought those voices into our homes; TV brought the rest of the performer, repackaged for fresh rules of engagement. Home video let us own the stars and watch them when we wanted; video cameras allowed us to play at being stars ourselves. The Internet has merely completed the process by providing an instant worldwide distribution and exhibition platform for our new star-selves, however many of them we want to manufacture.

In addition, an extremely profit-driven group of entertainment conglomerates now keeps the popular culture rapt in a feedback loop of movie stars, TV stars, pop stars, rap stars, tweener stars, reality stars, and Internet stars, all mutable, all modeling ways in which consumers can alter their own homemade identities for maximum appeal to friends and strangers. The revolution is complete. One hundred years ago, Charlie Chaplin, Mary Pickford, and a handful of others became the very first living human beings to be simultaneously recognizable to, in theory, everyone on earth. Today, a twelve-year-old child can achieve the same status with an afternoon, a digital camera, and a YouTube account. We have built the mirror we always dreamed about, and we cannot look away.

Part of the original impulse behind this book was to fashion a memorial for the old ways—for a cultural coin that had such worth for so long and that still retains value. The classic star system—as created by the Hollywood studios in the teens and twenties and sustained through the 1960s and, although much diminished, into the present day—was modern humanity's Rorschach test. We looked at those inkblots on the screen and saw what we needed: proof of discrete, individual, desirable human types. The system evolved, with stars falling away and new ones rising as necessary to the cultural demands of the time. Marlon Brando would have been unthinkable before World War II, and yet postwar Hollywood would be unthinkable without him. Each era has its own yearnings, pop star responses, and technological developments that change how the machine works, and each is a further step toward where we are now.

Where *are* we now? A way station, I believe, on the way to someplace very different, more truthful in some aspects, profoundly less so in others. A century of mass media and the concept of "stardom" have changed human society in ways we can barely encompass, but the one constant has been an urge toward personal fulfillment and freedom of identity that would have seemed perverse, if not sacrilegious, to our grandparents' grandparents.

Centuries ago, the common man's worth was marked primarily by duty—how hard he worked and how hard he prayed. The notion of "ego," of something unique within each individual person that needed to be expressed, was alien. What stars there were tended to be generals and kings, religious leaders and charlatans, and you didn't aspire to be like them. You simply followed where they led, or you kept your head down and worked the farm.

The movies helped change that. (All votes for movable type, the Enlightenment, the decline of the agrarian state, Sigmund Freud, and the rise of constitutional self-government will be counted.) The new medium tricked us, though, because it turned flesh-and-blood actors into dreamlike phantoms writ large on a wall. They didn't speak at first, either, so you could impose upon them any voice, any meaning, you wished. The stars thus became better versions of ourselves, idealized role models who literally acted out the things we wanted to do but didn't dare. If they died, as Cagney always seemed to, we still got safely up and went home.

Somewhere along the line, after many decades, we learned *not* to trust these role models anymore. Technology is inextricable in this, because each new medium effectively disproves the one preceding it. TV is somehow "better" than the movies, video and cable are "better" than network TV, the Internet is "better" than five hundred channels of Comcast. "Better" means less restricted in location and time, more portable, and more directly serving the immediate needs of you and me. We plug into star culture and its discontents on our cell phones now. The latest slice of the Lindsay Lohan/Mel Gibson/Charlie Sheen Meltdown Show is right there any time we want it.

When a specific medium is put out to pasture, so are its most representative figures, as the stars of the silent era would be the first to tell you. At the same time, that primal ache has never gone away. If anything, it has gotten stronger, because each wave of technology doesn't always make our lives better. Busier, yes, and faster. More than anything else, it just brings us closer to the mirror in which we reflect ourselves to the world. We still each in our own way ache to be somebody, to make our mark, to stand out from the crowd, *to be seen*. Otherwise, who are we? What's life for? Uniqueness of identity is the promise movie stars hold out to us; if they're able to separate themselves from the swarm of humanity, so might we.

I wonder what Marlene Dietrich would make of all this. *There* was a woman who knew from desire and who trusted a cameraman to keep her secret—that the magnificently shadowed creature of all those early-'30s classics was an ordinary German girl with bedroom eyes. Or the other Hollywood gods—what would they think? Archie Leach and Ruby Stevens, Frances Gumm and Marion Morrison and Norma Jean Mortenson.

Who? Well, yes, you know them as Cary Grant and Barbara Stanwyck, Judy Garland and John Wayne and Marilyn Monroe. Those original names were left in the closet, along with Roy Scherer's—excuse me, Rock Hudson's—homosexuality. Entire pasts were abridged or erased because they didn't jibe with the luxuriant beauty onscreen, the gorgeous lie. The movie moguls kept the secrets, and the press played along because they understood that, really, we didn't want to know.

With some exceptions, though, the mystery that surrounded movie stars for the better part of a century is now highly suspect. Indeed, many pop consumers consider it their duty to pull down the idols and pass their dirty secrets around the Web. How can we trust Tom

Cruise the movie star when we can Google the "real" one bouncing on Oprah's couch? We now have as much control over the idea of celebrity as the studio publicity departments once did, and is it any wonder that movie stars are ruthlessly mocked while our own sweet selves are headlining on YouTube?

Is this something like revenge? Or is it just the evolution of a species gradually conditioned to narcissism? For a century we accepted stardom as a blessing visited on those more gifted than we, a state of grace to which you and I in our drabness could not, and should not, aspire. We knew our place, and it was in the fifth row of the Bijou, worshiping as MGM chief Louis B. Mayer handed out the communion wafers. In 1919, when Chaplin and Pickford joined with Douglas Fairbanks and D. W. Griffith in creating United Artists, the first movie studio run by the talent, the other movie moguls complained "that the inmates had taken over the asylum." If only they knew. Sometime in the past two decades, between video and pay cable and the rise of the World Wide Web, the walls were breached and the masses poured in. The asylum is now ours.

You could see it coming a long way off, actually—since the late 1960s, with their anarchic overturning of the old ways. (Or maybe even further back, when Elvis arrived—an outsider who didn't need a new name.) The acknowledged motto of the new star order is Andy Warhol's much-abused announcement in the catalog of a 1968 Swedish art show that "in the future everyone will be world-famous for 15 minutes." A better, more concise variation came a year later, when Sly Stone recorded the number one pop hit "Everybody Is a Star."

The song's title was offered in a spirit of blissful hippie democracy, a counterculture version of the same promise that had lured tens of thousands of men and women to California and the entertainment industry over the decades. That promise said that you are the center of the universe, if only you can get the rest of the world to see it. Sly tweaked it enough to take the desperate edge off. Stay home, the song advises, and take heart. You are *already* your own star. Technology would eventually prove Stone correct. In effect, he predicted the Internet down to the size of a blogger's bedroom.

What happens to stardom, then, when we at last become stars ourselves? It mutates and spreads in a thousand directions. From our new perch we can now ridicule stars like Cruise, Gibson, Christian Bale, disseminating their audiovisual missteps to the world at large. We can lightly or wholly fictionalize our existence on Facebook or Second Life, developing plot threads, heroes, villains as we go: life not lived but shaped and produced. The new rules have also helped establish the half-lit world of reality TV, with its stars who are not stars because they are us (or less), as well as grotesque mash-ups of fame-mongering like *I Want a Famous Face!*, the 2004 MTV series that featured regular folks who volunteered to undergo surgery to look like their favorite celebrity. One wonders what these people felt when they came out of anesthesia and found they were still the same inside.

It is a long and fractured line from Charlie Chaplin to *I Want a Famous Face!*, but it *is* a line, and this book will try to trace it. I propose a cultural biography of modern stardom, a journey through the permutations of celebrity as it began with the founding of the first global delivery system for fame—the movies—one hundred years ago, all the way to the early twenty-first century, when stardom means something very different and not wholly understood. We'll see how the very concept of the movie star was an audience urge forced upon the first movie producers against their wills, and we'll see how that urge formed the transactional base—the primary unit of value—for an immense industrial system of production and consumption from the 1920s through the post–World War II era and, with various modifications, up to the present.

Some of those early figures are now forgotten—would you believe it if I told you that Norma Talmadge meant as much to women of the 1920s as Anne Hathaway or Natalie Portman mean to our daughters?—but they're crucial to an understanding of those who followed. The silent stars fashioned the original archetypes of Good Girl, Bad Boy, Action Hero, and Drama Queen, and it is their DNA that has been passed down from generation to generation, crossing mediums and mutating as necessary. Can one fully appreciate how

Angelina Jolie functions in our popular culture, as a figure of both iconic power and tabloid absurdity, without understanding her persona's roots in the movies' original man-eater, Theda Bara? Probably, but it's so much more instructive, not to mention fun, to do the math. So the first generation of superstars—the Pickfords and Valentinos, Chaplins and Swansons, Gishes and Gilberts—take up a good-size chunk of the early chapters. You need to know these people if you want to understand their children and grandchildren.

You need to know their parents, as well—the movie studios and the men who ran them, crudely brilliant businessmen who mastered the paradoxical art of mass-producing unique personalities. I've tried to trace how changes in technology, whether affecting the production, distribution, or exhibition of entertainment, gradually changed what kinds of stars audiences wanted, usually before the executives themselves figured it out. There's a fair amount of industry history here—the initial scrambles for dominance, the crisis of the talkies and the rise of the great studio factories, their decline and absorption into the towering corporate colossi that decree what we see and hear and buy today. These are the necessary girders that have supported a century-long system of celebrity. This is what lies on the other side of the screen.

Nor is this book solely about the movies. As we move forward through the decades, the gates open to different kinds of stars, TV tailoring celebrity for the small screen, pop music becoming the primary locus of new personas during the 1950s and '60s, and the Internet brokering fresh relationships between fame and "real life." You can't discuss the 1950s without Elvis and Lucille Ball, the 1960s without the Beatles, or the new millennium without lonelygirl15.

That said, I've had to draw the line somewhere. Athletes and aviators are out, despite what Charles Lindbergh meant to the 1920s. (And yet I've broken my own rules, since the changes in African American star persona in the 1960s are inconceivable without Muhammad Ali.) Socialites, too: this will not be the place to speculate on the cultural meanings of Barbara Hutton or Paris Hilton. I haven't been able to give hip-hop and its slow-growing conquest of the music industry (and, to a large extent, the entire entertainment business) the space or analysis its performers deserve. In fact, your favorite star may well not be in here. Given the span of time and scope of inquiry, drive-bys are inevitable. The details can be fascinating, but the larger journey is the point.

That journey could be defined as one from distant adoration to engaged self-actualization. Alternately, it could be described as a long trek from grand illusion to functional delusion. If there's a thematic through-line, it's in the ways the gods and goddesses of Hollywood were yanked off their thrones over the years as audiences increasingly demanded stars who looked and acted like them—i.e., people who seemed real rather than fake—and as the industry got better at the job of providing those stars. In 1949, Marlon Brando made every other Hollywood actor look like a fraud; twenty years later, Dustin Hoffman, Jack Nicholson, and Robert De Niro served as the new benchmarks in realism. Today it's the cast of *Jersey Shore* who are signifiers of actuality at its most extreme—a "realness" that makes us feel better about our own.

Yet the classic movie star lives on—has to live on, if only to give us something better to aspire to than Snooki and the Situation. We still have a varied buffet of star types before us, from the impenetrable Hollywood gloss of Jolie and Brad Pitt to the scruffy approachability of recent arrivals like Ellen Page and Joseph Gordon-Levitt. Younger audiences respond to those last two because they speak and act in ways that resonate with how people their age actually see themselves, as Hoffman did in the 1960s, as Mickey Rooney did in the 1930s. We want performers who reflect our reality—who seem to order that reality, comment on it, laugh at it, blow it up. The ones who do so with an appealing consistency of persona across a range of movies or other forms of media are those we call stars.

A distinction can and should be made between stars and actors. All stars are actors one way or another; not all actors are stars. Great actors—the true master craftsmen and -women—transform themselves in role after role, and if the projects are successful and the actor is celebrated enough, that changeability becomes his or her persona, whether it's Lon Chaney in the silent era, Alec Guinness after World War II, Meryl Streep in the 1980s, or Cate Blanchett today.

Stars, by contrast, don't hide themselves. On the contrary, the great movie stars each construct an image that is bigger than their individual films even as it connects those films in a narrative of unfolding personality. This is important. A concept we'll return to over and over in this book is that every successful star creates a persona and within that persona is an idea. The films are merely variations on the idea. The idea can be expressed as action or as attitude or simply as an unstated philosophy of how to live and behave in this world (or how not to live and how not to behave) that the player embodies in charismatic, two-dimensional human form. You could call it identity, too, but it's identity so contained, defined, and appealing that moviegoers grasp at it in an attempt to define their own senses of self.

Bette Davis acts out an ongoing drama of difficult women in a constraining society. Clint Eastwood shows time and again how macho toughness is affected by the stress-fractures of morality, even tenderness. Jimmy Stewart and Tom Hanks represent good men in an unkind world, but where the former responds with troubled decency, the latter wields ease and bonhomie. The idea can be as simple as Angelina Jolie = Amazon Queen, or Tom Cruise = Action Hero. It can be as complex as Johnny Depp, who projects shyness, mercurial daring, rebellion, eccentricity, and old-fashioned sex appeal, and whose persona can probably be best expressed as *maverick idol*.

There are many performers who don't convey an idea at all, whose star identity remains in flux. Matt Damon is an ambitious, well-liked actor who makes interesting choices in roles and has been rewarded with box office hits and critical approval, yet he doesn't convey a persona outside the movies other than as a smart, hardworking guy. In a sense, Damon's lack of persona *is* his persona, one that 2001's *Ocean's Eleven* and its sequels had great fun with by making his character the butt of jokes from Brad Pitt and George Clooney, two genuine stars who project, respectively, surfer-dude poise and devilish charm tempered by gravitas.

Again: each star is an idea of how we could be or should be or might want to be. The other important concept to keep in mind as you read this book is that each star-idea often has little to do with the person acting it out. James Cagney played bastards onscreen, but he was known and loved as one of the nicest guys in the movie business. Cary Grant, the studio system's Perfect Man, privately raged against the Academy for not giving him an Oscar and experimented extensively with LSD. Read between the lines of their existing biographies and the mythic love affair of Kate Hepburn and Spencer Tracy turns into a problematic tale of alcoholism, enablement, and emotional cruelty. I'm pretty sure Tom Hanks picks his nose.

In other words, these are human beings whose flaws we in the audience suspect and ignore, torn as we are between venerating the larger projection and wanting to pull down the screen. Even the stars themselves had mixed feelings about what they had created. "Bogart's a helluva nice guy until 11 p.m.; after that, he thinks he's Bogart," said a Hollywood restaurateur who knew the star well. But most famous actors recognize the size of the gap between person and persona. The ongoing mistake of the moviegoing public is to confuse the two and to ascribe great psycho-mythic power where there is usually only very good playacting. This is the mistake that fuels fan mail, Web shrines, and celebrity stalkers alike—that the star is exactly who we see—and it masks the ignored but necessary pleasures of the ordinary.

Remember the ordinary? It's passé right now, in our brave wired world of enabled fantasy. Maybe it's headed for extinction. Still, it's worth asking: What's so terribly wrong with us that we need to be someone else? This isn't a question that concerned our ancestors in the same way. If you asked a ten-year-old in nineteenth-century America what she or he wanted to grow up to be, the answers would doubtless have revealed the limits of cultural expectations and the immediate horizon: farmer, merchant, teacher, tradesman, soldier, mother, cop. Maybe a preacher or a rabbi. The adventurous ones dreamed of cowboys and explorers.

Ask a modern ten-year-old the same question, and you'll hear pop singer, athlete, actress, model, star. All variations on being noticed. On that level, this book isn't a history or a pop celebration or an anthropological thumbsucker. It is an inquiry and, in its later chapters, an intervention. It wants to know how we got here from there, who was important on the way, where we are now, and why that matters. It hopes to honor those performers and personas who really do seem indelible and who live on in the culture long after their physical deaths. And it suggests that for a great many people, fame—the act of seeing, the desire to be seen—has come to matter most of all, that culture is now hostage to celebrity, and that a massive, profit-driven corporate oligarchy considers it very good business to keep it that way.

Some of the questions we need to ask ourselves are the same as they've been for decades. Why does a particular star speak to one era but not another? How much of any celebrity is his or her own invention and how much our projection? Other questions are vastly different from those of a century, half a century, even a decade ago. Why do we pay to see famous actors in a movie theater, then go home and make fun of them on the Web? Why do we still need Hollywood's manufactured identities when we can create them for ourselves? Am I my Facebook page, or the other way around? Why, oh Lord, do we Google ourselves? And how are we supposed to stop when it feels so good?

If there are answers, they begin with Florence Lawrence.

GODS LIKE US

1.

The Star Is Born: From Edison's Blobs to Florence Lawrence

Here is the hardest part to understand: one hundred years ago, the movie star was a radically new idea.

Think about that. In the new millennium, a movie can gross a hundred million dollars on the strength of Will Smith's or Johnny Depp's name alone. A film without a star remains a nearly impossible sell; dreadful ideas are green-lit only because a famous face is attached. Although the rules have changed over the decades and fads have come and gone, movie stars still drive the commerce of mainstream narrative filmmaking and have done so seemingly forever.

"Forever" in Hollywood is relative, though. At the beginning, the movies were driven by anonymity. While there were actors onscreen in 1908, you probably didn't care who they were, and even if you did, they were unbilled and unknown. But maybe you had seen the same face reoccur from one one-reeler to the next, and you found that, in a strange way, you were attracted to it. The actor, whoever he or she was, registered feelings the way you did, in closeup and without gesticulating to the back of the balcony. At the same time he or she seemed to magnify those emotions and lend them a deeper, more forceful permanence. What they felt *felt* bigger.

You discovered that you wanted, maybe even desperately, to see this person again, not because of the part he or she played but because of who he or she *was*. Or seemed to be—that was what was keeping you up at night. Actors and actresses onstage clearly played roles, no matter how charismatic the performances, but the giants up there on the nickelodeon wall weren't acting. Were they? You were so close to the performer and to the answer, closer than you'd ever been before. You had to find out. To do that, you had to know who he or she was.

Thus the first great secret in movies was a name, because not a single actor was credited for the first decade and a half of cinema. Nor were directors, producers, or screenwriters. All you got when the lights went down was the film's title and the name of the company that made it.

It wasn't enough. By the last half of the first decade of the twentieth century, early film studios found themselves buried under a growing avalanche of letters. The writers begged to know who that nice young man in *The Valet's Wife* was, or the girl with the curls. *What are their names?* Anxiety leaks out between the neatly handwritten lines. A 1909 letter addressed to "the lady who appeared in *The Ingrate*" asks, "Will you please answer this letter, a postal will do, just telling me your name, your real name not a stage one. I promise I won't tell no one." I'll keep your secret, and only you and I will know. That's how close the new breed of performers seemed and how directly they spoke to each member of the audience.

It seems perverse, but no answer came—or was allowed to come, or had a conduit through which to come—and as the mystery lengthened, the need to solve it became more urgent. Early moviegoers turned to nicknames, alternate signifiers of the physical and psychic bigness of the new figures. "In order to have some kind of name for you we called you 'The Queen of Sheba,' " wrote a fan to one popular actress, as if passing along a secret code.

Since most audiences identified players by the studios for whom they worked, this particular actress was more popularly known as "the Biograph Girl." When she was hired by another studio and other players filled her roles, fans resisted. "She is all right," wrote one man to an early movie magazine about the anonymous Marion Leonard in 1909's *Through the Breakers*. "But she is not the Biograph Girl, not THE Biograph Girl."

In fact, THE Biograph Girl was about to be given a name, but first, the overarching question: Why this code of silence? What counter-intuitive conspiracy was going on here? The mystery surrounding the early days of film isn't how the star system was born but why it took so long to come into being—fourteen years, if we count from the first public screening of a motion picture. It seems crazy. It *is* crazy. Couldn't the photoplay moguls understand that we go to movies to see the people in them?

No, because for a very long time we went to see movies for other, less needy reasons. The early film studios didn't think in terms of stars because the cinema was, in order, a scientific discovery, a novelty, a bust, and an industrial product aimed at a lower-class, socially undesirable audience.

Until the Biograph Girl, Florence Lawrence, came along. But we're getting ahead of ourselves.

Actually, the very first person in a movie shot in America was a blob. The date was June 1889, or maybe it was November 1890. The blob was an Edison lab assistant, either John Ott or G. Sacco Albanese. No one remembers. If there are records, they've been lost. Everything about him, whoever he is, is visually and historically indistinct.

The film is called *Monkeyshines No. 1,* and it consists of a ghostly image of a man waving his arms. Maybe it's a man. The focus is so fuzzy it looks more like an astronaut—some bioluminescent emissary from beyond time and space. What is he saying? What important message does he bear? The snippet lasts twenty-seven seconds, not long enough to decode. You can watch it over and over again on the Kino DVD set *Edison: The Invention of the Movies,* as if repetition will unpack its meaning. But it resists, other than to say: *Start here.*

Behind the camera was a man named William Kennedy Laurie Dickson—W. K. L. Dickson in the history books—who was the scientist/mechanic that Thomas Edison had assigned to develop his Kinetoscope project. By this point in his life, Edison himself, the Great Man, handled the broad theorizing and patent filing while leaving the day-to-day tinkering to employees. It is Dickson who should be rightly called the father—or perhaps the midwife—of moving pictures. From 1888 until 1895, when he left Edison to work with other inventors on a movie projection system and eventually cofounded the studio that would become Biograph, Dickson and his assistants ground out the first films to be produced in America.

The Kinetoscope was a boxy, single-viewer peepshow—you paid your money and cranked a small mechanical arm, looking through a slot that revealed a brief scene to you and you alone. The thrill of voyeurism, of secrets revealed in a private exchange, was thus established as the rock-bottom commerce of the movies.

Who was in these early films? Dickson himself was the "star" of the first shown at an 1891 public demonstration—less than a second of the dapper inventor sweeping a straw hat before him, as if to say *Welcome to a future that will ask you to consider Ashton Kutcher a major public figure.* The true novelty of the Kinetoscope, though, was in its recording of mundane reality, and of preexisting celebrities who existed in that reality. Dickson brought the barnstorming tent-show star Annie Oakley into Edison's New Jersey studios and had her fire off a few trick shots. He filmed boxing matches that the company sold to peepshow parlors at $22.50 a round; customers then paid a dime for each of the six rounds, moving from machine to machine until the final knockout—an early version of pay-per-view sports.

Vaudeville performers were ferried across the Hudson from Broadway to the Edison studios and asked to re-create truncated versions of their acts: Louis Martinetti, contortionist; Annabelle's Butterfly Dance; Professor Welton's boxing cats; Hadj Cheriff, Arab Knife Fighter. "Billy Edwards and the Unknown"—it sounds like a Beckett one-act, or an existential superhero comic—turns out to be more boxing.

Already sex, or the promise of sex, was an integral aspect of the new technology. (This had been true of photography, with the "French postcards" of the 1890s, and it would be true of the Internet; the common ground is the one-to-one privacy of the viewing experience.) In 1896 *The Kiss* shocked bluenoses by having stage actors John C. Rice and May Irwin cuddle and peck in unexpected closeup, and when Fatima the Muscle Dancer shook her fully clothed moneymaker for the Edison cameras, the film was released in both a censored version (with black bars across her naughty bits, as though you were peeking at her through a Venetian blind) and in an unexpurgated cut. Interestingly, the censored version feels dirtier.

Still, a critical element was missing: the audience in its plural sense. The entire history of theatrical presentation, from cavemen to Broadway impresario David Belasco, provided a template for communal entertainment—for mass dreaming—that the movies had to adhere to if they were to become more than an onanistic gizmo. Visions are meant to be shared. We needed to see the images as part of a crowd.

Thus Edison went to it—which included "borrowing" and buying ideas from other inventors—and a working projection system debuted at Koster and Bial's Music Hall in New York City on April 23, 1896, the date generally agreed upon as the starting gun for movie history proper. The next day, the *New York Times* described the scene: "A buzzing and roaring were heard in the [projector's] turret, and an unusually bright light fell upon the screen. Then came into view two precious blonde young persons of the variety stage in pink and blue dresses, doing the umbrella dance with commendable celerity. Their motions were clearly defined. When they vanished, a view of an angry surf breaking on a sandy beach near a stone pier amazed the spectators. A burlesque boxing match between a tall, thin comedian and a short, fat one, a comic allegory called 'The Monroe Doctrine'; an instant of motion in Hoyt's farce, 'A Milk White Flag,' repeated over and over again, and a skirt dance by a tall blonde completed the views, which were all wonderfully real and singularly exhilarating."

Here, in utero, are so many of the shards that would come to be part of the movies: scenic views, comedy, action, blondes. (And how, exactly, was the effect of pink and blue dresses achieved? Early color tinting?) The difference was that instead of bending to peer into a machine, the audience leaned back to see human beings projected onto a wall ("half life size," but that would change) and sharing the experience with everyone else in the room. Each inhalation of breath, each startled cry, echoed about the theater like sympathetic wave-forms.

But there still weren't stars, not as we know them. Projected movies found a niche in vaudeville in the final years of the nineteenth century and the first years of the twentieth, but primarily as a mechanical novelty, rolled on between the singer and the comedy act. The short films that were shown featured other vaudeville acts, U.S. presidents, famous battles (or, more often, unconvincing re-creations of famous battles), and nature shots. There were a few fictional vignettes, though—*The Burglar on the Roof* (1898), *The Life of an American Fireman* (1903)—and then came a breakthrough: the twelve-minute *The Great Train Robbery* (1903).

No stars there, but there was a man who went on to become one. Directed by Edwin S. Porter—after Dickson's departure the main movie man at Edison—*Robbery* has some of the elements that would come to define cinematic language, such as crosscutting and, at the very end, like a lightning bolt from the gods, a closeup. Playing at least three roles was a nice Jewish boy from Arkansas named Max Aronson who had taken the less ethnic stage moniker Gilbert M. Anderson. As "Broncho Billy" Anderson, he would soon become the first western star and an early movie mogul, forming the Essanay studios in 1907 and eventually directing and starring in close to four hundred early horse operas.

In *Train Robbery*, of course, he's unbilled, and he doesn't even get the movie's big scene. In the final frames, the bandit played by Justin

Barnes lifts his six-shooter, aims it directly into the camera, and fires it at us (in some prints the explosion was tinted red). The bit was a sensation, and it welded screen violence with the visceral charge that comes from an audience's sudden understanding that it can't be hurt. (Today's horror movies offer the exact same compact to teenagers, who think they've just discovered it for themselves.) Martin Scorsese consciously reprised the bit at the end of *Goodfellas,* Joe Pesci shooting into the camera as if finally answering the Great Train Robbers back, eighty years on.

Yet by 1905 or so, the movies appeared to be over. The novelty wore off; the crowds got bored. Vaudeville theaters began to put movies at the end of the bill as "chasers," handy for clearing out the house. Ironically, the passing of the first fad set the stage for the next and more lasting phase—the first dedicated movie theaters, known as nickelodeons. As the vaudeville houses sold off their unwanted equipment, immigrant entrepreneurs like William Fox, Marcus Loew, and Adolph Zukor decided to take a flyer on movie exhibition. Why not? Some of them had already made a killing on the peepshow arcades, and the new yet unwanted big-screen projectors were cheap enough. A savvy businessman like Zukor—a fur merchant who'd go on to create Paramount Pictures and keep a seat on the board until his death in 1976 at 103—could do the math. They opened small picture parlors, charged a nickel per show, and found that they made money without even trying.

One difference was that the audience was often made up of immigrants who spoke little English and could thus enjoy movies without the barrier of language. It is very possible that if talkies had existed from the beginning—and Edison and Dickson had certainly experimented in that direction—the movies as we know them would never have taken over America and the world. Unlike the legitimate stage, unlike vaudeville, silence made the cinema everybody's medium.

Because they were classless, movies were initially considered lower class, but the seeds of change were already present. Another key component of the early nickelodeon audience was the middle-class or lower-middle-class woman, ducking into the storefront theater between errands and maybe not telling her husband about it later. She was seeking diversion, a little time of her own, something to take her outside of herself. This is where the dreaming starts.

Things happened very quickly now. The number of nickelodeons exploded over the next few years, from a handful in 1905 to an estimated 2,500 two years later, and onward and upward in geometric progression. By 1909, there were an estimated 9,000 small theaters across the country specializing in showing movies.

After that, basic business physics took over. What happens when you have an unprecedented expansion in the number of screens? There follows an upsurge in demand for product to fill those screens. Studios needed to be built, stock companies of actors had to be hired. The exhibition and production ends of the early film business began a transformation from cottage industries to organized entities, as did the distribution companies, called film exchanges, which transported early movies from the people who made them to the people who showed them. And because the number of movies being produced, distributed, and exhibited ballooned, the nature of what was *in* those movies had to change.

And rapidly. The earliest moviemakers went out and filmed reality or fudged it in the studio—telling stories was only a fraction of what they were about. But when your exhibitors are screaming for twice, thrice, *ten* times as many movies per week as before and there aren't nearly enough wars or parades to film, you have to start thinking outside the box. Fiction, then, was a natural. You only had to cook up a story, or steal one from a play or a book, and put on a show in front of the camera.

Between 1907 and 1908, narrative movies—dramas and comedies—leapt from 17 percent of all film output (as opposed to documentary "actualities," vaudeville performers, and sporting events) to a full two-thirds of the total. The early film studios began to adopt the factory model to meet the demand, and part of this new order was the hiring of a stable group of professional actors.

And here, at last, is where it begins. You cannot have stardom without familiarity—without an audience encountering the same faces again and again on a regular basis—and you cannot have familiarity without an established system of production. We think of movie stars as aspects of charisma, unique and self-willed, but they would not exist without a group of businessmen in derby hats slowly coming to understand that making movies was as pure a profit venture as showing them and that actors were the best way to disguise the commerce of the thing.

And yet—still no movie stars, at least initially. Professional stage actors were embarrassed to be associated with the upstart medium, and producers didn't want to give performers a reason to ask for more money. Most important, the early studios were more focused on establishing their own brand names, the thinking being that if you're selling toasters you don't need to promote the individual slices of bread.

There was this, too: no one was really sure what people actually *did* in movies. What limited media coverage there was used verbs like "posing," "modeling," and "shamming," rather than "acting," to describe early film performances. The vocabulary and the mentality it reflected came from still photography rather than the theater, and as narrative storytelling turned from the exception to the norm, journalists of the era struggled to leap from one conceptual paradigm to another. "The repertoire actor has discovered a new use for his talents," wrote *Moving Picture World* in October 1907. "He is now a moving picture. That is, he now poses for moving pictures. By lying down, rolling over and jumping in front of the camera he is able to earn in three days a sum equal to a week's salary at his former industry."

"Lying down, rolling over and jumping in front of the camera"—not what you'd call "acting," is it? The silence that brought the early cinema to its first mass audience also cut it off from the respect afforded the legitimate stage. Everyone knew that real actors like Maude Adams, Sarah Bernhardt, and Edwin Booth spoke in fluent Shakespeare, with grandiloquent cadences designed to volley off the furthest balcony. The movies, by comparison, were mummery, playacting—a puppet show. These people weren't acting, they were simply *being*.

So established stage actors sneered at the infant medium, and that is probably the best thing that could have happened to it. No one understood that entirely different gifts of self-presentation were needed; that the camera, in effect, gave each member of the audience the most intimate seat in the house. Yet the men and women—mostly women—who would become the first movie stars intuitively understood that less is more, that being *was* acting, and that the naturalism needed for the screen brought them elusively closer to the audience than anyone had dreamed possible.

They also had less to lose. When they weren't rank beginners—office boys and neighborhood girls drafted to stand in front of the camera—early film actors tended to be unknown stage performers struggling to find regular work in New York or on the road. In many cases, stepping into the new Edison studios on East Twenty-first Street or going out to Vitagraph in Flatbush, Brooklyn, represented the difference between making a living and giving up. Other performers welcomed the chance to earn extra cash during idle periods. Much has been made of the fact that many of the first major stars came from broken homes—fathers long gone, stage mothers dragging broods from theater to theater, young girls becoming breadwinners for whole families. Movies were not something to be spurned. They put food on the table. They were an *in*.

From the audience's perspective, if you went to a movie in 1908, you knew only the title and the production company. The studio's name was the chief means of product differentiation: Edison, Biograph, Vitagraph, Selig, Kalem, Lubin, Essanay were the primary brands. Not that the product itself was terribly variable, but in a hangover from the Gilded Age, business profit was considered the only measure of success. The men who created these companies wanted very much to be taken seriously, and to that end the corporation was the star.

Moviegoers refused to play along and became obsessed, instead, with the actors *in* the movies. Some of the companies figured it out. As early as January 1909, Kalem published a trade ad identifying its key players. Others resisted, with the hidebound Biograph refusing to promote actors by name until 1914, despite the fact that from 1908 to 1913 D. W. Griffith was inventing modern movie storytelling at the studio and making stars of the Gish sisters, Blanche Sweet, Bobby Harron, Lionel Barrymore, Mary Pickford, and Florence Lawrence.

A new breed of upstart businessmen figured it out as well, and the first was Carl Laemmle, the future father of Universal Pictures. A Bavarian immigrant with a decided playful streak, Laemmle was hated by many in the young film industry, and he reveled in the role. He had a target, too. In 1908, in an Edison-sponsored effort to protect patents and profits, the early studios had formed the Motion Picture Patents Company, aka "the Trust." The Trust was serious business, prosecuting perceived infringement—i.e., anyone else making a movie on his own and trying to get it seen—with lawsuits and hired goons. Since the licensed companies had an exclusive deal with Kodak, you couldn't even buy film legally unless you were in the magic circle.

Against the Trust was a motley, unorganized group of companies, many founded by Jewish immigrants as opposed to the solid American burghers of Vitagraph and Biograph. From the start, class and ethnicity were crucial aspects of the struggle for control. The new men were collectively lionized and despised as "the independents," and since many of them had started out owning nickelodeons, they were able to witness and respond to audience reaction with their own eyes. They understood that a movie sold on the strength of its story and performances, not by its length in feet (the Trust's method of doing business). The fight between the Edison Trust and the tatty independents represented the first collision of the mainstream with an alternative in American movies. Who ultimately won? Look to the corporate credits of almost every Hollywood movie we see today: Paramount, Universal, Fox, and MGM were all started by the men who opposed the Trust.

"Uncle Carl" Laemmle was hilariously blatant about his desire to tip over Edison's applecart. He called his outfit the Independent Moving Picture Company—IMP—and chose as its logo a grinning devil, wielding a pitchfork presumably aimed at the Trust's fat rear end. Casting about for a way to build up his own business while driving the enemy crazy, he fixed on promoting a star. And not just any star. He stole the Biograph Girl. Naughty man.

It's difficult, one hundred years on, to understand why audiences responded so strongly to Florence Lawrence. Her very few surviving films reveal a statuesque woman, attractive in the preferred Gibson Girl mode of the day, with a prominent nose, broad face, serene expression. Her acting is histrionic without being overbearingly so, yet there's little that makes her jump off the screen the way a movie star is supposed to. The cultural context for her style of performance has vanished, and with it the tools to appreciate her. To watch Lawrence—along with most of her peers—is to see a female type that owes everything to nineteenth-century values and modes of expression. Perhaps that's why the crowds went mad. She was familiar but new, a known quantity seen from an entirely fresh angle.

In point of fact, Florence Lawrence was out of work when Laemmle came calling. In mid-1909, she and her husband, Biograph actor Harry Solter, had made the mistake of writing to Broncho Billy Anderson, offering to jump ship to his Essanay studio, which was then working out of a flyspeck California hamlet called Hollywood. Solter wanted to direct; Lawrence was getting enough fan mail by then to think maybe she was worth something, and, besides, she resented the speed at which Griffith and the Biograph brass insisted actors play their scenes. Like her colleagues, Lawrence worked hard, appearing in forty-six one-reelers in 1908, and sixty-two in the first two-thirds of 1909 alone. It's possible she simply wanted a break, or maybe some respect.

Biograph and Essanay were both part of the Trust, though, and management across member studios closed ranks against the hired help. In short order the Solters were ratted out, shown the door, and blacklisted from working at any other licensed company. Lawrence signed up with IMP because she had no choice. The first thing Laemmle did was put her in movies. The second thing he did was kill her off.

The actress was working in IMP productions as early as August 1909, but it wasn't until the end of the year that Laemmle started promoting that fact. At first he simply ran a photo of her face with the words "She's an IMP!" in a December issue of *Moving Picture*

World, the assumption being that fans knew her by appearance rather than name. The ground beneath the film industry's feet had been shifting all that year, though. Vitagraph had already advertised its one-reel version of *Oliver Twist* as featuring "Miss Eliza Proctor Otis as Nancy Sykes, the role which this eminent actress has made famous throughout the world." Edison was promoting the French mime artist Mlle Pilar-Morin in a series of shorts and even starting to list the casts for its prestige productions in onscreen credits. Early in 1910, Kalem released a lobby poster featuring eleven of its most popular players. The bomb had been assembled, but no one seemed to have a match.

In February 1910, Carl Laemmle lit the bomb. On the 19th, according to Lawrence's 1914 memoirs, her obituary, with a photo, appeared in a New York newspaper. To the actress's great surprise, she was dead, run over by a speeding automobile. Other sources say the story ran in a St. Louis newspaper and that she'd been mown down by a streetcar. It's possible the story didn't run at all; the main order of business was the correction that appeared in *Billboard* a week later, avowing that the actress was indeed alive. "Miss Lawrence has a one hundred percent health certificate that should keep her with us a long while," the writer said about "the queen of moving pictures."

Then Laemmle took off the gloves, running a full-page ad in the March 5th issue of *Moving Picture World* highlighted by Lawrence's photo and the headline "WE NAIL A LIE." The rumors of the actress's death, he claimed, had been started by IMP's rivals in the Trust because—well, *why*? So that audiences would no longer look for her in movies? That makes no sense.

It was all a big fib, the opening gong in a century of sweaty, hectoring studio ballyhoo. Laemmle possessed two characteristics that his opposite numbers in the Trust lacked: tastelessness and a willingness to exploit it. This proved to be crucial to the history of both the movies and twentieth-century popular culture, and it's why the Trust companies eventually died out. They wanted to make the movies into a proper business, while Laemmle understood that it is our improper urges that lure us into the dark over and over again. Nothing sells a star like his or her death; the 2008 pop detonation surrounding *The Dark Knight* and Heath Ledger's final performance is just a more recent example.

Lawrence, conveniently, was still alive. On March 6th, the *St. Louis Post-Dispatch* ran an unprecedented front-page story in its Sunday magazine, calling Lawrence "the Girl of a Thousand Faces" and illustrating the notion with copious photos and an interview with the actress. Never before had an article about a movie actor appeared in the non-trade press. The piece was uncredited, and surely it came from Carl Laemmle or someone close to him.

Now comes the brilliant part. In addition to giving movie fanatics of St. Louis all the information about Lawrence that her previous employer, Biograph, had withheld, the article announced that the actress would make a personal appearance in the city later that month, along with frequent costar King Baggot. "You've Seen Them On The 'Screen,' Come See Them In Person," ran an ad the day of their arrival.

And there it is. Consciously or instinctively, Laemmle had divined the desire hovering beneath the surface of Florence Lawrence mania—the burning need to prove she was real. Since no box office records of the era survive, we don't know how much money her movies made, but we do know that given the chance to see the actress in the flesh, the public went crazy.

The St. Louis appearance was a mob scene, the first directly caused by a movie actor. Hundreds pressed onto the platform to glimpse the actress, and when she left the train to get into a car, reported the *St. Louis Times,* "there were enthusiastic shouts from female voices, and a rush of well-dressed women to get a closer view of the little woman in a close-fitting blue dress whom they instantly recognized as Miss Lawrence, their heroine." According to Laemmle's biographer, fans started "tearing the buttons from her dress, the trimming from her hat, and the hat from her head"—an early instance of the weird piranha frenzy that celebrities can experience when swallowed by a crowd. Everyone wanted a piece. Everyone wanted *their* piece.

Lawrence became agitated and reportedly fainted; once her party made it to the automobile, fans surrounded the vehicle and refused to let it move. "I had no idea that so many people were interested in me," she later told the *Times*. "It seems so strange that so many people would gather at the train to welcome one they had never seen, only in pictures." No one understood what had just happened, least of all the woman at the center of the rapture. Seeing Lawrence in person seemed profoundly necessary in order to prove that she really existed and that the emotions she stirred up weren't illusory. She was *there*. It wasn't a trick.

There existed no parameters for this sort of popularity, and the impact of a star like Lawrence, onscreen and off, was both scary and exhilarating. Stage actors had always been faraway figures, glamorous but distant, encrusted in a sort of exaggerated gentility. By contrast, the new "picture personalities" often dressed like the people who paid to see them, and they certainly acted like them. The settings of the stories were often bourgeois and domestic; there were even slum dramas like Griffith's 1912 *The Musketeers of Pig Alley*, arguably the first urban gangster film. Even before the closeup was established, successful movie performance didn't broadcast emotions but embodied them in a new and unprecedented naturalism.

Journalists and average moviegoers struggled to articulate what was going on. "We do not know the lady's name," wrote one reviewer about *Resurrection*, a 1909 Lawrence Biograph, "but certainly she seems to us to have a very fine command of her emotions and to be able to express those emotions before such an unemotional thing as a camera. A very ordinary person can indeed act before a crowded house of interested men and women, but it takes a genius to do so with real feeling on a moving picture stage." Suddenly it was the stage actors who were "ordinary" and the once-shunned film actors who were "geniuses."

But what relationship did the genius onscreen bear to the actual person? Was it an act? Was it actual? If the essence of a moving picture player seemed to stream directly off the screen—and moreover seemed constant from film to film—wasn't that proof of something inherently special in the actor? This was what was untested. This was what had to be found out.

Executives at the other studios, no fools, saw what Laemmle had done and followed suit. In April, Vitagraph released a lobby poster of its stock company and sent its own Florence—Florence Turner, alternately "the Vitagraph Girl" and "the Shadow Girl"—on a series of personal appearances in Brooklyn. Reported *Moving Picture World,* "That those who pose for the Silent Drama gain a tangible hold on their audiences we were aware. That the popularity of the Shadow Girl would cause a small riot by reason of the eagerness of those who knew only the 'shadow' to greet the reality was, to say the least, a surprise."

The surprise was short-lived. Over the next few years, the building blocks of the star system fell quickly into place, and actors became the primary object of value in promoting movies and forging a contract between studio and audience. Lawrence benefited, but not for terribly long. Before 1910 was over, she had left IMP for the Lubin studio, subsequently quitting that company and sailing to Europe claiming nervous exhaustion (another first: the star as rehab-ready victim), then returning to found her own independent mini-studio (*another* first), then quitting again in 1913 to cultivate roses, only to stage a further comeback later that year. She offers ground-entry evidence that creating movie stars can lead to rampaging neurosis, diva fits, and trouble. Also, that it's generally worth it, for the producers and the audience, if not for the star herself.

If Lawrence's appeal had roots in the nineteenth-century past, the movie stars that quickly came to dominate pointed forward. The two decades from "WE NAIL A LIE" to the onset of the Great Depression in 1929 saw a seismic cultural shift, no less than the overthrow of the Victorian Age for the Modern Era. America was no longer an agrarian society, for the country's urban population, 20 percent of the whole in 1860, had crossed the 50 percent line for good in the 1920s. With the move to the cities, small-town codes of behavior were left behind, as were the social contracts that governed village life.

In the city, men and especially women were free to reinvent themselves, *had* to reinvent themselves, since they were cut off from roles established over many decades of postcolonial American society. If they were lucky, the new urbanites had a good job, decent hours and wages, and leisure time—a fresh concept—in which to spend those wages. The manufacturing companies and the nascent advertising industry rushed to fill the gap; the great consumer culture shuddered to life. Average household spending tripled between 1909 and 1929, while the total volume of magazine advertising doubled that, growing 600 percent between 1914 and 1929. Personal identity ceased to be a matter of societal context, of where you belonged in the continuity of a small town. More and more, you were what you owned and what you wore.

World War I, meanwhile, hardened and made worldly the wholesome young men who fought it and the proper young women to whom they returned. Sex was suddenly in the air, and Freud, and a hectic sense that one's duty was not to one's parents or to God but to oneself. "My candle burns at both ends," wrote poet Edna St. Vincent Millay, and many followed her example. We like to think the 1960s invented the sexual revolution, but if you knew what your great-grandparents were up to, you'd probably be shocked.

The movies' place in all this is problematic, busy, and crucial. The cinema both reflected these social changes and helped cause them, decried them and egged them on, sold audiences a lifestyle to which they could aspire and then criticized them for aspiring to it. The movies were the iconic battleground between old and new—the stage on which the great change played itself out—and they were, more and more, available and necessary to everyone.

In the period immediately after IMP and other forward-looking studios consciously built the star system on the bones of the Trust's ignorance, the movies began to seriously court the middle and upper-middle classes. The number of theaters in New York City increased eightfold between 1910 and 1930, and some of them were astonishing palaces. By 1913, at least three stage theaters in the Herald Square–to–Times Square axis had converted to movies, and in early 1914, Vitagraph reopened the Criterion with a mighty Wurlitzer organ to give sonic accompaniment to the dancing shadows.

They were all shown up by the April 1914 opening of the Strand, a neo-Corinthian temple on Broadway and Forty-seventh Street that was built by the Mark brothers specifically to attract a high-class crowd. The Strand was managed by impresario Samuel "Roxy" Rothafel, whose nickname would itself go on to adorn countless theaters—a signifier of smart uptown pleasures in even the smallest villages. Roxy kicked off the Strand with cannon fire, the American flag, baseball footage shot that morning in Brooklyn, a Keystone comedy, and the nine-reel, 135-minute William Farnum western *The Spoilers*. The opening-night glitterati were astounded, and a *Times* reporter wrote, "If anyone had told me two years ago that the time would come when the finest-looking people in town would be going to the biggest and newest theater on Broadway for the purpose of seeing motion pictures I would have sent them down to visit my friend Dr. Minas Gregory at Bellevue Hospital."

It was all changing so fast. The movies were changing, too—becoming longer, more lavishly produced, better told. D. W. Griffith's 1915 *The Birth of a Nation* is generally considered the first true movie sensation—never before had a strip of celluloid become Topic A on all levels of American society from the president on down—but it was far from the first feature-length production. Multi-reel films exhibited in installments were being produced as early as 1909, and some 1910 theater owners experimented by showing Vitagraph's five-reel *The Life of Moses* in one sitting, to record business. By 1913, even before Griffith ran into front-office resistance to his four-reel *Judith of Bethulia,* longer films were becoming more and more common. (Once again, Biograph seems curiously unable to have predicted the future; as a result, the company's prized director finally up and quit.)

Griffith's true revolutionary spadework had already been accomplished in the hundreds of short films he made for Biograph from 1908 to 1913, in which he hammered out the cinematic grammar with which we still live. The director didn't invent crosscutting or the closeup or editing for suspense or atmospheric long shots, but he was the first to use such devices consistently, consciously, and artistically. He was the first person to think *as a filmmaker.* It's in his camera lens that the modern star was born.

The closeup, for example. When he tried it out in a Biograph film his bosses were horrified. "We pay for the whole actor, Mr. Griffith," he was scolded. "We want to see all of him." As the director brought his camera closer, though, strange things began to happen. Audiences found they could read an actor's thoughts. Actors discovered they didn't really have to act, at least not in the accepted stage style. They had to focus and remain open and *be.* In a 1921 pocket book called *Screen Acting,* actress Mae Marsh described the process and hinted at the vanishing border between player and role. "Good screen acting," she wrote, "consists of the ability to accurately portray a state of mind. . . . It never pays to imitate anyone else's interpretation of any emotion. Each of us when we are pleased, injured, or affected in any way have our own way of showing our feelings. This is one thing that is our very own."

Galumphing about and windmilling one's arms was passé, even if the old style held on in the form of famous stage personalities lured before the cameras. The celebrated nineteenth-century actress Sarah Bernhardt starred in a handful of French photoplays that found great success when Adolph Zukor brought them to America in 1912; he subsequently produced a number of filmed stage productions with established Broadway stars under the company name "Famous Players in Famous Plays." Made a bundle doing it, too, even if the movies themselves were dreadful.

Zukor was nothing if not smart, and he understood that Bernhardt's semaphoric acting style didn't suit the new medium. Instead, he had his eye on a young girl appearing in a Belasco play. "I knew Mary Pickford had had picture experience, because she had been with Biograph a couple of years before and knew the camera," the mogul told the audience at a 1927 Harvard Business School lecture. "We tried people who were well advanced on the stage, but the director could not make them do things to suit the camera. I felt if we could get people who had experience on the stage and also had some camera experience, the results would be much better."

This sounds a little like Sam Phillips's early-1950s comment that if he could find a white kid who sang like a black man, he might make a killing. And in fact Mary Pickford was the Elvis of early movie stardom, the figure who completely rewrote the rules for audience investment in a person appearing in motion pictures. She was the first global media star—the first person to be famous across the entire planet at the same time. She was the first star to take control of the business of herself. And she was the first star to be held prisoner by her onscreen image—the original celebrity victim of persona.

2.

The First Goddesses: Mary Pickford, Norma Talmadge, Flappers, and Virgins

The nostalgic mistake most of us make, sitting here in our twenty-first-century catbird seat, is that the silent era was all one thing, a blur of black and white scored to an immense ballfield organ. This is nonsense, and complacent nonsense at that. The gulf between a 1908 Griffith short and anything released in, say, 1927—a melodrama like *Seventh Heaven* or an art film like *Metropolis* or *Sunrise*—is vast. It's the difference between a toddler's first steps and a grown man's stride. The late-1920s talkie revolution dialed everything back to zero, but before it did, the movies achieved a remarkable artistic maturity even as the business of the star system gradually took it hostage.

In those first three decades, and for some time after, the industry catered primarily to women, a constituency for which celluloid dreams of consumption and fantasy proved irresistible. This was a largely conscious decision by the early studios to develop their most loyal audience, and the new industries of fan magazines and advertising also leaped upon it as the source of immense collateral profits. Plenty of men went to the movies, and plenty of them had favorite actors and actresses, but the urgency driving the star discourse, onscreen and in the fan press, was largely female. What set the cinema apart was its ability to dramatize and visualize a woman-centric universe that didn't exist in reality but that instead reflected the inner lives of millions of women across America. In essence, the medium provided an arena for consensual mass role-playing, with each female star a richly loaded icon of potentiality. What would these icons do, and would they be punished or rewarded for it? Come into the dark and find out.

So there were three primary periods of the silent era—infancy, maturity, decadence—and the only thing they had in common was Mary Pickford. She was huge in all of them. How huge? You wouldn't believe it if I told you. We are sold so many celebrities today, on such a regular basis, that the adjectives have become impotent. Because Pickford's rise to fame paralleled the birth of movie stardom itself—because no one had ever been famous like *this* before—the mania surrounding her was freshly minted, newly crazy. Florence Lawrence made St. Louis go nuts, but Pickford caused mob scenes in New York and the capitals of Europe during her 1920 honeymoon. The hysteria came from the lack of established guide rails—from the vertiginous sense fans had that they were operating in wholly new territory, one that granted a deeper (if illusory) intimacy with the worshipped idol. Pickford pioneered the frontier of movie stardom and mapped many if not all of its dimensions: art, entertainment, commerce, publicity. In the process, she changed how Hollywood and popular culture did business.

She was born Gladys Smith in Toronto in 1892 and, following the familiar path for early "picture personalities," had a bum for a father and a hard-jawed juggernaut for a mother. The former died when Gladys was six, not long before the girl made her stage debut with a local theater company. She hit the road three years later, at age nine, and was soon supporting her mother, Charlotte, and two siblings, Jack and Lottie, both of whom would have subsidiary movie careers of their own. At fourteen, tired of the touring life, Gladys turned up at the office of the great Broadway impresario David Belasco and harangued him until he gave in. Casting the determined little nobody in one of his plays, he insisted she at least change her name. Thus Mary Pickford was born out of a combination of curly-headed charm and ruthless drive.

In 1909, she decided to try movies at the urging of her mother. Pickford dropped into Biograph and informed D. W. Griffith that five dollars a day wasn't good enough but that ten would do. She was hired; something about her youthful imperiousness hypnotized people into bending to her will. Within a year, Pickford was the new Biograph Girl, already known to dazzled audiences as "Little Mary." In 1910, during the first flush of movie star mania, Pickford was the subject of a full-page spread in *Motion Picture World* in which she was called "an artiste of the highest rank in a field where there are few of her kind." This was mere marketing hype. She wasn't *that* famous yet.

Still, in the early Biograph one-reelers that survive, you can see why people responded to her: she was *there*. Pickford had—still has—a presence onscreen that is vivid and alive without ever seeming forced. She's a natural, and you can tell what's going through her mind simply by the emotions that pass quickly and easily across her face. In the 1912 Griffith short *The New York Hat,* in which she plays a small-town girl mistakenly assumed to be having an affair with the local pastor (a young Lionel Barrymore), Pickford's quicksilver vibrancy makes the whispering old biddies who oppose her look like nineteenth-century etchings. Wrote *Motion Picture World* in a review of one of her films, "It seems as though she was not acting at all, but was simply having a good time." In that one sentence is the defining difference between stage and screen performance.

She and Griffith didn't see eye to eye. Even if her time at Biograph offered her the greatest variety of roles she'd ever get to play—brides, villainesses, Native American princesses—Little Mary was too tough-minded for the idealized innocence the great director prized in actresses (and which he found at last when Lillian Gish showed up one day in 1912). "Mr. Griffith always wanted to have me running around trees and pointing at rabbits, and I wouldn't do it," she wrote later, and so she jumped to Carl Laemmle's IMP, then to Majestic, then back to Biograph, learning the fine art of salary negotiation as she went. Then, temporarily soured on the movies, she returned to Broadway. In 1913, she met the man who may have been her most natural match. Not Douglas Fairbanks; that was later and that was love. This was business, and the man was Adolph Zukor.

Zukor's Famous Players in Famous Plays production company was doing good business putting well-known names on the screen, but established stage actors didn't know how to play to the camera, and not a few of them were drunks. So Zukor invited Charlotte Pickford and her daughter to lunch at Delmonico's. In his 1953 autobiography, *The Public Is Never Wrong*, he recalled his pitch: " 'The screen public will choose its favorites,' [I told them]. 'There will be a star system rivaling—maybe outshining—that of the stage. As for money, we have shown with *Queen Elizabeth* and *The Prisoner of Zenda* that people will pay higher prices for better entertainment. Big salaries are not a dream, for we have already begun to pay them—have been roundly denounced in the trade for it. If feature pictures succeed—and of this I have no doubt—we expect to pay according to drawing power at the box office.' "

At last: someone who spoke Little Mary's language. Within a few days, Pickford and Zukor had negotiated a contract paying her $500 a week, an absurdly high figure for the time. "I did not quibble," wrote her new employer. "I knew her value for the future and I expected to be paying her more than that before we were finished." In fact, he would be paying her twenty times that amount—$10,000 a week—within three years. As in so many other aspects of the infant industry, Zukor saw what was over the horizon more cleanly and dispassionately than any of his rivals.

It took a few films to get the formula down, but with the early-1914 release of *Tess of the Storm Country,* Pickford became the kind of public figure for which there was no precedent. "Little Mary Pickford comes into her own," raved *Variety,* and the film was so popular that Famous Players brought it back into theaters up to eight times over the following months. She was twenty-two. It was her 196th film.

The movies tumbled out, feature-length now, seven in 1914, ten in 1915. Pickford was the subject of constant veneration in the new entertainment press, lauded in the *Ladies' Home Journal* as "the best-known girl in America." She had her own face cream on the market by 1915—Pompeiian Skin Cream—and a daily newspaper column that same year, ghostwritten by screenwriter Frances Marion. Letters poured in, to the actress and to the fan magazines, in which you can feel both the intimacy of the star/fan bond and the dispiriting distance between idol and idolater. "If I could grow up to be one hundredth part as sweet and lovely as Mary Pickford, my dearest wish would be fulfilled," wrote one fan to *Photoplay,* not having the faintest clue what the real Mary Pickford was like. But everyone was making that mistake just then.

What Pickford didn't convey was sex, at least not in public. The Pickford persona—the one that would harden into marble by the early 1920s—was that of a smart, sassy girl-child on the cusp of adolescence. The titles of the movies themselves tell us what the audience wanted to see and what Pickford the canny businesswoman was happy to give them: *Little Pal, A Girl of Yesterday, Little Peppina,* and of course her hugely successful run of classic-lit adaptations, *The Poor Little Rich Girl, Rebecca of Sunnybrook Farm, The Little Princess, Pollyanna,* and so on. By the time she played the rough-and-tumble slum kid of 1925's *Little Annie Rooney,* the actress was thirty-three years old. Pickford was the original American Girl.

That is why she was loved by men but rapturously adored and ultimately imprisoned by women. As the new medium of cinema pulled its audience blinking into the twentieth century, Pickford became a visible icon of nineteenth-century storytelling and virtues. Not the sort of gauzy Victorian ideal that Lillian Gish would come to embody and elevate, but something tougher, closer to Tom Sawyer than Becky Thatcher. There's a lot of Twain and Dickens in all those little girls (and boys) she played, but there's even more Horatio Alger: pluck and determination, fast wits, a saving sense of humor. When a Pickford movie gets sentimental, surprisingly little of it comes from the actress herself. Onscreen and off, she was nobody's victim, but she still functioned as a psychic safe zone for audiences that couldn't begin to articulate why they needed one.

The cultural continuity she stood for—the sense that the hectic Now was still grounded in a comforting Then—took on a nearly desperate necessity in the wake of World War I. As the variety of female roles available onscreen (and as models for women in the audience) exploded to include vamps and tramps, clotheshorses and waifs, working women and wandering wives, Pickford held down the center, setting the terms for the culture of her day by seeming somehow bigger than that culture. As would be the case with the Beatles in the 1960s, there was Pickford and there was everybody else.

Like Chaplin, she prompted the sort of praise reserved for civic statuary. Writing in a 1917 issue of the *New Republic,* the poet and early film critic Vachel Lindsay titled his review of Pickford's *A Romance of the Redwoods* "Queen of My People" and said, "[T]o reject this girl in haste is high treason to the national heart." To not like Mary Pickford wasn't just in poor taste, it was un-American.

But what if the girl wanted to become a woman? As the teens moved into the twenties, Pickford struggled to emancipate herself in different roles. The public would have none of it. In magazine polls and in letters, they demanded their Little Mary because that's who they thought she was. If she grew up, they would have to grow up and let go of an innocence that was slowly slipping away. Pickford represented a deepening and more necessary nostalgia, and she understood what was happening. "I became, in a sense, my own baby," she later admitted.

Even Zukor recognized the injustice, while also realizing it was great for business. "It is ironical, I suppose, that Mary could not portray on the screen the indomitable woman who was one part of her," he wrote in his autobiography. "In 1916, Mary was twenty-three, had been married for several years, and was being paid more than the President of the United States. Yet to the public she was a little girl somewhere between the ages of twelve and eighteen. We did nothing to discourage the illusion."

Mary Pickford could do whatever she wanted, obviously. She chose not to, because for her the public was to be obeyed. To a woman who had been a working actress since the age of six, any other response was unthinkable. The notion of the "rebel star" that would take shape during the sound era and blossom with Marlon Brando in the post–World War II era didn't yet exist. Anyway, Pickford was too good a businesswoman to play with fire.

What she did do, in a number of 1917 and 1918 movies and periodically into the 1920s, was play two roles per film: young girl and grown woman. It's shocking to watch *Stella Maris* (1918) and realize that the fairly boring title character and the warped, abused orphan Unity Blake are in fact played by the same actress. One woman glows, the other skulks; one is graceful and shallow, the other is a quirky, pathetic instrument of vengeance. This is more than hair and makeup. Directed by Marshall Neilan, a talented, hard-drinking party boy who became Pickford's preferred director, *Stella Maris* may be the star's best film. Yet Unity Blake is a testament to the artistic skills her fans didn't actually want from her. (Nor did Zukor: one story goes that he turned pale when he saw Pickford in costume as Unity until she reassured him, "Don't worry, I die before it's over.")

Besides, there were so many other new women to fill the niches Little Mary wasn't allowed to. She may have held the mountaintop, but on the promontories just below were stars of equal psychological necessity: melodramatic fashion plates like Norma Talmadge and Gloria Swanson, the ethereal Lillian Gish, and the two faces of the flapper, plucky Colleen Moore and hypersexual Clara Bow. There were major male movie stars of this era—see the next chapter—but attention must first and foremost be paid to the actresses, because they served a critical function for the movies' most critical early audience. To a nation (and a world) of women in the dark, the female stars showed what could be thought and felt and possibly done. As models of behavior and misbehavior, they were nothing short of revolutionary.

Theda Bara was first, a thoroughgoing sensation in 1915's *A Fool There Was*. The actress was a former Chicago shopgirl named Theodosia Goodman who had come to the attention of ambitious producer-exhibitor William Fox, who hyped her new name as an anagram of "Arab Death." The movie is primitive and Bara's kiss-me-my-fool writhings now look ridiculous, but the public was ready to be ravished by foreign sirens, and the imposture took. (The success of *Fool* also made Fox an industry player, and the studio chief's name lives on as an entertainment and cultural brand decades after he himself went bust in 1929.)

More important were the real deals: Pola Negri from Poland, Alla Nazimova from Russia, and eventually Greta Garbo from Sweden, in her silent MGM films a pitiless gray-eyed goddess of destruction. Swooning and cursing, driving stupid men to their dooms, these women of the world acted out all the emotions a good American girl was supposed to keep to herself, and all the sexual gamesmanship as well. Never before had the fantasy of conquest and revenge seemed so close.

A Woman of the World was even the title of a 1925 Negri vehicle, one that playfully explores the space between American heartland simplicity and jaded Eurotrash sophistication. It's a comedy but an indulgent one that likes all its characters, and it shows how far American society (and, by extension, American moviegoers) had come by the mid-1920s. The foreign vamp was no longer a threat, no Arab Death, but rather a cool survivor who might teach us all a few things.

Negri was a fascinating presence onscreen—with her black hair, mocking smile, and heavy-lidded eyes, she seems almost proto-Goth. In *A Woman of the World,* she plays the Countess Elnora Natatorini, who flees a Continental romance gone sour to a distant cousin's house in a small American hamlet called Maple Valley. In short order, the town's crusading district attorney (Charles Emmett Mack) has fallen for this black-dressing arriviste from abroad—the countess thinks he's pretty hot, too—and the townspeople are buzzing about the black skull tattoo on her arm. (She "did it for love," which all the small-town characters nod at in sympathetic understanding.)

It's a fun movie, and it shows how deeply the figure of "the other woman" had become embedded and even forgiven in the discourse of the movies and popular culture. *A Woman of the World* pretends to be about the collision of small-town American values and "foreign" morals, but it's really about the two coexisting in a post–World War I world that's much, much smaller than it had been ten years before. Somewhat radically, it says you can be a European countess if you live in Maple Valley, USA—even if you've never been to Europe. More and more the new movie stars offered their audiences choices; less and less they seemed to judge.

This fresh sophistication influenced the portrayal of all-American girls, too, especially in the dramatic dilemmas of Norma Talmadge and Gloria Swanson, each of them critical to the evolution of female stardom in the postwar years. Both actresses could play for laughs or tragedy, and both functioned as paper dolls for the fashion fantasies of the women who paid to see them. Swanson now seems the smarter, sharper figure—not especially beautiful (with that regal jaw that would seem so paranoid thirty years later in *Sunset Blvd.*), but perceptive and chic. The series of "daring" social comedies she made with a very young Cecil B. DeMille for Zukor's new Paramount Pictures put her over: *Don't Change Your Husband* (1919), *Why Change Your Wife?* (1920), the ripely bizarre *Male and Female* (1919), with Gloria as a rich girl getting down with hunky butler Thomas Meighan on a desert island, complete with left-hand turn into ancient Babylonian flashback, Swanson stepped on by a live lion. She acted out all the sex and adventure that fans were beginning to realize were their due, her films both feeding on that desire and creating it with newly impatient visual splendor.

Norma Talmadge was, if anything, even more important to women of her time, which is one reason she's entirely forgotten today: the curse of the actress who embodies her generation is that she means almost nothing to the generations that follow. When talkies arrived, Talmadge was quickly swept away in the new noise, and that seems to have been fine by her—she'd had a great run, and she knew it. Behind the elegant onscreen attitude was a Brooklyn attitude and a Brooklyn accent; the latter was scrubbed away with speech lessons, but the effort was obvious.

Talmadge had a sister who was a star, too—Constance, who appeared mostly in comedies as opposed to Norma's dramatic vehicles. (There was a third sister, Natalie, who wasn't much of an actress and who was relegated to opening her sisters' fan mail until she married the great slapstick artist Buster Keaton in what turned out to be the defining mistake of his career.) More important, the Talmadge girls had another of those dreadnought stage mothers who yanked her daughters out of Brooklyn and across the river to the Vitagraph studios starting in 1910. (Dad, again, was a loser and long gone; Mama Peg referred to him as "that skunk.")

Most important by far, Norma Talmadge had Joseph Schenk, the studio executive nineteen years her senior who married her in 1917 and immediately set about improving his investment. Norma had been languishing at Vitagraph; a good and easygoing presence on film, she nevertheless lacked a persona. She portrayed the new modern girl in all her youth and silliness, shamed into shoplifting a dress to keep up with her sorority in 1914's *The Helpful (?) Sisterhood,* playing a shallow, cigarette-smoking society woman (named Lesbia!) in the same year's *John Rance, Gentleman.* She was dark-eyed, dark-haired, and pretty, though—she registered.

After hopscotching from Vitagraph to National to Triangle, Talmadge had her breakthrough in a delightful 1916 comedy called *The Social Secretary.* The triumph belongs as much to screenwriter Anita Loos, who was probably the brightest and smartest of early Hollywood's young women screenwriters. Loos would go on to write the classic *Gentlemen Prefer Blondes,* and her script for *Secretary* similarly acknowledges sex appeal while making a joke of it, putting Talmadge in glasses and frumpy frocks in an effort to keep the title job. (Think *Ugly Betty* eighty-five years early.) Loos's opening titles wittily sketch out the daunting new twentieth-century universe facing women while suggesting a way to navigate it: "New York, the magnet that draws countless thousands of working girls; where temptation abounds at every hand, but where a good girl can be just as good as she can be in Wichita."

A year later Norma met and wed Schenk, who set her up in her own Norma Talmadge Film Corporation. Although the marriage looked like a business arrangement, there was real feeling there. Schenk was ugly, sometimes crude, but he had ideas and dynamism—writing in her gossipy 1978 book *The Talmadge Girls,* Loos gushingly described him as "an outstanding example of the fascination that comes from power."

Schenck knew star persona could be fudged by opulence and big budgets. Surround Norma with ritzy sets, swaddle her in couture or costume exotica, give her good directors and writers and publicists, handsome leading men, and stories long on martyrdom and escapism—and the women will come. And they did, starting with 1917's *Panthea,* the first of Talmadge's Schenk productions, and all the way through to her last silent, *The Woman Disputed,* eleven years and thirty-eight movies later. The biggest hits were *Smilin' Through* (1922) and *Kiki* (1926), but all of her movies did well and in a sense were merely one long film called *Norma Talmadge Dresses Up and Suffers for Your Entertainment.* The star was the new Hollywood lifestyle, and each movie, each magazine article, was a window through which that world could be glimpsed by us, the plebes, greasy palms against the glass.

Talmadge's career path is important for a number of reasons. As one of the first movie actresses to demonstrate the value of having a powerful and intelligent sugar daddy, she paved the way for Marion Davies (the longtime mistress of media baron William Randolph Hearst), Norma Shearer (who married MGM's boy genius Irving Thalberg and prospered), and dozens of other female stars over the years. In this, Talmadge was the anti-Pickford, perfectly content to rely on others to handle the business of her business.

She wasn't the first wholly manufactured star—Theda Bara gets that honor—but Schenk was the first mogul to get it right. He seems to have understood the gestalt of movie star creation, that it was the whole package that mattered, on and off the screen. Norma wasn't a particularly incisive movie personality, but she was lovely to look at and to clothe, and she was a pretty good actress, especially in lighter dramatic roles. In the context of her time she was even considered a "great actress," because Schenk varied the parts and, in addition to American heroines, let Norma dress up as Chinese, Arab, Native American, and, in 1921's *Love or Hate,* a character named "Acacia, the Passion Flower."

Crucially, Talmadge was the first movie star to truly sell herself as a lifestyle, one to which her fans could and should want to aspire. Women wanted to be Mary Pickford, but they wanted to dress like Norma Talmadge—and drive the same cars and live in the same sort of mansions. They couldn't afford such things, of course, but they could afford the beauty creams and makeup, and they could remodel themselves on Norma's lines, with her help. Those lines, when it came to clothing, should be "soft and inconspicuous," and the walk should be poised, or so advised the actress in a 1922 *Photoplay* article titled "Miss Talmadge Says," one of many in which the actress functioned as a makeover oracle.

What Miss Talmadge said was that it isn't how you feel, it's how you look. This jibed with a larger shift in popular opinion. Perception—the way other people see you—took on a vast and almost desperate importance in the teens and twenties. Such qualities as honesty and inner strength, moral conviction, duty to God and country, came to seem passé; what mattered now was "personality." Did you have it? If not, how could you get it? During this era, magazines and pamphlets and mail-order booklets crowded in like primitive spam, all promising to show the reader how to magnetically charm other people with "personality." Look them in the eye; smile at them. Say what you think they want to hear. Who you really are isn't important; it's who they *think* you are that matters. Pretend, and you will become.

It's impossible to think that the movies didn't play an immense part in this. Because the early films were silent, and because they loomed so large, they put a premium on presentation—on how the stars looked. Perhaps audiences already sensed that what they saw was a false front, that the actors were just the same as you or I, but what a beautiful false front, and how could we get some of that for ourselves? By looking like the stars, obviously, and by aping their pearl-toothed charisma. The silent era is when the leisure and advice industries first came into their own, with consumer role-playing enabled by the glamorous possibilities enacted on the screen. The promise was simple: Follow Norma's rules (dress like her, act like her), and you can be your own star. Better, you can be your own movie. To daily lives as starved of melodrama as the average American filmgoer's, this was better than good. It was a bargain, dreams made real on the cheap.

The old truisms didn't just go away, of course. While the movies offered endless iterations of the modern woman—comediennes like Marion Davies and Constance Talmadge, beauty queens like Barbara La Marr, plucky heroines like Mae Murray and Mae Marsh—the struggle to define acceptable female behavior was the dominant obsession of the culture and the cinema. What made a bad girl bad? Could a good girl be true to her hopes and desires without *becoming* bad? In the movies, the dialectic took the form of two archetypes, one phasing out, the other phasing in. The former was the fragile virginal innocent, a vestige of nineteenth-century America, and while many actresses played it, Lillian Gish came to embody the persona, provided it with a spine, and, by the late 1920s, had become the archetype's conscious artistic remnant.

The other archetype was the modern American girl, the one called the flapper, after the unfastened galoshes in which she and her friends stomped around. Olive Thomas laid the groundwork, Colleen Moore served as the epitome, and Clara Bow acted out the dangers of taking the character too far. (Louise Brooks, who many today consider the greatest exponent of the type, haircut and all, was unappreciated in her own time—a popular but not all that necessary screen flapper who had to go to Germany to make the movies for which she's now rightly venerated.)

Gish first, and not just because she was the last to go, dying in 1993 at the age of ninety-nine—still cogent, still kind, the living cameo in the attic chest of pop culture. Gish mattered because the quality she projected, a stunningly graceful moral purity, was an old-fashioned concept she successfully ported into the modern era with the help of director D. W. Griffith. At first she embodied it unself-consciously; then, as she matured and the culture coarsened around her, she took upon herself the role of the Last Good Woman in the movies.

There was nothing judgmental in this at all. It seems to have been simply who Gish was, and she was smart enough to recognize it as a market niche. What a young Queen Victoria she might have made, or a Jo March; as it was, the star of 1933's *Little Women,* Katharine Hepburn, carries much of Gish's cinematic DNA, which itself has roots in the long-vanished America of the New England Transcendentalists. Few movie stars practiced Emersonian self-reliance as well as Lillian Gish.

For all that, few fell apart onscreen like she did. The closet scene in D. W. Griffith's *Broken Blossoms* (1919) is the one that sticks out in early film history like a broken tooth, and it has an immediacy that renders it still frightening. Gish is playing a London slum girl beaten and bullied by her sadistic father (Donald Crisp); in the film's climax, she locks herself in the closet to hide from his wrath, and as he batters down the door with a hatchet, Gish enacts a harrowing display of panic collapsing into madness. She spins in tighter and tighter circles, mouth quivering, eyes widening and turning up in her head. This is art and it's obscene; you feel every blow upon the door of a young girl's fragility. The film was a Paramount production, but when Adolph Zukor saw a print, he was horrified: "You bring me a picture like this and want money for it? You may as well put your hand in my pocket and steal it. Everybody in it dies." A few days later, Griffith put $250,000 on Zukor's desk and bought back the rights; *Broken Blossoms* went on to make a killing.

Gish could rein it in, too, underplaying the baptism of her dead newborn child in *Way Down East* (1920) and making you weep at her stoicism, but her true métier may have been innocence cracking under pressure. *The Wind* (1928) is probably her best movie (despite a lousy happy ending insisted on by the exhibitors; even she hated it), and as the sexually repressed girl from back east whose mind snaps in the endless Texas winds Gish again makes emotional meltdown horrifyingly real. Because she looked so angelic, she seemed to have farther to fall.

You can see this in Gish's very first film, 1912's *An Unseen Enemy*. It's an exceedingly strange Biograph short about burglars terrorizing two young sisters in the next room by sticking a loaded pistol through a vent in the wall. Gish, eighteen, and her sister Dorothy, fourteen, had shown up at the studio on 11 East Fourteenth Street one day with their mother—once again, father was long gone—impressed that their onetime backstage friend Gladys Smith had reinvented herself for the movies as Mary Pickford. As Lillian tells it in her autobiography, Griffith scooped the sisters up into a rehearsal room, dubbed one "Red" and the other "Blue" when he couldn't remember their names, and goaded them into hysterical nervous breakdowns by enacting the scene he wanted to film. "Tell the camera what you feel," he yelled. "Fear—*more fear*! Look into the lens!" For added insurance, the director pulled a loaded gun from his pocket and fired into the ceiling, then calmly told the Gishes, "You have expressive bodies. I can use you."

The pert, adored Dorothy would have a successful movie career with and without her sister, but Lillian became something larger, muse to the father of the movies and proof that his disappearing America could register on film. Today, she seems a visual correlative of all the pre–World War I sensibilities that were then dying out, and Gish may have understood that better than her mentor. To the end of her life she defended Griffith's problematic breakthrough, *The Birth of a Nation* (1915), against charges of racism, even though it's easy to read between the lines of her autobiography for her true thoughts on the matter.

And she was willing to do anything for the Master, including lying on an ice floe on Vermont's upper Connecticut River for hours during the filming of *Way Down East*. The temperature was subzero; icicles formed on her eyelashes and her hand grew numb as it trailed in the water (for the rest of her life, she said, it bothered her in the cold). Bounding across the breaking ice to rescue her, costar Richard Barthelmess fell in the water and nearly drowned. Years later, he said to her, "We could have been killed. There isn't enough money in the world to pay me to do it today." And Gish, writing calmly in her book as if murmuring to herself, replied, "But we weren't doing it for money."

That is something different. That is what Lillian Gish brought to the table. *We weren't doing it for money.* Can you imagine Mary Pickford saying such a thing? She would have screamed and called for her lawyers. Other actresses might provide moving testimonials about inspiration and art, but most of them were primarily interested in job security. Gish genuinely believed that the cinema *was* art—not one derived from stagecraft but a form with its own beauties and rules and dark meanings—and she devoted herself to that idea like a nun at the altar.

She never married. Today rumors would accrue (and, since her death, have accrued) around that domestic omission; while she was alive, the prevailing image of Gish was of a woman married nobly to her art. When MGM's Irving Thalberg, desperate to loosen her image in the late 1920s, offered to arrange a scandal for her, she graciously declined, returned to the New York stage, and every so often dropped in on the movies like a stern but kindly conscience. Her last movie was 1987's *The Whales of August,* and when a costar expressed sorrow that Gish hadn't been nominated for an Oscar, the ninety-four-year-old actress shrugged and said, "It could be worse. Suppose I'd been nominated and lost to Cher?"

There *is* something inherently chiding in her insistence that the movies can and should be better than themselves—something vaguely medicinal, like all those 1980s Meryl Streep performances that were nominated for Oscars because they were Good For You. Or maybe that's just the guilt of audiences who know they're mostly in it for the trash. Gish understood her worth, though, and also the weight of being the cinema's chaste grandma. "Oh, I'd *love* to have played a vamp," she said in 1983 about her silent years. "Seventy-five percent of your work is done for you. When you play those innocent little virgins, that's when you have to work hard." And yet her performances seem weirdly sophisticated now next to the actresses who, in the years following World War I, were the very model of the new American girl.

The term "flapper" today conjures up an image of an impossibly slim young 1920s woman with bobbed hair, a cloche hat, fringed dress, unsnapped galoshes. She smokes a cigarette from a long holder and swigs illegal gin from a small flask in her rolled-up stocking. She dances the Charleston, necks in the rumble seat of a Ford, goes to "petting parties," has sex. She doesn't break rules so much as exist outside of them: in this sense, the flapper is a forerunner of the hippie chicks of the 1960s and the riotgrrls of the 1990s. She is, quite clearly, great-great-aunt to Ellen Page's Juno, smart-mouthed and possibly aware that she's a little lost. And for a long while she's surprisingly hard to find in the movies.

Which is to say that there's a 1920 film called *The Flapper*, starring Olive Thomas, but the title character bears no resemblance to the cultural cliché outlined above. If anything, Thomas comes off as an oversexed Heidi, sneaking out of her boarding school to woo an appalled older man and quickly revealed as a young girl out of her depth. She's an immature prankster, not a New Woman, and one senses the movie and the culture that produced it dancing around a character they're too nervous to confront.

Colleen Moore, on the other hand, was a John Held drawing come to life: wide eyes, Kewpie-doll lips, and a sense of mischief that did seem like something new and unfettered. *Flaming Youth* (1923) cemented the image of the flapper, with Moore as its face. Scott Fitzgerald wrote, "I was the spark that lit up flaming youth, and Colleen Moore was the torch. What little things we are to have caused all that trouble."

Actually, she kept the torch from burning down the house. In *Flaming Youth* and its hastily produced follow-up, 1924's *The Perfect Flapper*, Moore tamed a dangerous persona—editorials were being written about these sexually frank young women—and made it palatable for market consumption. Her characters Patricia Fentriss in *Flaming*

Youth and Tommie Lou Pember in *Perfect Flapper* dance the shimmy and go to petting parties but they're fundamentally good girls because Colleen Moore herself was one—a nice Irish kid from a happy family (for once!) who worked her way up in the movies, invested her money wisely, and eventually died content, wealthy, and old in 1988. In the twenty-odd films she made from her 1923 breakthrough into the early sound era, she neutered the image of the Wild Child and rendered it adorable. In language your daughters might understand, Moore took Lindsay Lohan and turned her into Anne Hathaway.

In so doing, she reconfigured the flapper into a figure of consumer fantasy and wish fulfillment. Moore's slimness and the geometric lines of her hair and dresses were part of the appeal—she's almost more fascinating to look at in still photos than in motion—but so is a wholesomeness that softened and mainstreamed the archetype. In *Orchids and Ermine* (1927), a typical Colleen Moore film of its time, she plays "Pink" Watson, a big-city hotel telephone operator looking for Mr. Right. There's a silly comedy plot about a handsome but mild-mannered oil millionaire (Jack Mulhall) who switches places with his valet (Sam Hardy), not to mention a brief and wholly bizarre appearance by a seven-year-old Mickey Rooney as a midget, but the main order of business seems to be the friendship between Pink and her friend Ermintrude (Gwen Lee).

Ermintrude is what the flapper was before Colleen Moore got hold of her: She exudes sex like it's BO. She's blond and blowsy, her posture is terrible, and she checks out all the men in the movie with long glances that seem to weigh their wallets and everything else down there. *Orchids and Ermine* says, Girls, don't be like her. Be like Colleen—sweet and funny and flighty, rooted in the common morals that have sustained us, lo, these many centuries. In her 1920s films, Moore prefigured such sassy yet fundamentally nice girls as the Mary Tyler Moore of the 1970s and the Sandra Bullock of the 1990s. The one thing she *didn't* do was put out.

But Clara Bow—oh, dear sweet Jesus. If Moore worked her way up to stardom and consciously fashioned her image (or had it fashioned for her), Bow was a blat of raw sexual energy from outside the system.

Her performances are galvanized by a vivacious electricity that's bigger than sex but that clearly includes it, and *all* of it. In her sense of joyful carnality and the sadness that lurks beneath, Bow looks ahead to Marilyn Monroe, but where Monroe had a dreamy slowness to her (the sensuality of both the come-on and the afterglow), Bow's motor seems to rev uncontrollably into the red. There's something a little desperate about this kind of jazz-baby gusto; that's the excitement and the danger, and it rendered her suspect in the eyes of commentators and even many of her fans. She most certainly did not have sex with the entire USC football team, as one rumor went, but it was easy for people to believe she could have.

Bow was another Brooklyn kid, but more desperately poor than most. In 1921, she won a fan magazine contest offering "Fame and Fortune"; first prize was a train ticket to Hollywood and a part in a movie. She was sixteen years old, and grabbed onto the film business as the lifeline it surely was. In 1922, she appeared in two films, one a quasi–whaling documentary funded by the town of New Bedford, Massachusetts. In 1923, she made four films and met B. P. Schulberg, the executive who would steer her career. In 1924, she made eight films. In 1925, *fifteen*. You can feel Bow clawing her way up the ladder, never once looking down.

Mantrap (1926)—the title's the name of a town, but it's obviously selling Clara, too—was the film that put her over, and 1927's *It* made her a sensation. *It* was originally a lurid best seller by Elinor Glyn, the Jackie Collins of her day, and "it," for all the mystery and Glyn's own self-promoting hoodoo, was old-fashioned sexual magnetism. (*New Yorker* wit Dorothy Parker, as usual, cleared the air around the subject: "It, hell," she said about Bow. "She had Those.") Bow's movies all have sleazy titles—*Dangerous Curves, Rough House Rosie, The Fleet's In* (the implication of the latter being that Ms. Bow will be otherwise engaged for the next week or two). She also starred in the first movie to win a Best Picture Oscar, 1927's *Wings*, and she was Paramount's top draw for a few years. It didn't get her much respect.

To watch her in a film—*It* is available on DVD, and recommended—is to understand why: Bow is uncontainable. She's a wild thing, and you can tell that it scares even her a little. Today, that sort of energy would be celebrated. Actually, today, Bow would probably be a rock star, channeling her craziness into acceptable noise. In 1927, watching this lascivious little animal prepare for a date with her boss in *It* and almost shimmying off the screen to a Charleston only she can hear must have caused acute sexual discomfort in at least half of America's moviegoers. She behaved vertically the way women weren't even supposed to behave horizontally.

So Bow was leered at and mocked, and when she sued her secretary for embezzlement in 1931 and the secretary retaliated by telling sordid tales of Clara's sex life in court, heads nodded and lips pursed everywhere. She was still naive enough (only twenty-six by then) that it hurt.

The unspoken implication—and this is where Clara Bow matters most—is that maybe she didn't deserve stardom after all. Maybe she was just a fan who got lucky. Bow hadn't come up through the theater like Florence Lawrence or Mary Pickford, and she didn't come to film as a young professional like Colleen Moore or Gloria Swanson. She won a contest. She was one of us. No wonder she always played shopgirls.

There was at this time a great deal of public anxiety about young female outsiders crashing the Hollywood dream palace. It's forgotten now that the startling success of the new medium created a mass emigration to Los Angeles by thousands upon thousands of would-be actors and actresses in the teens and early twenties. The urge goes back to the earliest days of the industry, a plea to be seen that is almost embarrassing in its intensity. "Miss Lawrence, have you a protégé?" a fan beseeched Florence Lawrence in a 1914 letter. "I would like very much to act and I am going to act. . . . The very soul in me seems to cry out for the chance to express what it has concealed for years."

Hear her need: *a chance to express what it has concealed for years.* Multiply that sentiment by a thousand, a million, and you begin to sense why the young movie industry and keepers of the public morals panicked as droves of young women arrived in Hollywood looking for work. There is such aching frustration in that letter, and the movies both soothed the frustration and fanned the flames. In her head, the Lawrence fan was already a star, but since no one in her daily life saw that stardom, it didn't really exist and neither did she. Movies proved you weren't really a star—you didn't really matter—unless you were seen. All those women flocking to the movie factories just wanted an audience to validate what they already felt.

It should be noted, though, that Lawrence's letter writer perfectly misunderstands what film acting (and acting in general) is about. Acting is not the art of expressing yourself at all. It's the art of expressing somebody else. When Carl Laemmle and Adolph Zukor built the star system on the faces of Lawrence and Pickford, they fudged what was really going on—a craft of pretending—and instead gave the audiences the dreams of self they clearly wanted. (And don't think they didn't know it, especially Zukor.) The new system placed value on the "picture personality," not the particular film or performance, so of course it seemed as though the new movie stars were "expressing what they had concealed for years"—an extension of who they already were.

That was a lie and it still is, the great mistake upon which celebrity culture was built during this time and by which it continues to operate. Even the movie stars who don't seem like actors, who mint consistent personalities that carry over from film to film to film—the Pickfords and Cary Grants and Joan Crawfords, all the way up to the George Clooneys and Anne Hathaways—are playing pretend. If we in the audience mistake what they do for a reflection of who they "really are," we do so at our peril.

So over a hundred "extra girls," as they came to be called, arrived in the movie capital every week during the teens and twenties, and the film studios did everything they could to scare them off. "Out of 100,000 persons who started at the bottom of the screen's ladder of fame, only five reached the top," warned industry ads placed in newspapers across the country in the mid-1920s, while a 1927 four-part *Photoplay* series titled "The Truth About Breaking Into the Movies" ended with the blunt warning, "Don't go to Hollywood!"

The great unspoken fear, of course, was sex. A movie-struck girl alone in a big city with no income might turn to prostitution or become prey to the sexual underworld. Maybe her morals would just erode from lack of work. One article quoted a weary Extra Girl who had been invited to share living quarters with an actor: "I guess I know what that means, but I'm tired of going hungry."

The reality of striving for stardom was often banal and sometimes ugly. Bow found out the hard way, and she was one of the success stories. In a very real sense, she was the Extra Girl who got through the studio gates and lived the dream, but she never quite learned the rules, one of which was that embodying untempered sexuality in a society deeply messed up about sex will both raise you up and bring you down. They will love you and hate you for turning them on. Bow's mistake was that she showed herself to audiences as she *really* "really was," assuming, perhaps, that that's what first prize in a "Fame and Fortune" contest meant. It wasn't that she was a bad actress—she wasn't. Being Clara Bow just came more naturally to her. The audience's mistake lay in assuming that a woman who acted like she slept around actually did.

So Bow got to "express what she had concealed for years"—you can see it come pulsing off her in waves of nervous excitement in the early roles and you can see it slowly dull over time. And at the end, when Bow retired from the screen in 1933 after a dozen or so talkies—she never got used to the microphones—she said to the press, in words that could have come from all the girls buying bus tickets home, "It wasn't ever like I thought it was going to be. It was always a disappointment to me."

3.

The Matinee Idols: Charlie, Doug, Rudy, and More

All right, what about the men? They were there, and many of them were immensely popular, but only a handful changed the culture's prevailing winds. It may be that movies in their first decades simply meant more to women. The post–World War I change in feminine roles, morals, and modes of behavior was played out onscreen in a crucial if unarticulated dialogue between industry and audience. Female stars in female-oriented stories offered transformative ways of being; they said you could be *this* or *this,* or if you did *this,* here's what might happen. By contrast, male stars offered classic modes of behavior: the cowboy, the clown, the hero, the lover. In melodramas aimed at female audiences, men often served as the status quo against which female characters reacted—husbands and flirts, bosses and daddies, worshippers and ravagers. Such roles didn't change the social narrative but, equally important, confirmed it.

For male performers, the métier tended to be action rather than emotion. (For actresses, this was true only of the stars of popular cliff-hanger serials, such as *The Perils of Pauline*'s Pearl White, or the rare comedienne like the gifted, troubled Mabel Normand.) It's a generalization, but most male moviegoers didn't feel a pressing need to "express what they had concealed for years." They didn't even have to conceal it. Men could express much of how they felt right out in the open, in the day-to-day activity of their lives. They didn't need to dream, because they got what they wanted from the waking world, whereas the cinema, as a mass projection of secret inner life, mattered more to the half of the population without power. In truth, the social structure of mainstream America *was* how men expressed themselves.

So the very first male stars were handsome Arrow Collar Boys like King Baggott or manly Shakespearean stage types like Griffith favorite Henry B. Walthall. The first actor who seemed born to the movies rather than the stage was Wallace Reid, who had already appeared in one hundred films by the time Griffith cast him as the blacksmith in *Birth of a Nation*. Boyishly gorgeous, unpretentiously virile, a master of onscreen action, Reid was the model for all the can-do idols who have followed down the decades, from his immediate heir and rival Douglas Fairbanks through Errol Flynn and Steve McQueen all the way to Tom Cruise.

He was the all-American guy, beloved and untouchable. Reid wrote screenplays, played multiple musical instruments, raced cars on and offscreen (as Paul Newman would do). *Motion Picture Magazine* called him "the screen's most perfect lover," which no one seriously considered an overstatement. And from 1919 until his tawdry death three years later, he was a morphine addict. There was, in fact, a level of dark and painful secrecy to stardom of which the public had no concept, and it was about to erupt into view. But we're not quite there yet.

As the medium evolved over the teens and postwar years, other male archetypes emerged, each played by an overlapping group of actors: the suave dandy (Conrad Nagel), the intelligent hunk (Thomas

Meighan), the macho man (Francis X. Bushman), the Latin lover (Antonio Moreno and Ramón Novarro), the sensitive swain (Richard Barthelmess). The now-forgotten Charles Ray carved out a successful and profitable niche in the teens as a young country-bumpkin hero—often in baseball plotlines, prefiguring Kevin Costner—starting with 1915's *The Coward*. In 1923, Ray gambled his career on a big-budget historical romance called *The Courtship of Miles Standish* and saw his career dry up overnight, an early example of the perils of fiddling with persona.

Still, many of these types existed onscreen only in relation to the female characters they tempted, wooed, seduced, or saved. In the world according to the movies, men had little agency of their own—a pleasing inversion of life outside the theater. Reid and Ray tended to drive their own films, and there were action heroes like Rod La Rocque and Lloyd Hughes, but even they stopped dead for romance.

The exceptions were the westerns, which had been a man's world for decades. The great star here, after Broncho Billy Anderson laid down the ground rules, was William S. Hart, a former stage Shakespearean who approached the genre with understanding and respect. Hart had grown up on the frontier, in Dakota territory, and had labored on farms and worked cattle; he knew how to portray the old West because he *was* the old West. Hart films like *The Toll Gate* (1920) and *Tumbleweeds* (1925) remain striking to a modern viewer because they're brooding and violent—they understand what living beyond civilization does to a person. Movie westerns got dumbed down and neutered fairly quickly, but Hart's work anticipates the tough, mature horse operas that returned after World War II. You can see through him to the John Wayne of *The Searchers* and, even further, to Clint Eastwood in *Unforgiven*—a legacy of good men doomed to do bad things.

The other major cowboy star, Tom Mix, was everything Hart wasn't: flashy, uncomplicated, fun. *Riders of the Purple Sage* (1925) and *The Great K & A Train Robbery* (1926) were breakneck entertainments with none of the historical weight Hart consciously put into his films, and they were insanely popular with young boys, many of whom grew up believing that all cowboys dressed in clean buckskins and rode unnaturally intelligent steeds like Tony the Wonder Horse. Mix gutted the western of complexities and made it safe for the singing cowboys of the next generation. Where a Hart hero is often his own worst enemy, a Tom Mix film assigns all men into categories labeled "Good Guys" and "Bad Guys" (and women into a box labeled "Wimmen"). Thus the movies repackaged the narrative of American expansion with the unflattering bits sifted out. It sold, and it sold well.

There were other outlier figures, some of them unexpected. For a while, the Japanese actor Sessue Hayakawa was a bona fide romantic lead in American movies, a representative of kinky foreign pleasures starting with Cecil B. DeMille's *The Cheat* (1915), in which he brands and nearly rapes Fannie Ward. Racists objected and so did the Japanese Association of Southern California; the character magically became Burmese for the 1918 re-release.

This was interesting stuff, though—a sexually irresistible ethnic villain. Hayakawa turned his new fame into a solid run of films made by his own production company; most were much less nasty than *The Cheat* and some are quite wonderful. *The Dragon Painter* (1919), recently rediscovered and released on DVD, is a startlingly poetic example of a star road not taken: the early-twentieth-century rage for orientalism extending to romantic and sexual fantasy.

It was also asking a little too much of bourgeois American audiences. Outside of Hayakawa, "exotic lover" types remained Latin or European, and with an early-1920s rise in anti-Asian sentiment, the actor left Hollywood for his native Japan, then traveled to France, and ping-ponged among the three countries for the rest of his career, eventually picking up a Supporting Actor Oscar nomination as the POW camp commander in *The Bridge on the River Kwai* (1957).

Other unique male stars? John Barrymore and Lon Chaney, two sides of the same Master Craftsman coin. Barrymore was the Great Profile, a matinee idol of the New York theater who came to film with a pedigree—his parents were well-known actors and his grandfather was the celebrated Civil War–era Shakespearean John Drew. (Our own generation's representative of the clan, Drew Barrymore, carries both lineages in her name.) Barrymore's 1922 performance of *Hamlet* on Broadway would become legendary, but he was in movies as early as 1912, following the example of his older brother Lionel. In 1920 he stunned film audiences with a *Dr. Jekyll and Mr. Hyde* that was a triumph of makeup and character psychology.

Barrymore was quickly differentiated from the pack of movie leading men as someone with deeper gifts and a more profound mastery of an ancient and respected craft. In him, Adolph Zukor's old idea of "famous players" finally bore fruit, not through an aging stage dinosaur airlifted into a new medium but via a young, attractive star who straddled and understood both worlds. You could only hear Barrymore's classically trained voice in a theater, but it seemed to ring out even in his silent films, so charismatic was his bearing. This is a pose that can't be held for long, however, and the Barrymore of the sound era tapered off into self-parody and booze—albeit with a handful of terrific performances on the way down.

In fact, he's arguably the first of the modern "great actors" in the cinema, trading on our snobbish suspicion that the stage really *is* more important than the movies. From Barrymore flows Olivier and the other British knights (Alec Guinness, Ralph Richardson, all the way to Sir Ben Kingsley and Daniel Day-Lewis) and a more homemade school that insists that some movie performers are artists rather than stars: the Robert De Niro of the 1970s, the Edward Norton of the 1990s, the Ryan Gosling of the 2000s. Marlon Brando may have given them their animal magnetism, but Barrymore was the first to intimate that acting was a higher calling worth the occasional spiritual maiming.

If Barrymore imported the values and verities of the New York stage to the movies, Lon Chaney, the "Man of a Thousand Faces," came up with something wholly new. Like Chaplin, Chaney was an irreducible singularity—there was no one like him before and there has been no one like him since. Most of the actors in this book created types that were then followed up by others, who in turn adapted those types to serve their own purposes. Chaney stood alone in his insistence that acting was total body transformation. Boris Karloff became the Frankenstein monster, but he didn't create the makeup, and he spent the rest of his life running from the role. Chaney, by contrast, took pride in doing all his own work, pushing himself far past what others thought wise or necessary. His art was creative masochism, and the fascination for audiences was how far he'd go. (Again, the only possible modern correlatives may be the De Niro of *Raging Bull* or the Christian Bale of *The Machinist* and *The Fighter*—self-conscious artists who martyr their body to their craft.)

Chaney is still the face of the Hunchback of Notre Dame and the Phantom of the Opera to people who've never seen the movies. Even his lesser-known films are about twisting the actor's instrument past the grotesque into a weird twilight zone of the soul: the fraudulent amputee lusting after a young Joan Crawford in *The Unknown* (1927), the *real* amputee and criminal mastermind of *The Penalty* (1920), the humiliated professor turned circus clown of *He Who Gets Slapped* (1924). Chaney's movies say that the world is cruel and that cruelty in return is an all-too-human response.

Without the makeup, he was handsome in a durable tough-guy way, and he appeared in dramas and even a few romances. But Chaney lives on as a rebuke to the entire concept of movie stardom. Most audiences prize consistency in their favorite actors: we go to a Harrison Ford movie expecting to see Harrison Ford. Audiences in the 1920s went to a Chaney movie having no idea who he'd be this time—and that was the thrill. Eerily, his life was bounded on all sides by quiet. His parents were deaf-mutes, and Chaney grew up communicating with them through sign language, facial expressions, and mime. He was a major headliner up to the dawn of the sound era but made only one talkie, a remake of 1925's *The Unholy Three*. In 1930, he contracted a throat infection and lapsed, once more, into silence and death.

Over all these performers towered four men, the key quartet of male stardom in the medium's early days. Two of them took existing character types and made them newly perfect for the movies and the times: Douglas Fairbanks, the action hero, and John Gilbert, the ardent Romeo. The other two invented entirely new types. More than just the latest "Latin lover," Rudolph Valentino was the first object of mass female sexual hysteria in modern culture, a figure whose *lack* of traditional he-man qualities caused men to sneer in homophobic panic and women to dream of being sensitively ravished. Chaplin—Chaplin was only the first genius of the form, proof that Edison's clattering machine was capable of an art that owed nothing to previous models. He was also, by a long shot, the biggest star of them all.

"He is, I believe, the most widely known man in the world," wrote a reporter for the *New York Herald Tribune* in late 1917. "They know him almost as well in Japan and Paraguay and Spain as we do here. Because of that he has attained an almost legendary significance in the eyes of millions of people; they give him something akin to the homage given to Bernhardt and Shakespeare and John L. Sullivan. These millions could never have that feeling for a Senator, a diplomatist, a millionaire."

Those words were written only two years after Charles Chaplin's ascension to fame and one year after he hit his creative stride with the twelve shorts he made for the Mutual Film Corporation in 1916. Already he existed on a level beyond other public figures; a decade later, by the time of *The Gold Rush* in 1925, he seemed bigger than popular culture itself. Admonished Virginia Cherrill, who played the blind flower seller in *City Lights* (1931), "Charlie was a god, you forget."

Other comedians defined themselves through what Chaplin was not. Buster Keaton never smiled, and the joke in his movies is about a small, stoic man in a big world of machines and nature, not Chaplin's ballet of personal pluck. Harold Lloyd did imitate Charlie for a while, with a rip-off character named "Lonesome Luke," and was finally too chagrined to carry on; he slapped on a pair of glasses and created a highly successful (and very funny) slapstick variant on Douglas Fairbanks's all-American go-getter. Laurel and Hardy existed in a bubble of infantile purity whereas Charlie was consciously part of the world; Mack Sennett's Keystone Kops got laughs from speed and violence rather than speed and grace; Fatty Arbuckle aspired to nothing more than ruthlessly efficient comedy. There were dozens of others, all working hard for the boffo, not one of them concerned with the art of the thing. (Keaton achieved it anyway; arguably Stan Laurel, too.)

It wasn't just comedians who were mesmerized by Charlie, though; everyone was. Griffith may have proved with *Birth of a Nation* that movies could produce a work felt on all levels of society, from president to plebeian. Pickford and Fairbanks were idolized by filmgoers around the globe. But Chaplin cranked everything up another notch—or five—because he was simultaneously hilarious and meaningful.

This was simply unheard of: a movie actor adored by the crowds and the intellectuals alike, and for the same reasons. You could laugh until you couldn't breathe at a movie like *One A.M.* (1916) while marveling at the formal brilliance of Charlie all by himself in a film, coming home drunk and trying to get to bed while every prop in the house fights him off, one by one. You could go to see a knockabout comedy called *The Kid* (1921) and find yourself moved to tears by the panic of a man losing his beloved adopted child.

Chaplin was the first figure in American popular culture to successfully unite high and low culture; with his arrival, great writers and thinkers began to talk about the movies as if they mattered. The painter John Singer Sargent, who regularly took his patron Isabella Stewart Gardner to see Chaplin movies, spoke to the mystery: "He does things, and if you're lucky you see them." Sigmund Freud and George Bernard Shaw weighed in on Charlie, and Hart Crane wrote poems about him. Most people thought of Chaplin as a kind of poetry himself, and that, too, was unprecedented. In the end, it may have ruined him as an artist.

First, though, he was just very, very, very popular, and it came on with a suddenness that was a critical part of the thrill. As would happen with the Beatles, part of the joy of Charlie-mania was that it infected everyone all at once. You can even pinpoint when the madness started: the first few months of 1915. Prior to that, Chaplin had escaped London and a childhood to make one weep—an actor father who drank himself to death, an actress mother in the insane asylum, young Charlie and his older half brother Sydney in foster homes and workhouses before finding employment in music hall revues—and he was touring America with Fred Karno's troupe when someone told Mack Sennett's partners at Keystone about him. A telegram duly went out—"Is there a man named Chaffin in your company or something like that?"—and in December 1913, Chaplin was signed up for the head-spinning amount of $150 per week. "A year at that racket and I could return to vaudeville an international star," he figured.

His first experiences at Keystone were unpleasant. He argued with the director and his best bits were cut from the finished film; Sennett and the others weren't sure the awkward young Englishman would work out. One day, Sennett saw Chaplin standing around the set in his street clothes and told him to go to wardrobe and pull together some sort of a costume; they'd work something out in front of the camera.

"I had no idea what make-up to put on," Chaplin wrote in 1964's *My Autobiography*. "However, on the way to the wardrobe I thought I would dress in baggy pants, big shoes, a cane and a derby hat. I wanted everything a contradiction: the pants baggy, the coat tight, the hat small and the shoes large. . . . I added a small moustache, which I reasoned, would add age without hiding my expression."

"I had no idea of the character," Chaplin continued, "but the moment I was dressed, the clothes and the make-up made me feel the person he was. I began to know him and by the time I walked onto the stage, he was fully born."

In other words, a star was born, for it was the Little Tramp, not Charlie Chaplin, who was to become the true mass idol—the one recognized around the world and across the generations. Show a twenty-first-century kid a picture of the Tramp and there's a good chance, a century after the comedian walked into the Keystone wardrobe room, that he or she will say that's Charlie Chaplin. The image remains everywhere—in advertising and on the Internet, at costume parties and in video stores. The Tramp has long since entered the public domain; no sooner was he born than he was part of the common cultural consciousness.

This is an extreme version of what was already happening with the other major movie stars of his day, but only because Chaplin's costume, a clown's costume, was extreme. Mary Pickford had a "costume," too—the golden-curled girl-child, America's Sweetheart—and it, too, was distinct from the woman who wore it and mistaken for the real thing by millions of moviegoers. Valentino's "costume" of the rapacious foreign lover was at odds with the bland dandy he seems to have been, as was Clara Bow's "costume" of the girl who had ants in her pants. It's true that the costume was sometimes so close to the actual person as to be nearly street clothes. Douglas Fairbanks willed himself to be a perfected version of himself onscreen, and I doubt Lillian Gish guzzled bathtub gin and entertained multiple lovers when the cameras weren't rolling. (It feels wrong even typing those words.)

But Chaplin *wasn't* a bum. The Tramp filtered a concentrated version of Charlie's restless comic invention, with precision moves and a deliciously ironic take on the world, but it was only one version. Since so few people saw any other, they assumed that creator and creation were the same.

To see photos and home movies of Chaplin out of the Tramp costume is a shock. The 1983 documentary *Unknown Chaplin* collects rehearsal footage and other rarities, some of which can be seen in their entirety as extras on the Chaplin DVDs released by Warner Home Video in 2004. These are revelatory. In an outtake during the filming of 1917's *The Immigrant,* Chaplin briefly puts on a pair of glasses, and it's as if someone had drawn nipples on the Mona Lisa—a violation of the known order of things. An unreleased 1919 short called *The Professor* shows Chaplin trying out a completely new character: a grumpy, down-at-the-heels proprietor of a flea circus, with flyaway black eyebrows, wide moustache, top hat, corncob pipe, and dowdy morning jacket. It's . . . interesting. If five years earlier the comedian had come out of the Keystone wardrobe room wearing this outfit, would the course of film history have been entirely different?

Chaplin did understand what the stakes were. In *How to Make Movies,* a 1918 behind-the-scenes-of-my-new-studio short shot by Chaplin and not intended for general release, there's a great gag in which Charlie's butler opens the studio's walk-in safe and emerges with the Tramp's shoes, tattered and precious. A title card calls them "His Greatest Treasures," and Chaplin pulls out a special pillow upon which to place them. As well he should, for the shoes—and the hat, the cane, the jacket, the moustache—are the pieces of the star that Charlie was. Without them, he's just a pleasant and clever young man who has done very well for himself.

In one snippet of this Chaplin arcana, you can actually see the transformation occur. The comedian liked to roll the camera when famous people visited his studio, and one such scene features the young Crown Prince Frederick of Denmark clowning around with the comedy superstar. Charlie is playing the genial Hollywood host, and then, under the goading of his royal friend, he takes on the Tramp persona. The shoulders hunch, the face turns slack, the eyes go dead, the feet assume that instantly familiar perpendicular shuffle. The change is genuinely eerie. Chaplin is putting the costume on from the inside out.

What became famous, then, was one of infinite possible Chaplins, or perhaps just the one that came out that day at Keystone and got locked into place. He played other characters in the early years, but the Little Tramp was the one that everyone loved, and it did seem to fire his comic invention while inviting a new kind of sympathy. Chaplin's physical movements were small, defined, and funny, and he was always turning something into something else through his mime. The classic instance is the scene in 1916's *The Pawnshop* in which Charlie examines an alarm clock and treats it as everything from a sick patient to a can of sardines. The world turns marvelous in his hands; in *The Gold Rush* (1925), dinner rolls become dancing feet and boots become food. Chaplin's comedy is the delight of unexpected metaphor.

Uniquely, he made eye contact with the audience. Dramatic actors couldn't do that without breaking the illusion of independent narrative, but Charlie will glance into the camera with a playfully deadpan stare, inviting us to share his disbelief. It's an invitation to the dance, acknowledging that A) we're out there in the dark and B) Charlie and we are on equal footing. Such flattery! But it was also a new kind of intimacy, cementing the relationship between star and audience in a secret compact, unseen by any of the other characters onscreen.

By the end of 1914, Chaplin was chafing under the Keystone rule that every movie had to end with a frantic chase, and the sooner you got to it the better. He signed with another company, Essanay, for $1,250 a week, almost ten times his previous salary, and shot his initial film for them on January 14, 1915. For the first time, he was properly publicized, and within months the entire country, then the world, went nuts for all things Chaplin.

Poems about him ran in newspapers. His shorts were sellouts; exhibitors and audiences couldn't get enough of them. The Ziegfeld Follies staged a number called "Those Charlie Chaplin Feet," and music publishers rushed out the sheet music for songs like "The Chaplin Waddle," "The Chaplin Strut," "The Chaplin Wiggle," "The Chaplin Glide," and "The Chaplin March Grotesque." There were Charlie lapel pins, hats, socks, ties, Christmas decorations, cards, comic strips, and dolls, very few of which Chaplin himself saw a penny from. Marcel Proust had his moustache trimmed "à la Charlot." *Motion Picture Magazine* called the whole thing "Chaplinitis." He was a fad built for the long haul, for while his comedy provided the immediacy of laughter, his poignancy hinted at the durability of art.

Oddly, the man at the center of this storm of public interest was so busy making movies that he had no real idea of its extent until he traveled from California to New York by rail in February 1916. As the train pulled into Amarillo, Texas, midway through the journey, Chaplin was in his underwear preparing to shave; he glanced out the window and was surprised to see a vast crowd milling about the station. Bunting and flags hung everywhere, and refreshments sat on long tables. The comedian assumed that a foreign dignitary was passing through until the mayor of Amarillo got on board and made him come meet his fans.

In fact, telegraph operators had been keeping a fascinated nation posted as to Charlie's progress as he crossed the country; bigger crowds awaited him in Kansas City and Chicago. "People were standing at railroad junctions and in fields, waving as the train swept by," Chaplin wrote in his autobiography. "I wanted to enjoy it all without reservation, but I kept thinking that the world had gone crazy! If a few slapstick comedies could arouse such excitement, was there not something bogus about all celebrity? I had always thought I would like the public's attention, and here it was—paradoxically isolating me with a depressing sense of loneliness."

By the time he got to New York, the mobs were so thick at Grand Central Station that the chief of police asked Chaplin to disembark at 125th Street. A newspaper blared "HE'S HERE!" in a typeface reserved for sinking ocean liners. His brother, Sydney—by now Charlie's business manager—greeted Chaplin with the news that he had completed a deal with a new company, the Mutual Film Corporation. Charlie would make $10,000 a week, plus a signing bonus of $150,000. The figure was so large that for weeks it became an obsessive cultural topic of its own. In all of America, only the president of U.S. Steel made more money than Chaplin. The entire Supreme Court earned 19.5 percent of his yearly salary. Mary Pickford immediately went to Zukor and demanded equal pay (she got it, too). The public conversation began. How can a mere movie star be worth that much money?

When he's an artist, obviously. The first two years of Chaplin's ascension to public godhood also saw a battle to define what he meant and whether physical comedy could be compatible with the loftiest aesthetic ideals. To some people, the question didn't even make sense. Art was refined; it led away from the body to the higher sensibilities. In 1916, though, an influential article ran in *Harper's Weekly,* written by a respected stage actress named Minnie Maddern Fiske, that was among the first to put forth the claim that the comedian was, in fact, an artist of the first order. "Chaplin *is* vulgar," Mrs. Fiske acknowledged, "[but] vulgarity and distinguished art can exist together."

Well, of course they can. We know that now. Out of that sentiment flows much that is great in twentieth-century popular art and culture. The Marx Brothers, Robert Johnson, Alfred Hitchcock, Elvis Presley, Marilyn Monroe, Andy Warhol, Robert Rauschenberg, the Ramones, Public Enemy, and on and on and on. Chaplin got there first. Chaplin planted the flag.

The trouble with being praised as a visionary, though, is that you start to believe it. By 1920, Chaplin was telling the *New York Times,* "My clowning, as the world calls it—and I dislike the word clown, for I am not a clown—may have esoteric meanings. I prefer to think of myself as a mimetic satirist, for I have aimed in all my comedies at burlesquing, satirizing the human race—or at least those human beings whose very existence is an unconscious satire on this world." In this, Chaplin established another precedent, becoming the first comedian who wouldn't rest until everyone took him seriously. He planted the flag for Woody Allen, too—and Jerry Lewis, Robin Williams, Jim Carrey, and all the other restless geniuses who don't see that what they do with comedy is often much richer and more meaningful than the solemn drama toward which they contort themselves.

The madness continued. A return visit to New York in 1921 resulted in a melee at a movie premiere in which Chaplin had his hat and tie stolen and a piece of his pants cut off by a fan; the police eventually passed him over the heads of the crowd so he could escape. From there he went to London, where thousands met him at Waterloo Station and the press and public shadowed him everywhere as he visited the shabby scenes of his childhood. All levels of British society fell at his feet. He met and became good friends with the author H. G. Wells, and a whore on the street confessed to him that *The Kid* had made her cry.

That was the thing, though. If Chaplin was moving toward a greater self-consciousness and even pretentiousness, the movies remained brilliant. *The Gold Rush* in 1925 balanced epic sadness and hilarity, and 1931's *City Lights* is a comedy of both monumental ego and astonishing humanity, no more so than in its almost unbearably moving final shot, an extreme closeup that in itself is an endless inquiry into the mysteries of stardom. No one else could have dodged the coming of the talkies—not even Pickford or Fairbanks—but Charlie convinced us that what he did was capital A Art and that Art rested on silence. He went where Mary didn't have the courage to go and Doug didn't have the imagination. He made his own rules and insisted we follow.

Like Chaplin, Douglas Fairbanks rose with triumph from a broken childhood; it was one of the many bonds of the real friendship between the two men. Why does this seem necessary to so many early star biographies? Does a miserable youth gun the engine for playacting and self-invention, either as camouflage in a hurtful world or as a way to win over adults who could never be pleased? Fairbanks's father was abusive and his stepfather abandoned the family, and all you get from the star is that dazzling, confident grin. He was the first actor to be called "the king of Hollywood" by his peers as well as fans and the press. Before then the industry hadn't even realized it needed crowned heads, but all the subsequent "kings of Hollywood"—beloved and untouchable, they run from Clark Gable to Jack Nicholson to George Clooney—are cut from cloth that Doug Fairbanks tailored.

What unites them? Ease, assurance, self-mockery. The latter especially—that little extra wink—is what Fairbanks invented that was original. The wink said heroism in the movies could be fun, had to be fun, for it to matter in the twentieth century. The fast editing and closeup camera shots of the films pulled the rug out from under stagebound pomposity, and if you showed you were in on the joke, you invited the audience along—a partnership that seemed stunningly novel and delightful at the time. (It seemed so again ninety years later, when Johnny Depp did it in *Pirates of the Caribbean*.)

The wink—often it was nothing more than the obvious pleasure Fairbanks took in doing his own stunts—performed a function that was important but largely unnoticed. It separated the star from the movie in which he was starring. To watch one of the actor's early comedies like *The Matrimaniac* (1916), or one of his later costume epics like *Robin Hood* (1922) or *The Thief of Bagdad* (1924), is to engage in a game in which the movie is just the latest obstacle Doug has to surmount. Fairbanks himself *is* the movie, a crucial step in the development of the screen star as something distinct from and bigger than anything that had come before.

There are two separate periods to his career. He arrived in Hollywood in 1915 an established Broadway name—he was already thirty-two, the opposite of a juvenile lead—and was lucky to land at Triangle, where the tiny, clever Anita Loos and her future husband, director John Emerson, took him under their wings. There followed ten high-spirited adventure comedies in two years, in which Doug plays an average American boy who wants to get ahead or impress his girl and ends up in a spiraling farce of chase scenes and complications. The films are breezy, fast, ridiculously enjoyable, and they established the star as a modern fellow breaking free of the fusty concerns of the previous generation. There's no fat on them, and no cynicism, either. They blur together in the best possible way.

In 1920, Fairbanks began his run of groundbreaking swashbucklers with *The Mark of Zorro*. He did eight in all, including *The Three Musketeers* (1921), *Robin Hood* (1922), *The Thief of Bagdad* (1924), and *The Black Pirate* (1926), and even if these stories had been done in piecemeal fashion by earlier directors, they were now wholly owned by Fairbanks. The sets were gargantuan and yet he filled them. There is not a buccaneer movie made since that does not owe 95 percent of its DNA to *The Black Pirate,* and, yes, that goes double for Disney and Depp.

Fairbanks was proof that force of personality can exert a gravitational pull of its own. He was nice looking but too solidly built and thick-necked to be a conventional matinee idol. That constant tan—another new idea—wasn't so much an attraction as an intriguing affectation. Yet he was universally loved because he mastered the trick of never doubting himself while never seeming to take himself very seriously. In an era when "personality" was the most important quality a modern young person could have, Douglas Fairbanks provided a fully functioning example. He didn't just have it. He *was* it.

Another critical thing to understand about Fairbanks: he saw himself as a brand and sold that brand accordingly. Even Pickford considered herself an actress first with a few profitable sidelines. Doug, by contrast, got the big picture. He cut a publishing deal and authored pamphlets on how to live right, titled *Laugh and Live, Wedlock in Time, Making Life Worthwhile,* and so forth. These were tremendously popular, as were his monthly "Douglas Fairbanks' Own Page" columns in *Photoplay*—no matter that many were written by his secretary, Kenneth Davenport. The explicit message of all his lifestyle advice was that with the proper attention to good grooming, moral rightness, and can-do attitude, you, too, could be like Doug, and he was more than happy to help you get there. The movies themselves were merely proof of what was possible—advertisements for a new kind of healthy living. In a sense, the primary transaction was buying into the Fairbanks philosophy.

Which was ultimately another big fat lie, no matter that Fairbanks himself believed it on many levels. He had to believe it, or it wouldn't have sold, but in 1917, there he was in a Manhattan hotel during a war bond drive with Mary Pickford by his side, staring out the window at the starstruck crowds below. She was his lover by then, they were each still married to other people, and the hordes were waving Doug's latest self-help book, a manual on the benefits of staying faithful to your spouse.

If Doug and Mary were big separately, together they were without precedent. The couple met at a party in the early teens and got to know each other during the bond drives of World War I. They were attracted to each other's professionalism and to the enjoyment each took in professionalism—it's no coincidence that they both loved what they did. When Pickford and Fairbanks joined forces in 1919 with Griffith and Chaplin to found United Artists, it was their acumen rather than their affair that prompted them to go in on the venture. (Pickford had the better head for business, but Fairbanks knew a good opportunity when he saw it.)

And there's the sense that both might have been lonely. Pickford was no longer living with her husband, actor Owen Moore, whose problems with alcohol may or may not have been exacerbated by the pain of being Mr. Mary Pickford. Fairbanks was estranged from his wife, socialite Anna Beth Sully; his only real friend was Chaplin. There were not many people who could have understood what being adored by a global audience was like. There may, in fact, have been only two—three if you count Charlie—so it's lucky they got along. They seemed to have been a good match anyway, Doug's bluff good cheer taking the edge off Mary's nervous anxiety that it might all go away at any second. (She once said she expected that "every year might be my last in pictures.")

They worried, Pickford especially, that the fans would turn against them when the truth about their affair came out. Adolph Zukor fretted over the couple's delight in motoring around the New York area "disguised" in driving goggles and dusters. A businessman to the core, he was terrified that his investment would be destroyed by the public who had bought it. "Fairbanks will survive," he told Pickford's mother when the relationship came to his notice, "[but] if Mary appears to fail the public's trust, it will punish her." And when the two did marry in 1920 and the news was announced, anyone who cared could backtrack through the divorces and note how often the couple had appeared together in public over the previous three years. The math was easy, and it was done by a number of journalists and other professional busybodies.

What happened, though, was unexpected: the world exploded with joy. The timing, in fact, was perfect. Two years later, during the wave of sex and murder scandals that rocked early-1920s Hollywood, either Pickford or Fairbanks would have been cast as a villain in the suddenly suspicious eyes of the public. Just to be safe, the Reverend J. Whitcomb Brougher of L.A.'s Temple Baptist Church (possibly at the behest of Mr. A. Zukor of New York City) released a statement assuring the public that the Pickford-Fairbanks nuptials were "scriptural."

It probably wasn't necessary. In 1920, their union was confirmation of several things, not least the notion that stars were special creatures made of better stuff than you or I and therefore deserving only of each other. It made such good sense on so many cultural and psychological levels, since the King of Hollywood should obviously be enthroned with America's Sweetheart. Alistair Cooke, who wrote about and befriended Fairbanks, called it "living proof of America's chronic belief in happy endings."

But it wasn't just America. The Pickford-Fairbanks marriage served notice that these were planetary gods. The couple's transatlantic honeymoon was like a royal tour of the colonies. Mobs surrounded their New York hotel (Fairbanks turned a handspring on the roof to give them a thrill); mobs stormed the gangplank when their ship docked in Southampton, England ("[their idols] had materialized . . . they had become human," wrote one reporter); London traffic snarled for miles around their hotel. (King George V's limousine was reportedly caught in the crush, and there you have the centuries-old ruling class helpless before the new crowned heads.)

Pickford opened the patio door in her nightgown one morning to find a wall of applauding British fans. At a garden party, a seething crowd pulled her out of her car while Fairbanks and the police fought them off; in photos, Mary is clearly terrified. "I touched her dress!" shouted one fan, and again we see the restless throng convulsively ripping something it loves into a million souvenirs. The couple took to seeing the sights of Europe by moonlight.

What the public was saying as it threatened to adore Mary to death was simple: You belong to us. The gods are owned by those who worship them. The dream is not the property of the figures in the dream but of the person having the dream. Zukor understood that. It was the democracy of the new movie stardom, and it was tyrannical. In the end, Mary and Doug reigned for sixteen years from their Hollywood mansion, Pickfair (what else could they call it?), divorcing sadly but without much fanfare in the sound era. They drifted apart, as kings and queens do when they understand that their subjects need them more than they need each other.

Where Doug and Mary had the misfortune to age past their moment, Rudolph Valentino had the great pop luck to die at the peak of his. As with many icons of mass lust—Marilyn Monroe is another—his legend is more potent and dangerous than any of his movies. He was a lower-middle-class Italian kid named Rodolfo Alfonzo Raffaele Pierre Philibert Guglielmi who left home for Paris by the time he was seventeen. A year later he was in New York, where he made his living as a landscape gardener, dishwasher, petty thief, dancer; maybe he hired himself out for less pretty things, too. He was the immigrant experience looking for a place to land.

In Hollywood, he found work playing villains and extras, gradually working his way up to bigger villains and extras. *The Married Virgin* (1918) casts him as the blackmailing gigolo Count Roberto di San Fraccini and lets him pitch passionate woo to the errant wife played by Kathleen Kirkham. "What's the matter with Ethel?" someone asks her husband (Edward Jobson), who responds, "I wish I knew. If I understood the female mind, I would be richer indeed." It's already clear that Valentino knows, even if he's jowly and circumspect and still not much of an actor; when Kirkham divulges her heinous plot to him, he just sits there, stolid as a packhorse.

What he does have is authority, and a kind of forward-leaning eagerness, as if he might pluck the chastity from a woman at any moment. The early Valentino is always thinking about the next act of seduction. In the following year's *Eyes of Youth,* he's still a brilliantined heavy—the credits call him "Clarence Morgan, a cabaret parasite"—but he's more sharply defined now. His sexuality cuts.

The screenwriter and MGM executive June Mathis saw *Eyes of Youth* and chose Valentino to play the wastrel tango artiste in the 1921 epic *The Four Horsemen of the Apocalypse.* Mathis had to fight to get him the role, and she quickly became the young actor's mother hen. He brought that out in women.

The film was a hit but Valentino was a sensation, and the release of *The Sheik* later that year created pandemonium. It's a ridiculous movie—it was ridiculous in 1921—but when Valentino as the desert warlord Sheik Ahmed Ben Assan bugs his eyes and spirits Agnes Ayres (playing "the orphan daughter of a British poet") off to a fate worse than death, every woman's filthy thoughts followed. *The Sheik* vulgarized an already vulgar fantasy—that what women really wanted was to be raped by a primitive Third World prince—and it sold like crazy, mostly because Valentino was incredibly sexual without being especially masculine. *The Son of the Sheik,* made five years later, is the better movie, but the original was the atom bomb, proof that women dreamed of being conquered and would pay to see it safely enacted onscreen.

As you can imagine, this terrified the menfolk. Valentino very quickly became an idol of teenagers and college boys, who adopted his slicked hair, his slit-eyed slouch, the slave bracelets he wore. A "sheik" became the preferred term for any studiously hip young man looking to get into his girlfriend's pants. And just as quickly, the older generation found everything to laugh at in the Valentino image, particularly its effeminacy. The most famous instance was the "pink powder puff" dustup of June 1926, when a Chicago newspaperman saw a young "sheik" use pink talcum powder in a men's room and wrote an inflamed editorial blaming Valentino for the queering of American manhood. The Valentino backlash is probably the first recorded instance of pop homophobia in American culture, curious only in that it settled on a figure half the population took to be stridently heterosexual.

The problem was that Valentino himself didn't seem to understand his image, or he misunderstood it, or he took no particular interest in maintaining it. (Today he'd have consultants, handlers, and publicists all working around the clock. Today he'd be Brad Pitt.) A nice, rather passive young man who liked to cook spaghetti, Valentino allowed his life and career to be controlled by strong women. After Mathis came his wife Natacha Rambova, a languorous demi-star who functioned as Rudy's muse, gatekeeper, and self-styled artistic equal. Rambova herself was a fiercely willed self-invention, a "woman of the world" who had actually begun life in Utah as Winifred Hudnut, the descendant of a Mormon elder.

Rambova, in turn, was a protégée of the flamboyant Russian actress Alla Nazimova, and the public implication was that Rudy was a limp plaything in the hands of these sybaritic near lesbians. The slave bracelet he wore was from Natacha (she wore a matching one); she dressed him up as the god Pan and took photographs (more snickers); his 1923 book of poetry, *Day Dreams,* was a best seller that could have been written by a tremulous teenage girl. ("Alas / At times / I find / Exquisite bitterness / In / Your kiss.") When Valentino quit Paramount in a contract huff in 1922, he and Rambova embarked on a two-year national dance tour, a financial success that delivered the idol to his public in the attenuated flesh, road-show style.

Before their divorce in 1925, they were an oddly controversial power couple. The failure of 1924's *Monsieur Beaucaire,* a film made under Rambova's artistic control, was laid at her feet. They were perceived as the celebrity and his succubus, a dynamic that, unfairly or not, has cropped up time and again in the culture: John and Yoko, Kurt and Courtney, on and on.

The difference was that Valentino just wasn't a very creative personality. Given the right vehicle—*Son of the Sheik,* or 1925's romantic adventure *The Eagle*—he could be wonderful onscreen, full of sinuous energy and self-mocking vigor. In other films, he would just posture or, worse, mope. *Cobra,* also from 1925, starts as a sharp, funny farce about the travails of being a human aphrodisiac, with Valentino playing the descendant of generations of Spanish lovers. In one period flashback, he plays his own grandfather with a neat little goatee, looking surprisingly like Ben Affleck.

Then the film goes awry, sending Valentino to the U.S., where he falls in love with a pert working girl (Gertrude Olmstead) while fighting off the advances of his friend's Eurotrash wife (Nita Naldi). This wasn't what the heaving fans wanted to see—Rudy conquered and laid low by America. They wanted it the other way around.

His death may not have been his greatest performance, but it certainly was the biggest show. In August 1926, Valentino had lunch with Paramount's Zukor and patched up their differences; the executive left with "the feeling that here was a young man to whom fame—and of a rather odd sort—had come too rapidly upon the heels of lean years, and he hadn't known the best way to deal with it." A few days later, Rudy was in the hospital with a burst appendix. He died on the 23rd, at the age of thirty-one.

The cultural hysteria that followed still dwarfs later public outpourings of grief for John Lennon, Princess Di, et al. A Valentino fan in London committed suicide upon hearing the news. A New York woman sat down among a pile of his photos and shot herself. Thirty thousand people descended on the funeral parlor at Broadway and Sixty-sixth Street to view the corpse. The scene devolved into a riot, plate glass windows smashed and angry fans rubbing soap on the street to make the police horses slip. "The confusion was indescribable," wrote a *New York Times* reporter. "Women yelled in fright and ducked about, afraid of the horses. Men were no better." Ten black-shirted men from the Fascisti League of America arrived to help restore order, reportedly at the orders of Benito Mussolini himself.

On the day of the funeral, a hundred thousand people lined the streets. The pallbearers included Zukor, Joe Schenk, Douglas Fairbanks, and *Photoplay* editor in chief James Quirk. Valentino's final lover, actress Pola Negri, attended, heavily veiled and swooning. Mary Pickford sobbed in black next to the Talmadge sisters, Norma and Constance. "Film producers, too, sat with brimming eyes throughout the solemn requiem high mass," said the *Times*.

It was the death of the movie star as invincible pop totem and the birth of something new: the martyred idol. No one quite put it into words, but the air was humid with the crocodile tears of the public. Had Rudy died for our sins of disbelief? Because women loved him too much and men despised him? Of course not; he died of peritonitis. Yet the riots outside the funeral parlor were in part a carnival of mass guilt for not appreciating him enough while he was alive. Somehow *we* did this to him, as we would to Marilyn Monroe and Judy Garland. Or so it seemed, and seeming mattered. The crowd rioted and then fell silent at its revealed power. The self-absorption of it all still astounds.

After Valentino's passing, the mantle of great screen lover passed to John Gilbert, an altogether different figure. Both played brooding, tempestuous men onscreen; both had difficulty controlling their careers off. Gilbert was American, though, and his dark and dashing good looks dovetailed with more traditional notions of manliness. He wasn't macho, but he wasn't a drawing-room dandy either.

For a while, he was as hot as can be. Every subsequent generation has had its variation on Gilbert's theme of tall-dark-and-handsome, and on the female enchantment that follows. He was the original dreamboat, the sigh-guy, with a directness that stood in contrast to Valentino's oblique Continental charms. Clark Gable came along in the early sound era and created a schism in the Gilbert persona: after Gable, there were Dangerous Men and Great Lovers. Of the latter, Robert Taylor was a pallid Gilbert photocopy in the 1930s, Tyrone Power was dull but absolutely gorgeous in the 1940s. Cary Grant looked the part, but he was too complicated under the smooth exterior and a better actor, not to mention funnier. The best the 1950s could do was Rock Hudson, problematic on so many levels.

Still, there are pieces of Gilbert in every new ardent movie swain that comes along; Robert Pattinson, for instance, is just version 18.0. The through-line is the world-weariness with which Gilbert balanced his romantic mooning. As befits a postwar romantic idol, he seemed to have been around the block. This is a man, not a boy, even with his trim moustache shaved off in the 1925 World War I epic *The Big Parade.* The drama of his movies is that love rejuvenates Gilbert and makes him idealistic all over again.

Parade, along with Erich von Stroheim's *The Merry Widow* that same year, made Gilbert a star. *Flesh and the Devil* in 1926 made him a pop force. The latter paired him with MGM's new Swedish discovery Greta Garbo, who plays a coldhearted man-eater in the film. The two fell in love offscreen, and their scenes together have an eroticism that's still startling and that must have felt like nuclear fusion back then. Unlike Valentino in *The Sheik,* Gilbert never seems like he's faking it—the thrill is in the quivering emotionalism, the downright lust, that overtakes a man who should know better. "It seemed like an intrusion to yell 'cut!' " recalled the film's director, Clarence Brown. "I used to just motion the crew over to another part of the set and let them finish what they were doing. It was embarrassing."

Seen today, Gilbert is a baroque, over-the-top actor—a ham—but that was what the times and the medium called for. The movies had evolved from Griffith's low-rent picture plays to bloated epics with huge sets and thousands of extras. Filmmaking in the late silent era was passing through maturity into decadence, and Gilbert walked this line perfectly. The big trick in his arsenal was the Stare, in which the actor's jaded eyes would pop with renewed purpose—when he first sees Garbo in *Flesh and the Devil*, say, and passion comes flooding back into the character's every pore. It looks silly now, but that's one reason it worked so well then. There was risk to such a florid performing style, and risk can be attractive.

Gilbert was an intelligent, well-liked, and troubled man, with many marriages, a growing fondness for drink, and a vanity that cloaked a gnawing insecurity—he was a modern movie star in that as well. Garbo was the stronger partner in their relationship; for reasons that have never been entirely clear, she left him standing at the altar in 1927. MGM head Louis B. Mayer had an intense personal loathing for Gilbert, but it's doubtful the mogul sabotaged the dialogue tracks of the star's first talkies, as has often been rumored. Rather, Gilbert suffered for being the last of the silent lovers, a breed that looked and sounded ridiculous when you could actually hear one of them speak.

He was through by the early 1930s, alcoholic, sad, and unemployable. There was a reunion with Garbo in *Queen Christina* in 1933—she seems ageless, he seems old—and a final film called *The Captain Hates the Sea* that Gilbert shot almost 100 percent drunk. On January 9, 1936, he had trouble sleeping, was given an injection by a private nurse, and sometime during the night choked to death on his tongue, the very muscle that had laid him low. Even Mayer would have found the irony hideous.

4.

Sodom: The Silent Star Scandals

The Hollywood scandals of the early 1920s altered star culture forever by taking its narrative off the screen and into the dark. Ten years earlier, the first great secret of the movies—the unknown that propelled feverish audience curiosity—had been an actor's name. Starting with Florence Lawrence, the names became known, and then the personalities behind the names. Over time, the fan magazines began to give us glimpses of the stars' personal lives, scrubbed clean but still tantalizing.

Lifestyles were marketed, tie-in products sold, and the story we were fed was that the stars were exactly like you or I, just with more money, bigger houses, better cars, sweeter breath. To read the old *Photoplays* and *Moving Picture Worlds* is to discover a realm where everyone is happily married, living lives far more stable than in the nomadic world of the theater, and indulging in hobbies from embroidery to cooking to motoring. These stories sold happy, "normal" living far beyond the means of the average reader, and they urged us to imitate and to buy in.

We wanted to know more, though. The fascination with stars is in large part a desire to unlock the nagging puzzle of identity—who *are* these people who we know so well and not at all? Identity sits at the intimate core of being, and it's easy (and entertaining) to confuse it with sex. That was the big secret, after all the others had been divulged. In the teens, fans were obsessed with knowing who their favorite stars were married to, and what they really wanted to know was who was sleeping with whom. The violence done to Mary Pickford and Charlie Chaplin by the mobs in the public square was on some level a rapacious desire to unclothe them, flay them, burrow to their essence. What is the innermost riddle? Something naked and hidden—something we're not meant to see. And perhaps there was resentment mixed in there, too, as if an unspecified envy toward these actors who pretended to be gods called for them to be brought down a peg. Scandal played to all audiences.

Hollywood obliged, eventually. The first hints that something was not right were the September 1920 deaths, five days apart, of Griffith actor Bobby Harron and Olive Thomas, the former Ziegfeld girl and beautiful star of *The Flapper.* Thomas was married to Jack Pickford, Mary's brother, and during an argument in a Paris hotel room she swallowed mercury bichloride in what may have been a melodramatic gesture or a genuine suicide bid. Four days later, she was dead, the first of Hollywood's mysterious exits and hardly the last. Harron died of a self-inflicted gunshot; it may have been genuinely accidental, but the weirdness was gathering.

The next year and a half saw the demons come out. Over Labor Day weekend of 1921, the gifted comedian Fatty Arbuckle held a party in a San Francisco hotel suite; much boozing and "jollification" ensued, and at the end of it a young actress named Virginia Rappe was dead of a ruptured bladder.

It was the revenge of the Extra Girl. Overnight, Arbuckle's image changed from a pudgy scamp to an obese pervert, pressing his obscene weight down on the struggling victim or (as one rumor had it) defiling her with a Coke bottle. Two trials ended in hung juries and the third in acquittal—the judge went out of his way to say a great wrong had been done to Arbuckle—but his career was over the moment the first headlines ran. The shock was the double-edged nature of star persona, and how easily every positive aspect of an actor's image could be instantly converted to its own negative.

Early the next year, on February 1, 1922, the eminent director William Desmond Taylor was found shot to death in his Westlake Park apartment in what proved to be an even bigger field day for the press than the Arbuckle affair. Not one but two young actresses were implicated—the comedienne Mabel Normand, who may or may not have been the dead man's lover and was the last person known to have seen him alive, and Mary Miles Minter, an ethereally virginal nineteen-year-old starlet who most definitely was the forty-nine-year-old Taylor's lover and happy to admit it. The rest of the cast was patently bizarre and included Taylor's ex-con chauffeur, his bisexual valet, Minter's overly possessive mother, and the general manager of Paramount Pictures, who arrived at the apartment shortly after the body was found and removed certain unknown items. The case remains unsolved, its details now leaching into the Internet era on a number of fetishistically detailed Web sites.

Less than a year later, matinee idol Wallace Reid died at thirty-one, technically of the flu but mostly from the effects of the morphine addiction he had acquired after being injured in a 1919 train crash. Rather than sweep the true nature of his demise under the rug, Reid's widow, Dorothy Davenport, went public, embarking on a lecture tour on the dangers of addiction and coproducing a film, *Human Wreckage,* with which she toured the country.

Sex orgies, murder, now drug addiction—it was a veritable trifecta of secrets vomited forth onto the shores of the public consciousness. Within two years, Hollywood had become engulfed by a perfect storm of scandal, and the reverence with which most of the press had treated movie stars was whipped away. Reformers who had been agitating for film censorship at the local level—thirty-six states had bills on the table regulating the content of movies—were suddenly able to take their argument national. The June 29, 1922, issue of the *Congressional Record* published a politician's speech that reveals the class fears driving much of the debate: "At Hollywood is a colony of these people where debauchery, riotous living, drunkenness, ribaldry, dissipation, free love seem to be conspicuous. Many of these 'stars' it is reported were formerly bartenders, butcher boys, sopers, swampers, variety actors and actresses, who may have earned $10 or $20 a week. . . . These are some of the characters from whom the young people of today are deriving a large part of their education, views of life, and character forming habits. . . . Rather a poor source, is it not? It looks as if censorship is needed, does it not?"

In other words, if we make stars out of the "wrong" people—working-class, undereducated, *undeserving*—they will drag the young down to their level. It's an argument that is evergreen and will always play well to worried parents and editorialists. Whether it's from rap lyrics or inadvertent breasts on national TV or the sight of Fatty Arbuckle, the 266-pound Monster from the Id, the children must be saved.

The film studios stalled for time. They formed a lobbying group called the Motion Picture Producers and Distributors of America (MMPDA)—in time it would become the Motion Picture Association of America, our MPAA of the curious film ratings—and in January 1922 hired the former postmaster general of the United States, a nerdy, capable Presbyterian elder named Will Hays, to clean up the industry's image. Carl Laemmle described the position as "a dictator of principles," and in short order Hays banned Arbuckle's films from being shown (an empty gesture, since no one wanted to see them), prodded the Los Angeles YWCA to plan a one-hundred-bed facility for Extra Girls, and, if rumors are to be believed, interceded in the domestic disputes of cowboy star William S. Hart and his wife.

More to the point, Hays was an outsider who would be listened to, telling the worried nation that "nothing is wrong with moving pictures—except youth. Picture play making is a matter of less than

20 years of age—and it really cannot be expected to have the splendid stability, poise and standards of, for example, the press, which has reached its present state only after six hundred years."

God love a politician.

If Hays helped quell the fires of outrage, though—and if movie producers began seriously vetting their stars for breaches of morality and legality—the beast had been loosed. The news media leapt upon the scandals with glee, fed by a postwar tabloid mentality that would turn everyone in 1920s culture into stars (Charles Lindbergh, Albert Einstein, café hostess Texas Guinan, Prohibition cops Izzy and Moe, gangster Al Capone—the list is endless, each personage his or her own genre). Poor Mabel Normand had it rough. She was a Friend of Fatty, her various addictions (including an opium-laced cough syrup she called her "goop") became public knowledge during the Taylor murder trial, and in 1924 her chauffeur killed a rich socialite with Mabel's gun. The Ohio attorney general, for one, had had enough, and banned all films from "this film star [who] has been entirely too closely connected with disgraceful shooting affairs."

What the journalists knew—what even the smarter studio heads must have understood—was that the audiences out there in the dark loved all this dirt. *Loved* it. It was proof of so many things. That stars weren't perfect beings, but flawed like the rest of us. That stars had *worse* flaws than the rest of us, and maybe we could do better if we had the chance. That money and fame either can't buy happiness or can lead directly to unhappiness (or at least the sin of having a really good time). That you could, or should, be punished for daring to rise so high. It was schadenfreude and it was a new kind of entertainment, yoked to the movies but delivering higher highs and more thrillingly vicious lows.

The star scandals also brought into alignment the changes that were occurring in society and perceptions of the actors who were enacting those changes on the screen. Morals *were* loosening, women *were* living freer and more sexual lives. Prohibition had galvanized an underground national party since going into effect in January 1920. (And if booze was illegal yet available everywhere, how bad could cocaine or heroin or morphine or "goop" be?) Not to acknowledge these changes, as mainstream popular culture and especially the smiling Hollywood publicity machine were doing, was a sign of hypocrisy at best, delusion at worst. The scandals helped resolve this paradox, and in a strange way reassured the public of what it already knew.

(Or maybe not, since some topics remained resolutely beyond the pale. When Gloria Swanson sickened and had to be hospitalized shortly after her 1925 marriage to a French marquis, newspapers published the details of her rising and falling fever, and fans feared the worst. What would they have said if they knew she was suffering the results of a botched abortion? Swanson, at the peak of her success, was earning $7,000 a week at Paramount; Adolph Zukor had a lot riding on her. If he had known that she had gone and gotten pregnant before getting married—if the public had known, if *Will Hays* had known—the tower would have come crashing down. As it was, Zukor got plenty of free publicity out of his star's "illness." Swanson, according to her autobiography, got a lifetime of guilt.)

Scandal turned out to be addictive. Going forward, the movie-star discourse—the many levels of public conversation connected to famous people onscreen—was inextricable from what we all suspected the stars did when the cameras stopped rolling. That became the other movie, the shadow drama: the drinking, fornicating, homicidal ghost in the machine. For some it became the only movie that mattered, precisely because it was the one we weren't supposed to see.

When, in the early 1930s, the Production Code of movie rules and regulations was laid down and eventually enforced—no more couples sleeping in one bed—the film industry turned actively neurotic about policing the chasm between screened life and real life. This was an untenable position over the long haul, and the years following World War II slowly brought the movie playing in theaters back into sync with its shadow version. By the late 1960s you could pay to watch naked movie stars swearing and smoking dope. You could even call it progress; many did.

In the 1920s, though, it was as if a bucket of maggots had been upended on the banquet table at Pickfair. Suddenly the bright miracle of movie stardom could end in death. Mabel Normand succumbed to tuberculosis and her addictions in 1930, a dead-eyed wraith. Actress/writer Barbara La Marr was gone in 1926 from heroin; the papers called her "The Girl Too Beautiful to Live," as if it were the title of her own shadow biopic. Broadway and film star Jeanne Eagels fell victim to some sort of speedball in 1929, and Jack Pickford was dead by 1933 of alcohol and drugs and disappointment. This became a critical aspect of the star drama, too—the ugly exit followed by chest-beating audience repentance—and it's the part where the weekly checkout line orgy of *People* and *Us* magazines still makes money.

It has to be asked. *Is* there something in fame that presses a person, or some people, toward self-destruction? Scandal is now an accepted part of the narrative thread of entertainment culture, easily able to go prime-time when a celebrity like Charlie Sheen hogs the microphone. A great part of the public fascination, though, lies in the inability to comprehend why those who have everything (and in America, fame *is* everything) would be unhappy enough to let addictions or despair get the better of them. This is the resentment, the inner complaint, that pairs with the dark enjoyment of watching a celebrity flame out. Why aren't the stars grateful for what they have, we grudgingly wonder, as we certainly would be if we had a chance at fame?

A number of reasons suggest themselves. For one, consumers and fans don't often consider the grinding effects of simple, daily boredom in the entertainment industry, either on the set waiting for the next camera setup or at home waiting for the next project. The unstructured life extends into the evening, when a poor nobody who has just become a semi-wealthy Somebody can move easily from party to dinner to nightclub to party, hoisted by hangers-on, coasting on an enabling current of liquor, drugs, sex, adoration. True, this is why some people become movie stars in the first place, but what happens when it still doesn't fill the hole inside?

Most disorienting of all must be the sense that everyone except you knows who you are. A star's persona is a construct agreed upon by all who consume it and all who profit by it, and that construct is taken as fact (or at least useful fiction) by everyone except the star, who knows but may not want to admit how temporary the persona truly is. No less a god than Cary Grant went famously on the record about this, writing in an autobiographical magazine article, "I have spent the greater part of my life fluctuating between Archie Leach and Cary Grant; unsure of each, suspecting each." If it was hard for him, imagine how psychically discombobulating it must have been for someone like James Murray, who was plucked out of the ranks of extras to play the lead role in King Vidor's dark 1928 masterpiece *The Crowd*?

The movie is precisely about the urge of the common man to become uncommon, and Murray's John is a handsome young blowhard who insists that "everything will be roses when my ship comes in" until he has to face the fact that he's just another human in the throng, that dreaming doesn't make it happen. *The Crowd* destroys the fantasy of stardom in a burst of diamond-hard social realism—unsurprisingly, the movie was critically admired and a commercial failure—and Murray conveys the shallowness at the start of John's pilgrim's progress, the neurosis in the middle, and the bleak acceptance at the end. (It's true, by the way. Most of us aren't seen or celebrated by those who do not personally know or love us. *The Crowd* implies that to wish otherwise is the business of fools, not that anyone wanted to hear that then or wants to hear it now.)

Murray was praised by Vidor as "one of the best natural actors we had ever had the good luck to encounter." His career was set, starring roles presented themselves, yet the new star rapidly unraveled. Given the actuality of fame, he retreated to the pipe dream; by the early 1930s he was an alcoholic panhandling for spare change on the street. When Vidor bought him lunch and offered him a part in 1934's *Our Daily Bread*, Murray cursed him out and stalked off. He was dead by 1936, drowned in the Hudson River after drunkenly clowning around and falling off a pier. Was it the suddenness with which he was raised up that undid Murray? Did he identify too closely with his *Crowd* character's insecurities, or was this simply a case of a person becoming a star with no inner psychological core, no sense of self, to support the new edifice? Haunted, Vidor later wrote a screenplay based on Murray's life; called "The Actor," it was never produced. Who'd play the part, anyway? Who would want to star in a role that exposed stardom as a useless trick at best and a destroyer at worst?

If some embraced immolation, simple disillusion claimed more. The arrival of the talkies in 1927 swept the movie industry clean in a kind of cosmic industrial reboot, but for many of the earliest "picture personalities," it had been over for a long time. The very first superstars were also the first to learn that stardom doesn't last forever, may not even last the decade. By 1924, "Vitagraph Girl" Florence Turner was just another stock player at MGM, that most glamorous of new movie studios and the epitome of the inhuman vertical industry Hollywood had become. An article called "Poverty Row" in a 1926 issue of *Motion Picture Magazine* showed Henry B. Walthall, star of *Birth of a Nation,* grinding out quickie films.

And what of the Biograph Girl, the actress with whom it all began in 1910? Florence Lawrence didn't have Little Mary's head for business, and her career was for all intents and purposes through by 1916. There were comebacks that didn't stick, a back injury that took her further out of the limelight. In 1924, Lawrence turned up in the regular *Photoplay* feature "Stars of Yesterday." She told the writer, "It is hard to feel that you have given the best of your life to motion pictures—and that they have no place for you."

The occasional bit part still came Lawrence's way, and for a while she ran a makeup store called Hollywood Cosmetics on Fairfax Avenue; a 1928 photo shows her posed outside the shop window with a stylish blond bob. She's a world away from the nineteenth-century drawing rooms of her Biograph days. She's one of us again, outside looking in.

But she had been inside, once. In 1931, she and her onetime rival Florence Turner were among the 750 nonspeaking roles in Paramount's *Sinners in the Sun*. They were Extra Girls now, and then they weren't even that. Shortly after Christmas of 1938, ill and worn out at the age of fifty-two, Florence Lawrence mixed herself a glass of cough syrup and ant poison, drank it, and died.

5.

Judgment Day: The Movies Speak

In the brief three-year period from late 1927 to the end of 1930, the U.S. film industry stopped making silent pictures and started making sound films. This period was called the "talkie revolution," but it wasn't a revolution at all, except in the sense that consumers rose up against an unspeaking medium for which there was suddenly no perceived cultural or monetary value.

The arrival of sound should be understood as an industrial calamity—a forced ground-up reinvention of an entrenched method of production that affected every level of the business, especially the manufacture and maintenance of movie stars. By 1931, the silent movie was not merely dead—no more were being put into production—but a remnant of an earlier era that was already considered primitive, even embarrassing. "[The talkies] have 'gotten me' to the extent that a silent picture actually bores me nowadays," a fan wrote to her favorite magazine in 1929, and in this she spoke for everyone.

We think of the movies as an infant industry in the mid-1920s, but in fact they were at the peak of their first maturity, a muscular engine of entertainment and profits. By the end of the silent era, there were 42,000 people employed in Hollywood, a town that was responsible for 82 percent of the world's total film output. The business as a whole was worth $2.5 billion, most of it tied up in theater chains. Yet within months—weeks, even—every single aspect of that industry was cast into turmoil. Imagine all the U.S. automakers having to convert from gasoline-burning engines to cars that run on Mazola—not gradually introducing them over the course of a decade, but either overhauling factories within the space of months or going out of business. Imagine the computer business switching over to holographic projection displays at user gunpoint. Imagine the newspaper industry having to go online in less than a decade or perish. Ah. Well.

All right—why? Silents had served for three decades, yet there was a sense that the movies were moving into an uncertain middle age. Box office revenue was down across all the studios. The culture was moving on. People wanted something new. More to the point, talk was suddenly being heard in an entirely different fashion. Radio had arrived and it was the wonderful new toy the movies had once been. By the end of 1920, only thirty broadcasting licenses had been issued, but events like the 1921 Dempsey-Carpentier fight helped sell the novelty, and by 1923 there were six hundred licensed stations. The exact years of the talkie revolution are also those of radio's gathering into the country's preeminent communications force. Having newly heard the drama of the human voice—at home, for free—audiences found silent movies very much lacking.

See how closely the two mediums intertwine. On August 6, 1926, Warner Bros.—a small-time studio with only one star, and that star a dog named Rin-Tin-Tin—risked it all on the first Vitaphone release: *Don Juan*, a three-hour extravaganza starring John Barrymore. It featured synchronized music and sound effects only, no talking. ("Who the hell wants to hear actors talk?" Harry Warner asked his brothers.) Three months later, David Sarnoff of the Radio Corporation of America launched his new network, the National Broadcasting Corporation, with nineteen stations; by 1928, NBC would have nearly sixty outposts. One of the first NBC shows, an all-star "Big Broadcast" that aired the night of November 11, 1926, proved so popular that movie attendance was down as much as 30 percent in the network's footprint. Audiences wanted to hear what the famous *sounded* like.

In January 1927, the Rose Bowl game was heard on the country's first coast-to-coast hookup. On May 2nd, William Fox released the first of his immensely popular Movietone shorts—footage of a West Point marching drill and Charles Lindbergh taking off on his transatlantic flight, both with "live" sound. In June, NBC aired the Paul Whiteman Orchestra in the first of sponsored weekly broadcasts for which the jazzman received $5,000 an hour. In October, *The Jazz Singer* had its premiere, a mostly silent film that gave star Al Jolson a handful of songs to sing. When he interpolated some talking patter—including his famous catchphrase "You ain't heard nothing yet!"—audiences broke into cheers.

The foundations, then, had been laid. The attractions of human speech were quite literally in the air, making the puppet show of silent film look tired. It helped a great deal that Jolson was an established star of the stage, already legendary for his eccentric high-voltage energy and ability to sell a song. And there was something about hearing real people realistically talk and sing that genuinely excited audiences. Barrymore in *Don Juan* had been a hit the year before, but the real draw was the program of Vitaphone shorts that preceded the film: primordial music videos featuring violinist Mischa Elman, banjo player Roy Smeck, Marion Talley the "Kansas City Canary," Anna Case and the Cansino dancers (featuring the young Margarita Cansino, one day to become Rita Hayworth), and a speech by none other than Will Hays. The *Don Juan*/Vitaphone shorts program broke the single-week record for a Broadway movie house and Warner Bros. stock soared. A second program of shorts included one of Jolson singing three songs. The pump was primed.

The Jazz Singer was a hit, but it wasn't the runaway smash enshrined by movie history; Warners' less remembered 1928 Jolson follow-up

The Singing Fool was the film that drew huge audiences and saved the faltering talkie from early extinction. But *The Jazz Singer* was the game changer—the movie that convinced theater owners that sound films would attract an audience and that it was worth investing in the speakers and the wiring. Other studios looked at the Warners—those pishers—and agreed to go in together on any sound technology *except* Vitaphone. (Zukor, bless his black heart, had already tried to buy his way in, but the Warners wanted too much money.) Several seasons of part-talkies and music-and-effect "soundies" ensued, almost all of them dreadful beyond measure and almost all of them popular and profitable anyway. In fact, the new sound films were often the only pictures making any money at all.

Lights of New York, released in July 1928, was the first all-talkie, and it notably featured no stars—just vaudeville players and future character actor Eugene Pallette in a woebegone fifty-seven-minute gangster story. When the villain tells a thug to take the hero for "a ride," the scene is hilariously slow by today's standards, as though a cast of five-year-olds were being prompted by an offscreen schoolmarm. Yet the sound was crystal clear, and audiences stood and applauded after each awkward, overacted scene. The technology, not the actors, was the star. This hadn't happened since the dawn of film; it wouldn't happen again until (arguably) the rise of TV and (certainly) the coming of the Internet.

The talent in Hollywood panicked. Why shouldn't they, when the lovely Dolores Costello was unintentionally making audiences roll in the aisles in 1928's *Tenderloin* by telling the villain, "Merthy, merthy, have you no thithter of your own?" The line became a sardonic catchphrase for a few months, an early example of the mockery that can envelop stars who have suddenly lost their power.

Costello appeared in the same year's *Glorious Betsy,* a Warners part-talkie that premiered to a packed, nervous audience of Hollywood screen royalty. Writer-director William DeMille—Cecil B.'s older brother—was present and later described the reaction of the assembled silent stars when an onscreen actor opened his mouth: " 'Ladies and gentlemen,' he said. *He said!* A thrill ran through the house. The screen had spoken at last: an operation had been performed and the man, dumb from infancy, could talk."

A turgid period romance about Napoleon's brother and the woman he loves, *Glorious Betsy* was, not to put too fine a point on it, junk. Every time Costello moved, the rustlings of her silk dress boomed like a windstorm over the speakers. Costar Conrad Nagel tried to maximize the script's romantic intensity by saying the title character's name over and over—"Betsy, Betsy, *Betsy*!"—drawing hoots from the audience. Yet the movie was a hit, and three weeks after it was released, Paramount, United Artists, and MGM signed deals to install sound recording equipment in their studios and amplification systems in their theaters. By the end of 1928, a thousand theaters were wired and ready to go, six hundred more than there had been six months earlier. A year later, at the end of 1929, there were 8,700 talkie houses—a 2,100 percent growth curve in eighteen months—and every sound film that was released was making money. That is how fast it all happened.

The way the studios manufactured and maintained their movie stars underwent a convulsion, too—had to, as stars were the most visible part of the machine, the bait that set the hook. As sound came roaring in, it rendered each and every screen career suspect, turned every star's value upside down. There wouldn't be this decisive a break in what a movie star meant to the studios, to individual moviegoers, and to the culture as a whole until the birth of the youth audience in the postwar years. Even then, the rise of Brando and James Dean was only a shift in fashion. The arrival of the talkies was a wholesale reinvention, and there's a sense of helpless exhilaration in the pace and cruelty with which stars and their associated meanings were elevated or destroyed.

The irony, though, is that the studios came out of the talkie transition with a much firmer control over the process of making film—and, by default, the process of making stars. With the appearance of sound film at the dawn of the 1930s, the Golden Era of the movie factory is upon us. The players that would dominate for the next thirty years are assembled: the major companies (Louis B. Mayer's MGM, Zukor's Paramount, Laemmle's Universal, the newly flush Warner Bros.), their smaller rivals (Harry Cohn's Columbia, Republic, Monogram, and so on down into Poverty Row), and a few late-arriving upstarts in RKO, funded with New York radio money and New York theaters to take advantage of the talkie craze, and Twentieth Century-Fox, cobbled together in 1935 by Warners' former house genius Darryl Zanuck from his new Twentieth Century production unit and the bankrupt pieces of William Fox's massive holdings.

These were the companies and the men who would tame the mystery of movie stardom and turn it into a nearly predictable business—a factory of luck and attraction and desire. They would build on the archetypes established over the course of the Silent Era—the Great Lover, America's Sweetheart, the Femme Fatale, and so on—and adapt them to changing times by packaging them, maximizing the glamour or the sex or the comedy, and sending them out to make money. The moguls understood: one movie can be a hit, but one star, properly put forth, can be a hit across many movies—can lead the public happily from one property to the next. If you put the pieces together right and cross your fingers, everybody wins.

Only it's not always that easy. Against the studios' star-making machinery is the apposite urge of the consumer, which is simply (and not so simply) to consume—to take the pretty object for oneself and into oneself. The history of modern fame, from the first movies to today, is a struggle for control between the people who make the product and the people who buy it. What did Bette Davis mean to Jack Warner and what did she mean to the women in the back row of the Bijou, and how were the two meanings different? Davis spent her early years fighting Warner Bros. for better roles; in effect, she created her own star persona—a nervy, neurotic modern woman living on the vibrant edge of feeling—that was closer to her fans' desires than the studio's more simpleminded shady ladies.

Nor was she alone. If some of the new stars arrived fully formed—after three decades on the stage, Mae West was already resplendently herself in her first film, 1932's *Night After Night*—others found their most resonant persona by accident or on loan-out to another studio, or, like Humphrey Bogart, had to weather a decade or so before charisma settled in. None of this proves that the studios were bad at what they did, only that they couldn't predict chance—and chance, the element of the unknown, is what keeps us coming back to the theater. Louis B. Mayer could sign an Eleanor Powell, say, and he could arrange for her to be clothed and groomed and coached and photographed and publicized to her best advantage, but the rest was between Powell and us, an audience lured in by perhaps the most technically adept dancer the movies have ever seen.

This tug-of-war waxes and wanes depending on any number of variables, but the wholesale remaking of an industry at the end of the 1920s saw the studios at a particular loss. The early talkies, in fact, show the American public exerting more control over the way movies are made than in any other era, including the panic over TV in the 1950s and the rise of the counterculture in the 1960s. With a suddenness that was terrifying, talking pictures were the only pictures audiences wanted to see.

In Hollywood, the actors read the writing on the wall and heard the sound waves in the air, and they huddled for warmth. Voice teachers like Felix Hughes and Mrs. Paul Sloane became stars to the stars. *Time* magazine panned Norma Talmadge's first talkie, 1929's *New York Nights,* saying she sounded like an elocution pupil. By her second sound film, 1930's *Du Barry, Woman of Passion,* the same reviewer remarked that the actress had improved—she now sounded like an elocution *teacher.*

It was a seller's market. By July 1928, there were seven colleges of "voice culture" in Beverly Hills. The audience of movie actors who attended an Academy of Motion Picture Arts and Sciences seminar held by two college professors learned that performers' voices could be classified into the following categories: euphonic, allisophonic, eulexophonic, rhythmophonic, and dynophonic. In short, nobody knew anything, least of all the studio heads.

What to do with the old stars, and who would be the new? Foreign-born icons of the silent screen were in jeopardy and reacted accordingly. Pola Negri scorned the talkies—"Eet is a fad, a curiosity"—and promptly dropped from sight. Emil Jannings, the great hambone star of *The Last Command,* for which he had won the very first Best Actor Academy Award, packed up and went home to Germany, where he eventually became one of the Third Reich's favorite actors. Overnight, the brooding European femme fatale became an endangered species, for how seriously could you take Olga Baclanova and Vilma Banky when you couldn't understand a word they said?

Greta Garbo, though, was a special case—a hugely popular hothouse flower—and Louis B. Mayer kept her on ice in silent romances until 1930, when he launched *Anna Christie* with the PR campaign "Garbo Talks!" She did, too, with deep and weary tones that matched her persona; still, as the actress herself later said of the film, "Did you ever hear any Swede talk like that?"

For other long-established stars, the arrival of sound was a challenge to which they rose, triumphed, and then quickly faded from the scene. Mary Pickford, now a ripe thirty-seven, leapt at the chance to remake her image. Her final silent, 1927's *My Best Girl,* is one of her best movies, but still she was stuck playing poor, young, and plucky. The talkies offered the break with the past she longed for, and so Pickford hacked her long Victorian tresses into a flapper bob—the fan magazines reeled from the scandal—and played the lead in 1929's *Coquette* with a thick southern accent.

The movie was a hit, and Pickford won a Best Actress Oscar, but she appeared in only three more sound films before retiring to produce a few pictures over the years, divorce Douglas Fairbanks in 1936, marry Buddy Rogers Jr. in 1937, and count her money and real estate holdings. Of her remaining talkies, one was Hollywood Shakespeare (*The Taming of the Shrew,* her only pairing with Fairbanks), and the other two were remakes of Norma Talmadge silents. Talmadge's, it turned out, was the image Pickford had yearned for all those years. By the time she got it, it was too late.

Talmadge, for her part, appeared in *New York Nights* (1929) and *Du Barry, Woman of Passion* (1930) before calling it a day; despite critical barbs, her voice wasn't all that unsuited for sound—in no sense was she the screeching Lina Lamont of *Singin' in the Rain*, for which Talmadge is sometimes cited as an inspiration. But her popularity was already on the wane, and an opulent period romance like *Du Barry*—love among the aristos—was exactly what audiences didn't want to see in the months following the stock market crash. The star accepted that her moment had passed with the graciousness of a grand diva. Writer-director Joseph Mankiewicz recalls seeing Talmadge come out of the Brown Derby restaurant in the early 1930s and blithely wave off a crowd of photographers with the words "Go away, you little bastards, I don't need you anymore."

Where was Chaplin in all this? Dithering and making orotund pronouncements to anyone who would listen about silence and art and the ruinous encroachment of modern technology. Chaplin talked, all right—he was said to chatter away at Hollywood parties until five in the morning—but he wouldn't utter a comprehensible word onscreen until 1940's *The Great Dictator*. As the talkies grew like kudzu, Al Jolson scoffed, "What [Chaplin has] really got is a gentleman complex. He's afraid he talks too nice to fit the screen." In this he came close to the truth of famous people terrified that their voices would reveal their real selves and thereby bring down the tottering edifice of persona.

What Jolson half sensed and Chaplin and his fellow stars possibly didn't understand is that their "real voices" were as much an invention as any other part of their persona. Charlie's ornately verbose way of speaking—"forever talking the dictionary," in critic David Thomson's marvelous phrase—was the mask of a self-educated man behaving like the genius everyone assured him he was. His voice wasn't the voice of the Tramp at all, but the self-willed tones of the man who had created him within and for a world of silence. It may be that the invention of the Tramp itself was such an occasion of serendipity—Charlie stumped in the costume department, hurry up, we're shooting in ten minutes—that he could never figure out a proper voice to go with it. So he went with the voice he invented off camera, that of a high-minded and achingly earnest pseud.

Most were willing to risk the game, yet if Pickford and Talmadge and Swanson had adequate voices (and they had), why did their stardom fade? Primarily because it was founded on and inextricable from silence—a delicately maintained illusion that sound's hiss destroyed. Sound revealed them as human and hastened the audience's desire to move on to the next new thing. Because all three women had been so very popular, so intrinsic a part of post–World War I popular culture, they were lashed to the mast of their era and went down with it. The break was complete and it was ruthless. Talkies needed fresh stars for whom the vocal component was part of the initial impact. That meant the established stars had to die off. You cannot retrofit an old dream into a new fantasy.

So younger, less formed performers had an easier time of it. Norma Shearer had been acting in movies since the age of seventeen and was rising at MGM under the guidance and care of production chief Irving Thalberg, whom she married in 1927, but she had never developed a tightly defined persona during her silent years. Instead, she was a high-end studio utility player, able to do glam or vamp as necessary. Shearer made her all-talkie debut in *The Trial of Mary Dugan* (1929) as a showgirl accused of murder; the film was a success and Shearer's voice proved to be a fluty and regal instrument that solidified her position as Queen of MGM. (Did it help that her brother, Douglas Shearer, was the foremost sound engineer in Hollywood?)

The talkies eventually allowed Shearer to ascend her throne in productions like *The Barretts of Wimpole Street* (1934) and *Marie Antoinette* (1938)—a decade earlier they would have starred another Norma, Talmadge—but in the early sound years she could play both uptown and sexy, throwing herself into Clark Gable's arms in *A Free Soul* (1931) with an eroticism that's still startling in a movie executive's wife.

A similar if harder path was forged by Joan Crawford, who evolved from the rowdy silent flapper of *Our Dancing Daughters* (1928) and *Our Modern Maidens* (1929) into a tough-as-nails Depression tootsie. Crawford's first talkie, *Untamed,* cast her as "Bingo, wild woman of South America," but her voice was richer than the parts she got and it led irresistibly to the classic sound-era Crawford: clipped and impatient, hiding vulnerability behind a wall of melodramatic bravado.

Crawford quickly became an onscreen match for Gable, the most potent of the new generation of stars. Unlike Gable, though, Crawford kept reinventing herself decade by decade, driven by a raging, if hazily articulated, need to stay on top. That drive is there in her voice, in the stance, in Crawford's pop-eyed avidity, and how much was a conscious invention and how much was just naked, get-me-the-hell-out-of-the-gutter ambition has never been fully explicated.

For a while, it looked as though Conrad Nagel might be the greatest star of the talkies. He was nice looking, he could act—better, he could speak, and after appearing opposite Dolores Costello in *Tenderloin* and *Glorious Betsy,* he popped up in an astonishing twenty-nine films in two years. ("I was an epidemic," he said later.) John Miljean appeared in four all-talkies and eight part-talkies; John Boles gave female audiences the vapors with his handsome looks and mellifluous singing voice in *The Desert Song.* One fan, writing to *Photoplay,* compared him to Valentino. "We have been looking for Rudy's successor for a long time. We need look no farther." By December 1929, Boles's fan letters to the magazine outnumbered John Gilbert's.

Yet by the mid-1930s, he was back playing dull male love interests opposite ballsy women like Rosalind Russell in *Craig's Wife,* Barbara Stanwyck in *Stella Dallas,* even Shirley Temple in *Curly Top* and *The Littlest Rebel.* The studio heads went mad with frustration. What did audiences *want*? They wanted talking pictures, but what *kind* of talking pictures? What was the talking supposed to sound like?

Was it supposed to sound like Broadway? Desperate to have talents on hand who were trained to speak—as opposed to movie stars, who presumably spoke without knowing how or why—the studios rushed to sign up actors, directors, writers, and composers from the New York stage. They even briefly reopened their old East Coast studios, hedging a bet that film production would shift back to the city in which the industry had taken its first steps.

The Warners negotiated to film entire Broadway shows along with their casts, and MGM rehearsed *The Trial of Mary Dugan* before live audiences. Yet the Broadway rush petered out because the crisp drawing-room enunciation of stage actors turned out to play poorly onscreen: mannered, twee, laughable. These people were, simply, not movie stars. They had voices but no faces; they lacked the signal intimate force of movie personalities. MGM tested a hundred Broadway actors and signed only one. (Gwynne Stratford; remember her—or him? Me neither.) William Fox brought thirty-two of New York's finest out west, but the only ones that took were the cowboy philosopher Will Rogers (whose dry prairie shtick allowed him to lob darts of astute social commentary, making him a cultural link between Mark Twain and Garrison Keillor), and a handsome young man named Paul Muni.

The latter, born Muni Weisenfreund, came from the Yiddish stage and was an expert in costumes and makeup; he played seven characters in one eight-minute screen test, prompting the studio to boast that it had found "a Chaney who talks." In effect, Muni wanted to be an anti-star, famous for looking like anyone *but* himself. And it's true that he ended up doing a run of stuffy Great Man costume pictures for Warner Bros. that eventually won him an Oscar (for 1936's *The Story of Louis Pasteur*). Muni asked for respect along with his gallery of putty noses, and Jack Warner gave it to him.

Yet the star's two best performances came in other genres and without makeup, and they say something about what sound brought to the table. One was the original *Scarface* (1932), a gangster movie pushed by director Howard Hawks toward opera and the Borgias, with Muni as big a buffoon ham killer as Al Pacino was in the 1982 remake. The other was a classic Warner Bros. social-problem film, *I Am a Fugitive from a Chain Gang* (1932), where the star for once reined it in and played realistic as an innocent man on the run from a grindingly cruel southern penal system. The movie was based, and based closely, on a true story, and the ending is chilling in its talkie genius, the hero's girlfriend asking the retreating fugitive how he survives and his whisper coming back from the dark of the night: "*I steal.*" That's what the silents couldn't give you—the slap in the face, the sting that came from sound wedded to image in ways that popped the equation into three-dimensional shape.

The novelty of the talkies, though, precluded star personality at first and instead celebrated effect—the machine that could do new, more lifelike things. So very, very few silent stars made the leap and became bigger. Ronald Colman was the rare case, moving up from second-grade John Gilbert status to a tough but suave heartthrob on the strength of 1929's hit mystery *Bulldog Drummond.* Colman stayed close to the top for the next decade, his smooth British tones a mark of intelligent sophistication that had its own sex appeal; he was the thinking woman's hunk.

Most silent stars became smaller, or just something different. John Barrymore briefly used his theatrically trained cadences to bolster his great-actor image in *General Crack* (*Cinema* said "the sound of his voice puts something gritty and muscular back into him"), but the star was already past his prime by the early 1930s and well down the neck of the bottle; after a solid run of dramatic leads, he sloped off into character roles—many extremely funny—and legendary offscreen carousing that ended in a drunkard's death. Barrymore's public persona became that of the Great Wreck, a vast talent knowingly and helplessly squandered.

It may be best to compare two actors passing each other on the escalators of fame, John Gilbert and William Powell: one lost everything because of sound, the other gained a new persona and a new career. Gilbert's flameout is encrusted in conspiracy mongering and exaggeration, but the indisputable fact is that the Great Lover's first talkie, *His Glorious Night* in 1929, reduced audiences to helpless fits of laughter. It was the romantic scenes that did it, Gilbert mooning, "I love you, I love you, I love you" to Catherine Dale Owen with a passion that had worked blissfully when no one could actually hear it but that aloud prompted—what? Nervousness? Surprise? The shock of disconnect? *Variety* wrote, "A few more talker productions like this and John Gilbert will be able to change places with [slapstick comedian] Harry Langdon."

The issue was never Gilbert's voice. He had appeared with Norma Shearer in a *Romeo and Juliet* parody in the all-star talkie *The Hollywood Revue of 1929*, and no one had covered their ears and checked for blood. But *His Glorious Night* was a badly misdirected movie, its feet glued to the floor by the limitations of early sound-recording technology. The "I love you" scene came in the midst of one endless seven-minute static shot; the laughter very probably sprang from relief.

More important, the dialogue was all wrong, and it was delivered all wrong. Nothing Gilbert said could match what rapturous silent-era audiences had played out in their heads, each moviegoer hearing a different script tailored to his or her private hopes and sexual dreams. Fans had a proprietary interest in their stars, especially the romantic idols. They owned them, like dolls, and like dolls they used them for fantasy play. Dolls don't talk back, not in their own words—not in florid dialogue that mocks the banal, unspecific love talk we all want to hear directed solely to us. With *His Glorious Night,* Gilbert stopped talking to each individual audience member and spoke instead to the crowd, and in this the ego-lie of the privileged star-to-moviegoer relationship was exposed. Of course his career was over. How could it not have been? He had cheated on each of us with everybody else.

Now look at William Powell. A simpler and happier story. His dark looks, gray eyes, and broad-shouldered physique had typecast him as a silent villain, emphasis on the suave and Continental (although he did play the pathetic cuckold George Wilson in the 1926 version of *The Great Gatsby*). The actor's second sound film was *The Canary Murder Case* (1929), in which he starred as detective Philo Vance, and suddenly here was the Powell we now know—the worldly, capable, funny class act who would solve Thin Man murders and lead Carole Lombard by the nose in *My Man Godfrey.*

Sound made this happen: the gentle acid click of Powell's tongue against his teeth, the tone in his voice—was it allisophonic or eulexophonic?—bespeaking a native intelligence that has seen it all and found it highly amusing. It was a new voice, a sensible voice; it was an *attractive* voice in ways for which there was no precedent in movies. "I heard my first talking picture a few days ago," a fan wrote to *Photoplay* (note the verb: the movie was not seen but heard). "It was *The Canary Murder Case*. I thought it was great! William Powell had always been fixed in my mind as a villain of the screen until then. He will never seem the same to me again and I am glad of it, because I like him so much better this way. He has a really remarkable voice. It is so easily understood and contains such a soothing quality. Let's hear and see more of him!"

So easily understood and so soothing; who had ever asked that of a silent star? No wonder Powell and Myrna Loy were a hit as *The Thin Man*'s Nick and Nora Charles, 1930s Hollywood's classiest and sexiest married couple. Their voices, and the droll worldview those voices conveyed, dovetailed perfectly; theirs was an onscreen marriage of diphthongs and knowingness. Loy had been transformed by sound, too; silent films cast this cat-faced girl from Montana as an exotic princess or a vamp, and she was still playing characters named Narita, Azura, Yasmani, and Nubi into the early talkies. *Manhattan Melodrama* (1934) let her finally and decisively make the leap. She begins the film as Gable's gun moll—a more sensible gun moll you'll never meet; you can imagine her doing his taxes—and by the end she's paired up with Powell, on the right side of the law and with the right star by her side. They are the gin and tonic of early Hollywood cinema.

There was a lesson here—naturalism works—but the studios were slow to pick up on it. Instead they spent the early sound era competitively testing out one genre after another. A raft of courtroom dramas (all talk, no action) was followed by a wave of primitive musicals, then all-star revues (Warners' *Show of Shows* featured seventy-seven "names," a promotional tactic that stretches the meaning of the noun to the breaking point), then westerns shot with new mobile equipment on outdoor locations, the microphones literally hidden in the cacti. Each new genre was seized on by all the studios at the same time, exploited, and discarded, and the technology got better each step of the way. But still the moguls couldn't see it. The audience wanted movie stars who sounded like themselves.

They wanted it so much that they became a little paranoid. At a certain point during the early talkie craze, moviegoers realized that actors could be dubbed with the voices of other actors, and a brief panic over star identity broke out. It became known that one Johnny Murray provided the singing voice of star Richard Barthelmess in *Weary River*, and there were even rumors that Douglas Fairbanks, the king himself, had been dubbed in *The Iron Mask*'s opening and closing scenes. Whose voices were really theirs? How could you tell? The sudden need for proof roiled popular culture, to the point that Colleen Moore released a notarized affidavit stating that the voice in *Footlights and Fools* was actually hers.

Curiously, one of the bigger sensations of the early talkie years was a Fox newsreel appearance by the seventy-one-year-old British playwright George Bernard Shaw. It was a delightful short in which Shaw, standing in the grounds outside his home, casually addressed the camera as if it were a new friend and cracked mischievous little jokes about the whole experience. The sense was that the audience was seeing Shaw as he was—it was a performance, of course, and the format was the aging author's own idea—and his ease made the stick posturing of the Broadway imports seem unbearable. For a few months, Shaw was as much a movie star as Conrad Nagel.

Sound, then, called for a new realism that jibed with the new, post-Crash sensibility. Flowery speech was out, since audiences couldn't emotionally afford it anymore. Wisecracks and cynicism and terseness and directness were the new coin, even when the settings were the suites and dance floors of the very rich. As radio brought the aural world into the living room, so the talkies brought movies closer to what people's lives felt and sounded like. It was the initial technological baby step toward giving the audience control of the machine, the first stirrings of the beast that would become the decentralized, consumer-driven media Omniverse of today.

6.

The Stars Who Talked: The Great Singularities of the Studio Era

Not all of what was heard on the screen was pretty, and that was the point. The Warner Bros. gangster movie served as a luridly controversial site of cultural truths, the gangsta rap of its day. New stars like James Cagney and Edward G. Robinson kicked you in the face with a viciousness that felt nasty and honest; they seemed to have lurched in from the streets. Actresses like Joan Blondell and Barbara Stanwyck—the former Ruby Stevens from Flatbush, Brooklyn—sold an earthy sensuality that cut through the posturing of upscale talkie dramas. They'd slept around and liked it; you could hear it in their voices.

For a brief moment, before she became a cartoon, Mae West was that raw sexual urge expressed on film. She came with saucy baggage, decades of mortifying the bluenoses of Broadway by writing and starring in plays like *Sex* (about the rise of a hooker to polite society) and *The Drag*, the latter featuring a cast of forty openly gay men and so beyond the pale that it closed in Bridgeport without ever making it to New York. Not until Madonna sixty years later would a female performer rub her audiences' noses so insistently, and with so few apologies, in the sins of the flesh. And for Madonna, *Sex* was just a book.

West was almost forty when she arrived in Hollywood in 1932. Thirty-two of those years had been spent onstage slowly accreting a legend as a truth-telling bawd. When *Sex* was busted in 1927 for "corrupting the morals of youth" and the star went to jail for ten days, the New York papers treated it as her latest production. Even the august *Times* chipped in: "For Miss West the change from the silks, crepes and sheer stockings of the average well-dressed woman . . . to the prison outfit was a shock." West's 1928 stage hit *Diamond Lil* cushioned the carnality by setting it in the Roaring Nineties—Grandpa's era, easy to mock and digest from a distance—but it was still a work of inspired smut. The Hays Office put its foot down: *Diamond Lil* would never be turned into a movie, and don't even think about *Sex* and *The Drag*.

Enter—who else?—Adolph Zukor. Unlike his fellow moguls, the Paramount head was still working out of New York City; he knew what West meant to local theater audiences and how she spoke to her various eras. She was not only great friends with the notorious 1920s nightclub hostess Texas Guinan, Mae was Guinan's show-business analogue. In a silent film, though, West wouldn't have transferred—you had to hear that drawling, do-me-big-boy voice to understand how far she pushed the edges of propriety.

In his autobiography, Zukor wrote, "No one believed that the Mae West of the stage could be transferred almost intact to the screen," and it's probable he didn't believe it either. But what did he have to lose? Paramount posted losses of $21 million in 1932, and its stock was in the basement. The studio's most valuable holdings were its theaters, but 1,700 of them faced conversion to office buildings.

So Zukor signed a rushed contract with West—$5,000 a week for ten weeks—and threw her on a westbound train, hoping something would come of it. The first result was *Night After Night,* a melodrama about a gangster (George Raft) who owns a brownstone speakeasy and falls for a slumming society girl (Constance Cummings). West was handed a supporting role as an ex-girlfriend of Raft's, a high-living party babe, and as soon as she turns up it's a completely different movie.

West was a quick study. Onstage, she had made a habit of slowing her line delivery down to a lazy saunter, to stand apart from the other actors. She realized that actors in early talkies, by contrast, spoke slowly, so in *Night After Night* she revved her performance up. It works; the film shifts gears and leaps ahead whenever her character, Maudie Triplett, is onscreen. *Night After Night* hopes to capture the glitz and grit of early-1930s New York, the collision of classes amid economic turmoil, and the simple thrill of not giving a damn. West is the only person in the movie who acts like she knows that life. Movie audiences had never seen anyone so fresh, in both senses of the word.

Zukor moved fast, somehow getting the censors to pass Paramount's reworking of *Diamond Lil* into West's second film, *She Done Him Wrong.* The star cut some of the play's more salacious lines and wrote new ones just as suggestive. ("Have you ever met a man that can make you happy?" "Sure, lots of times.") The resulting film broke box office records and made $2 million in its first three months. *I'm No Angel* (1933) broke *those* records; at Brooklyn theaters, the police had to be called out to restore order. A Boston reporter wrote, "The street outside [the theater] gave the effect of a run on the neighboring bank. . . . The round-up inside was as overwhelming, and when the languid hoyden slithered into view, every inch of seating and standing room was taken." By 1934, West had the highest salary of any woman in America.

What people responded to was her lack of pretense and her insistence on blunt, down-to-earth commonalities. Mae West was a signboard that said Everybody Does It, and the novelty was in her refusal to gussy that up with even the tiniest notions of romance. The

Depression had no time for romance; romance was for the swooning silent-movie and Broadway drama queens, who suddenly seemed out of step. West was American; she was fleshly; her curves stood in for all the carnal opulence that was hard to find in real life. "Mae West," wrote Elza Schallert in a 1933 *Motion Picture Magazine* profile, "is the first real Waterloo of the Garbo and Dietrich schools of sultry, languorous, erotic emotions. Because she has made them appear slightly foolish—as if they didn't know how to get a 'kick' out of life . . . she spells absolute doom to the hollow-eyed, sunken-cheeked, flat-chested, hipless exponents of the neurotic."

Ironically, West herself was never able to take her breakthrough anywhere. Her career and her persona had arguably peaked onstage in the late 1920s, and her movie success was primarily an aftershock. By *I'm No Angel,* "Mae West" had already hardened into a wax figure that had little to do with the breezy, electric West of *Night After Night.* From now on, she'd undulate and drop leering puns out of the side of her mouth, but there is nothing about her that suggests a real woman experiencing real desire. She's "sexy" without being remotely sexy. A *Variety* writer famously and accurately called her "the greatest female impersonator of all time."

So Hollywood missed the period of her most interesting creativity, catching instead only the final ossification. Yet West's persona outlived her commercial viability and outlives it still; passé by the late 1930s, she remains a household word today. And Zukor kept Paramount from bankruptcy, which for him was all that mattered.

Clark Gable, the era's other exponent of unbridled sex, fared better. He was younger, he was male, and he wasn't hobbled by years of stage mannerisms. The great thing about Gable, in fact, was that he came out of nowhere and seemed freshly minted. He was the first genuine sensation of the talkie era and the first evidence that sound could create stars as potent as the silent cinema.

More potent, in fact. Early Gable was brutish and threatening and sexually alive, dangerous in a way that fed into the most impolite fantasies of female moviegoers. When he pops up in Warner Bros.' nasty little 1931 melodrama *Night Nurse,* as a thug chauffeur dressed in gleaming black leather, he's a figure out of an S&M fantasy. In one scene he socks Barbara Stanwyck hard on the chin, a moment so transgressive that even the camera pivots away in shame.

That was the closest Gable got to playing with the kink of his appeal. Mostly he worked for MGM, a much less daring studio than Warners or Paramount, and he worked hard—twelve films alone in 1931, the year he popped loose. The one that turned the trick was *The Easiest Way,* which made audiences sit up and wonder who the hunk playing the laundryman was. If Warners thrived on grit and subversion and Paramount on cosmopolitan chic, MGM was the self-conscious dream factory, and Louis B. Mayer did what any factory owner would do: he gave consumers what they wanted while constantly tweaking and improving the product.

So in those twelve films Gable played a gambler (*Sporting Blood*) and an attorney (*Possessed*), a Navy pilot (*Hell Divers*) and an architect (*Susan Lenox: Her Fall and Rise*), two gangsters (*A Free Soul* and *Dance, Fools, Dance*), and a Salvation Army officer (*Laughing Sinners*). The studio played mix-and-match with costars, placing their new stud opposite Norma Shearer, Joan Crawford, Jean Harlow, even Greta Garbo, to see which pairing struck the most interesting and profitable sparks. Not surprisingly, the Garbo film, *Susan Lenox,* is the worst of the bunch; her Euro-disenchantment makes Gable look naive and his all-American vitality makes Garbo seem like a drag. The film was a legendary struggle to make, with twenty-two writers working on the script and Garbo storming off the set in a diva fit no fewer than six times, and already we're as far from Gable's unstudied earthiness as it's possible to get.

In the Shearer film, though, *A Free Soul,* he brings out a vibrant and unexpected heat in the Queen of MGM—what did Thalberg think as he watched the rushes?—and in the three 1931 movies he made with Crawford (*Dance, Fools, Dance*; *Laughing Sinners*; *Possessed*) Gable found his onscreen mate as clearly as William Powell found Myrna Loy. Gable and Crawford are both strivers, and they're both frankly, honestly sexual (not dirty—Mayer wouldn't have that—but healthily carnal). And they're of the people. You sense, through their playing together onscreen, the hard roads both actors had to travel to glamour, as well as the compromises and favors they may have had to trade.

Crawford's early sound heroines have pasts, and they weigh her down—the drama is in whether she'll be allowed (by men, by society) to rise above them, and that drama was close to the hearts of her audience. Gable, by contrast, shucks his past with a smile and a shrug of his impossibly broad shoulders. In *Manhattan Melodrama,* he's the friendliest, most self-confident gangster imaginable, going to his death with a flippant wave of his hand.

If Crawford is a fellow striver, Jean Harlow, with whom Gable made *Red Dust* in 1932, was a fellow playmate. Crawford carried over a sense of sin and melodrama from the silent era; Harlow, by contrast, was something new, a brassy blonde with Clara Bow's sexuality but a greater, more confident sense of self. (In fact, she came close to being Mae West as an actual woman.) She arrived on the half shell of sound, for Howard Hughes had taken so long obsessing over his World War I dogfight movie *Hell's Angels* (1930) that talkies arrived and rendered his Norwegian star, Greta Nissen, obsolete. The eighteen-year-old Harlean Carpenter took her place, picking up a new name in the process. In turn, John Gilbert was supposed to star in *Red Dust,* a steamy bit of nonsense set on an Indochina rubber plantation, but can you see him popping his eyes at the casually braless Harlow? Gable just grinned like he'd met dinner.

It's nearly impossible to convey how psychologically crucial Gable was at a time when America's sense of itself was prostrate. Millions of men were out of work in 1931; as family providers in a capitalist economy, they had become functionally impotent. Yet here was this man, a commoner, so different from the capering boys of the silents, who walked in like he owned the room. Gable was proof, when proof was needed, that male vitality still existed, and he gave women dreams about which they couldn't begin to tell their husbands or boyfriends.

It was the size and the ease of the man—the sense that he could reach out and swallow a woman whole. A Palm Springs waitress who once met him in real life spoke for many when she said, "He was so gorgeous, so clean. He looked like chocolate melting in your mouth." They called him the King because they needed one.

But here, too, we have a studio taking rough clay and fashioning it into something the audience didn't even know it wanted. The twenty-one-year-old Gable left Akron, Ohio, and an overbearing father in 1922, working in oil fields, freight-hopping from one place to the next, lumberjacking here, selling neckties there. He was living on a beach in Oregon around the time he met Josephine Dillon, an acting teacher fifteen years older who took him to Hollywood, coached him to speak in a deeper voice, paid for his new dentures, and—once he began to resemble something like Clark Gable—married him.

Like Valentino, Gable liked the company of powerful women; he just hid it more successfully from the sneers of newspapermen. So there was Dillon, and there was Jane Cowl, a Shakespearean stage actress and impresario who gave Gable a walk-on in her L.A. stage production of *Romeo and Juliet* and a major role in her bed. There was the aging silent star Pauline Frederick—another rumored model for Norma Desmond in *Sunset Blvd.*—who wore Gable out sexually while promising to help with his career. In 1931, there was a second wife, Ria Langham, seventeen years his senior. Crawford and Harlow were Gable's onscreen mates, and, importantly, they were his peers; offscreen, the picture was more complicated. There were steamy back-lot affairs with Crawford and Loretta Young, but the movie's new Dangerous Man mostly wanted mothering.

MGM's publicity department existed to banish such idiosyncrasies and build a dream that could be shared by millions of moviegoers, to each of whom that dream spoke alone. Interestingly, men in the film industry understood far better what Gable meant as a star and an investment. The women were too busy gaping. Two quotes from actresses named Joan testify to the female response. Blondell: "He was boyish, mannish, a brute—all kinds of goodies." Crawford: "I don't believe any woman is telling the truth if she's ever worked with Gable and did not feel twinges of a sexual urge beyond belief."

But it was male MGM executives who did the math after seeing their secretaries giggle and blush whenever the young actor came by the front office, and even they developed crushes on Gable. *Red Dust*'s writer, John Lee Mahin, wrote to producer Hunt Stromberg, "There's this guy, my God, he's got the eyes of a woman and the build of a bull . . . he and Harlow will be a natural." (The unspoken assumption is that John Gilbert, by this point, was *un*natural.) MGM publicist Howard Strickling recalled that Gable "was the biggest man I ever saw. His hands were tremendous. His feet were tremendous. He had a tremendous big head. His ears were tremendous. He was the biggest guy I ever knew, and I would say one of the most powerful. . . . There was nothing effeminate about him. Nothing actorish."

Strickling was a crucial figure in the seeding, feeding, watering, and flowering of the new star. He and Gable became close personal friends, and the publicist realized that the actor welcomed the chance to have the factory define him for the masses. "He was willing to be molded," Strickling acknowledged, so the MGM PR department reimagined the footloose boy as an outdoorsman, releasing a series of photos of Gable in flannel shirts, toting fishing creels and shotguns. It worked so well that the actor went hunting and fishing for real; he rode polo ponies, too, until the front office forbade him for fear he'd break his neck.

In his personal life, Gable tried out different wardrobes and sports and hobbies. He took up photography, raised purebred Chows, learned how to play gin rummy. In all this, there's a restless search for identity, any identity, that might come close to the one that America and the world found in him.

This was more common than you might think—actors reverse-engineering personalities from their onscreen personas. It was perfectly understandable, too. They were young people, uncertain, mostly undereducated, and then they were told they were gods and goddesses. Imagine that you have been you more or less contentedly all your life and one day you wake up to magazine headlines that insist "The Great American Male Has Hit the Screen at Last" and "What a Man, Gable!" Who is this person? you might think. How does he relate to the unexamined me? The hobbies and the clothes and the lifestyle changes were Gable's way of looking into the mirror of his celebrity until he saw what we saw.

In other words, even the stars wanted to be like the stars. "We learned a lot from acting," Joan Crawford once said. "I would rehearse lines I had in a picture and use them for myself. . . . The trick is not to lose your identity." But what identity *is* that?

Never a reflective man, Gable professed to see his stardom as so much nonsense, and that brusque dismissal fit his man's-man persona neatly. A few years before his death, he told a reporter, "You know, this king stuff is pure bullshit. I eat and sleep and go to the bathroom just like everyone else." For all his efforts, he never did quite see what everyone else saw, always viewed stardom as a fluke. The Dangerous Man knew the dangers of his audience; once, in the early stages of Gable-mania, he was mobbed by fans in the Venice Amusement Park and had to hide, trembling, in the reptile house. When he toured South America, his rooms were stripped for souvenirs.

It was all vaguely embarrassing—not proper employment for the kind of man Clark Gable had become after years of struggling. He gave his philosophy of acting in the early 1930s to a reporter: "Before I did this, I was shoveling. It's no different from any other job. I start at seven in the morning, when I finish at the end of the day, that's that." This isn't the attitude of an artist or even an actor of normal creative curiosity. It's the attitude of a day laborer, and it goes some way to explaining why Gable spent the rest of his career coasting, quite successfully, on the fumes of his initial explosion.

He made thirty movies in his first five years and thirty-six over the course of the next twenty-five. He was loved and admired and, in 1939, crowned king of the world and of Civil War history in *Gone With the Wind,* but he was always more star than actor. Unlike, say, Jimmy Stewart, he didn't have a postwar second act in which he grew the persona in different directions. Strickling, his friend and publicist, knew it, and he knew Gable knew it: "Clark would have given his right arm to have been recognized as the actor's actor, you know—what Spencer Tracy was. But Clark Gable was Clark Gable. That was one of the tragedies of his life; he couldn't play character parts."

Saving his studio from financial ruin would have to be good enough. At Gable's peak, MGM was paying him $7,500 a week and it wasn't nearly just compensation—his movies brought in $500 million for the studio during the same period. With productivity and profits slumping during the worst years of the Depression, the star was absolutely critical to MGM's bottom line. Nor were he and Mae West the only flagship brands to pull battered studios through the storm, since Shirley Temple performed the same function for Twentieth Century-Fox.

Other performers were only slightly less important, yet there suddenly seemed to be dozens of them. New icons were being forged from the psychic needs of the times, figures too direct and honest to seem like calculated studio product. While periods of peace and plenty tend to give us regal stars, eras of cultural and economic turmoil result in the birth of dynamic and individualistic public figures—stars who speak and move in wholly fresh ways. These can be of two types: the groundbreakers whose energy and meaning is then copied by others, or the singularities, figures of such irreducible individuality that they can't be imitated. They are *sui generis*.

West was one of the latter, at least by the time the movies got hold of her. If anything, star singularities force a need for their persona in the culture rather than the other way around. There was no call for Fred Astaire before Fred Astaire existed. The Marx Brothers and W. C. Fields invented their own genres out of specific comic worldviews. The young Katharine Hepburn seemed so eccentric to mainstream audiences that it took fifteen years for them to come around. Edward G. Robinson looked like a toad and was built for character parts and ethnic caricature, but he had the crude forward momentum of a sex symbol; he was a star because he acted like one.

Shirley Temple similarly created a need for herself, although in a completely unself-conscious way. That unself-consciousness was her value to the public; unlike every other star out there, she couldn't be accused of faking it. How can a child be anyone but herself? To Depression audiences desperate for anything optimistic that wasn't a lie, Temple was a lifeline.

There had been kid stars before and there would be kid stars afterward, but Shirley became something much bigger, as inimitable as Chaplin and that other new talkie sensation, Mickey Mouse. Temple epitomized innocence and survival, the hardiness of the openhearted child. At the age of six, she functioned as a national pulse. If she was healthy, so were we.

And, really, it seemed she could work miracles. It was reported that a mute girl in England saw 1934's *Bright Eyes* and spoke for the first time in twelve years. The loaves and fishes extended to the bottom line; by the end of 1934 Fox was $4 million in the black almost solely on the strength of her movies. As Temple noted in her 1982 autobiography (both an enjoyable read and a wonder of fiscal probity), "During 1936, almost 90% of reported [Fox] corporate net profits were attributable to earnings of my four most recent films." As with Gable at MGM and West at Paramount, the studio rode on her back.

The public merely beat down her door. Temple-mania brought out the weird in just about everyone. Women approached her father and offered money to sleep with him, hoping to birth their own Shirleys. The Ideal Toy Company sold thirteen different official Shirley dolls, and that's not counting the hundreds of illegal knockoffs. There were Shirley berets, overcoats, hair ribbons, headbands, soap, dishware, sheet music, sewing kits, pocket mirrors, paper tablets, playing cards, anklets, barrettes; she promoted GE model kitchens, Packard automobiles, insurance, Wheaties, flour, Grunow Teledial radios, Quaker Puffed Wheat. Temple was the perfect product spokesperson, since the artless naïveté of her brand defused the crassness of the sell. Everyone wanted a piece of her.

But that was it; everyone could potentially have her. Unlike adult stars, Temple was within reach. You could own a doll or you could have your own child or you could make your existing child into a Shirley Temple. Many mothers did, tormenting their daughters' hair into curls and signing them up for dancing lessons, trying to make their child into the star they themselves were too old and fallen to be. Part of Temple's appeal was that she was tantalizingly close to home, displaying the artless self-assurance of a real kid without any of the actorly fussiness. She *was* your daughter, only better: less whiny, more famous.

As with other major stars, this need to touch, to embrace, could turn ugly. Temple constantly received kidnapping and extortion threats, and the perpetrators almost invariably turned out to be young men and women, bored and maybe resentful and certainly wanting a little attention for themselves. Perhaps they just wanted Shirley, or the millions who loved her, to notice them.

En masse, star love was dangerous. When ten thousand people turned out to meet Temple outside Boston's Public Garden in 1938, the crowds broke through police barricades and nearly swallowed up the eight-year-old actress. Wrote Temple in her autobiography, "I suddenly saw only a mosaic of arms and faces, mouths gaped open and shouting. Hands reached up to claw along my bare legs, tug at my shoes, and pull at my dress hem." Later, when she asked her mother why people behaved so, Mrs. Temple said, "Because you make them happy." It's asking a lot of an eight-year-old to process that, but Shirley did. "A fundamental fact of life began to sink in," she wrote. "No matter its brilliance or how remote its location, any star can be devoured by human adoration."

Delight and greed are both addictive, and while a child eventually has to grow up, fans and the front office want to put maturation off as long as possible. "Now she's lovable," Fox head Darryl Zanuck told Temple's mother early on. "The less she changes, the longer she lasts." Zanuck protected his asset by keeping to the formula, casting Shirley in rehashed Mary Pickford vehicles and opting not to loan her to MGM for *The Wizard of Oz*. It wasn't until Temple turned fifteen that she was told she was actually sixteen—Fox had shaved a year off her age when signing her up eleven years earlier, the better to make her appear a prodigy.

This is the private struggle of any child actor. Judy Garland came through it disastrously—the uppers and downers that MGM doctors fed her didn't help—but Temple kept her balance. As a child and an adult, she seems to have been wholly lacking in neuroses, a surprising quality in an actor until you realize Temple wasn't really an actor at all. She was adored for herself because she instinctively knew how to be herself—or a compelling make-believe version of it—in front of the cameras. Her handful of post-childhood performances are pleasant and largely unnecessary.

An actor like Clark Gable might invent himself from the pieces of his MGM persona, but Temple's gift, and the source of her appeal, was that she always knew exactly who she was, and who she was was a normal girl. Fame and Fox did everything to convince her otherwise, but when she finally left Hollywood at sixteen to enter a boarding school, it was with relief. "Tears came to my eyes," she wrote about her arrival. "I looked at all those girls and knew I was one of them." As if she had ever been anything else.

Such were the singularities. The groundbreakers—new stars who refashioned established archetypes into something fresh and powerful—came to prominence in the early to mid-1930s, as the studios regained control of the machine after the chaos of the talkie conversion. These stars embodied a mass urge, filling a cultural hole and giving shape to it. James Cagney transcended mere gangsters to become a powerhouse of criminal restlessness. Bette Davis updated the silent drama queens with neurotic, self-destructive venom. Cary Grant rose from a swamp of good-looking juveniles to achieve perfect moral and physical balance. Spencer Tracy was an average Joe who became not just a great actor but the sound era's first great movie actor, with perceived gifts not found on Broadway but within the subtle observances of the closeup.

They answered the call for performers who drew on visual and sonic talents but, above all, had the impact of coherent personalities that lay behind individual roles. The shock of Gable was in finding the virile, functioning man the culture hadn't known it was seeking. No matter who Davis was playing, what came through was her self-lacerating honesty, an actorly refusal to cut the corners of feelings. They kept the bargain of the great silent stars—persona is greater and more important than any one film—but they brought a new immediacy that had everything to do with being heard as well as seen.

In many cases, that personality came together either by accident or in direct opposition to studio planning. Warner Bros. executives screened the dailies of *The Public Enemy* (1931) and quickly realized that Cagney, the actor playing the main character's best friend, was wiping lead actor Edward Woods off the screen. Their job was to recognize talent, and so they switched the roles; everyone went home happy except Edward Woods.

Cagney's gift was threat—a storm cloud of imminent violence that broke with a frightening sense of joy. The breakfast-table grapefruit sailing out of nowhere into Mae Clarke's face in *The Public Enemy*—that was based on an incident involving a real New York gangster (who had actually used an omelet), but it was Cagney's innate genius to slam the gesture right into the dark crack between cruelty and comedy. Like Gable, he seemed the real thing, a thug just in from hanging on the corner with the boys, and what a pity he didn't live to be filmed by Scorsese. He was a smarter, more agile player than Gable, though, with a dancer's demonic delight in timing that none of his imitators captured. Cagney saw the limitations of gangster roles and fought hard to be cast in a variety of parts; he knew and respected the kinds of movies he was loved in—thus the astonishing *White Heat* as late as 1949—but made sure to challenge himself as much as possible. If Gable had had the interest, the encouragement, and possibly the brains, he might have had a career like this.

Once they had recognized and signed talent to a contract, though, the moguls could be blind to its potential. Or perhaps they just were innately conservative businessmen who had difficulty thinking creatively. Bette Davis landed at Warners after Universal had failed to do anything with her, and there she languished, seething, while playing minor molls and insipid ingénues. Studio head Jack Warner was already terrified of her ("an explosive little broad with a sharp left" was his way of complimenting her), but Darryl Zanuck, at that point still Warners' production guru, saw and appreciated her grit.

At first, she was just too fast for movies. Reviewing her debut Warner Bros. production, 1932's *The Man Who Played God,* the *New York Times* complained that Davis "often speaks too rapidly for the microphone." In her 1974 memoir, *Mother Goddam,* Davis concurred: "It was always difficult for me to speak slowly on or off the screen, always difficult for me to do anything slowly." Bette was ready; it was the technology that had to catch up to her.

So did Jack Warner; so did the world. She hacked away at the studio chief to loan her to RKO for an adaptation of Somerset Maugham's *Of Human Bondage* (1934); the role was that of Mildred, a nasty, consumptive waitress who abuses the upper-class twit (Leslie Howard) obsessed with her. Warner got Irene Dunne in exchange and thought he had the better end of the deal. Who wanted to watch this odd, pop-eyed girl in a sadomasochistic romance?

What Davis understood was the vicarious thrill to be found in a horrible woman charismatically played. Audiences gasped when, in the emotional climax of the film, Mildred the slattern tells the hero what she really thinks of him—"After yuh kissed me, I always used to wipe my mouth. *Wipe my mouth*"—and they applauded when he finally tells her off. They applauded at the end of the movie, too, not for Howard but for Davis. *Of Human Bondage* is far from a great movie, but Mildred burns the screen with the violence of an actress staking her claim.

And still the studio cast her in roles that were a man's idea of a dangerous woman, when the point about Davis was that she was best at showing how women could be a danger to themselves and to others. In 1936, fed up with pleading for better parts, she broke her contract and fled to England. The last straw appears to have been Jack Warner's offer of the lead in *God's Country and the Woman,* in which she was to play a lady lumberjack.

The studio sued, and Davis very publicly lost in a British court, returning to Hollywood contractually chastened but with her larger point made. Warner may have owned the actress, but the actress owned her persona. The fan magazines were behind her ("Our little Bette craves something with guts, and wishes to leave the sweets to the sweet," wrote *Silver Screen*), and finally Jack Warner started listening, acceding to her wish to play a spoiled southern belle in 1938's *Jezebel.* Davis wrote later, "He insisted no one would want to see a film about a girl who wore a red dress to the New Orleans Comus Ball. The custom was to wear a white dress. I told Warner only 10 million women would want to see this film. As it turned out, I was right."

Thus began her great late-1930s/early-1940s run of melodramas in which Davis explores, time and again, the effects of a woman's will when it is thwarted. Does it make her a murderer, as in *The Letter*? A spinster who sacrifices her life for the married man who teaches her to live, as in *Now, Voyager*? Should she destroy her family (*The Little Foxes,* or the nutty, sexually subversive *In This Our Life,* in which Davis schemes her way into her creepy old uncle's lap)? Is death the only cure for egotism (*Dark Victory,* Davis's shallow socialite going nobly into the darkness of an inoperable brain tumor)?

She understood, perhaps better than any star before or since and certainly better than Joan Crawford, that the tension for a woman in a society run by men is between self and selfishness, that it is often impossible to explore the former without being accused of the latter, and that there is drama and hard truth to be mined from this. Of course Jack Warner and Darryl Zanuck didn't get it, since as moguls and men they were responsible for the tension in the first place. (Zanuck especially, with his daily afternoon "naps" in which he'd be joined by a starlet from the lower ranks and the entire Fox lot would shut down for an hour while everyone just went off and screwed.)

So Davis made herself, with the help of sympathetic directors like Michael Curtiz and couturiers like Orry-Kelly; she knew an audience was out there for what she had to say, and she played to it until it answered back. Other actors, by contrast, had to weather a while before the elements gelled, being typecast and typecast and typecast until a role came that twisted the typecasting a half turn to the left, or, better yet, gave them the space to create something new.

Humphrey Bogart was the clearest proof that some movie stars should be allowed to age a bit, like firewood or scotch. Eleven years in the business, five for Fox, six for Warner Bros., and none of the thirty-nine movies he made in that time let him be *Bogart,* which is to say a figure of sympathetic menace and accumulated mastery. How could they have? He hadn't accumulated it yet. It took two 1941 movies, *High Sierra* and *The Maltese Falcon,* to turn his luck around; in the former, he plays an aging gangster just trying to find a little peace, and in the latter, of course, he is private eye Sam Spade, corroded beacon of honesty in a fallen world.

Up to then, Bogart had mostly played thugs because his jowls and those ferrety teeth seemed to offer no sex appeal whatsoever. In mid-1930s terms, that was correct; he was not leading-man material. Neither was Edward G. Robinson, but there the latter is as the star of *The Amazing Doctor Clitterhouse* (1938), playing the title role of a mild-mannered society doctor who becomes a gangster as a matter of academic curiosity (and earning the love of an attractive lady fence in the bargain). It's a comedy, more or less, but Bogart, as the doctor's surly gangland rival, keeps dragging the movie back toward something uglier. When he's killed at the end, it's almost a relief. There seemed nothing comedic in Bogart as there was with Robinson—nothing to render him lovable.

Warners tried. They put him in westerns, a horror movie, cast him as a sensitive Irish stableman opposite Bette Davis in *Dark Victory,* and you can see the desperation growing in his eyes as the late '30s kick in. Maybe that's what turned the trick and gave *High Sierra*'s Roy "Mad Dog" Earle a sadness that broadens our conception of what a movie gangster should be. The character was hardly the first sympathetic bad man in a Hollywood movie, but Bogart exudes a bone-deep weariness that is purely a function of time and experience.

Earle has been running so long he has outstripped gangster-movie clichés. He just wants to go somewhere and lie down. Similarly, Bogart plays the character with the knowledge of all the other bad men he has been and the troubles they have seen. The role has a sense of distance, between Earle and the straight world, between Bogart and his past roles, and it flatters us into seeing and sharing that distance where the film's other characters see only a hoodlum.

So the sourness that had always been a part of the Bogart persona acquired meaning and moral dimension, and *The Maltese Falcon,* in which he's the one guy with the long view among a gallery of greedy freaks, sealed the deal. The darkness now had weight, the cynicism now was tinged with bleak comedy, and Bogart's sense of command looked like sex appeal of a fresh and unexpected type. It's the sexiness of someone who has been around the block, who has seen things and knows better than to talk about them. The mystery is in everything that's withheld, the long pause before the leveling retort. "You know how to whistle, don't you?" Lauren Bacall famously asked him in *To Have and Have Not* (1944). Bogart knew. (And what a lovely irony that the actress who matched him stride for stride onscreen and in life was all of nineteen years old when they met, already in possession of the assurance it had taken Bogart four decades to gather in.)

Another actor who had to find himself was Cary Grant. He was more self-motivated about the process than Bogart, leaving Paramount after four years of solid but unspectacular buildup and becoming a free agent in 1936, signing nonexclusive contracts with both RKO and Columbia. This was unheard of in a town where everyone was owned by one studio and one studio only, but if Grant's business plan was unorthodox, the persona he began to develop was even more so.

Paramount had originally signed him in 1932 as a threat to Gary Cooper, who was balking at assigned roles and had decamped to Africa for an extended sulk. For a long while, Grant seemed to be a mannequin version of the bigger star. To see him opposite Mae West in *She Done Him Wrong* and *I'm No Angel* is to wonder who the impostor with Cary Grant's face is. He's attractive, smart, easygoing enough, but what's missing is that sense of play, malicious and engaged, that animates even his most serious later roles.

Ironically, Grant would discover who he was in one of the most notorious movie bombs of the 1930s, a whimsical slice of what-the-hell called *Sylvia Scarlett.* The film put a further nail into the young Kate Hepburn's career; she plays the title role of a young woman who travels through a storybook England with her con man father (Edmund Gwenn), dressed as a boy much of the time and pining for a rich man (Brian Aherne) who can't understand his "queer feeling" for her.

Grant plays Jimmy Monkley, a Cockney wastrel who joins Gwenn and Hepburn in their picaresques—at one point they form a theatrical troupe called the Pink Pierrots, oy vey—and maybe because it's a character part instead of a romantic lead, Grant seems freed for the first time onscreen. Virile, cruelly funny, acrobatically poised, naturally superior, he's at last the Cary Grant who would dominate the 1940s and 1950s—his own man, insofar as even Cary Grant was uncertain who that man was.

Sylvia Scarlett was universally hated, but Grant came away with good notices, and after a few more Paramount flops, he was loaned out to Universal to play a devil-may-care ghost in *Topper* (1937), a big hit. Then he went free agent, and would he have risked such a novel course before *Topper* proved his commercial viability or *Sylvia Scarlett* consolidated his persona? Grant always professed to have cobbled what we call "Cary Grant" from the pieces of the boy born Archibald Leach and all of the men that boy had wanted to be over the years, and in this he was hardly alone. So many of the stars are unconscious creations consciously arrived at, paintings where each brushstroke is a product of instinct and calculation and luck. Even John Wayne, whose persona was founded on the rock of all-American directness—whose fans don't even think of him as an actor—confessed to working hard on what he called "the Wayne thing" when he started out. "It was as deliberate a projection as you'll ever see," Wayne said late in life. "I practiced in front of a mirror."

All stars have their version of that quote; it's the closest they come to admitting that identity itself may be a con. Grant's version, much cited and hard to attribute, is "I pretended to be somebody I wanted to be until I finally became that person. Or he became me." Because he was an acrobat by nature and early training—Grant arrived in the U.S. from England as part of the Bob Pender circus troupe—the hallmark of his screen personality became balance. Every movement is aligned, loose yet controlled; the strain never shows but the mind is forever sharpening its blades. Grant was also an ambitious man with ambivalent feelings about fame and privacy. Decide for yourself whether he was gay, straight, bisexual, or omnisexual (there's at least one biography for every theory) and note, too, that a sense of hidden depths, of multiple levels to the persona (and we're just seeing the top two or three) ground his mature performances and keep him from seeming like an empty tuxedo. Far from it; Hepburn once described Grant as "personality, functioning," and in his best performances (*Notorious, Only Angels Have Wings, His Girl Friday, North by Northwest*) he is just that: a Whole Man, balancing shades of darkness and light in a way no other classic-era actor achieved.

There's something of a paradox, in fact, in what audiences wanted from Cary Grant (elegance, class, lightness) and what he offered (a continuing and often profound essay on moral dexterity). Like Bogart, he has aged well. Unlike Bogart, Grant has yet to be fully reckoned with, for his very ease works against a full appreciation of his meaning. The more our culture values bluntness, crassness, classlessness, the more his grace seems necessary.

7.

The Factory: How Stars Were Made

The average movie star during the classic studio era wasn't Cary Grant or Shirley Temple, of course. The average movie star didn't begin a movie by gunning down her lover in cold blood, as Bette Davis did in *The Letter,* or end it by going up in a screaming fireball, like Cagney in *White Heat.*

Instead, the average star offered comforting, entertaining variations on archetypes established in the silent era, refashioned for the talkies, and tweaked throughout the 1940s and into the postwar era. Such performers were even more necessary to our identification with the onscreen fantasy, enough like us to seem within reach yet still big enough to dream about. These were the demigods of the A-list, B-list, and beyond, who in the studios' view functioned as box office bait and promise of consumer dependability. If you liked one Robert Montgomery movie, this promise went, you would like them all, and equally. The star's presence on a marquee told you what kind of film you would be seeing and what sort of pleasures it would offer. It even told you how the movie would end, more or less. Hard-bitten Ida Lupino might not go gently into that good night, but sweet Alice Faye would hit the final credits singing with a smile and a tear. These were brand guarantees not to be idly tampered with.

The groundbreakers and the singularities may have offered a template by which the studios could do business, in other words, but the workaday stars—the Fred MacMurrays and Miriam Hopkinses, the Van Johnsons and Ann Sotherns—were the business plan. If you couldn't mass-produce Gables, at least you could try, and even if the knockoffs didn't have the snap of the real thing, they could still be profitable.

So there was plenty of tall, dark, and handsome in the 1930s and '40s, and most of them didn't take a left turn into Cary Grant. More likely, they were performers like Tyrone Power, Fox's gorgeous leading man and utility player (specialty, shallow right field). There were actresses who worked the turf between what Norma Talmadge had done and what Bette Davis was doing, suffering and causing suffering in other people, acting out the smaller dilemmas of the women who paid to see them. There were female fashion plates like chic Kay Francis in the early 1930s, available simply to be beautiful, and quick-witted ladies like Irene Dunne. Each of these successful workaday stars possessed a particular energy that made him or her stand out and that continues to glow to those still paying attention: Margaret Sullavan's edgy intelligence, say, or William Holden's macho insecurity.

The process of creating new stars was absurdly uncertain. How much of an actor's potential for being recognized by both studio and audiences as a reliable commodity was inherent in his or her personality? How much was granted by the audience based on physical appearance? How much was talent, studio publicity, dumb luck? What made one actor a top-rank name and another a valuable but lesser type?

To pick just one player out of the pile, Ralph Bellamy was tall and likeable—standard screen-idol stuff. He could and did play leads. Yet he also had an earnest aw-shucks drawl that marked him as a necessary sap in the cynical moral universe of 1930s screwball comedies. In

The Awful Truth (1937) and *His Girl Friday* (1940), Bellamy's every man who's not smart, fast, sexy, or mean enough to be Cary Grant. (In 1935's *Hands Across the Table,* he's not even mean enough to be Fred MacMurray.) The comedy—and it's gleefully cruel—is in watching a nice guy finish last. Bellamy played many other types of parts, but this was his most lasting role in the cultural fair.

His female analogue is Jean Arthur, whose career goes back to the late silents and earliest talkies but who comes into her own in 1930s comedies as a raspy-voiced, no-nonsense best pal to male stars like Jimmy Stewart, Cary Grant, and Gary Cooper. She's the tough-minded babe with heart of mush, one of the boys who turns into a beautiful, pining girl in time for the final clinch. Arthur played leads in dramas and comedies—she's marvelous in the screwball *Easy Living* (1937)—but she functioned best in relation to other, bigger stars.

The history of "average" stardom during Hollywood's Golden Age, then, is that of themes and variations. Here is the Singing Teenager: MGM calls her Judy Garland and both profits by and remains oblivious to her trembling emotional intensity. Universal, by contrast, has Deanna Durbin, unruffled and cheerful, merging pop tunes and classical numbers and towing half of America behind her.

Or Pep Boys, those juveniles with restless, unquenchable energy. Warners briefly cultivates Frankie Darro—a sort of junior league Cagney—in early-1930s dramas like *Wild Boys of the Road.* MGM hits pay dirt with the unstoppable, unkillable, inconceivable Mickey Rooney, who during his tenure at the studio rises from *Andy Hardy* movies and teen musicals to become the number one box office attraction in the country but whose career looks back to starring in his own silent comedy series at the age of six and ahead to gangster noir, character roles, Broadway success, and, at eighty-six, a character part in the family film *Night at the Museum* (2006), in which he resembles the world's angriest garden gnome. There's a distinct possibility that Mickey Rooney *is* the history of American movie stardom.

Or the all-American female sex symbol. Over the course of the studio era, the type evolved along with the rhythms and desires of the larger culture. In the 1930s, we see Depression amorality ceding to renewed glamour as Jean Harlow (uncomplicated, blond, fast) gives way to Carole Lombard (complicated, blond, funny). In the 1940s, wartime goddesses like Rita Hayworth (dreamy carnality) and Betty Grable (wholesome fun) give way to film noir heroines like Veronica Lake (bruised, moody) and Jane Greer (treacherous, brunette). Postwar sirens like Ava Gardner (sophisticated, erotic) hint at a new frankness, and so on into the breast-obsessed 1950s, through Marilyn Monroe (blond, dreamy, more complicated than we thought) and up to Elizabeth Taylor, who insists, starting with 1951's *A Place in the Sun,* that it's *all* about sex, baby, and don't bother pretending otherwise.

But that was a long time arriving. For two-plus decades, attractive young actresses staked a claim on one corner of sexual persona or another and hoped for the best. Some of these variations are forgotten yet still potent. To stumble upon a movie starring Ann Sheridan (*Torrid Zone, I Was a Male War Bride*) is to sit up and appreciate an actress who fused sex and irony like few actresses in studio-era Hollywood—a familiar type (hot tamale) with enough distinctiveness (cool humor) to make audiences want to see her again.

Some female stars, like Jeanette MacDonald in the 1930s or Kathryn Grayson in the 1940s, were just pretty people who could sing, and that was fine; each movie personality had a devoted fan base to whom he or she spoke most clearly and a wider audience that accepted them as slightly more perfect versions of ourselves.

On the other hand, which Jeanette MacDonald are we talking about? The playfully sexy star of early Paramount musicals like *The Love Parade* (1929) and *One Hour with You* (1932), or the stiff, virginal MacDonald of MGM operettas like *Naughty Marietta* (1935) and *Rose-Marie* (1936). House style—the worldview of a particular studio that was often (but not always) set by its top executives and that permeated the outlook and message of its movies and the meaning of its stars—is too often an overlooked variable in Hollywood histories. To properly understand many of the stars, you have to look at the company that put them forth.

The young Katharine Hepburn, for instance—angular, eccentric, and headstrong—could have flourished at no other studio but cosmopolitan RKO, and neither could that Art Deco swizzle stick, Fred Astaire. Cagney and Robinson and Bogart were the snarling dog-soldiers of Warner Bros.' proletarian street symphonies. Where MGM's Clark Gable was Olympian and unconquerable and Warners' Gable was a brute, director Frank Capra at raffish Columbia brought out the star's class-leveling sense of humor in *It Happened One Night* (1934). That movie did the same for Claudette Colbert, who was a chic soubrette at sophisticated Paramount.

MacDonald's case is instructive, for she simply meant different things to different studios. At Paramount (which tended to lean Euro where RKO kowtowed to New York), she was adorably loose, trilling light romantic arias in a slip while looking at Maurice Chevalier as if she wanted to jump on him right there. She represented Continental sexual freedom, whereas Mayer's MGM corseted MacDonald and sold her right back to America, putting her next to the astonishingly dull Nelson Eddy for a series of popular musicals in which sex is not remotely an option, despite a hit song titled "Indian Love Call."

The clamping down of film censorship in 1934, in the form of the Production Code Administration (the forerunner of the MPAA) and its new enforcer, Joseph I. Breen, was only partly responsible for the neutering of MacDonald. We are seeing, instead, Louis B. Mayer's unease with female eroticism winning out over the more benign understanding of the Paramount team (Zukor in New York, B. P. Schulberg and Y. Frank Freeman running the studio in L.A.) that sex exists and has sold movie tickets since the days of the nickelodeon.

True, some movie stars seemed to lead their stardom. Every role Barbara Stanwyck played was another chapter in an ongoing saga about a savvy but emotionally vulnerable city girl's dealings with men, and the author of that saga was Stanwyck, no matter which director or studio she was working for. Other actors seemed to be led by their stardom, like Lana Turner dully acquiescing to every stop on her journey to fame: the fabled discovery at Schrafft's lunch counter, the Sweater Girl, the heroines of noir and melodrama, and so forth. Or Rita Hayworth, who once complained that men went to bed with

Gilda (her most famous role, in the film of that name) and woke up with her.

Jimmy Stewart was the rare example of a pliant studio functionary who went to war and came back harder, more interesting, open to risks as an actor. Of his early career he later said, "MGM was a wonderful place where decisions were made on my behalf by my superiors. What's wrong with that?" That's the sound of the cog thanking the machine for allowing him to spin, but on returning to Hollywood from a war service in which he flew more than twenty bombing missions and experienced death at close hand, Stewart sat down and screened some of his old movies. In his own words, "[I] couldn't believe what I was watching. One of them, [1936's] *Born to Dance,* made me want to vomit. I knew I had to toughen up."

Thus the Stewart of the Anthony Mann westerns and Alfred Hitchcock thrillers of the 1950s, in which the all-American boy hero of 1930s MGM is buffeted by doubts and madness. This is unusual in Hollywood stardom during the studio years: a popular actor consciously and carefully altering his public image. In modern terminology, it was a reimagining of the Stewart brand, and it paid off commercially and artistically, in no small part because it rested on both our established fondness for the actor and our understanding that the world had changed around him. *Vertigo* (1958) is Alfred Hitchcock's most heartbreaking film in part because Stewart lets us see, buried under all his character's neuroses, the sweet, simple, lost Jimmy of an earlier era.

That younger Stewart, though, was as much a necessary product of his time as the post–World War II Stewart was of his. The late 1930s saw the studio factory system mass-producing bulletins of astonishing optimism and cheer, making them so well and so seductively that they seduce us today, even when we're aware of the lies they tell. Bolstered by Breen's enforcement of the Production Code Administration, in which every villain was punished, no married couple copulated, and homosexuality did not exist, the American movie industry painted the world as a playground in which all audiences were to be treated like children.

This limitation was both curse and blessing. Films of the classic studio era, from the early 1930s until the late 1950s, don't always harp on lightness, but they allude to the dark mostly through lighting, music, melodrama, and scripted innuendo, and especially through stars whose onscreen personalities hint at forbidden pleasures. Even then, the endings demanded by Breen and the front office usually wrap up the plot in a logic-denying pretzel, such as Ray Milland cheerily quitting booze after the rest of *The Lost Weekend* (1945) has shown, with clinical specificity, that his character will surely drink himself to death.

That was a Paramount production, and Paramount saw stars through the lens and gaze of its directors. Think of Josef von Sternberg obsessing over Marlene Dietrich across seven increasingly bonkers cinematic fever dreams, or Ernst Lubitsch chuckling over the silly sexual games played by the casts of his arch Continental farces. Think of the vastly underrated Mitchell Leisen guiding his Paramount troupers—Colbert, MacMurray, Stanwyck, Milland—through the erotic comedy and melodrama of his 1930s and '40s films. Of writer-director Preston Sturges, his gonzo-literate dialogue the true star of movies whose names on the marquees included McCrea, Colbert, Stanwyck, Dick Powell, and Veronica Lake. And, obviously, think of Billy Wilder merrily putting the screws to everyone from MacMurray in *Double Indemnity* (1944)—a sleazy MacMurray radically different from the grinning ramrod of Leisen's films—to Jack Lemmon in *The Apartment* (1960).

This isn't to say that stars didn't prosper at Paramount. Of course they did; you couldn't run the business without them. But the studio tended to entrust stars to the directors and then let the directors be. By contrast, MGM wholly gave itself over to the manufacture and promotion of screen actors, boasting that it had "more stars than there are in Heaven." In truth, Mayer's company specialized in quality as well as quantity, for MGM's stars were the most inarguably godlike. The studio had three queens—Garbo, Norma Shearer, Joan Crawford—and a king, Gable, who was acknowledged as such by the entire industry. A list of MGM contractees reads like the Pantheon: in addition to the above, there were Jean Harlow, Spencer Tracy, Judy Garland,

James Stewart, William Powell, Myrna Loy, Oscar-winning character actress Marie Dressler, dancing top Eleanor Powell, teen heartthrob Van Johnson, Lionel Barrymore, Mickey Rooney, Margaret Sullavan, Robert Young, Franchot Tone, Robert Taylor. All top stars of their day; all money in the bank.

When the Marx Brothers and Katharine Hepburn flamed out at Paramount and RKO respectively, MGM commercially rehabilitated them by sanding the eccentric, audience-unfriendly edges off their personas. They Metroed them: the Marxes were cast as romantic advisers to dull young lovers starting with *A Night at the Opera* (1935), while Hepburn won back moviegoers by being paired with Spencer Tracy in a series of comedies and dramas that explicitly took the starchy, feminist Kate down a peg. In *Woman of the Year* (1942), Hepburn's sportswriter is humbled by her inability to make breakfast for her husband, the kitchen turning into a series of widening culinary disasters. The inescapable conclusion is that she's being punished for straying outside a woman's proper domain.

Even if Louis B. Mayer didn't personally okay the script, he certainly approved of the sentiment. His was a sunny, maudlin America where every woman knew her place until she became Mother, at which point she was sanctified. How different this is from the roles Hepburn had become known for at RKO, all those headstrong aviatrixes and nineteenth-century feminists, tempest-stirrers and botherers of men. *Bringing Up Baby* (1938) is the one screwball comedy that comes closest to real anarchy because, as dizzy heiress Susan Vance, Hepburn embodies the chaos principle with joy but without sentimentality. Her craziness cuts. No wonder the film was a box office failure; no wonder it became a classic only years later, well after Hepburn had won over mass audiences through her teaming with and taming by Tracy onscreen and off.

Everything at MGM was about the proper care, grooming, positioning, and sale of stars. Mayer and his minions understood that actors were the studio's primary products and movies only the boxes they came in. Upon signing an MGM contract, a player was given over to a factory that controlled every aspect of his or her life. This is not exaggeration: the studio executives had a chart tracking the menstrual cycles of all its actresses, the better to know who wasn't feeling her freshest at any given moment or who might be using that as an excuse.

Newly invented names were handed out, cooked-up biographies written, fraudulent interests and hobbies assigned. What nature hadn't bestowed, wardrobe, diet, hairstylists, and the intervention of MGM doctors and dentists corrected. If you flagged from too much work, like the young Judy Garland, the doctors gave you speed pills to get you through the day and sleeping pills for when the day was over. If you were married but a sensation with young women, like Johnny Weismuller of the *Tarzan* movies, the studio might even pay off your wife to get a divorce.

In truth, MGM didn't do anything different from the other studios. It just did it bigger and better. Once the executives had hit on a strategy, a way of packaging a particular star, the factory specifications were locked in. William Powell and Myrna Loy went after *The Thin Man* in five increasingly limp sequels. Weismuller was Tarzan in six MGM movies, and then went off to make six more for RKO. The *Andy Hardy* series, so dear to Mayer's heart in its steamrolling Americana, ran to fifteen entries. The one area where adherence to formula paid creative as well as financial dividends was in the MGM musicals unit of the 1940s and '50s, overseen by a former Tin Pan Alley tunesmith named Arthur Freed with a solid team behind him. Their run of films includes *Meet Me in St. Louis, On the Town, An American in Paris, Singin' in the Rain,* and many others.

Perhaps the reason the musicals are the studio's greatest legacy is that they're the one genre in which an MGM star can actually cut loose. The Freed films explode with the exuberance of sharp, gifted people working at the top of their game, song and dance numbers providing an outlet for energies the studio tamped down elsewhere. The musicals transform Mayer's corn and clichés into something as beautifully strange as Gene Kelly tap-dancing on roller skates while singing

"I Like Myself" in *It's Always Fair Weather* (1955) or as deeply emotive as Garland singing "Have Yourself a Merry Little Christmas" in *St. Louis*.

Otherwise, the big lie with which Joe Breen and his Production Code blanketed the movies—happy endings all around and no sex for anyone—found its most enthusiastic proponent in Mayer, who really did believe in Mom, apple pie, and virginity with the fervor of a converted New England junkman. By contrast, Darryl Zanuck's Twentieth Century-Fox embraced all-American corn because it was good business. Zanuck, the rare non-Jew to run a major studio during the Golden Age, was a Presbyterian from Wahoo, Nebraska, and he was as cynical and energetic as the tough little movies he wrote and produced by the dozen at Warner Bros. in the early 1930s. When he jumped ship to form his own studio, it would be logical to think the new company would pick up where Zanuck had left off.

But because Fox's theater holdings were more rural and middle American than Warners' urban chains, the new studio head had to change course. Zanuck's Fox purveyed a wholesome, bland, and profitable worldview embodied in stars who weren't as chic as the Paramount crew, nor as godlike as MGM's stable, nor as caustically urban as the Warner Bros. mugs, nor as elegantly sassy as RKO's players. A prototypical Fox star was Loretta Young, virginal and gorgeous and graciously sweet (no matter that she had become pregnant with Clark Gable's baby while shooting *Call of the Wild* for MGM; the daughter, who had her dad's ears, grew up being told she was adopted). In *The Farmer's Daughter* (1947), Young plays a naive Swedish American farm girl who runs for Congress, winning the day against the Beltway insiders with her no-nonsense populism. She won an Oscar for the role, and in truth it perfectly embodies the Fox philosophy: Hicks know best.

So Zanuck's big stars were homespun truth-teller Will Rogers in the 1930s and girl-next-door Betty Grable a decade later, modest lothario Tyrone Power (Valentino with a sense of decency, and where does that get you?), and perennially heartbroken Alice Faye, the small-town girl made good. Eventually, Fox got to Marilyn Monroe and had no idea what to do with her, marooning her bodaciousness in westerns, suspense melodramas, and other hapless outings that rarely tapped into the weirdly innocent sadness that gave her depth. Monroe is the clearest proof that a star can end up at the wrong studio.

Henry Fonda was at Fox, too—plainspokenly gorgeous, he was the studio's answer to Paramount's Gary Cooper. Unlike Cooper, Fonda had room in his persona for a social conscience that dovetailed, occasionally, with Zanuck's own. The star chafed at many of the roles he was handed, but Fonda's *Young Mr. Lincoln* (1939) and his Tom Joad in *The Grapes of Wrath* (1940) are evidence of how creatively rich Fox's Americana could get when necessary. Both were directed by John Ford, who made his home at the studio before venturing out to do more complicated work for others (*The Searchers* at Warner Bros., the "Cavalry Trilogy" of *Fort Apache, She Wore a Yellow Ribbon,* and *Rio Grande* in the late 1940s for RKO).

Ford's métier was westerns, and his favored star after 1939 and *Stagecoach* was John Wayne. Although it didn't really happen until the culture had shifted around him in the 1950s and '60s, Wayne became the line in the sand for everyone who had an opinion about where America was going. Wayne the movie star became a litmus test; how you felt about him derived from your cultural and political views more than any other perspective. Either he was a standard-bearer for vanishing values or a pigheaded reactionary, a proud American or a bully. Wayne became the most extreme example of the movie star whose persona is mistaken for the man, in part because in swagger and sentiment he embodied the myth of the country that produced him.

In the 1940s, though, he was just a cowboy star, finally on the A-list after a decade of trying. The shot that introduces the Ringo Kid in *Stagecoach*—the young outlaw god against an endless canvas of high desert, Ford's camera rushing up and halting in awe—delivered Wayne to the moviegoing public like Venus on the half saddle. He had made sixty-four movies in eleven years; this was close to his last chance. And because he had spent so much time refining "the Wayne thing," it was fully formed by the time he was borne into major stardom in *Stagecoach*. A useful analogy (though his fans might shrink from it) is to the Beatles, who erupted first in England's consciousness and then in America's after invisibly forging their rock-and-roll chops in the basements of Liverpool and Hamburg. What looked to us like innate grace was in fact mastery achieved through forethought, practice, and years of work.

It bears repeating that what we came to call "John Wayne" was a false front as two-dimensional as any western set, although you could argue that the actor turned it into a real building over time. Born Marion Morrison, Wayne was raised not in the Wild West but in the Los Angeles suburb of Glendale. He didn't particularly like horses. He starred in combat movies during World War II while expending an unusual amount of energy trying not to enlist; in the end, he never served. His relationship to John Ford, an autocratic director who used mind games, pranks, and verbal abuse to make his crews squirm, was that of a submissive, often insecure son.

So Wayne *was* an actor, nothing more but nothing less, and a very good one within the limits of his persona. He was a great one, in fact, if you consider "John Wayne" to be Marion Morrison's primary performance, an original role conceived with care and deepened, at times brilliantly, over the course of one player's life. In *The Searchers* (1956), Wayne's Ethan Edwards is the kind of American icon we hate to admit was necessary to the settling of the West. He's cruel, racist, single-minded, and effective, and consequently he's isolated by the civilization that follows. The character is Ford's achievement and screenwriter Frank Nugent's, but in the particulars and paradoxes it is Wayne's—or, rather, Morrison's. As an exploration of the dark side of a star's core persona, it's as morally alert as Cary Grant's coldly romantic user in *Notorious* or Jimmy Stewart's paranoid lover in *Vertigo*.

To an extent, though, what the actor did with his persona was his business. Above all, the Hollywood movie factory demanded reliability—the reassurance that John Wayne would be John Wayne no matter where you put him, and maybe just enough better than the last time to keep the crowds coming in. Star persona, the celluloid divinity that drew us to the church, was the one mystery beyond the studio heads' control. They could assemble the pieces brilliantly but they couldn't force us to buy. This was the challenge, and the history of the studio era is the narrative of their attempts to rise to it.

8.

Monsters, Scarlett Women, and Other Characters

There was one way to ensure that the studio kept control: make the part the star.

Universal specialized in this inverted but profitable way of doing business with its double cycle of horror movies, first in the early 1930s and again at the dawn of the 1940s. *Frankenstein* (1931) was named after the mad scientist played by Colin Clive, but the world quickly applied the name to the monstrous man the scientist created, as though the little child inside us all called the bogeyman under the bed by the first word that came to mind. The shambling creation was "the Frankenstein monster" everywhere but in the popular culture, where he was simply Frankenstein. Eventually the movies themselves acknowledged as much, with *Abbott and Costello Meet Frankenstein,* and so forth.

This Frankenstein—monster, not man—wasn't played by Boris Karloff so much as inhabited for a time by him, sparked into life with grunting sympathetic menace. The visualization came long before Karloff was cast. Universal's resident makeup genius, Jack Pierce, spent weeks fretting about false eyelids and cheesecloth layers of skin, rationalizing the monster's flattened head (the good doctor being an amateur surgeon, he'd adopt the expedient pop-top mode of brain transplantation), steel struts for the pants and eighteen-pound boots. Only when Pierce was satisfied did he allow director James Whale to proceed with screen tests.

Whale, for his part, found his man eating lunch in the studio commissary: a large, muscular Englishman with gracious bearing and soulful eyes. William Henry Pratt was forty-two and had dug ditches and driven trucks when he wasn't finding stage or screen work. Born in London to prosperous middle-class parents, he changed his name to Boris Karloff in part to spare them the embarrassment of having an actor in the family. Whale told the actor he wanted to test him for the Frankenstein monster, and Karloff remembered three decades later that "it was a bit shattering, but I felt that any part was better than no part at all." Pierce went to work, a mad scientist in reverse, sculpting a dead man from live flesh. The makeup took three to four hours to put on each day and almost as long to take off.

And when the film was done, the studio did the best they could to hide the actor at its center. Karloff was billed in the opening credits of *Frankenstein* as "?," and he wasn't invited to the Hollywood or New York premieres with the other stars. Producer Carl Laemmle Jr. and the Universal brass worked overtime to preserve the mystery and present not a performance by a human player but an authentic, unspeakable mockery of biological life. The Laemmles were still working the old ballyhoo—but, significantly, reversing the process "Uncle Carl" had instigated only two decades earlier with Florence Lawrence. Now anonymity was the trick.

They hadn't counted on Karloff providing the monster with the one quality the part didn't require—a soul. The immense success of *Frankenstein* served as a sharp rebuke to conventional stardom and a reminder that we go to the movies as much to gaze at the freaks (and feel sorrow and kinship with them) as to lust after beauty. Audiences saw and responded to the pain beneath the monster's latex half eyelids—the wounded fears and hesitant joys of a giant, dangerous baby—and in moviegoers' mixture of revulsion and empathy was the echo of Lon Chaney's greatest successes. Karloff's fame was assured.

Yet the makeup so disguised the man that the public ultimately associated that wounded soul with the role rather than the skill of the man playing it. Karloff may have been a star, but the monster was always the bigger one. The actor was quickly typecast as eldritch villains of either limited intelligence or evil brilliance. He was *The Mummy* (1932); a scarred, mute butler (the model for Lurch in *The Addams Family*) in *The Old Dark House* (1932); an effete Satanist in *The Black Cat* (1934); a mad surgeon with an Edgar Allan Poe fixation in *The Raven* (1935), and so on until the end of his life—even beyond, since four Z-grade Mexican horror movies Karloff appeared in were released to theaters only after he had died in 1969.

He was a journeyman player, in other words, and it was the beast that got top billing in the culture. A child of five knows the Frankenstein monster through pop osmosis alone, even if he or she has no idea who Karloff is, let alone Jack Pierce. Physically and psychologically, the monster turned out to be big enough to be played by any number of actors. Karloff held on through the brilliant, parodistic 1935 sequel *The Bride of Frankenstein* and 1939's *Son of Frankenstein*, and then Lon Chaney Jr. put on the size twenties for 1942's *Ghost of Frankenstein*, followed by Bela Lugosi in *Frankenstein Meets the Wolf Man* (1943), and stuntman Glenn Strange for *House of Frankenstein* (1944), *House of Dracula* (1945), and *Abbott and Costello Meet Frankenstein* (1948). That is how thoroughly the character came to overshadow the actor: the Monster could be brought to life by his own stuntman, the stand-in filling the hole where a movie star usually is.

All the Universal monsters were the marquee attraction, not the men playing them. Claude Rains found fame as *The Invisible Man* (1933) but had to go to Warner Bros. to become recognized as the premiere character actor of his era. Poor Lon Chaney Jr. was such a team player that he'd play anything you asked him to: the Wolf Man (his most famous role), the Frankenstein monster, Dracula, the Mummy (in a three-film Universal series of the mid-1940s). He was born Creighton Chaney; even his stage name coasted on the fumes of his famous father's career.

Lugosi, too, never found his way out of Dracula's coffin. He and his horror movie peers were trapped between above-the-title stardom and character acting, not taken seriously outside their signature roles but not critical to them, either. Even those actors initially typecast in gangster roles—Cagney, Robinson, Bogart—had more latitude, since their menace derived from personality and skill rather than costume. For the men who played the bogeymen, there was no place to go but down—Karloff in his Mexican cheapies; a pathetic, drug-addicted Lugosi wrestling with a rubber octopus in the infamous *Bride of the Monster* (1955); and Chaney crooning the title song of the grindhouse classic *Spider Baby* (1968) before going out in a sputter of ignominy as the mute assistant in *Dracula vs Frankenstein* (1971), a film in which the Universal horror formula is finally boiled down to sludgy drive-in swill.

Claude Rains escaped, though. *His* final role was King Herod in *The Greatest Story Ever Told,* George Stevens's 1965 A-list biblical epic, a fitting send-off for the man who had given us nasty King John in *The Adventures of Robin Hood* (1938) and the morally fluid police chief of *Casablanca* (1943). Because Rains's Universal horror breakthrough three decades earlier had never been a matter of costume—*The Invisible Man* is creeptacular for its special effects, for director Whale's subversive wit, and for the star's mellifluously evil voice—the actor had no visual expectations pinning him down. He could be anyone he chose to be, and so he was.

Certainly Universal tried straitjacketing Rains in horror movies, or movies that at least sounded horrifying. *The Man Who Reclaimed His Head* (1934) promised audiences a sequel to *Invisible Man* but turned out to be a solid, provocative antiwar drama, no monsters anywhere in sight. *The Mystery of Edwin Drood* (1935) is the reverse: it sounds like Dickens but is, in fact, studio pulp, with Rains twitching through his role as a mad strangler. He must have been glad to get away to Warner Bros., where an initial supporting splash as the murderous Spanish aristocrat in *Anthony Adverse* (1936) set his course.

Rains's métier was likeable malice, so cleverly played that audiences came to recognize and treasure him. This in turn allowed him to take on roles of great kindness, as Bette Davis's godlike psychiatrist in *Now, Voyager* (1942) or the faithful husband *Mr. Skeffington* (1944), the latter a rare title role. Typically, though, Rains gives that film back to Davis as his grasping, immature wife.

He was, in other words, the perfect character actor, a reliable bet no matter what he looked like but always working to define what the main characters are and do. (Ironically, one of his few leads was in the 1943 remake of *Phantom of the Opera*—a horror role, and a masked one at that.) Rains's Captain Renault in *Casablanca* is the embodiment of the title city's endemic corruption, and he represents its pleasure principle as well, bedding the more attractive émigrés (or trying to), shocked, *shocked,* to discover gambling at Rick's, and softening Bogart in our eyes while making sure the star comes off the more honorable man. He gives Rick an out at the end, too—that stroll off the tarmac into a beautiful friendship is one of the most perfect Hollywood endings, in part because it satisfies our suspicion that not every story has to twist itself into a final romantic clinch.

What's the difference between a star like Bogart and a character actor like Rains? Between, say, Bette Davis and Thelma Ritter in *All About Eve*? Age and looks have a little to do with it, but in truth they simply have different audience needs to answer and jobs to perform. One explanation is that the star is who we want to be, or at least who we briefly imagine ourselves to be while he or she works out dilemmas onscreen. The character actor, by contrast, is usually part of the dilemma—an integral aspect of the situation the star must resolve one way or another on the way to the words "The End."

In *Casablanca,* Rains is Bogart's obstacle—one of them, anyway—as the French police captain working for the Nazis. Only a miraculous change of heart, hinted at by their friendship, brings him around. The actor was adept at these climactic 180-degree turns: in *Mr. Smith Goes to Washington,* Rains's character, a cool politician nicknamed "the Silver Fox," is stricken by conscience and, most improbably, confesses all on the floor of the U.S. Senate.

Thelma Ritter, who played maids, cleaning ladies, and street-corner buttinskys from 1947 to 1968, illustrates the other crucial purpose of the character actor: to provide a running commentary to the main action. In *Rear Window* (1954), she's Jimmy Stewart's masseuse, standing in for the audience as she voices her fears and ghoulish fascination with the possible killer across the way. In *Pillow Talk* (1959), she's Doris Day's comic-drunk cleaning woman, cracking wise and passing out. Backstage dresser Ritter tends to Broadway star Margo Channing (Davis) in *All About Eve* (1950), but she's also the one person who stands up to her, as though her Brooklyn accent gave her diplomatic immunity.

Ritter's six Oscar nominations included her performances in *Eve* and *Pillow Talk,* as well as her most vivid role, as the doomed stool pigeon Moe in the tough little film noir *Pickup on South Street* (1953). All Supporting Actress nods. She never won. Same with Rains: nominated four times, never won. Peter Lorre, the German star of *M* and a figure of effete derangement at Warners for years? Never even nominated. The same goes for countless other valued supporting players. No one ever wanted to *be* Rains, or Ritter, or Lorre, even if they're great fun to imitate and contemplate. We don't project ourselves upon the great character actors, or even the hardworking ones, but they do intensify the beam we shine on the stars.

In the early years of the Motion Picture Academy, supporting actors were awarded only a certificate of merit; a full statue wasn't instituted until 1943. Those who won during the studio years tended to be young talents on the way up (Van Heflin in *Johnny Eager*), old men (Charles Coburn in *The More the Merrier,* Walter Huston in *The Treasure of the Sierra Madre*), or Walter Brennan (three wins in *five years*). The women awardees played mothers (Anne Revere in *National Velvet,* Jane Darwell in *The Grapes of Wrath*) or villainesses (Gale Sondergaard in *Anthony Adverse,* Claire Trevor in *Key Largo*) or doomed young women (Teresa Wright in *Mrs. Miniver*). Gifted utility players like Lorre were rarely noticed because that, in fact, was their function—to fill out the studio dreamworld without calling attention to themselves, except in those one or two scenes in which they leap out and engage with the leads before moving back into the background. They were the mortar that held the bricks.

Every studio had its full complement of character actors spanning the generations from youth to age, from Freddie Bartholomew to Lionel Barrymore, and spanning as well an infinite variety of human types: waspish (Clifton Webb), stupid (Grady Sutton), avuncular (S. Z. "Cuddles" Sakall), meek (Donald Meek), and so forth. This was the gene pool in which each studio movie swam, its respective vision of mankind. Some directors, like Preston Sturges at Paramount, wallowed in the pleasures of character actors and virtually gave their movies over to them, so that *The Palm Beach Story* is as much about tiny Jimmy Conlin, crabby William Demarest, and prissy Franklin Pangborn as it is about ostensible leads Joel McCrea and Claudette Colbert. Or W. C. Fields in *The Bank Dick*, positing a worn-down character hero in a universe of aggravating, marvelous freaks with names like Og Oggilby (Sutton), J. Pinkerton Snooperton (Pangborn), Joe Guelpe (Shemp Howard), and Filthy McNasty (Al Hill). To Fields, we're *all* character actors bedeviling each other's movies—that's the great, lacerating joke of existence.

Interestingly, character actors were allowed to sin—often, in fact, *had* to sin so the leads wouldn't. In *Casablanca*, where would Ingrid Bergman and Paul Henreid be if Peter Lorre's Ugarte hadn't murdered his way into possessing the letters of transit? The letters give Bogart's Rick the power that sustains him through the movie, and for his crime, Ugarte is killed off in a shrieking fit (Lorre's preferred method of exit). Character actors either take the bullet or just fill out the screen. They're either functional or they're furniture.

Most often, they're used to represent a singular human attribute. Berton Churchill specialized in pompous small-town bankers, from *Heroes for Sale* (1933) to *Stagecoach* (1939). Pangborn, ever a bottom-

ABOVE: Florence Lawrence, the first movie star to be publicized by name, in 1911's *A Girlish Impulse*. The act of dressing up—and *seeing* oneself dressing up—was mirrored by an audience of women desperate to know her identity.

LEFT: The inmates take over the asylum: Douglas Fairbanks, Mary Pickford, Charlie Chaplin, and D. W. Griffith announce the founding of United Artists, February 1919. Of the four, Pickford had the head for business.

BELOW: Mae West and the man whose company she saved from bankruptcy: Paramount founder Adolph Zukor. West sold sex—or the idea of it—to moviegoers craving sound and bluntness. Zukor just sold stars, brilliantly.

ABOVE: The power of cute: Shirley Temple writes her name for posterity outside Grauman's Chinese Theatre, 1935—just a normal kid who created obsessive mania in millions.

RIGHT: Clark Gable as Hollywood wanted us to know him: not an actor but a virile king of men. Gable was taking notes and retrofitting his personality to his studio persona.

BELOW: Vivien Leigh officially becomes Scarlett O'Hara under the watchful eyes of producer David O. Selznick and co-stars Leslie Howard and Olivia de Havilland, 1939. Every woman in America dreamed of playing the part.

ABOVE: The young Marlon Brando poses for a 1950 wardrobe test for *A Streetcar Named Desire*. In attitude and bearing, in the hostility radiating from his eyes, this was a new kind of star—one who didn't need us.

LEFT: Marilyn Monroe in a still from *How to Marry a Millionaire* (1953), contemplating, perhaps, the many different Marilyns available to her: sex goddess, sex toy, actress, photo op, woman.

BELOW: St. Sidney: Sidney Poitier as the slum doctor in 1950's *No Way Out*. As the first African American leading man permitted by the system, Poitier had little latitude to spread his talents.

ABOVE: Elvis Presley around the time of his ascension. He was the Brando threat made manifest in music, coming right into your house to seduce your children. More to the point, he was wholly unmanufactured.

BELOW: Dustin Hoffman, boy prince of the new *menschlichkeit*, in 1967, the year of *The Graduate*. He was thirty, but a younger generation seeking its own stars claimed him as its own.

ABOVE LEFT: Jane Fonda, second-generation Hollywood royalty, the way the film industry saw her in 1955: Hank's little girl, ready for her close-up (after a little hair and makeup).

ABOVE RIGHT: Jane Fonda as she and her 1960s peers saw her, in *Klute* (1971): radical in politics and acting choices, and nobody's plaything, least of all the studios'.

BELOW: Robert De Niro around the time of *Mean Streets* (1973): craft and mystery and enigmatic rage—the Brando threat reconstituted for the New Hollywood

ABOVE: The return of glamour: Harrison Ford as Han Solo in *Star Wars* (1977). He brooded and winked like other post-sixties stars, but he had Gable's swagger and an old-school charisma that felt freshly invented.

RIGHT: Meryl Streep as we admired her in the 1980s: the tormented, impeccably acted heroine of *The French Lieutenant's Woman* (1981).

BELOW: Meryl Streep as we love her in the new millennium: the lusty matriarch of *Mamma Mia* (2008). It's one of the most startling changes of persona in the history of movies.

LEFT: Tom Cruise the way he wants us to see him, as the can-do flyboy and apotheosis of Reagan's America in 1986's *Top Gun*.

BELOW: Tom Cruise the way we actually see him, after the Internet got hold of the infamous 2005 *Oprah* couch-jumping incident. It's proof that star persona is now controlled by a wired and enabled public.

BOTTOM: The paparazzi empress and her chosen consort: Angelina Jolie and Brad Pitt. The two embody stardom for a new century, built on the old archetypes but less dependent on movies than on the gossip-sphere.

ABOVE: Brando 5.0? Ryan Gosling, the most recent iteration of the macho-mysterioso hunk craftsman, in 2011's *Drive*.

BELOW LEFT: Lindsay Lohan, teen-actress-turned-reality-star. She acts out the same bad-girl dilemmas that Clara Bow and Elizabeth Taylor did, only now they take place in our blogs and Twitter feeds.

BELOW RIGHT: Anne Hathaway, Hollywood's reigning good girl, demonstrating the eternal class argument of grace and propriety. No mug shot for her. Yet.

waggling store manager, was where gayness went for the duration of the studio era. Marjorie Main—Ma Kettle—was the plain-talking sticks, George Sanders untrustworthy urbanity. Eve Arden: sarcasm. Margaret Dumont: high-society cluelessness. Fay Bainter: maternal warmth. Agnes Moorehead: neurotic angst. You could drop these players into any script and they'd perform their designated task like a software macro. Executives and audiences alike valued them for their reliability.

One last way of looking at the matter: if the studio stars were stand-ins for us, the character actors were all the other people who give us hope and trouble throughout the day. Their exaggerations make sense to us because that's often how we see the world, as a gallery of familiar types within which our misunderstood dramas or comedies play out. They're the nasty teacher who gives us too much homework, the sympathetic friend, the dithery mother, the cruel father—or the nasty mother, the dithery father, the sympathetic teacher, the cruel friend. Each variant had its specialist at one studio or another. Character actors are not the stars, but they enable the stars, and their quotidian weaknesses (character flaws, if you will) underscore the grander, more perfect struggles of the leading players.

The consensus among cineastes and historians is that the Hollywood studio system peaked in 1939, the year of an unusually high number of movies that were recognized as great then and that have lasted: *Stagecoach, Mr. Smith Goes to Washington, The Wizard of Oz, Wuthering Heights, The Women, Destry Rides Again, Only Angels Have Wings, Ninotchka, Gunga Din.* The mother of them all, of course, is *Gone With the Wind,* and from the novel's publication in 1936 to the movie's opening day, the casting of Scarlett O'Hara was its own outsized drama, and probably the more culturally important one. David O. Selznick, a producer whose ego was far too big to fit under a studio roof (he'd boy-geniused his way through Paramount, RKO, and MGM before going out on his own), brilliantly orchestrated the search, testing half the actresses in Hollywood and drawing out the suspense until the country was simultaneously obsessed and sick of it all. Then Selznick threw the sucker punch. He cast a woman no one had heard of.

It was a rare case of the factory opening its doors, not only allowing the public to see how stars are manufactured but turning the process into narrative, contest, fantasy. More than that, *GWTW* gave the American public a say in what kind of woman they wanted Scarlett to be, which in turn said much about what kind of woman was valued and feared in American culture. Whether Selznick intended it as such, the search for Scarlett was a pop experiment on a grand scale, and one of the very few times before the arrival of the counterculture when audiences and the film industry interrogated each other about what, exactly, a movie star meant.

Everyone had an opinion. Bags of mail arrived at Selznick International Pictures and the secretaries kept tallies. By July 1938, there were 300 votes for Ann Sheridan, 228 for Miriam Hopkins, 61 for Katharine Hepburn, 58 for Joan Crawford. The chief Hollywood gossip hens, Hedda Hopper and Louella Parsons, clucked and strutted and took the search as their own, weighing in on every contender and proposing to speak for millions of women. If Tallulah Bankhead got the role, Parsons wrote, "I personally will go home and weep because she is not Scarlett O'Hara in my language, and if David O. Selznick gives her the part he will have to answer to every man, woman, and child in America."

"She is not Scarlett O'Hara in *my language*"—here was the insanity of the thing. Selznick had to translate the heroine of Margaret Mitchell's novel into millions of private languages and emotional landscapes, each of which had to agree with the others. Today this is a common cultural parlor game, gossip magazines and Web sites speculating endlessly on who would make the "best" Edward Cullen, Lisbeth Salander or Katniss Everdeen. In 1939, it was new and it was thrilling.

The character's physical appearance was the least important aspect. *Gone With the Wind* opens with the famous line "Scarlett O'Hara was not beautiful, but men seldom realized it when caught by her charm." Everyone understood that would be the first thing to go. A heroine can be fascinatingly plain in a book—often has to be if she's to hook the projected fantasies of an average-looking mass readership—but the studios worked hard to sell beauty because the moguls understood that we go to the movies to see pretty people. We love them for it and hate them for it, but we pay. It is the foundation of the movie business. So Scarlett, whoever she was, would be a looker.

Much more critical was her psychological profile. As she staggers across the story's epic Civil War backdrop, Scarlett is by turns a spoiled child, a bold vixen, a manipulative lover, a war refugee, a murderess, a victim of marital rape, a mourning mother, a user, a giver, a survivor. Her crime—shared only by all the women in the audience—is wanting too much, and the War Between the States is her punishment. She's a classic bitch-heroine who crosses the lines of social propriety so we don't have to, and the fascination lies in seeing what Scarlett wins (her pride, the land, self-sufficiency) and what she loses (children, family, love). And if Rhett Butler has to carry her upstairs for a good, forced husbandly shagging, well, she was asking for it, wasn't she? The entire culture understood that much in 1939—if only because it was Gable doing the carrying—and so does Scarlett, glowing happily in the morning-after sunrise.

And there was the way the character mirrored the emotional and actual emancipation of women in the post–World War I era—an evolution, in critic Molly Haskell's words, "from seductress to woman of action [that] exerted an enormous pull as a fable for working women." On top of that was an additional element of sexual willfulness that made the novel a deliriously racy read for adolescent girls of the era. Until Rhett comes along, no man chooses Scarlett—she chooses the men. As sexually repressed as she is, Scarlett has more potency than anyone else in Margaret Mitchell's South.

How could an established actress be overlaid on a character matrix this complex? The star personas of Hollywood's golden era allowed for a handful of emotional postures and positions, but not this many at once. Garbo embodied romantic fatalism, Shearer was tastefully headstrong, Crawford exuded sheer will; that was all, or almost all. Some were better actresses than others but their meanings at the box office were limited by what the public paid to see and what the studio heads were willing to let them do. Bette Davis seems the closest fit, but Jack Warner wouldn't loan her to Selznick without Errol Flynn as Rhett, and no one, including Davis, thought that made any sense. The actress ended up playing her own Scarlett, the Confederate belle Miss Julie in 1938's *Jezebel*. She won an Oscar for it, too, but the loss of *Wind* forever nettled her. Years later she wrote regally, "It was insanity that I not be given Scarlett, but then, Hollywood has never been rational."

Bankhead didn't win the part, either; she was too old and distinctly unvirginal. (Selznick later thought to offer her the role of Aunt Pittypat and immediately thought better of it.) Norma Shearer was a candidate until the producer leaked her name to gossip columnist Walter Winchell to test public reaction. It wasn't good; Mitchell herself felt the widow of MGM's Irving Thalberg "had too much dignity and not enough fire for the part." Everyone correctly sensed that a dull Scarlett would be disastrous.

Katharine Hepburn was in the running on the strength of her period-film résumé, but she was in a career downturn and Selznick perceptively saw no eroticism in her. "I think Hepburn has two strikes against her," he wrote in one of his endless memos. "First, the unquestionable and very widespread intense public dislike of her at the moment, and second, the fact that she has yet to demonstrate that she possesses the sex qualities that are probably the most important of all the many requisites of Scarlett." Like Davis, Hepburn built a private mythology around the loss, saying in 1990, "I was too strong for it. [Director] George [Cukor] said I was too noble."

Other well-known actresses considered or tested included Jean Arthur, Miriam Hopkins, Margaret Sullavan, Ann Sheridan, Joan Crawford, Barbara Stanwyck, Paulette Goddard, Joan Bennett, Frances Dee, Loretta Young, and a very young Lana Turner ("completely inadequate," wrote Selznick). It got to the point where Lucille Ball was called in for a reading; there was still a decade to go until *I Love Lucy*, but Ball was no one's idea of a Scarlett, even her own.

For the fans who followed the search obsessively, the real thrill was the possibility that Selznick would cast from the crowd—would pick one of *them*. Aided immeasurably by his head of publicity, Russell Birdwell, Selznick sent his troops across the land looking under every bushel for the perfect Scarlett O'Hara. One executive held auditions in the east and north, another covered the western states, while Cukor himself headed south, to the crucial proving grounds. When he arrived in New Orleans, the local newspaper devoted more front-page space to him than to the abdication of Edward VIII. In Atlanta, socialites and debutantes turned out en masse to try for the role. Susan Falligant, a University of Georgia senior, was granted a week's leave of absence to travel north for a screen test. Women's colleges let their students skip classes for auditions.

Then there were those who crashed the party, like the woman who followed Cukor from New York to Atlanta and was apprehended as she stalked him on the train trip back. "I must see Mr. Cukor," she wept bitterly as she was taken away. "If I talk to him he will realize I am the only Scarlett. This is the turning point of my life." Back in Hollywood, a would-be actress arrived at Selznick International in a packing case marked "OPEN AT ONCE"; she ran into the producer's office and started reciting Scarlett's speeches while peeling off her clothes. One day a truck pulled up in front of Selznick's Summit Drive home, in the back of which was a giant replica of the hardcover edition of *Gone With the Wind*. The cover opened to reveal an actress in a hoopskirt, who literally stepped from the pages of the book.

It was, for a year or two, a genuine phenomenon, one in which women who hoped to become the star they were in their own heads projected that need onto Margaret Mitchell's heroine. Winning the role of Scarlett would have been the perfect triangulation, would have closed the loop, and if you believed in it strongly enough and were delusional enough, it must have seemed absurdly close. This was as near as the classic Hollywood star machine ever came to democracy (which wasn't close at all), and it prefigured the mania that surrounds reality-TV contests: the recognition, at last, of the inner immortal.

Selznick never intended on casting a rank amateur, obviously. There would be too much of a learning curve and not enough onscreen presence. Famous movie stars, being *too* well established, carried the opposite burden. The producer fretted that "all we have to do is line up a complete cast of such people as Hepburn and Leslie Howard, and we can have a lovely picture for release eight years ago." A professional was called for, but she had to be unknown, or from someplace else, like Mars. Or England.

Overall, Selznick spent $92,000 to interview 1,400 women and give 90 of them screen tests, at the end of which he still hadn't found his "new girl." He was leaning strongly in the direction of Paulette Goddard, who tested very well and possessed a sharp, minx-like quality. She had sex and cleverness, but what she didn't have was warmth or mystery. Also, she was married to Charlie Chaplin, or living with him, or something—it wasn't very clear. Sexual scandals and leftist pronouncements had made the comedian increasingly unpopular in the late 1930s; Goddard, costar of Chaplin's *Modern Times* but yet to appear in *The Women*, was considered his latest "discovery," quote marks very much intended.

She was, and would turn out to be, more than that, but Selznick knew he couldn't drop a morally compromised Scarlett O'Hara on the country. Was she married or not? Goddard fudged: they had been wed aboard a yacht in the Pacific but the documents had been destroyed in a guerrilla attack . . . or maybe they'd been married by the mayor of Catalina, an island that turned out to have no mayor. When Louella Parsons started referring to the actress as "Scarlett O'Goddard" in her column, women's groups across America began write-in campaigns complaining that *Gone With the Wind* couldn't possibly star an actress who was the mistress of a suspected communist. The word "boycott" was mentioned more than once. Scarlett may have been many things, but she wasn't a pinko slut.

To the rescue at last came Vivien Leigh, springing like Athena from the head of the producer's brother, Hollywood agent Myron Selznick. The long-accepted legend is that Myron showed up the night David filmed the burning of Atlanta, years of old movie sets going up in flames on the Selznick back lot, and suddenly there appears a dark-haired, wild-eyed young Englishwoman with fire reflected off her features, Myron cackling to his kid brother, "Here's your Scarlett."

As legends go, it's close enough to the truth that no one minds much. Leigh wasn't completely unknown to David, though. He had screened one of her British films, *Fire Over England,* when looking for someone to star in his 1938 feature *Young at Heart* (ironically, Goddard ended up with the part). Selznick also knew Leigh was in town, not just to accompany her lover, *Wuthering Heights* star Laurence Olivier (they were both married to other people but couldn't keep their hands off each other), but to sniff out whether the role of Scarlett O'Hara was within her reach. One story has Olivier passing her to his agent, Myron Selznick, who passed her off to one of his associates, Nat Deverich, who took Leigh to the local racetrack where he chatted up Selznick International executive Daniel O'Shea, who went back to the office and asked his boss, David, if *he* might ask Cukor to test Larry Olivier's girlfriend. As a favor to Myron.

So when Myron said, "Here's your Scarlett," Leigh was already written down in David's calendar for an upcoming audition. No matter. The producer saw and was besotted, as was Cukor the next day, as was Margaret Mitchell. ("Naturally, I am the only person in the world who really knows what Scarlett looks like, but this girl looks charming. She has the most Irish look I have ever seen with the word 'Devil' in her eye.") The women of the great American South declared themselves satisfied that the role had gone to an Englishwoman, since that meant it wouldn't go to a northerner. Myron Selznick quickly signed Leigh to a contract and moved her out of Olivier's bedroom into an apartment with one of his secretaries.

And the public acquiesced. Out of all those women from the South who had desperately auditioned, only one, Alicia Rhett, got a small role, as Ashley Wilkes's sister. Yet it was fine, all fine. Selznick had courted the audience and flattered them with the length and seeming seriousness of the flirtation, but Leigh was exactly what everyone wanted. She was a new star but one born full-sized. The actress stepped naturally into the role because she brought so little baggage, and she was generic enough to fit everyone's dream of Scarlett O'Hara while remaining specific enough to make the part her own. Or did the part make her? The peculiarities of their twinned arrival keep actress and role in eternal tension. We can't not think of Scarlett without Leigh's face, and the remaining eight films of Leigh's career mostly measure the distance traveled from Scarlett and, in the case of *A Streetcar Named Desire* (1951), the perilous journey back.

9.

The Afternoon Shift: Postwar Studio Stardom

The problem with gods who look and act like us is that they get old like us, at which point they cease to be gods. So we continually choose new ones as young and as beautiful as we hope we are when we look in the mirror. Each freshly born divinity is a reflection of who we think we are at that moment in time and culture, or, more precisely, who we might want to be.

The Hollywood factory years were not monolithic, then, but fluid. Modes of behavior and the stars who embodied them in movies, on the radio, in real life, changed over the decades from the rise of talking pictures through the slow decline of studio hegemony in the 1950s. Some people simply fell out of fashion, like the early-1930s hothouse orchid Kay Francis, or Paul Muni, who finally ran out of famous men to play. Others, like Shirley Temple and Mickey Rooney, grew up, betraying both the fans who thought they owned them and the moguls who did. A few appeared and disappeared like supernovas. Luise Rainer, "the Viennese Teardrop," won two Best Actress Oscars in a row (for 1936's *The Great Ziegfeld* and 1937's *The Good Earth*) and was virtually forgotten by 1940. (She's still going strong at 102 as of this writing, as if to spite Hollywood's neglect by outliving it.) Some just imploded, like Frances Farmer, a Hollywood rebel who was institutionalized for the crime of fighting the machine two decades too early.

One sign that the first generation of talkie stars had run its course was an ad that appeared in the trade magazine *Independent Film Journal* in February 1938. Written anonymously by Harry Brandt, the gadfly president of the Independent Theater Owners of America—and thus the spokesman for every movie theater that wasn't owned by one of the studios—the ad railed against the prestige costume pictures the majors forced independent theaters to show in exchange for getting at more populist (and profitable) fare. (This practice was known as "block booking," and it proved crucial to the overturning of the studios' monopoly by the U.S. Supreme Court in the 1948 Paramount antitrust decision, the first serious blow to the system.)

Brandt's broadside read, in part, "Wake up Hollywood producers! Practically all of the major studios are burdened with stars—whose public appeal is negligible—receiving tremendous salaries necessitated by contractual obligations. . . . Among those players whose dramatic ability is unquestioned, but whose box-office draw is nil, can be numbered Mae West, Edward Arnold, Greta Garbo, Joan Crawford, Katharine Hepburn, Marlene Dietrich, and Fred Astaire."

This was the infamous "box-office poison" ad, a yawp of protest from small-town movie theater proprietors at the urbane creatures their paying customers had no interest in seeing. None of the listed stars worked for homespun Fox or gritty Warner Bros.; all, instead, came from sophisticated Paramount (West, Dietrich), glamorous MGM (Arnold, Crawford), metropolitan RKO (Hepburn, Astaire). They were favorites of the critics and educated big-city audiences, the Sean Penns and Meryl Streeps of their day.

Industry reaction was swift in some cases. RKO gave Hepburn $200,000 to end her contract and go away, and she arrived at her family home in Old Saybrook, Connecticut, just in time to see it destroyed by the hurricane of '38. (Four men ultimately saved Hepburn's career: Philip Barry, who wrote her Broadway return, *The Philadelphia Story*; boyfriend Howard Hughes, who gave her the money to buy the film rights; old friend George Cukor, who directed the movie; and Spencer Tracy, who starting with 1942's *Woman of the Year* mellowed the actress in the eyes of both the industry and the public.)

Within a few years, many of the stars labeled "poison" were working at different studios, trying on different personas to replace the ones that had soured. Crawford landed at Warners and played a more victimized, noir-ified version of Bette Davis in *Mildred Pierce* (1945), which finally won the actress an Oscar. Astaire, who had less genre range than his partner Ginger Rogers, bounced around a bit before settling in at MGM, where Freed's musicals unit understood his great worth. Dietrich, desperate to change her image after her run of coldly brilliant Josef von Sternberg melodramas, hopped to Universal and a western comedy, of all things—*Destry Rides Again* (1939), a huge hit that both diminished Dietrich's star power by making fun of her and saved her career by showing she could take a joke. West merely slipped from view, a fossil.

Greta Garbo was the sole member of her generation to simply say the hell with it. Disillusionment had been the actress's métier since the silent era, and the almost cosmic faith in disaster in which her characters and public persona trafficked seemed increasingly mannered to the general public and to Louis B. Mayer, the man who had brought her to America in 1926. MGM put the star in a Lubitsch comedy, *Ninotchka* (1939); the ads said "Garbo laughs!" and she did, but it looked like it hurt.

By the time of 1941's modern-dress screwball romance *Two-Faced Woman,* which isn't as bad as its reputation but isn't much good either, Garbo saw the writing on the wall. The studio wanted her to be like other women, and what was the point of that? Mayer wasn't sad to see her go, since the European audiences that increasingly sustained her salary had been cut off by the war, and the scene in *Woman* in which the star dances the "chica-choca" was met by critics with derision. *Time* magazine likened it to "seeing your mother drunk." Of course Garbo quit. The mystery, her stock in trade, had been compromised.

Through her leaving, oddly, Garbo's persona was strengthened and confirmed. She really *didn't* need us. Over the subsequent decades, until her death in 1990, the star was a human rebuke, the ghost in the machine. She resisted comeback offers from Norma Desmond in *Sunset Blvd.* to the Mother Superior in *The Trouble with Angels*. A Garbo sighting in Manhattan became the celebrity equivalent of glimpsing the Loch Ness Monster, proof that an Olympian landscape of myth existed parallel to our shabbier world. More than that, Garbo's refusal is the great slap in the face of the audience-star contract, a negation of the idea that famous people want to be watched and loved and worshipped. How stupid, responds Garbo. How incredibly, uselessly stupid. No wonder she's still potent. We never get over the lovers who get over us.

In truth, the moviegoing audience had simply outgrown what Garbo initially meant, as it outgrows all stars. The cultural demands made on actors and actresses changed as America emerged from the Depression, capsized into World War II, then emerged into the postwar years hardened, wiser, and more paranoid. Every generation distrusts the previous generation's version of—well, "cool" isn't the right word, since that concept won't even be invented until the next chapter. But the signal attributes that make a pop artifact like a movie culturally successful—its pacing, language, the sound of that language, the characters it employs, and the values those characters embody, how it resolves its narrative and who wins—generally have a half-life of a decade or so, even without a drastic contributing factor like a global war.

Which is to say that a *Gold Diggers of 1933* (sassy, straightforward, clear-eyed, hopeful) is almost unimaginable by the late 1940s and early 1950s, when the smiles on all those Fox and MGM musical heroes were stretched to the breaking point. The brooding shadows of film noir, Val Lewton's suggestive horror masterpieces at RKO, and Billy Wilder's disenchanted farces were creeping into the mainstream. We want to feel that movies, and the people in them, are telling us the truth about life, but truth is a moving target, subject to so many variables of current events and attitudes and technology that each cultural decade is a world unto itself, a link in an ever-mutating daisy chain of ephemeral meaning.

So the war years matured American moviegoers, taught them a new sense of duty, and brought them into a larger world where isolationism served little purpose. The movies made by the Hollywood studios during World War II translated that political reality into cultural terms, both consciously—under constant pressure from the Office of War Information's Bureau of Motion Pictures, a well-intentioned propaganda arm—and subconsciously. New stars served as vessels of these new meanings. Greer Garson became instantly famous and won an Oscar as *Mrs. Miniver* (1942), a stoic middle-class London wife and mother surviving the Blitz and reminding American audiences that the British were Just Like Us.

Or Van Johnson in *A Guy Named Joe* (1943), flying successful bombing runs while being guided by the ghost of dead pilot Spencer Tracy to the right targets and to Tracy's girl Irene Dunne. Young, cute, easygoing—wholesome without being a jerk about it—Johnson caused a panic among teenage bobby-soxers; of course Tracy's character had to die so his could live, the 1930s legend ceding ground to the new kid. In reality, it was almost the other way around. Johnson was involved in a serious car accident during filming and came out of the hospital with a pair of metal plates in his head; only Tracy's intervention saved his job and career. Ironically, Johnson's new 4-F status kept him in Hollywood starring in hit war dramas while most other male stars were off fighting.

Despite Johnson's middle-American appeal, a growing awareness of ethnicity can be seen in the movie stars who came to prominence in the decade from the late 1930s to the late 1940s. John Garfield—born Jules Garfinkle on the Lower East Side and a veteran of New York's

Group Theatre—made female moviegoers swoon as the rebellious musician in 1938's *Four Daughters,* mostly because he was so radically different from everyone else in the movie's slim, golden universe.

Dark-haired, short, gloweringly intense—Harry Warner must have wondered who in hell let this *grober* in—Garfield was for the longest time the only recognizably Semitic romantic lead in American movies, and the chip on his shoulder was part of his allure. The splendidly overripe melodrama *Humoresque* and the perverse film noir *The Postman Always Rings Twice,* both from 1946, use Garfield's edge to erotically reinvigorate the personas of established Hollywood queens Joan Crawford and Lana Turner.

Ethnicity was sex, in other words. It's an assumption that runs all the way back to America's origins as a slave-owning society, that has tunneled beneath our culture and always will, popping out disguised as the jitterbug or doo-wop or rap. The young Frank Sinatra looked like a freshly hatched ostrich but his singing voice promised a slowly cresting big-band orgasm, and he drove parents crazy because he was so clearly from the wrong side of the tracks. (Brando, with his sweat stains and mumbles, became the quintessential postwar Visigoth, but we're not quite ready for him yet.)

In addition, there was a new knowingness to star persona by the end of the war, a weariness that spoke of having been through the fire. The male idols were truculent and distant, with no interest in winning over an audience. Alan Ladd became a sensation as a grim avenging angel in *The Blue Dahlia* (1946), while Glenn Ford chased Gilda and her men through halls of mirrors and watched his wife get blown up in *The Big Heat* (1953). William Holden was too full of doubts to be a conventional leading man; Montgomery Clift even more so with his blue neurotic stare. Then came even darker heroes, like itchy Kirk Douglas, bitter Robert Ryan, gracefully hulking Burt Lancaster, Richard Widmark in pulpy B films punching at fate when he wasn't pushing old ladies downstairs, and Robert Mitchum, whose entire being radiated a lazy *Screw you.* All of them men to disturb the sleep of female moviegoers and Louis B. Mayer.

The women became more sexually alert, too. Start with Lauren

Bacall, offering to come for Bogart whenever he whistles in *To Have and Have Not* (1944): Mae West's old promise in a body and a sensibility that actually makes sense. Then work your way through the growing frankness of Ava Gardner (possibly the sexiest woman in classic Hollywood cinema), Susan Hayward (urban and no-nonsense, like Barbara Stanwyck's hard-ass kid sister), Jane Russell (Howard Hughes's great gift to breast-obsessed American men; even the pioneering push-up bra he designed for her role in *The Outlaw* became a star), and so on to Marilyn Monroe and Elizabeth Taylor, the alpha and omega of eruptive '50s movie sex.

Even the good girls seemed to know their way around, like Grace Kelly massaging Jimmy Stewart's back in *Rear Window,* classiness with a promise of sin. Yes, in MGM musicals, Debbie Reynolds and Gene Kelly sublimated sexuality into song and dance so well that it completely vanishes, until Ann Miller shows up, or Cyd Charisse. In general, though, the growing split personality of popular culture in the postwar era—demanding lockstep good cheer on one hand while hinting at all the things repressed—was reflected in the movies. It was the rare new star who managed to rise above this hidden culture war and achieve consensus.

The only one to do so, in fact, was Audrey Hepburn, whose unstudied elegance was and remains so powerful that the Motion Picture Academy fell at her feet with her first major film, 1953's *Roman Holiday,* and she adorns T-shirts and calendars sold to twenty-first-century girls.

Hepburn is one of the very few timeless pop figures—a performer who could potentially have flourished in any century or culture. More important, as one of the few female star singularities coined during the postwar era, Hepburn turned out to be tremendously necessary. Male movie stars in America are allowed to age, while female movie stars are sent out to the ice floes of character parts and horror movies. This remains so, as Harrison Ford and Michelle Pfeiffer will be the first to tell you. Hepburn, therefore, was wooed onscreen in her late twenties by men old enough to be her father: Bogart (age fifty-four) in *Sabrina,* Astaire (fifty-eight) in *Funny Face,* Gary Cooper (fifty-six) in *Love in the Afternoon,* Cary Grant (fifty-nine) in *Charade.* Only the two actors whose personas are predicated on physical elegance—Astaire and Grant—were able to pull this off without seeming like dirty old men.

What did audiences ask of stars in the 1950s? The same as always. They wanted someone who told them the truth about life—or, rather, told them fictionalized truths that gave their lives shape and made them bearable. The only difference was that those truths had to seem rawer. Hepburn was the great exception, proof there was still space for centered, natural poise. Moviegoers and the media looked to her as evidence that grace existed on earth even after Hitler (it mattered that Hepburn was European), and also that the old stallions of Hollywood—and the culture and industry they represented—still had potency. This she did without the threat of actual sex; she was perhaps the only one of the new stars to play by the old studio rules of carnal displacement and disengagement.

A carnally alive performer like Elizabeth Taylor, by contrast, simply wouldn't have been believable within the same frame as Bogart or Astaire or Grant; she would have exposed them as aging neuters and they would have made her look like a tramp (or merely a tramp). Even Van Johnson, the bobby-soxers' dreamboat, seems daunted by Liz in *The Last Time I Saw Paris* (1954). Paul Newman or Montgomery Clift could at least play believably in Taylor's sandbox before getting chased out, but it took the new frankness of the 1960s for Taylor to find a costar—Richard Burton—who could match her stride for ripsnorting stride, onscreen and off.

Audrey Hepburn, though, was proof of the perceived constancy of classiness, of a Continental taste that seemed suddenly youthful and right within the broader stage of the Marshall Plan era. Hollywood and older audiences loved her because she seemed to carry the banner of the Production Code's buttoned-up morality into the present; there was nothing at all *vulgar* about her.

Yet Hepburn isn't sexless, and her star persona allows for much more sophisticated readings than the cartoon virginity of, say, Doris Day, or even Monroe's much mocked curvature. Astaire and Hepburn in *Funny Face* aren't about sex, but neither are they *not* about sex; both players understand that Hollywood movies are metaphor rather than the thing itself, and they both know that pleasure is to be found in the dance (real and metaphorical)—that the stepping stones in the movie's final shot lead on past the words "The End" to a place the audience isn't privy to and doesn't need to be. No matter how hard the studios tried, the real work of romance and seduction can't be produced anywhere but in our own imaginations.

Anyway, it's not as if there weren't enough scandals to keep the prurient busy. The postwar years saw sex, drugs, and rock and roll erupt everywhere while the studios tried desperately to stuff them back into their boxes. The tenor of movie fan magazines shifted from conspiratorial to adversarial, from the wide-eyed re-mulching of studio PR typified by *Photoplay* to the sardonic investigative sleaze of Robert Harrison's *Confidential,* which from 1952 until its effective muzzling by the studios in 1957 reported on the sins of the stars with the most salacious headlines the editors could cook up: *Why Liberace's Theme Song Should Be, "Mad About the Boy!"* or *Orson Welles, His Chocolate Bon Bon and the Whoopsy Waiter.*

Some of these sins were true, others pure rumor, and all strove to give readers a picture of the "real" film industry behind the wholesome studio exterior. The longer the Production Code and its cheerful lies remained in place, the louder the scandal magazines bayed; in the gap between was the growing divide between the movie factory and the culture moving further from its walls.

Audiences were more forgiving of certain infractions than in the past, but, crucially, only if the star's persona permitted misbehavior. Robert Mitchum, the sleepy lion of film noirs like *Out of the Past* and *The Big Steal,* was busted for pot possession in 1948, did a month and a half in jail (with photographers snapping him mopping the floors), and came out a bigger star than before. Marilyn's nude photos were in circulation even before Hugh Hefner used them to launch *Playboy* in December 1953, and her casual acknowledgment that a girl's got to pay the rent *somehow* became part of the public fantasy that Monroe was. In both her and Mitchum's cases, the straightforward honesty with which they faced the public—very much against their studios' wishes—won them a greater respect.

Errol Flynn was similarly blessed, but in his case the general public understanding was that all women, even underage ones, wanted to sleep with him, and he couldn't actually be expected to say no. The star's 1943 trial for the statutory rapes of Betty Hansen, seventeen, and Peggy Satterlee, fifteen, was a smirking public Flynn lovefest—the crowds outside the courtroom pulled at his buttons, as if to seduce him en masse—in which Warners attorney Jerry Geisler successfully portrayed the girls as generally confused, more or less willing, and certainly easy. Flynn, thirty-four, denied everything and was acquitted; after the verdict was read, a little girl rushed up to present him a bouquet of flowers.

Of course he did it. Flynn did it with everyone. Actor David Niven once called the star "a magnificent specimen of the rampant male," and he didn't even like the man. Jack Warner, who owned him, said, "You know Flynn, he's either got to be fighting or fucking." Thus he was allowed to be in life—or mediated life—what he had established on the screen, and audiences implicitly understood that life was crueler and rawer than what the Production Code let them see. Geisler knew what he was doing when he packed the jury with women. The star was our designated satyr, our smiling national billy goat. After 1943, if you were about to get lucky with a girl, you were "in like Flynn."

God help you, though, if you were a famous left-wing comedian with a taste for younger women. Jerry Geisler was back in Los Angeles court in 1944, defending Charlie Chaplin, age fifty-five, from accusations of violating the Mann Act, i.e., transporting a woman across a state border for the purposes of sex. The case was brought by an overzealous local prosecutor in the name of Joan Barry, an emotionally disturbed would-be actress with whom Chaplin had carried on a brief affair. At one point toward the end of their relationship, Barry broke into the star's house in the middle of the night and held a gun on him; he talked her into putting the weapon down, then had sex with her. Common sense was never Charlie's strong suit.

Geisler easily got the comedian off, but everyone in Chaplin's circle underestimated the anger that had been building both in the public and in Washington, where Chaplin's pro-Soviet speeches during the wartime alliance with Russia hadn't played at all well. Once beloved, Charlie was now considered vain, arrogant, even predatory; there were rumors that various interests in the capital were out to get him. (By 1952, the FBI's files on Chaplin ran to thirteen volumes, more than half of them devoted to the comedian's "moral conduct.") Nevertheless, when Barry's lawyers filed a paternity suit—she had given birth to a girl in 1943—Chaplin was so confident that he didn't bother to bring Geisler back, hiring another attorney instead. Blood tests had proved he couldn't be the father, so how on earth could he be found guilty?

Yet he was, after one hung jury and then a second trial in which the prosecutor raged against this "cheap Cockney cad," a "gray-headed old buzzard" who was "a master mechanic in the art of seduction." The jury found Chaplin guilty, eleven to one, of fathering a child he could not possibly have had, and while legal experts called it a gross miscarriage of justice, the press and the public weren't outraged, only curious. Hadn't Charlie in some way brought this on himself, by his lusts or his politics or (ah) by forgetting that we only wanted him to make us laugh? Flynn stayed within the lines of his assigned meaning and got off scot-free. Chaplin colored outside the lines of his and had to pay $75 a week to Carol Ann Barry until the child turned eighteen, a commitment that, so far as anyone knows, he kept. Joan Barry ended up in a mental institution.

But all the old gods were aging poorly by the late 1940s. The silent stars by now were almost completely forgotten, a mere twenty years after the first talkies. In 1949, when Gloria Swanson was tapped to play Norma Desmond in *Sunset Blvd.*, she was earning $350 a week as a television talk show host in New York. She promptly divorced her fifth husband and got on the first train west, and she hadn't even read the script.

Give credit to Swanson. When she did read the script, and realized this sordid tale of a delusional silent-film icon was a brilliantly cruel parody of her own career arc and most of her peers', she recognized it as both true and a hell of a part. Reportedly, Billy Wilder and his cowriter Charles Brackett had originally approached Mae West, but the idea of playing a has-been struck her as an insult, possibly because it was close to the facts. There was a phone call to Pola Negri, who took affront in such a thick accent that Wilder realized she wouldn't do.

Most deliciously, there are stories of a pilgrimage to Pickfair, where Wilder and Brackett pitched the plot—cobwebs, insanity, murder among the film industry's living relics—to Mary Pickford herself. Accompanied by her second husband, Buddy Rogers, Pickford sat listening, wide-eyed and earnest, and quickly realized that the role of Joe Gillis, the young screenwriter Norma entraps in her mansion, was as important as Norma herself. No, no, this will not do, the great star said—if I am to appear in this film, Norma must be the central character. Wilder gamely plowed ahead with the pitch and then, in his words, "I suddenly stopped reading and just said, 'You know, Mary, you can play anything. You really can. You can act rings around any actress. But, Mary, I just realized this is not on your level. It's not up to your caliber.' " And he skedaddled out of there, realizing he was closer to Norma Desmond than he wanted to be.

Swanson looked much younger than her fifty-two years and was as vain as a deposed queen, bristling at the idea of making a screen test (for Paramount, the studio she had helped to *build,* for Christ's sake) until her friend George Cukor told her to shut up and behave. Learning that she'd have to wear old-age makeup, she smilingly asked Wilder if costar William Holden couldn't be made up to look younger instead?

But she got the irony of the thing, and the horror, and all the many levels of its daring. Wilder and Brackett (with help from cowriter D. M. Marshman Jr.) concocted a hall of mirrors that reflected back to audiences the one thing they didn't want to know or see: *that movie stars grow old.* In 1950, the cinema had been around a half century, give or take. This was a new idea.

Worse, *Sunset Blvd.* says that movie stars continue on even after we're done with them, turning in on themselves to gnaw on the adoration they once received from the world. Inside Norma Desmond's Hollywood haunted house is a brutal concordance of Wilder fiction with wilder reality. Norma's butler, Max—her former husband and director—is played by the director Erich von Stroheim, and the film they screen one night is *Queen Kelly*, the notorious, unfinished 1928 fiasco von Stroheim made with Swanson. Using the film was von Stroheim's idea; so were the fan letters Max secretly writes to convince Norma that people still care. He got it too, and all too well.

So did the "waxworks" Wilder hired to play Norma's bridge group: Anna Q. Nilsson and H. B. Warner, both major draws during the silent era (Warner had played Christ himself in Cecil B. DeMille's *King of Kings*), and Buster Keaton, at that point a recovering alcoholic wreck several years away from rediscovery. "Waxworks is right," deadpanned Keaton between takes, and the rest of the group got the giggles. Swanson, meanwhile, sat down and designed a hat for Norma's meeting with DeMille (playing himself) that consciously echoed one she had worn in 1919's *Male and Female,* directed by DeMille. The actress later described *Sunset Blvd.* as "a modern extension of Pirandello, or some sort of living exercise in science fiction," both of which seem perfectly reasonable.

Hollywood took it well, all things considered. After one of the screenings Paramount held for industry tastemakers, Barbara Stanwyck got down and literally kissed the hem of Swanson's gown, a wonderful we're-not-worthy moment that briefly reinstated the old Hollywood order. Louis B. Mayer had a different reaction. The MGM head followed Wilder out of the screening and shrieked, "You bastard! You have disgraced the industry that made and fed you! You should be tarred and feathered and run out of Hollywood!"

Wilder's response has been variously reported as "Fuck you" and "Go shit in your hat," but how can he have been surprised by Mayer's horror? The man helped create the system that *Sunset Blvd.* exposed as a meretricious folly, one that leads only to soullessness and dementia. Worse for him, Mayer still believed in that system—was, in fact, probably the only mogul to buy into the happy lies he peddled. As such, he was as deluded as Norma Desmond, and as unnecessary. Within a year, he would be forced out of MGM.

Mary Pickford was at that screening, too, but disappeared quickly afterward. Someone told Swanson that Mary was too "overwhelmed" to stay around. Was she upset at missing out on a great comeback role? Or was the movie simply too painful to watch for a fifty-eight-year-old woman who had once owned the planet and now rarely left her house?

The comeback had its own problems for Swanson, who got work but not enough to sustain a second film career, and who realized too late that the role had eclipsed the actress in the public's eyes. She lost the Oscar that year to Judy Holliday in *Born Yesterday*, and as the reporters clustered around her afterward, "It slowly dawned on me that they were unconsciously asking for a bigger-than-life scene, or, better still, a mad scene. More accurately, they were trying to flush out Norma Desmond."

This is from her memoirs, *Swanson on Swanson*, which remains a great read for its clarity, honesty, and colossal star vanity. No matter how much she played the diva, Swanson understood the game and her part in it. "During my years of obscurity," she writes, "the public had forgotten Gloria Swanson. In order to spring back to them in one leap, I had to have a bigger-than-life part. I had found it, all right. In fact, my present danger seemed to lie in the fact that I had played the part too well. I may not have got an Academy Award for it, but I had somehow convinced the world once again of that corniest of all theatrical clichés—that on very rare artistic occasions the actor actually becomes the part. Barrymore *is* Hamlet. Garbo *is* Camille. Swanson *is* Norma Desmond."

And so, for most people, she remains. Norma was her last major role, which has something to do with it. More to the point, Norma was Swanson's greatest role, the one that embodied all those aspects of celebrity the culture assiduously avoids until it's time to feed on the bones. *Sunset Blvd.* is about the quiet after the acclaim and the madness that can accompany it, the absolute egotism necessary to sustain stardom, and—worst of all—the idea that famous people need us more than we need them. Norma Desmond, forever ready for her closeup, represented the old rules of celebrity engagement at the exact moment that new rules were being written.

10.

Barbarians at the Gates: Brando Changes Everything

Every once in a while, there comes an event that breaks the history of a culture in half. A *before* and an *after* come into existence, with the *after* completely unimaginable during the *before,* and the *before* wholly untenable once there's an *after.* We are ushered into a new country, necessitating a new vocabulary. Once the Beatles arrived, for instance, it was impossible to readily remember what the world previously sounded like.

Additional examples are everywhere. The music establishment couldn't turn back the clock once Stravinsky premiered *The Rite of Spring* to a rioting Paris audience in 1913, nor could art unthink Picasso's Cubist breakthrough once *Les Demoiselles d'Avignon* had come out of his brush. In 1976, *Never Mind the Bollocks, Here's the Sex Pistols* changed what rock and roll could mean as surely as Joyce's *Ulysses* changed what literature could say in 1922. The shower scene in Alfred Hitchcock's *Psycho* transformed commercial cinema from a vehicle of narrative sentiment to a canvas of cathartic sensation; our children treat its progeny as date movies. You could play this game all day.

In 1951—a year after *Sunset Blvd.* killed off the silent star for good—the event was called Marlon Brando, and the movie was *A Streetcar Named Desire.* The modern, democratic era of stardom begins here, with the arrival of an inscrutable figure who seems to have stepped from the audience itself. The 1960s start here, too, because with Brando the search for meaning is no longer directed at the outer world but inward, toward some mysterious kernel within that will explain everything.

Or, rather, the 1960s start around here. What appeared to be an explosion was actually a series of widening detonations, beginning with Brando's first performances on the New York stage in the mid-1940s and peaking in 1955 with his Oscar for playing Terry Malloy in *On the Waterfront.* It's hard to pinpoint the exact moment Brando emerged as the most exciting, baffling, charismatic actor in the history of the cinema, but the September 29, 1951, premiere of the film version of *Streetcar* serves as a convenient epicenter. If nothing else, the film finally let the entire country experience what Broadway and New York already knew: that Brando was not only a new kind of performer but an entirely new kind of star.

Suddenly, those words meant separate things. "Performer" indicated what Brando did, "star" meant what he was, and his impact was equally, if differently, profound in both arenas. As an actor, he replaced presentation with essence, craft with intuition, preparation with spontaneity—or at least the illusion of spontaneity, since the young Brando did do his homework. On the surface, though, he appeared to possess none of the tools or skills commonly accepted as necessary for becoming an actor. He just *was*—or seemed to be. This was near to the dream flickering in every moviegoer's greedy, attention-starved heart: that you could just get up there, be yourself, and greatness would shine through. For a while, before he threw it back in our faces, Brando was our representative at Olympus.

As a star, he was even more conflicted. Brando shattered the rules of how to behave in public and to the public, spurning the offering of fame and in that spurning seeming to stand for a higher calling, noble and troubled and freshly attractive. Celebrity was worthless, he implied, and the kind of acting he was after wasn't the high-toned poetry of an Alfred Lunt or a Laurence Olivier but something earthy and real. Not entertainment, not even art, but Truth.

This is more than Garbo's "I want to be alone." This is an inarticulate contempt for celebrity that was redefined—to Brando's considerable confusion—as the next new wrinkle *in* celebrity. Was it his gift that drew us in, or his loathing (of himself, of Hollywood, of us gawking out there in the dark)? Ultimately, they're inextricable. Watching Brando act is like watching a man try to crawl out of his own skin.

This posture was disconcerting as well to audiences in the early 1950s—the battles over Brando's meaning were loud and impassioned—but it slowly absorbed into the mainstream as the youth audience grew in power over the next fifteen years and a counterculture emerged. It continues to be a defining stance. Brando's assumption that stardom is a burden both terrible and ridiculous is now the common coin of any actor who wants to be taken seriously. Not to adopt the position, consciously or otherwise, is to risk being taken for a lightweight. Think of our modern movie stars—Sean Penn and George Clooney, say. Who do you consider the "greater actor"? Why? At the bottom of your reasoning is Brando, the actor who rejected grace for torment, ease for grim seriousness, and celebrity for a greater engagement with the world—or at least the pose of engagement.

Was it coincidence that the late 1940s of his apprenticeship on Broadway and in Stella Adler's dramatic workshop at New York's New School were also the years during which Jackson Pollock became famous for explosively dripping paint onto canvas? Brando was an action painter in performance terms, setting up the parameters, the framing timbers, of a role and then letting himself be guided by instinct and chance. He reacted to the straitjacket of sudden fame much as Pollock did, too, not with alcohol but an equal measure of self-hatred, mercurial behavior, and womanizing. In a sense, he was luckier, since Hollywood was an easier and more forgiving target than the New York art world. As long as you made money, you could bait the moguls as much as you wanted.

So naturalistic was Brando's acting at first—so naked and accidental—that it could get embarrassing. The film critic Pauline Kael famously wrote of seeing him onstage for the first time in 1946's *Truckline Café* and thinking that a young player was having a seizure right there in front of the audience; then she understood it was performance and recalibrated her shock into thrill.

You hear that slack-jawed awe often in early descriptions of his acting. Brando arrived in New York after getting expelled from military school, and he signed up for the drama classes out of boredom. He wouldn't take the exercises seriously, hung out at the back of the theater chasing tail, and then there he was in a workshop presentation of a play called *Hannele's Way to Heaven,* and, in the words of classmate Mae Cooper, "People suddenly started looking at him. It gave you the chills, it was so good, so quiet, like the dawn of something great. . . . It was like suddenly you woke up and there's your idiot child playing Mozart. It made your hair stand on end."

Offstage, Brando continued to romp around New York, but he realized he had something special in him and, in a disorganized way, began to focus. He spent a lot of time at the movies, particularly classic revivals at the Museum of Modern Art. He took in a great number of Chaplin films, and it's intriguing to speculate on what he saw there, some wordless piece of persona he might possibly try to take into himself. (It didn't help, sadly, when the great comedian cast Brando years later in the almost unwatchable *A Countess from Hong Kong.*) He bought a pet raccoon and slept with any girl who looked at him twice.

His first Broadway part was as the son in the nostalgic hit *I Remember Mama,* and the line between *before* and *after* became immediately apparent. "The curtains went up," said one witness, "and there were [stars] Mady Christians and Oscar Homolka acting up a storm. Suddenly, in the back, down the stairs comes this kid munching an apple. Here were these two great professionals emoting, and then this kid who really looked like he *lived* upstairs in that house. He started to say his lines, and I said to myself, 'It's a stagehand. Someone's just wandered onstage, or maybe it's an understudy. The fellow that's supposed to play the part isn't here, and this guy, he's not acting.' "

He's not acting. Certainly not in any terms that were understood by audiences and the entertainment industry. So what was Brando doing? You have to look at the pieces of it. Where other actors articulated their roles or consciously tried to feel their way into them, he was naturally intuitive. His choices were wildly imaginative yet had the ring of honesty—they were novel but right. During a classroom exercise in which the teacher asked students to imitate chickens during a nuclear attack, most of the students ran around squawking their heads off. Brando calmly squatted and mimed laying an egg. After some confusion, they understood; of course that's what a chicken would do.

He insisted on a street-level realism in gestures, bearing, and—most celebrated and mocked—speech patterns, not through any thought-out philosophy of presentation but because to do otherwise was to play it false, and false was the enemy. (Later in his career, Brando would take the approach to extremes, refusing to learn his lines and taping them in hidden places all over the set. His rationale was that real people don't have their words memorized, so actors should subvert their way back to natural thought processes. Quixotic or just plain lazy, it drove crews and directors nuts.)

Brando didn't intend to rebuke centuries of accumulated stage wisdom, but because he was an outsider and because he didn't *aspire,* he saw no way but his. His fellow actor Martin Balsam said, "What you saw was the elements of truth being done up on that stage. He was being as honest, as close to reality as possible." "He's not acting," in other words. Which meant that he was one of us. Weirder still, he was the rare "one of us" who became famous while wanting nothing to do with fame. Who *was* this guy?

You could feel the thrill in your nerve endings, in part because of the actor's physicality and sheer animal beauty. When Brando performed a monologue in *Truckline Café* about killing his wife, the audience interrupted the play to cheer for two solid minutes. (Castmate Karl Malden said, "In fifty years in the business, I've never seen it happen before, and it's never happened since: He stopped the show.") And as rehearsals for the Broadway production of *Streetcar* wound on in the fall of 1947, anyone with eyes could see that Brando's Stanley was taking the play's focus away from Jessica Tandy's Blanche.

The play's director, Elia Kazan, said, "Hers seemed to be a performance; Marlon was living onstage. Jessie had every moment worked out carefully, with sensitivity and intelligence, and it was all coming together, just as [playwright Tennessee] Williams and I had expected and wanted. Marlon, working 'from the inside,' rode his emotion wherever it took him; his performance was full of surprises and exceeded what Williams and I had expected. A performance miracle was in the making."

The opening-night audience called the *Streetcar* cast back for endless encores, cheering and applauding, yet a funny thing happened. The next day's reviews virtually ignored Brando and focused instead on Tandy. While hers was a performance that could be described and understood in conventional terms, there were no models, no words, for what Brando was doing. Which suited him fine. After the opening performance, a friend called out, "You've become a star tonight." "Oh, shit, don't be ridiculous," he responded.

On his agent's advice, he turned down the offer of a seven-year MGM studio contract—tendered by Louis B. Mayer himself—and already professed to find the whole business of acting vaguely shameful. "The theater to me is just a job," Brando told the *New York Post* in 1948. "Just like slicing baloney. It's my favorite way of slicing baloney, the pay is better." (Gable had made similar protestations fifteen years earlier, but he did it defensively. Brando was the first star to go on the attack.) One night at a New York club, the emcee turned the spotlight on the new sensation and announced, "Ladies and gentlemen, Marlon Brando!" but Brando just sat there, wanly applauding himself and refusing to stand, refusing to play the game.

That set the course for the career, with Brando intermittently serious about acting while maintaining nothing but distaste for the business of stardom. He did go to Hollywood, first testing for an early version of *Rebel Without a Cause* that was never filmed, then immersing himself in the character of a paraplegic veteran for his 1950 debut film *The Men,* then moving on to the filming of *Streetcar,* this time with a Blanche, Vivien Leigh, equally willing to go out on an emotional limb. (A more consciously theatrical limb than Brando's—you could argue it was an entirely different tree—but the intensity matched what Brando was doing.) The *Rebel* test is available on a special-edition DVD of *Streetcar* and it's fascinating. Brando, clearly uncomfortable with the boilerplate dialogue, suddenly slams his fist on the table with a force that sends the sound levels into the red and seems to rattle the camera itself; later, he poses and answers questions for an offscreen studio employee with a polite smile that radiates hostility.

The problem was that Brando was never able to articulate what he wanted—out of life, out of acting—and rejected all attempts by anyone else to do it for him. A rebel to the core, he refused to play by whatever rules a given situation called for. To Hollywood, Brando extended a stiff middle finger, calling the two dominant gossip queens "the fat one" (Louella Parsons) and "the one with the hat" (Hedda Hopper). He drove down Sunset Blvd. with a prop arrow through his head. He told a reporter, "I'm not afraid of anything and I don't love money."

This was heresy. After an initial bout of curiosity, the industry responded in kind. One visitor to the *Streetcar* set was Humphrey Bogart, peering between the stage lights because he "wanted to get a pike at this kid Brando." Some months later, Bogart accepted the Best Actor Oscar (for *The African Queen*) that by rights should have gone to the kid. It was the first of several spankings administered by the Academy; many years later, Brando would opt to spank back.

There is plenty of evidence that he did care about his image. Brando always felt *Streetcar* typecast him as a Cro-Magnon—actually, his words were "a blue-jeaned slobbermouth"—and that the role was far from who he really was. "I was the antithesis of Stanley Kowalski," the actor wrote in his autobiography. "I was sensitive by nature and he was coarse." When the offer came to play Mark Antony in Joseph Mankiewicz's 1953 film of *Julius Caesar,* Brando jumped at the opportunity to remake his persona. He studied Shakespeare speeches on record and asked British stage legend John Gielgud, who was playing Cassius, to coach him through Antony's famous funeral oration.

The film and Brando's performance were triumphs, and the dismissive cynicism that had greeted his casting—comedians on TV mumbling their way through the Bard to big laughs—was replaced by a newfound respect from critics, audiences, and the film industry. It didn't take, because a respectful Brando was not the Brando anybody wanted. We wanted the animal, and maybe so did he. Six months later, there he was onscreen again as Johnny, the cruelly sexual leather-clad stud of *The Wild One,* and that was the image that burned into the culture's retinas. What are you rebelling against, Johnny? *Whaddya got?*

Brando himself never gave much more in the way of specifics. *The Wild One* is a lousy, simpleminded movie (and real motorcycle gearheads laughed themselves silly at the actor's outfit), but it may be the purest distillation of his early star persona: phallic and peremptory. Above all, it says that Marlon Brando doesn't need you to love him, and there may be no greater bad-boy turn-on than that.

If it were that easy, Brando might have faded into the woodwork with the other '50s relics. But he was also electrifying to watch, especially when he cared to be, which in the early days was often. The big movie of 1954 was *On the Waterfront,* and his performance remains one of the most artless yet exquisitely crafted in the history of the medium. The star plays Terry Malloy, a mook of an ex-boxer who has spent his entire life taking orders from people brighter than he. Over the course of the film he will become his own person, making his own choices.

What Brando does in *Waterfront* is shockingly organic, for Terry grows in stature before our eyes. It's as though we were watching a man slowly get to his feet after a life on his knees. The performance builds to the arc of the classic soliloquy, encrusted by years of parody but still honest and true when you encounter it in its proper turn. "You don't understand. I coulda had class. I coulda been a contender. I coulda been somebody. Instead of a bum. *Which is what I am.*" Everything in the movie leads up to that last sentence, the pivot on which

Terry's awakening turns, and you realize that the actor has sculpted the part this way from the beginning. In the simple, unforced clarity of his self-knowledge, Terry is finally a man, and what's most moving about the line is the quiet exhalation of relief with which he says it. No illusions.

That's what Brando's acting promised and every so often delivered: no illusions. Yet stardom and celebrity are illusions by definition, betraying a person's irreducible essence by confusing it with a bigger, more glamorous false front upon which that essence can be projected and played with. So what is a man like Brando to do with stardom? Abjure it, scorn it, eat until the bloat sets in. Take roles for the money and treat them like dirt, or give strange, wonderful performances that no one understands (see *Reflections in a Golden Eye, The Nightcomers, One-Eyed Jacks, The Missouri Breaks,* or any number of Brando-mysterioso acting jobs). Win an Oscar and shove it up the ass of the Motion Picture Academy, as he did when he sent Sacheen Littlefeather to the podium in 1973 to accept his statue for *The Godfather* and lecture America on its sins.

Still, celebrity clung to Brando, his initial gutter realism giving way to bizarre behavior. He was the first movie star as slow-motion car wreck, though he'd be far from the last. When he was on as an actor he had beauty and a knack for the brilliant, unexpected gesture. More important, for young audiences bored with the platitudes of Hollywood, Brando's arrogance was itself the gesture that was called for. There was an angry curiosity on our part, too—why does a man spurn the fame we all crave? Because he already has it? Because he knows it's worthless?

Crowds swarmed, most notably at the New York premiere of 1955's *Guys and Dolls,* where the star's automobile was almost crushed under the weight of the throng. In Paris, fans mobbed him and tore off his shirt. He began to grow paranoid. "His eyes changed," said a friend. "No more shyness, no more vulnerability. He looked at everybody with a lot of confidence. But also pity too. Like he felt sorry for you."

Soon enough, Brando attracted imitators. How could any idealistic young actor absorb performances so visceral, that seemed to cut through the dullness of the mainstream with such authority, and not want to do that? The star himself was upset by the idea of followers, and it's disturbing to read of his callous treatment of the young James Dean, who literally begged Brando for attention shortly after he arrived in Hollywood. Brando would listen to Dean leave long messages on his answering machine and make fun of them to friends, and when the younger actor hit it big in *East of Eden,* Brando told a reporter, "Mr. Dean appears to be wearing my last year's wardrobe and using my last year's talent."

He had a point, though, because the younger actor copied his idol's every mannerism. Brando played the bongos; so did Dean. Brando rode a motorcycle; so did Dean. The imposture extended to wearing the same kinds of clothes and even dating one of Brando's cast-off girlfriends, Maila Nurmi, the future Vampira of late-night television. At one Hollywood party, Brando coolly watched Dean enter and predicted to a friend that he'd fling his coat on the floor "because I do it." And Dean did.

Accordingly, Dean's own acting style proved to be a twitchy, neurotic variation on Brando's brooding power. It's completely fitting that *Rebel Without a Cause* finally got made in 1955 with the younger actor at its center, because, in truth, Marlon Brando was too mature for the role of a conflicted high school student. His are not the agonies of youth, even in a youth hit like *The Wild One,* but the battling impulses of a man. Dean, by contrast, realizes that the misery of *Rebel*'s Jim Stark comes from not knowing who he is yet. Even at twenty-four, he let us see right through to the contorted little boy flailing on the floor. Brando always seemed to know who he was even when his characters didn't; the difference was that he couldn't put it into words and considered any attempt to do so to be useless, fraudulent, foolhardy. The stuff of celebrity, not the stuff of acting—let alone the stuff of life. Life's what's not on the cue cards. There's a certainty to Brando's art if not his expression, whereas Dean was all about uncertainty and his inability to measure up. The culture needed and responded to them both.

Yet it's Brando's DNA that still courses through our young actors and movie stars, especially the ones who profess to take it seriously. Not until St. Marlon said, in effect, *You can't talk about this* did the posture of acting as sacred macho mystery come into play, the old Shakespearean player's romanticism imbued with a sexy new danger. His children are legion, taking difficult roles and building them from the guts outward: De Niro and Pacino in the 1970s, Daniel Day-Lewis and Sean Penn in the 1990s, Edward Norton and Leonardo DiCaprio and Ryan Gosling today. When *The Godfather* was released in 1972, producer Albert Ruddy looked at the supporting cast of Pacino, Robert Duvall, James Caan, and admitted that "Marlon created these guys."

Other stars took only the parts they wanted, like Steve McQueen's approximation of Brando's he-man cool, or Jack Nicholson's live-wire unpredictability, or the sneer of the young Elvis Presley (a major Brando idolater who carried the mutant strain into a new arena). Others still just ripped off the wardrobe and continue to do so. If the character of Stanley Kowalski dialed American male performance back to square one, his blue jeans and tight T-shirt did the same for fashion.

That was the unthinking genius of what Brando wrought. Because the pieces of him were so democratic, so within reach—everything but the art, and there you were on your own—he seeded the future. Moreover, by so fiercely embodying the present (the impatient modernity of postwar America as well as the lightning moment of performance), he created the notion of a dated, out-of-it cultural past, and *that* was a notion that grew until it swallowed the mainstream. Either you got what Brando was about, or you were gone, baby, gone. Here was a whole new thing—the establishment of a mass alternative defined primarily by age. Brando was the fork in the road, the line in the sand. Through him, the counterculture.

It didn't happen overnight, of course. The reigning culture—the mainstream pop industry—kept putting out movies and creating personalities, but the factory machinery was starting to rust. Divested of their theaters after the 1948 court decree, their audiences staying home and watching TV, the studios retrenched in fear. A-level movies suffered from gigantism—Cinerama and its little brothers—while the Bs often took the risks and brokered new faces. An edgy actor like Richard Widmark could be born in a high-end suspense thriller like 1947's *Kiss of Death,* playing a giggling cretin who pushes an old lady downstairs in a wheelchair, then move on to classic '50s noirs like the London-set *Night and the City* (1950) and Sam Fuller's *Pickup on South Street* (1953), playing flawed, heroic jerks and putting his thumb squarely on what no longer worked with the classic good-guy archetype (idealism, for one thing). But no one thought of Widmark as a star in the traditional fan-magazine sense. If nothing else, his smile was too scary—the sincere welcome of a barracuda.

Widmark played more typical heroes, too—he's excellent as the health services doctor tracking down plague carrier Jack Palance in *Panic in the Streets* (1950)—but he was made for the avid moral uncertainties of noir. Without setting out to do so, Widmark became a rebel star of the 1950s, as opposed to the status quo stars who anchored popular entertainment. Status quo stars were the figures who played by the old rules and who provoked uncomplicated responses of desire and emulation: the Doris Days and Grace Kellys, the Gregory Pecks and Tony Curtises and Rock Hudsons.

There was a youth wing, consisting of Sandra Dee and Tab Hunter, among others, and there were the old prewar Olympians, fighting marginalization in ways both creative and misguided. To watch Joan Crawford's 1950s movies is an often jaw-dropping object lesson in a Great Star refusing to acknowledge that the culture—and her assigned meaning in that culture—has irrevocably changed. 1953's *Torch Song* is Joan's response to Bette Davis's success in *All About Eve,* yet where *Eve* is largely about fears of aging and being discarded on the part of Margo Channing/Bette Davis, *Torch Song* denies time's passage for a rococo romance with a blind pianist, extreme Technicolor, and a rousing, eyeball-scorching blackface musical number. This is star obliviousness as high camp.

Other prewar stars understood that to survive as anything more than a curiosity, they had to break their own mold and redefine what they meant to the culture. James Stewart, as mentioned earlier, bravely plumbed the neuroses under his cheery all-American exterior. Bogart took a flyer on the part of a drunken mail boat captain in *The African Queen* (1951) and won an Oscar. Katharine Hepburn moved into spinster roles, exploring the drama of a stiff-backed woman learning to yield in movies like *African Queen, Summertime* (1955), and *The Rainmaker* (1956). After her *All About Eve* success, Davis played larger-than-life divas of Hollywood (*The Star,* 1952) and history (Elizabeth I in *The Virgin Queen,* 1955; Catherine the Great in *John Paul Jones,* 1959). She eventually and grudgingly joined Crawford in the camp horror *Whatever Happened to Baby Jane?* (1962), a movie that is very much about the madness of stars who don't understand that their moment has passed. Cary Grant and Fred Astaire got by on younger actresses and their own preposterous charm. Cagney saw the writing on the wall, retiring in 1963.

The studios still considered themselves in the business of building new stars, and there were more than enough actors happy to be built. Yet the demands of maintaining a two-dimensional studio star persona in an increasingly three-dimensional postwar universe created friction, rebellion, dissonance. The psychic heavy lifting it took the handsome, gentle, gay Roy Scherer Jr. to become the handsome, gentle, straight Rock Hudson was invisible and immense, but he put up with it to the point of entering into an arranged marriage with his agent's secretary after *Confidential* magazine threatened to reveal his sexuality in the weeks before *Giant* was released in 1955.

Hudson agreed because he was the go-along type, he wanted to be in pictures, and the system still emphasized toeing the line. Said actress Piper Laurie, a colleague of Hudson's, "When we weren't making movies, we were in school or on the road promoting the movies. We were told before going on these trips or being interviewed that we had to act a certain way, dress a certain way, say certain things, and not say certain things. . . . You could not discuss politics. It was all very prudish and reactionary. We couldn't be ourselves. That was one of Rock's problems all his life. He was manufactured from the day he got out there and he was under that pressure his entire life."

"We couldn't be ourselves," the lady says. The executives would have replied, *Who wants to see you be yourself?* The studio's job was to fit new performers into old archetypes, and if the fit was off, it was the actor who got trimmed. Yet there were enough performers with the strength of will and personality to push back, either through the fresh energy they brought to their roles, varying degrees of rebelliousness offscreen, or some combination of both. Marlon Brando was the first but he was also *sui generis*—few were going to follow him that far out onto the ledge. (And just in case they thought about it, there was that brutal 1957 *New Yorker* profile of Brando by a young Truman Capote titled "The Duke in His Domain," perfectly illustrating the dangers of "being yourself" in front of the press and/or diminutive geniuses with razor-sharp pens.)

Certain male actors predated Brando onscreen and subsequently developed spiky, intelligent personas as the 1950s deepened: Kirk Douglas as a vicious reporter antihero in Billy Wilder's *Ace in the Hole* (1951), or Burt Lancaster moving like America's ulcerated conscience through *From Here to Eternity* (1953), then playing the powerful Broadway gossip columnist in *Sweet Smell of Success* (1957) as a repressed incestuous freak. Robert Mitchum, blowing off his pot bust and playing a homicidal preacher in *The Night of the Hunter* (1955). Yes, Mitchum also played a Marine shipwrecked with a nun (Deborah Kerr) in 1957's *Heaven Knows, Mr. Allison,* but that was the point—the rebel star chose, or seemed to choose, his own destiny.

The aim was to break through the era's stifling decorum and have a little fun doing so. James Dean seemed headed that way before his death in a 1955 car crash, although you wonder how long he could have kept playing an exposed adolescent nerve before the novelty wore off. His role in the star pantheon was to be the first baby boomer star martyr, cut down by cruel fate—the embodiment of the quote "Live fast, die young, and leave a good-looking corpse," which most people think Dean said. Actually, it's a quote from the juvenile delinquent played by John Derek in 1949's *Knock on Any Door.* The words move to where they best fit, yet who would James Dean have become if he'd lived? An even more fragmented Brando? A counterculture hero, a tarnished wreck, a numbed survivor? I think the 1960s would not have been kind to him, nor he to them.

More '50s rebels: Elvis made his back-to-back best films, *Jailhouse Rock* (1957) and *Kid Creole* (1958), before disappearing under a wave of hair dye and cookie-cutter schlock, the movie industry taming what the music business couldn't. Frank Sinatra at last came into his full power as an actor, a star, and an interpreter of song; after a decade and a half in the business, his supporting Oscar for *From Here to Eternity* silenced the jeers of those who thought he was just a skinny fad from a bad neighborhood.

On the contrary, through the mediums of film and the new long-playing record album—put it on and settle in with your honey—Sinatra became a critical arbiter of cool whose movie choices could be daring. The heroin addict of *The Man with the Golden Arm* (1955) is one thing, the presidential assassin of *Suddenly* (1954) quite another. With Frank, the attitude was the persona and the come-on, too—a weary awareness, a refusal to be emotionally engaged, a belief in the momentary pleasures of a held note or a bedded dame. Anyone who doubts Sinatra's studied disdain for the era that most rewarded him needs to see Vincente Minnelli's *Some Came Running* (1958), in which his postwar novelist returns to a hometown that's a viper's nest of hypocrisy.

Jerry Lewis, the national id, was even more extreme. If the 1950s were about conforming, Lewis was the most outré example of the joys and dangers of letting it all hang out, and he was enshrined and mocked as everything the culture was desperately not. He was low-brow, impulsive, repulsive, *ex*pulsive, loud, bratty, abrasive; above all, he was enjoying himself. The comedian had had Dean Martin with him as ballast for years, but after the team broke up in 1956, Lewis embarked on a series of movies that are nearly miraculous in their ability to bend the laws of physics and humor. Of course he got no respect from the mainstream, yet the running gag that they love Jerry in France is really just a reluctant admission that there are depths of meaning to his comedy we're unable or unwilling to plumb. The idea behind Lewis—that you can never go too far in comedy—is one that's necessary but still culturally disreputable, as Sacha Baron Cohen has discovered to his pain and profit in the current era.

The most interesting rebel stars of the 1950s, though, were the women—tough noir babes like Gloria Grahame and melodramatic troupers like Susan Hayward, but also a youth star like the underrated Natalie Wood, whose performance in *Rebel Without a Cause* is subtler than Dean's and who created with 1961's heartbreaking *Splendor in the Grass* a female *Rebel,* and as such a rather more dangerous proposition. Wood's persona is the girl overflowing with a vibrancy that no one sees—certainly not the grown-ups and sometimes not even the boy—and whose playing is thus touched with nervousness and melancholy. When Wood's Deanie finally came unglued in *Splendor*'s bathroom scene, repeatedly shrieking through a terrifying smile, "I'm a *good* girl, Mama!," she spoke to the emotional panic of young women in the Eisenhower era, who were offered endless freedoms and punished for taking them.

Elizabeth Taylor took those freedoms and laughed in everyone's face. She began the decade as Spencer Tracy's pert daughter in *Father of the Bride* (1950) and ended it in full hypersexualized howl as Maggie the Cat in *Cat on a Hot Tin Roof* (1958) and Catherine Holly in *Suddenly Last Summer* (1959), the latter so threatening that she had to be lobotomized by Katharine Hepburn. Both those films were from the pen of Tennessee Williams, and Taylor was a key Williams woman, orgasmic and frustrated and mad as hell. That deep, deep well of carnal knowledge is there as early as 1951's *A Place in the Sun,* in which her delicate debutante—really, the nicest girl in town—pulls Montgomery Clift to her and whispers huskily in his ear, "Tell Mama. Tell Mama all."

Taylor's star persona quickly rippled off the screen into the gossip columns with her serial marriages (four in the 1950s alone) and tragedies (third husband Mike Todd's death in a plane crash; her own hospitalization and near death from pneumonia) and depredations (stealing Eddie Fisher from Debbie Reynolds). Very much the Angelina Jolie of her era, Taylor gave good copy, all the more so for not seeming to care who wrote what about her. Her personal drama became more entertaining than her movies—because it appeared to be more truthful—and it affected both the roles she played onscreen and the larger role she played in the pop circus.

She was the era's wanton, a beautiful voluptuary who did as she pleased, acted out our hidden desires, shocked the media's nosy neighbors, and whose glamour grew with each fresh sin. Taylor was an old-school star—in the sense that she was unlike us, everything we dared not be—but she was old-school unleashed. Even if the studio system hadn't been crumbling from within, she would have toppled it. She came close to doing so anyway when *Cleopatra* (1963) ran absurdly over budget, Twentieth Century-Fox responded with a boardroom coup, and Taylor ran off with leading man Richard Burton—husband numbers five and six, since she married (and divorced) him twice.

Then there's Marilyn, so simple and so complicated a figure that she's hardly visible for the static. Despite her titanic fame during life and cult status after death, Monroe remains a transitional figure. In her we see the sexy studio starlet struggling to adjust to a changing culture's changing attitudes about art and celebrity. She was just as manufactured as Rock Hudson—made-up name, hair dyed and teased into spun sugar, elocution lessons—but she became big enough to understand that she was bigger than her studio, and that someone *that* big should be the author of her fame rather than its victim. So, in the mid-1950s, Monroe traveled to New York, studied at the Actors Studio, married an intellectual Jewish playwright—himself a star of a world of high culture and urban drive—and tried to become her own person. Whatever that was.

In any event, a "real person" was not what we wanted from her. We wanted the Monroe the movies promised us: big tits and wide eyes, the irresistible combination of innocence and experience. Monroe quickly came to fill the dimensions of a crucial '50s male fantasy, the virgin who knows how. Everything in Monroe's voice, face, eyes projects naïveté; everything below the neck promises sexual obliteration. The mystery in Marilyn's persona lies in how the two halves connect. What buttons do you have to push for the girl to become a woman? In

The Seven Year Itch (1955), that's the specific concern of Tom Ewell, a cringing married-with-children executive stuck with a half-clad Monroe over the course of one long, hot Manhattan weekend.

As directed by Billy Wilder, the movie's a sniggering dirty joke in which Ewell is the subject and Monroe the irresistible and possibly movable object. It's not her best movie, but it's definitely the one that encapsulates what she meant to the era: the threat of unbuttoned lust in a buttoned-up time. Taylor meant something similar, but because she seemed to control her own sexuality rather than be controlled by it, her movies are bawdy dramas. Monroe mostly made comedies in which, more often than not, she's the joke—the child who doesn't realize she has a woman's bodacious body.

Only two movies she starred in are really any good—*Some Like It Hot* and *Gentlemen Prefer Blondes*—and only the latter was made at Fox. (And that was a Howard Hawks film before it was anything else.) Monroe had the misfortune to be a sex goddess at a studio ill-equipped to deal with sex, no matter that studio head Darryl F. Zanuck treated the lower ranks of starlets as his personal happy hunting ground. Fox's leading ladies tended to be blond and perky, like Alice Faye in the 1930s, and Betty Grable in the 1940s. Monroe was heir to the tradition but slinky, breathy, frankly sensual.

Discovering her as twenty-year-old magazine model Norma Jeane Baker in 1946, Fox gave Monroe a six-month contract and a new name, wasted her in nothing roles, and dropped her. She went back to modeling, shot some nude photos for ready cash money, then lucked into a short-term Universal contract. A break here, a break there, and suddenly she had two small 1950 parts that stopped their respective movies in their tracks: the crime boss's mistress in *The Asphalt Jungle* and the wannabe actress—her career "rising in the east like the sun"—in *All About Eve*. Zanuck, kicking himself, re-signed her to a seven-year contract and *still* couldn't figure out what to do with her. She was cast as a psychotic hotel babysitter in *Don't Bother to Knock* (1952) and a murderous femme fatale in *Niagara* (1953), both severe misunderstandings of her gifts.

Monroe, it turned out, meant more off the screen than on. It has been pointed out by others that still photographs distill her appeal more clearly than the movies, and it was a pair of photos—those 1949 nude shots—that put her over the top as a star in 1952. Or, rather, it was Monroe's response to the scandal that was novel and appealing, the Fox PR department in a panic because the photos, reprinted on a calendar, had resurfaced just in time for Monroe's first major films, and Marilyn saying, in effect, why not tell the truth? I needed the money and, anyway, it's not like I killed somebody.

Five years earlier, her career would have been over before it began. A different actress might have been packed up and sent home. Monroe's response, instead, won her notoriety and then sympathy. "Didn't you have anything on?" someone asked. "I had the radio on," she replied, and that quote, reported or tweaked or invented in *Time,* set the sexpot Candide persona in concrete. That she was dating and soon would marry New York Yankee Joe DiMaggio buttressed her image as someone more natural than manufactured—a creature who didn't quite follow the rules of the entertainment industry, or was unable to, because she was either dumb or unconcerned, and either way a good match for another of nature's wonders, the star baseball player.

He left her, it should be noted, over another photograph. Filming of the iconic subway-grate scene in *The Seven Year Itch* brought New York's East Side to a standstill and every news photographer out into the open at two in the morning to snap Marilyn with her skirt billowing up over her head. It was a PR orgy and probably planned that way; director Wilder ended up reshooting the sequence on a Hollywood soundstage and that's the version in the movie. DiMaggio watched from the sidelines livid with rage as the passing subways blew his wife's skirt up again and again for the cameras, Monroe laughing—*laughing!*—with hedonistic delight, playing for every one of those bulging lenses, and if getting it on with the entire world isn't cheating on your husband, then what is? The couple fought bitterly that night, announced their divorce two weeks later. When *Itch* was released the following year, a fifty-foot-tall photo of Monroe in the subway-grate pose towered over Times Square. Poor, conflicted DiMaggio. He was living with every man's fantasy and he only wanted her to be a wife.

Monroe is a throwback to those silent stars who came out of horrific childhoods seemingly undamaged, even triumphant. She never knew her father, and her mother was in the asylum by the time Norma Jeane was seven. She lived in orphanages, foster homes, and with friends of family from the age of nine. At one boardinghouse, no one believed the favored tenant had molested her. And so on. Was she a dumb blonde or just numbed by disaster? These unforgiving facts and more connect with her suicide in 1962 at the age of thirty-six: the unhappy marriages, the tales of presidential affairs, the trauma that acting was for her, a sense of restlessly wanting to prove herself as more than the fifty-foot Marilyn (although she loved being that, too)—all these things conspire to have turned Monroe, after her death, into the chief celebrity victim of twentieth-century popular culture. In this construct, we used her—we and Darryl Zanuck and the Kennedys and the Actors Studio and all our filthy little fantasies—and she died for those sins.

That's just another narrative, of course, one meant to explain a death and a life that aren't so easily resolved. It's also very good business, as Elton John and whoever makes those commemorative plates and bottles of Marilyn Merlot will tell you. What we don't understand, we commodify. Still, ask it: Who *was* Monroe? Not an actress in the usual sense, since performing in real time, as opposed to a photo shoot, filled her with terror. She showed up hours late on the set, repeatedly flubbed the simplest lines. The ballerina Irina Baronova, who knew her during the London filming of *The Prince and the Showgirl* (1957), observed that Monroe "has a quite unconscious but basic resistance to acting. She loves to show herself, loves to be a star, loves all the success side of it, but to be an actress is something she does not want at all. They were wrong to try to make one of her. Her wit, her adorable charm, her sex appeal, her bewitching personality—are all part of *her*, not necessarily to be associated with any art or talent." John Huston, who directed her last completed movie, *The Misfits* (1961), said, "She had no techniques. It was all the truth. It was only Marilyn."

Was Monroe the rare star, like Shirley Temple, who's exactly as we see her? That doesn't wash, either. What needs to be reclaimed is her collaboration in and enjoyment of the business of self-reinvention. Monroe remains more than a victim, more than a found object of helpless sexuality. Instead, she projects the struggle of the naturally sensual woman in a culture and an industry predisposed to distrust and control her. *Gentlemen Prefer Blondes* (1953) and *Some Like It Hot* (1959) both put the matter bluntly. How can a woman get what she wants (money in *Gentlemen,* love in *Some Like It Hot,* security in either case) without being punished for it? More than that, *why* is a woman punished for it? I'm not submitting a brief for Monroe as a protofeminist heroine; Gloria Steinem, who has written with acid sympathy about the star, wouldn't have that and probably neither would Monroe. (She once said, "I have always had a talent for irritating women since I was fourteen.")

That said, Marilyn spent her career being treated as an object ("That's the trouble, a sex symbol becomes a thing—I just hate to be a thing"), and these two movies are about a woman trying to become a subject, either by adorably shaking down the entire male gender for whatever diamonds she can get or by pulling herself out of despair against all better judgment to trust her heart (to a man disguised as a woman disguised as Cary Grant, no less). The first film is a comedy, the second a comedy in which Monroe's dilemma is embedded as a near tragedy; she has never seemed so delightful as in *Gentlemen* and never so sad, so exhausted, as in *Hot.*

There's the arc of a career for you: Monroe may have tried to define herself, by herself, until the effort just wore her out. She was a pretty girl in a still photograph who had the good fortune and the bad luck to move.

11.

The New Machine: Small Screen, Small Gods

Part of the reason Marilyn Monroe was a movie star was that she kept the original compact of commercial cinema as established in the early silent era. She was larger than life, overabundant—an object of desire so opulent that only CinemaScope could contain her. In other words, she was too big for television, and that was a relief to the men who made the movies.

There were three seismic shocks that transformed popular culture in the decade and a half following World War II. Brando's recalibration of male performance and Hollywood stardom was one. The rock-and-roll explosion was the second. The unstoppable rise of TV in the late 1940s and early '50s was the third, and without question it was the most transformative.

The essence of the broadcast revolution is simple: it offered a literal home theater. No longer did you have to go out to see the stars and be entertained. Now they came to you. This affected the kinds of stars who were created from the 1950s on, in the sense that the people you let into your house are different from the people you pay to see in a theater. They're more like you and me, for one thing, which also means you and I are more like the stars. For decades—until, arguably, the arrival of nighttime soaps in the 1970s and '80s—the most celebrated figures on the small screen evoked not glamour but ordinariness. They acted out comic and dramatic versions of our own dilemmas, or they filled history with life-sized personalities rather than the bigger-than-life stars of film.

The prototype figure of movie westerns, for instance, is John Wayne, subsuming genre into his own drawling, super-cowboy persona. The TV correlative is James Arness, whose celebrity was never larger than his role as Marshal Matt Dillon on *Gunsmoke*. Fess Parker, Carroll O'Connor, and Elizabeth Montgomery weren't stars so much as their characters were—Davy Crockett, Archie Bunker, Samantha Stevens. Audiences still went to the movies to see the people in them. They watched TV to see the shows. The first was adoration, the second ownership.

(That said, it's worth questioning who owned who. The fundamental business transaction propelling commercial television was and is fundamentally different from that governing movies and other localized mass audience events such as theater, concerts, and professional sports. With the latter, we're the consumers, the entertainment is the commodity we want to consume, and the ticket price is the unit of exchange. With network TV, the transaction looks similar but isn't. What in fact is being bought? Follow the money. Advertisers are the consumers, the price of a thirty-second spot is the unit of exchange, and we, the desirable viewers, are the product being purchased. The TV shows? They're just bait.)

The rapidity with which television became the dominant entertainment force in American culture is unparalleled. It took eighty years for the telephone to reach 35 million households. Radio was around for a quarter of a century before it achieved the same penetration. With

TV, it took a decade. Contributing factors to the medium's outrageous success included the nation's sudden shift from a wartime economy to a consumer economy; the ensuing rise of a consumer culture in which, more than ever, you were what you owned; the nesting impulses of millions of young Americans newly safe from overseas threat; and the related mass exodus from cities to a newfangled idea called the suburbs.

This final development proved to be crucial. No longer were urban entertainment centers—movie houses, theaters, arenas—easily available to families. On the other hand, there was this box in your house that brought everything right to you. Most families got rid of their living-room pianos, signifiers of old culture, and made the new machine the focus of their communal spaces and their lives.

Everything lined up. The baby boom delivered 76 million new audience members to the small-screen medium from 1946 to 1961, setting the stage for the supremacy of kiddie shows, TV westerns, and youth marketing. The money was there, and so was the desire to lavish it on one's home. Consumer spending on appliances and home furnishings increased 240 percent in the five years from 1946 to 1951, and two-thirds of purchasers of new TV sets identified themselves as "middle income."

By contrast, film attendance plummeted, from 90 million in annual ticket sales in 1948 to 51 million only four years later. We were getting what we needed, but it wasn't at the movies. The glamorous life that audiences had paid to see inhabited by Bette Davis and Cary Grant was suddenly theirs for the purchase, no longer on the screen but everywhere in the culture that surrounded it. Who needed the fantasy when you had a window on the world that was, in a manner very different from the movies, a window back onto ourselves?

Did TV have a primordial star—its very own Florence Lawrence? Not in the sense of someone anonymous suddenly acquiring a name and in that process changing everything. The rules of modern celebrity had already been established, and, besides, in the early days it was the technology that exerted the fascination. Television itself was the star. It didn't matter what was on—game shows, variety, wrestling, a test pattern. People watched.

If you had to pick a first, though, the honor might go to Helen Parrish, a former Hollywood child star who served as emcee for NBC's *Hour Glass* variety show, launched in May 1946. Or Jackie Robinson, whose Brooklyn Dodgers battled the New York Yankees in the 1947 World Series, the first postseason contest to be televised and a watershed moment for the new medium. (It wasn't the 3.8 million people who tuned in to the games during October, many via barroom televisions; it was the hundreds of thousands of TV sets that flew off the shelves in November.)

Yet there *was* a galvanizing personality, and his name was Uncle Miltie. On June 8, 1948, NBC premiered *Texaco Star Theater*, a variety show featuring a weekly rotation of comic hosts: Henny Youngman, Jack Carter, Morey Amsterdam, and Milton Berle. (Radio giant Fred Allen was asked but didn't want to commit to the infant medium.) Borscht belters all, they were New York entertainers with the flopsweat of years of vaudeville and nightclubs on their brows. They worked hard, but Berle worked hardest. By September, he was the show's permanent host. By the following May, he was on the cover of *Time*. They called him "Mr. Television," the star as a standard for the medium itself.

As standard, it was proudly crass. Every Tuesday night at eight, Berle would dress in women's clothing, schpritz water, fall down, bray his idiot guffaw, uncork wheezy one-liners, and audiences loved him—loved his manic *tummler* energy and willingness to do anything for a laugh. "It's not lappy enough," he'd hector his writers. "You gotta put it in their laps or they won't understand it." The show pulled in 5 million viewers—a full 75 percent of the total viewing audience—and urban legends circulated about New York's water pressure dropping precipitously during commercial breaks, the city going to the bathroom en masse. Berle had been a child star in the silent era (he appeared with Mary Pickford in the second *Tess of the Storm Country*) and had never stopped working in vaudeville, clubs, hotels, any room that would have him. Like the stage players who dared to try acting in silent pictures, he couldn't afford to be a snob, and, anyway, it's usually the case that the strivers who never got on top in an older medium are among the first to conquer the new.

And, too, early television was primarily an East Coast phenomenon—half of the TV sets in the country were in the greater New York area. The language Berle spoke was well understood by all those families in the city and the suburbs. He was Mendel Berlinger, a Jewish kid from the Lower East Side, with roots identical or similar to much of his audience. And he'd made good, like they were doing. He was called "Uncle Miltie" because a lot of his viewers probably *had* an uncle like him—loudmouthed, funny, given to broads and broad jokes. He was to the variety format what the early wave of ethnic shows like *The Goldbergs, I Remember Mama,* and *The Life of Riley* were to situation comedy—a reminder of home.

Berle burned fast, though. *Texaco Star Theater* was number one in the ratings from 1948 to 1951, and by the end of his run, a full third of all TV programming consisted of similar "vaudeo" shows. At the beginning, CBS had quickly counterattacked by launching *Toast of the Town,* a variety hour hosted by Broadway columnist Ed Sullivan. Sullivan was a curious case of an anti-star star, a figure so knock-kneed, so charisma free, that audiences and media commentators came to adore him in all his contorted woodenness. Comedian Alan King said, "Ed does nothing, but he does it better than anyone else on television."

In fact, Sullivan had the booking instincts of a master showman, and he knew what sold, whether it be Elvis Presley, the Beatles, or Topo Gigio the Italian Mouse. The very first *Toast of the Town* featured Dean Martin and Jerry Lewis, Broadway composers Rodgers and Hammerstein, and pianist Eugene List—a more broadly appealing party than Berle was hosting over on NBC and one that played to the audience that was slowly widening beyond the coasts and into the heartland. Berle was off the air by 1956. *The Ed Sullivan Show* (as it was renamed in 1955) rolled on until 1971, by which point Sullivan himself, fusty, smart, and beloved, had become the real Mr. Television.

No one wanted to *be* him, though—or Berle, or any of the other radio and film personalities who began to fill the programming schedule as their other careers dried up. At one point, *Look* magazine put "TV's Old-New Stars" on the cover: Fred Allen, Jack Benny, Bob Hope, Groucho Marx, Eddie Cantor, Jimmy Durante, Ken Murray, Ed Wynn, Bobby Clark, and Burns and Allen, all veterans of vaudeville, radio, and movies. Jackie Gleason was another face familiar from the corners of the movie screen, but as the host of *Cavalcade of Stars* he was a Berle without the sharp edges, and his idea to spin one of his sketches, about a blowhard New York City bus driver and his wife—more "real people"—into its own half-hour show was inspired. One turned on the television for entertainment rather than more complicated notions of glamour and transference, and here was comfort in known quantities.

All of which paves the way for Lucille Ball and *I Love Lucy*. The requirements are in place: an actress coming off a busy film career (seventy-five movies at four different studios) in which she never quite made it to the A-list; a character not swank but middle class, living in a dumpy New York apartment building with dumpy best friends. Ball was forty, so the movie thing was over, but she held a good hand of cards. She had begun to refine her gifts for comedy on a radio show called *My Favorite Husband,* which ran from 1948 to 1951, and she had a husband, Cuban-born bandleader Desi Arnaz, who was a fine comic actor himself and a sharp business mind.

CBS was convinced the show would fail. The network asked that the Arnazes bear most of the production costs and in return gave them full rights, a decision that would make the couple millionaires. Most crucially for posterity, the network allowed Ball to stay in Los Angeles and film the show rather than air it live from New York, with the result that *I Love Lucy* remains a classic to modern viewers on TV, DVD, and Hulu long after Berle and other unpreserved legends have been forgotten to all but cultural historians. Ball even hired a respected Hollywood cinematographer, Karl Freund, who came up with a lighting scheme and three-camera approach that remains in use on sitcoms to this day. In essence, she applied filmmaking professionalism to a ragged new medium, taking the first step in the TV industry's eventual move west.

Yet Ball's greatest stroke of genius was what she did in front of the cameras. Following the misadventures of Lucy Ricardo, stage-struck wife of New York bandleader Ricky Ricardo, *I Love Lucy* was straight-up situation farce, put over by pros with enthusiasm and expert timing. The real novelty was that Ball, a former movie star, was playing a woman who desperately wanted to *be* a star, and whose cracked attempts to make it into the spotlight always went awry, always geometrically progressed to a madness beyond her control, always sent her *wahhhhhh*ing back home to Ricky chastened and punished for our viewing pleasure.

I Love Lucy was explicitly about the distance between the average person and fame. The show acknowledged the hopes, resentments, egotism, and frustration central to the audience experience in the age of celebrity—the tension between worshipping the beautiful image and wanting to be worshipped. It just turned that tension into comedy, simultaneously feeding and defusing it. Lucy tries to horn in on Ricky's TV audition by disguising herself as a clown; Lucy takes dance lessons from a French smoothie to get into the club act; Lucy does herself up as the Maharincess of Franistan to get Ricky some publicity. In her crazy need to be seen, how different is she from the woman who jumped out of the giant *Gone with the Wind* book into David O. Selznick's lap?

It went further than Ricky's club show. In various episodes, Lucy tries to write a steamy novel, write a play, become a sculptress, appear in a commercial selling Vitameatavegamin. She doesn't just want to be somebody, she wants to be Somebody. A contender.

This could be tragic, but because it's Lucy, hectic and naive, we laugh. Still, which Lucy are we talking about, Ricardo or Ball? One of the reasons the show plays so well, even today, is that the matter's left unresolved. Actress and character couldn't have been more different, obviously. Ball was a successful TV star and businesswoman, a

Hollywood survivor whose sweetest revenge came in 1957, when her production company Desilu bought one of her old film studios, RKO, for $6.2 million. By contrast, Ricardo was an adorable ditz, whose ambitions and crashing, ridiculous disappointments fit neatly into a weekly half hour of comedy.

Yet to the culture, Ball and Ricardo were the same, or, rather, Ball receded behind Ricardo, suppressing glamour to play "real." She understood where others didn't that the new idiot box was too small for movie-size celebrity. Every episode of *The Loretta Young Show* may have begun with the long-established screen star swirling through a doorway in a couture gown, but the moment was as silly as it was grand—silly *because* it was grand—and was mercilessly parodied by TV comedians. By dressing down and playing middle class, Ball approached us on our own terms.

The confusion over which Lucy we actually loved deepened during the second season, when both actress and character became pregnant and in fact appeared to give birth the same day. On January 19, 1953, the episode "Lucy Goes to the Hospital" aired to an audience of 44 million (President-elect Eisenhower's inauguration the following day got only 29 million) and Ball had her baby delivered by caesarean section in a Hollywood hospital. Which baby was the actual one? It depended on whom you asked. Ball and Arnaz had Desi Arnaz Jr. The public had Little Ricky.

This was a different sort of stardom, established over the long arc of a TV series and with the lines between player and played hopelessly blurred. It fed a different hunger, too. With movie stars, the investment was in an actor's persona, the supposedly "real" person behind the characters he or she played. People went to see the *idea* of Humphrey Bogart or Rock Hudson or Elizabeth Taylor as it was brought to bear on a new situation, and each new situation was sold as the best yet. Studio publicity existed to tease audiences with the idea of perfection, the movie that finally made good on every promise Clark Gable offered, and the films themselves were always on some level a letdown, because the promise was an ideal we each carried privately. Our relationships with the great movie stars are so often deeply personal—we respond to the way they act out our own joys and unhappiness—but the movies, cruelly, insist we share them with others.

The contract that Ball and other protean TV stars offered to home audiences was nothing like that. If movies represented variations on the themes of its stars, television shows provided variations on the themes of its characters and their attitudes. The critical component was consistency, for each week Lucy Ricardo/Lucille Ball acted out a fantasy of self-aggrandizement, failed hilariously, and the next week it would happen all over again, the counter magically reset to zero. Each week Archie Bunker would confront the universe with blinkered bigotry, Samantha Stevens would use witchcraft to upend and save her husband's advertising career, Lucas McCain would reluctantly break out his gun and kill a bad guy on *The Rifleman,* and the *Mission Impossible* team would bring down another petty dictator with latex noses and baroque plots. What changed were the details; the essential situation remained the same.

Even the shows that implied time passing over the course of a series—soap operas, dramas—were predicated on repeating the same basic thrill in miniature over and over. TV was (and to a lesser extent still is) fractal, with each individual episode standing in for the show as a totality. To tinker with the basic concept—like letting two battling lovers marry and have a child in the fourth season—is to destroy the delicate balance that keeps viewers tuning in.

So Lucy stayed Lucy even when *I Love Lucy* ended its run in 1957. From 1962 to 1968 she was Lucy Carmichael in *The Lucy Show* and from 1968 to 1974 she was Lucy Carter in *Here's Lucy,* both further iterations of the same episode in which a lovable dingbat suffers for her ambitions. The lesson, always, is enjoy her but don't be like her, and this was because the show, like so many shows on TV, was closer to our own lives than anything we saw in the movies.

Movies took us to exotic places and reenacted moral dilemmas, but television was entertainment in the home about the home, and its homilies took the form of warnings. The wave of WASPy suburban middle-class sitcoms that dominated the schedule in the late 1950s and '60s included *Leave It to Beaver, Father Knows Best, My Three Sons, Make Room for Daddy, Bewitched, The Donna Reed Show, The Dick Van Dyke Show,* and *Ozzie and Harriet,* each show acting out the consequences of mildly non-normative behavior. What happens when Beaver Cleaver decides to play in the family car? He backs it into traffic, so, kids, don't do that. (Easier said than done; in a personal case of copycat violence, I watched that episode at age eight, went outside, and backed our family Rambler into traffic. What scriptwriters mean as warnings, audiences often take as imitative cues.)

This fit into a culture obsessed with fitting in, and it also flattered an audience that was largely female: during the 1950s, women represented 55 to 60 percent of evening viewers and a full three-quarters of the daytime audience. There were other genres, of course—westerns and spy shows, variety revues and doctor dramas, anthologies like *The Twilight Zone* with its cautionary tales of petty human sins resulting in cosmic retribution. In the 1960s a run of broad fish-out-of-water sitcoms stormed prime time, with critically derided hits that included *The Beverly Hillbillies* (hicks in Hollywood), *Green Acres* (richies in the sticks), *The Munsters* and *The Addams Family* (monsters in suburbia), *Bewitched* (cute witch in suburbia), *I Dream of Jeannie* (sexpot genie in Florida), *Hogan's Heroes* (funny guys in a POW camp), *Gilligan's Island* (seven caricatures on a desert island), and so on. All of them, at their core, wondered what makes a home and how someone "different" could fit into a "normal" setting, or vice versa. Even the westerns tended to contemplate domestic issues. *Bonanza* was essentially *My Three Sons* on the Ponderosa, while *The Rifleman* was a single-dad drama with live ammunition.

The stars of all these shows were talked about and liked and in some cases much loved, but they rarely prompted cultish attention the way movie stars did. Because he came into our living rooms and dramatized what happened there, there was little mystery to Robert Young in *Father Knows Best.* Young was never mobbed like Marlon Brando; instead, people stopped him on the street and asked for advice about their own children until he despaired of the attention. His star persona was approachable, life-sized, and because the character of Jim

Anderson lacked any idiosyncrasies beyond an unseemly fascination with the evening paper, he stood in theory for every father.

If you wanted to find TV actors who were genuine sensations, you had to lower your gaze. As with any technological advance, younger generations took to television most intuitively and with the least amount of psychological adjustment. En masse, American children stopped playing, came inside, and absorbed what streamed out of the box. Teachers, politicians, and cultural commentators all took notice; so, too, did advertisers. What they noticed was that televised cowboy shows abetted childhood playacting even more than radio, and also that you could make insane amounts of money selling accessories to that playacting. The four years from 1947 to 1951 saw $150 million in retail sales to children of western-related clothes, capguns, and other items, and that was only the beginning. *Davy Crockett,* a three-part miniseries on Walt Disney's new ABC show *Disneyland,* sold $300 million of related merchandise in one year, and, again, it was the character that moved the marketplace, not Fess Parker, the actor playing him.

If there was a star of *Disneyland,* it was Walt Disney himself, who finally had a stage on which to develop the persona of beloved corporate paterfamilias he had been building for decades. The idea behind Walt-as-star was *trust*; the man who invented Mickey Mouse and *Snow White* was a brand you could rely on, whether he was pitching coonskin caps, his new amusement park, or Annette Funicello, his personal choice for the Mouseketeers on *The Mickey Mouse Club.*

Plucked from obscurity when Disney noticed her dancing in a Burbank production of *Swan Lake,* the twelve-year-old Funicello turned out to be the most popular of the Mouseketeers when the show launched in 1955. Walt put her in spin-off serials and watched uneasily as she matured into an accidental teenage sex symbol. On one show, Funicello sang a song called "How Will I Know My Love," and it proved so popular that Disney released it as a single, the first of many gentle, unassuming pop songs sung by Annette in the late 1950s and early '60s.

In this she was hardly alone, for one of the remarkable things about early TV was the way it provided teenagers with a platform for both sound and vision—for stars like them singing the music that was theirs right in their very own homes. This phenomenon had roots so local that the distance between celebrity and audience could be a matter of blocks. With afternoon programs like Philadelphia's *Bandstand* and Baltimore's *Buddy Deane Show,* high schoolers could rush home from school and see kids from their English class dance to the latest hits. *Deane,* the inspiration for John Waters's 1988 film *Hairspray,* never went national, but in 1957 *Bandstand* crossed over to ABC, where it ran for thirty years and established host Dick Clark as a never-aging Dorian Gray of TV rock.

This youth market, established on TV and the airwaves far more than in the movies, created an unprecedented alternate star hierarchy, separate from the adult cosmology and governed by different rules of appeal and desire. More and more, these stars came from the world of pop music; the taxonomy of stardom that in the 1950s leapt from the big screen to the small was about to conquer a new medium, that of recorded music. The doors of celebrity were about to open wide to accommodate a whole new arena of emulation and projection.

Previously, singers whose fans were primarily young constituted only one wing on the house of stardom. Frank Sinatra in the 1940s might have given teenage girls fits, but he was a known and comprehensible quantity who, it was expected, would someday graduate from crooning into more respectable forms of singing and acting, just as Bing Crosby had done. Sinatra's early film roles, coming as they did in the constrained and controlled medium of the Hollywood musical, let him sing a number or two but made sure the grown-ups remained the main order of business.

The dance shows on TV, though—who cared about them? Only the kids watching them in cities and then across the entire country, a private after-school planet with new rules of dress and behavior and rhythm to which parents and other guardians of culture remained oblivious. These shows and the new rock radio stations were the first of the adolescent secret societies: jungle-drum telegraphs, playing tunes only fourteen-year-olds could hear. They took over where slang—a way of speaking out loud without being heard—left off and prefigured the hidden channels of communication our teenagers use today: IMs and texting and ringtones pitched at a sonic frequency adult ears no longer hear. Suddenly, star culture was stratified by age, and the strata spoke in different languages.

What this meant in TV terms is that many shows developed a singing teenager with spin-off hit singles: Ricky Nelson on *The Adventures of Ozzie & Harriet,* Paul Petersen and Shelley Fabares from *The Donna Reed Show,* Johnny Crawford of *The Rifleman,* whose five Top 40 hits included the deathless "Your Nose Is Gonna Grow." Except for Nelson's, the records were junk, cynical on some level or all of them, and designed only to tap the wallets of the 13 million teenagers who in 1956 had a total spendable income of $7 billion a year. Unlike the differentiated adult consumers, the adolescent market tended to act (and buy) as a mass, so if you could find the right artist, or manufacture the right artist, you stood to make a killing. The route was predictable and controllable and at worst you'd get a hit or two before the hormonal hordes moved on. And who knows? You might end up with another Elvis Presley.

Except that nobody had predicted Elvis Presley.

12.

Vinyl: The New Rock Celebrities and the Warhol Factory

Even Elvis didn't predict himself. What happened to him, or, more accurately, through him—the arrival of pop music as a radical new field of star persona—was inevitable but not in any way planned. When the nineteen-year-old truck driver showed up at Sun Records in Memphis on Monday, July 5, 1954, it was with a nebulous dream of becoming a star by singing country songs or pop songs or even a little gospel. Certainly not the rhythm-and-blues songs by black artists that Elvis and his friends so deeply grooved on, that had fed his wilder dreams since he was a boy. He was a child of the postwar American South, which meant you soaked up hillbilly artists with your parents, then stayed up nights secretly listening to Dewey Phillips play Elmore James's "Dust My Broom" on WHBQ or B. B. King spinning discs on WDIA, "the Mother Station of the Negroes." It meant you snuck out of Sunday services with your girlfriend to run to the colored church a mile away, where Queen C. Anderson and the Brewsteraires rocked the rafters. This double existence, one culture accepted and open, the other acknowledged but taboo, was the air through which Gladys and Vernon Presley's son moved. The black stuff was life, but it wasn't for public performance. You just couldn't *do* that. Could you?

Presley was a shy and distracted teenager—an oddball, for sure, with that greasy hair and those pink-striped pants—and while he toted his guitar everywhere and sung without being asked, it was with a soft, almost embarrassed intensity. He wasn't a showoff, but he still burned. Months before his first session, Elvis had paid $3.98 to cut a record at Sun and impressed owner Sam Phillips's motherly assistant, Marion Keisker—"impressed" isn't the right word; more like "oddly moved"—and eventually Sam rounded up two musicians, guitarist Scotty Moore and stand-up-bass player Bill Black, to see what the singer might could do in the studio.

The trio ran through a Bing Crosby tune and a country ballad called "I Love You Because," a big hit for Ernest Tubb a few years before. Phillips recorded take after take of the latter, well into the wee hours, and nothing was happening; the song just sat there, immobile. They took a break. Wired with nervous energy, Elvis started horsing around, singing Arthur "Big Boy" Crudup's gutbucket blues "That's All Right, Mama" in a wildcat tone. The microphones were off; he knew it was safe. Black joined in on the bass, then Moore on guitar, and then Phillips stuck his head out of the control room and said, "What are you doing?" "We don't know," they shrugged. "Well, back up, try to find a place to start, and do it again."

The point is that Elvis needed permission, and so did white America. Sam Phillips was the great enabler; he had long told Keisker, *If I could find a white man who had the Negro sound and the Negro feel I could make a billion dollars,* and here that singer was in front of him and the damn kid didn't know what he had in him. Back up, try to find a place to start, do it again.

And the boy listened. The reason that Elvis Presley redefined popular music and celebrity culture in his image, birthed rock and roll, infused the American mainstream with the impolite energy that jolted it back to life, is that he *did* listen. When Sam said okay, the lightbulb clicked on over that pompadour, and you can almost reach out and touch the joy that barrels through Presley's subsequent Sun singles: "Good Rockin' Tonight," "Mystery Train," "Baby, Let's Play House," all the rest. In their grooves lay something even bigger, a promise that the two broken halves of America might be made whole, and that the country might at last live up to its ideals of equality. *This* is the music Elvis heard in his head and had been too shy to sing. This was the fame too big to say.

We have to digress and look ahead for a moment, because we are moving beyond the visual mediums that have until now defined the parameters of stardom. With Presley and rock and roll, we come to the third of the tectonic shifts in post–World War II pop culture, one in which celebrity, and the penumbra of mania and need that surrounded it, suddenly extended to the world of popular music in wholly unexpected ways. The heat of new-star charisma—the impact of fresh voices and personas—was no longer on the movie screen but in the very grooves of the records you brought home and listened to in your bedroom.

All three of these cultural shifts were predicated on sudden breaches in accepted taste: Brando's funk and mumbling, the way television drastically reordered the domestic space, Elvis brazenly letting black music in through the front door. The latter was by far the most threatening to the status quo, even if it came with a white face. The *rhythms* were black and were possessed of everything the white mainstream desired and feared in blackness: freedom, sex, a good time—all promises purchased with the slaves and mightily repressed afterward.

By bringing America's shadow culture into the light, Elvis was in one sense only the latest wrinkle in minstrelsy, that long-standing practice of white artists adopting black styles to access what are generally perceived as greater emotional truths—feelings more "real," more experienced, beyond the limits of white Protestant culture. The practice is deeply entwined with the idea of American stardom, and it travels from the late eighteenth century through post–Civil War blackface, through Al Jolson and Elvis, all the way to Eminem and beyond. It is the great dialectic, the primal push-pull, of our country's popular culture and, since we're so good at selling it, it's the world's dialectic to a certain extent.

Yet Elvis was also a crucial integrator, openly citing his influences, placing credit where it belonged, discounting race and class as barriers or even issues with which to contend. It all came streaming through his sound and his energy—the melting pot, stirred together at last. Not that he could have or would have put it into so many words, but Elvis was the wild, classless idealism of the New England Transcendentalists, of Walt Whitman's "barbaric yawp," laid onto vinyl. He offered a vision that would eventually ground the coming counterculture, a sense that America was much, much bigger than its divisions—that it was in fact whole, entire, and straining for release.

Abandon. That was the idea that Elvis carried like a hip-pumping bacterium into the host culture's DNA. Abandon your racial definitions, abandon your frightened, uptight culture, give yourself up to the beat, to sexual abandon itself. There is not a note of "That's All Right, Mama" that isn't politically and democratically incendiary, and the miracle is that Presley appeared to be making it up as he went along. Stardom was no longer about accepted norms of talent or personal appeal. It was pure, unfiltered magnetism. You couldn't sell it so much as simply point to it. Or imitate it and hope for the best.

Crucially, the rise of Elvis let actual black music stars in the door. It was happening anyway. Deejays like Dewey Phillips (no relation to Sam) and Cleveland's Alan Freed were mixing the races on the air. But Fats Domino didn't cross over from the R&B charts to the pop charts until after Elvis hit. Little Richard didn't record "Tutti Frutti" until 1955. Ray Charles had made his soul music breakthrough on Atlantic Records in 1953 but it didn't bear commercial fruit until 1955's "I Got a Woman." Where Presley's impact may have been most felt, arguably, was in the rise of Chuck Berry, an intensely ambitious guitarist and songwriter who articulated all the crossover dreams Elvis knew but couldn't spell out. Would Chess Records have taken Berry on without Sam Phillips's example? Would the legendary house of Chicago blues have recorded and released "Maybellene" in May 1955 as a way to tap into the new teen audience if Elvis hadn't existed? After a million copies sold, it didn't much matter.

Presley influenced other white rockers, of course—he played Lubbock, Texas, and turned Buddy Holly's young life inside out—and he served as vanguard for a number of artists, like Carl Perkins, who were headed in the same direction. What shocked everyone, though, was how both Elvis's confidence and the audience for what he was doing kept spreading, infecting all it touched with a thirst for boogie and liberation. In 1956, Sam Phillips reluctantly sold Presley's contract to RCA for an unheard-of $35,000, and the first thing Elvis insisted on recording was a morbid blues number cowritten by journalist Mae Axton. Nobody believed in it, not even Phillips, yet "Heartbreak Hotel" sold a million copies within two months and topped the pop, country, and R&B charts. When the band played it live, Scotty Moore started getting scared by the violence of the audience reaction. "I guess it's just something God gave me," Elvis told a journalist about the screaming crowds. "Know what I mean, honey? And I'm grateful. Only I'm afraid. I'm afraid I'll go out like a light, just like I came on."

The other major development occasioned by Presley was the shift from movies to pop music as the primary locus of star explosions, a progression that intensified throughout the 1960s and served for three decades, until the rise of hip-hop, as the vehicle of the culture's most potent new meanings and changes. Inasmuch as this book is primarily concerned with movie stardom, those changes lie outside its purview. Still, it needs to be pointed out that the sonic reinvention embodied by Elvis—the radical disassembly and reintegration of racial and cultural assumptions—was taken to new heights a decade later by the Beatles, a rock group that proved you didn't have to be American to play American music, and all kinds, synthesized in wholly new ways.

The innovations brokered by the Beatles seem endless, starting with the fact that John Lennon and Paul McCartney wrote their own songs, a concept that in one stroke introduced the alien notion of self-expression into the factory production of popular music. Suddenly you meant what you sang, which meant, too, that you could be an artist, *had* to be an artist—an idea Bob Dylan quickly picked up and used to inspire the entire singer-songwriter movement. Pop stars now had even greater potential agency and impact than movie stars, because what movie star writes his own dialogue?

The single most revolutionary aspect of the Beatles, though, was that they were the first *star group*—the first popular phenomenon in which each of the parts was indispensable yet the whole was somehow far greater than the sum of the parts. To think of the Beatles without John (wit, depth, cruelty, rebellion, confusion) or Paul (craft, charm, cheek, prettiness, an unexpected pair of rock-and-roll balls) or George (poise, mystery, silence, lacerating humor, the grounding principle) or Ringo (the child, the clown, the rock, the adored ugly duckling) is to not think of the Beatles at all. As the critic Greil Marcus wrote, "You did not have to love them all to love the group, but you could not love one without loving the group."

You could see the pop culture machinery struggle to contain this new idea, from the Beatles' first appearance on *The Ed Sullivan Show*—Paul gets the closeups and John is barely even miked—to the first two films the Beatles made, *A Hard Day's Night* (1964) and *Help!* (1965). Elvis, of course, had quickly been subsumed into conventional Hollywood celebrity, his natural authority tamed and constrained over the course of thirty-one increasingly disposable films. To watch *A Hard Day's Night,* though, is to witness a movie actively grappling with which of its stars is *the* star before caving in to the inevitable realization that each of the Beatles is his own story line and, indeed, his own genre. When Ringo goes off on his wanderings late in the film, it could be a heart-tugging Chaplin silent. John's verbal sallies and disappearance down the bathtub drain are pure Marx Brothers anarchy. Paul's cheeky sex appeal has the confidence of a Depression-era juvenile lead like Dick Powell. George—well, the movie isn't sure what to do with George, who's quiet but sharp, so they turn him into a sort of cooler variant on Britain's Angry Young Man.

You had, in essence, four personas within one larger persona—a new idea that was already hardening into convention with *Help!*, and that probably would have reduced the Beatles to the Monkees if they had been at all serious about movies. In the second film, Ringo is more than ever the breakout comic figure—the Harpo, the Curly, the Jerry Lewis to the other three's combined Dean Martin—and you can tell it doesn't interest any of them. Still, the movies underscored how you could personalize your Beatles experience, and tailor its meanings to you alone, a way to achieve private intimacy on a mass scale.

To bring it down to the personal level, this writer was six years old when the group took off in America. My first recollection is of standing in the music section of a Boston department store, transfixed before a cardboard display on which the four Beatles' heads waggled back and forth on motorized pivots. I had no idea which Beatle was which or even who these people were, and then my mother reached over and picked up a copy of *Meet the Beatles* because my twelve-year-old sister had been agitating for it and had a birthday coming up.

In my memory, we cut to a few weeks later, and I'm sitting on my older sister's bed while she and my middle sister hold before me the back cover of *Meet the Beatles*. Their hands are covering the names under the big photo of the group, and I am grilled repeatedly as to which Beatle is which. Ringo is easy, and so is the hollow-cheeked George; it's the other two I'm having trouble getting straight. They keep at it until I get it right, and I have to imagine that a similar process is happening across the country, even around the globe, as people tweak their perspectives, widen their brains, to entertain the notion that everyone in a pop group is important to what it means.

Before they learned to tell John from Paul from George from Ringo, the hair was the only thing most people saw. It took on a strange life of its own, with everyone from New York cops to President Lyndon Johnson having his say on or off the record. The most popular merchandising tie-in of 1964 was the Beatle wig, a cheap mop of black plastic strands that you could buy either to celebrate or lampoon the Fab Four. These were manufactured at the rate of 35,000 a day and represented a keepsake of the mania and a stand-in for an actual lock of Paul's hair.

In general, the group lent itself to cross-marketing more naturally than anyone besides Chaplin, Shirley Temple, Mickey Mouse, and Davy Crockett. Like them, the Beatles were iconic, easily reduced to toy size. There were dolls and pens, edible albums, masks, games, bow ties, Beatle-nut ice cream. There were also innumerable rip-offs, including albums by hastily assembled session musicians dubbed the Beetles and the Bugs, designed to gull the very credulous or very young. The Beatles represented something so new in star culture that it took the marketplace and people's minds some time to adjust to the rules.

But adjust they did. Everyone came around eventually, and the ambitious among them reset their sails. As with the movie stars of the classic studio era, each successful pop artist or act now embodied an idea, which in turn implied a story that was played out in their successive album releases. Within the context of British bands, the Beatles sat above all, supreme and untouchable, while the Rolling Stones skulked about posing as Lucifer in exile. The Who illustrated the struggle between sensitivity and rock muscle, and the Kinks wept ironic tears over a vanishing England. Beneath these founding four were a thousand other bands settling into niches of blues, pop, rock. A solo star like Eric Clapton could emerge from the British blues freaks to forge a new idea, the Guitar Hero ("God," to his fans), while constantly measuring the distance between technique and artistry, sound and feeling, American black men and English white boys.

In America, much the same progression was occurring. The Doors served as a front for the overpowering, doom-laden sex appeal of Jim Morrison, whose myth was that he was mining the subconscious of America while coming for its daughters. Until the persona overpowered Morrison with booze and entropy, he was a star in a way Adolph Zukor might have appreciated.

Jimi Hendrix was America's own guitar hero (brewed in England), but he pushed further than Clapton or the others, doing things with an electric guitar no one had thought possible and thus creating the persona of the rock virtuoso. Janis Joplin was one of the very few compelling female rockers, a weary, ballsy, white-hippie heir to Big

Mama Thornton. That she, Hendrix, and Morrison all died within a few months of each other in 1970 and 1971 became part of the narrative too—the young, talented, and doomed, betrayed by the weakness in the counterculture argument that release brings bliss.

The most unsettling of them all was a nice Jewish kid, born Robert Zimmerman in Minnesota in 1941, who undertook a series of breathtaking star-making games, reinventing himself in persona after persona and discarding each like snakeskin. By the time the Beatles reignited his rock-and-roll dreams, he had already rechristened himself as Bob Dylan, a rising folksinger with a breakthrough song ("Blowin' in the Wind") and album (*The Freewheelin' Bob Dylan*) under his belt. Huge within the New York folk/protest scene, admired by the music industry cognoscenti, and in demand as a songwriter, Dylan nevertheless seemed destined to remain a cult figure, with a look (peevish, unkempt), a sound (goatlike), and a demeanor (seriously weird) that seemed impossible to square with conventional notions of celebrity.

Yet by yoking his music to the diesel engine of rock and roll at the 1965 Newport Folk Festival, Dylan annoyed all the right people (the elitists, the humorless, Pete Seeger) and attracted a huge new audience that didn't fully understand what he was talking about in "Like a Rolling Stone" but sent it to number 2 on the pop charts anyway on the strength of its irresistible chorus and unmistakable sneer. Here was Brando again, astride his motorcycle asking "Whaddya got?"—an attitude aped by Dylan on the cover of *Highway 61 Revisited*.

That was only one of his temporary faces, a brief stop in a shape-shifting career that Todd Haynes's 2007 film *I'm Not There* could encompass only by casting six different actors, including a woman and a young black child, as the various incarnations of "Bob Dylan." In its cataloging of personas and its acknowledgment that not one of them ever gets to the truth of this man or of any pop icon, *I'm Not There* may stand as the single most honest movie ever made about celebrity in America.

This music culture, a noisy but containable threat when codified by Elvis and the first generation of rockers, had widened and deepened until it stood, at the midpoint of the 1960s, as the expression of a defiant Other America. The twin engines of the counterculture were exuberance and disgust, the first conveyed by the Beatles and other pop voices, the latter driven by a sense that the parental society was wrong at its most fundamental levels. The growing war in Vietnam, the battle over civil rights in the South, the perceived fear and apathy behind much of mainstream popular culture provoked a profound generational disengagement that took decades to fully play out. You could speak to this generation—and Dylan did, taunting anyone who didn't get it as a Judas, a Mr. Jones, a fool living positively on Fourth Street—but at first you couldn't sell to it, because selling was what The Man did.

The exception was if you turned selling itself into art, as Andy Warhol was doing in his various "factories" around New York in the 1960s. Warhol was only tangentially involved in the music scene (through his sponsorship of the Velvet Underground, the minimally selling but widely influential rock group), but, ironically, his film work in this era fed into the discontents and strategies of the next few generations of pop musicians. A fiercely inquisitive mind behind his pose of affected boredom, Warhol rose out of the fashion world wielding a simple and inarguable truth: in a culture driven by money, everything is product. Art is a product, so a commodity like a Brillo box or a soup can is therefore art. Stars are products, too, and stars are art and art is a commodity and stars can thus be manufactured, like canvases or kitchen appliances or shoes.

Warhol set out to prove his case, ignoring the fact that Louis B. Mayer and the other Hollywood rajahs had made millions manufacturing stars decades before. But that was okay, because Andy appreciated the old glamour, its cheesiness and allure, and he wasn't out to make a political point at all (although if you wanted to supply one, that was fine by him). Andy *loved* stardom and money and art, so much so that he wanted to take them all apart and see where they connected with each other.

His first declaration was that a star is anyone who says he or she is a star. This was an inversion of the film studio philosophy, which said that stars are born and then perfected in-house. Warhol, by contrast, maintained that anyone who dreams is a star, anyone who seeks reinvention or simple presentation—anyone invested in the theater of the self. Which is, of course, all of us in the daily movie that is American life, more so in the twenty-first century than ever.

Warhol made that movie in snippets and in long, unforgiving swaths. In 1963, he shot poet John Giorno sleeping for five hours, as if to say *This is what Mayer didn't show you: Clark Gable when the lights are out.* He filmed DeVeren Bookwalter getting a blow job in *Blow Job* (1964), or seeming to get a blow job; the camera stays on Bookwalter's face for thirty-five minutes as it passes through various stages of contortion and boredom, and the audience is left to wonder what exactly is happening below the frame and is that what desire and release look like? Is that what I look like when I have sex or when I watch a film? Warhol admitted he wanted to implicate the audience, and his movies work in the space between the viewer and what he or she wants to see on a screen. Do we want to see ourselves? A beautiful movie idol? Ourselves transformed *into* a beautiful movie idol? Do we need *what is* or *what could be,* and how does one become the other? How do you tell the difference? By the simple addition of an audience?

Warhol collected a coterie of lost children, addicts, socialites, hustlers, and freaks, dubbed them his "superstars," and put them into campy, transgressive dramas like *Vinyl* (1965) and the epic, three-hour, two-projector *Chelsea Girls* (1966), in which Ondine and Nico and Mary Woronov battle each other for the attention of the viewer. The closest Andy came to creating an actual star as the rest of the culture might understand the term was Edie Sedgwick, a poor little rich girl who had the sort of nervous, wide-eyed magnetism the camera naturally loves. She really was his very own Clara Bow, jittery with speed and possibilities, adored and then jettisoned when she became too tiresome.

Warhol early on concluded that the act of filming itself was the fundamental building block of celebrity. I film, therefore you are. To that end, his most important movie work is the series of "screen tests" that he shot from early 1964 to November 1966. The format for each test is exactly the same: The subject sits motionless in closeup for the duration of one 100-foot roll of 16 mm black-and-white film. He or she is told not to blink. The films, shot at twenty-four frames per second, are then projected at sixteen frames per second; they last about four minutes each. Warhol made more than five hundred screen tests, and the subjects include all his superstars and much of the downtown artistic elite of mid-'60s New York. Edie is there, of course, as is the Velvet Underground's Lou Reed, critic Susan Sontag, British folkie Donovan, actor Dennis Hopper, avant-garde artist Yoko Ono (pre–John Lennon), poet Allen Ginsberg, and a very wary Bob Dylan.

Dylan gives nothing away, but he's about the only one. The deep, abiding fascination of the Warhol screen tests is that the subjects always begin by posing and then let their true selves seep through, or they begin by trying to project a true self only to fall back into posing, or some sublimated drama in between. Nothing happens in these films and yet everything does, because they're explicitly about what happens in our heads when we dream of being seen. In one stunning test, a dark-eyed beauty named Ann Buchanan stares down Warhol's camera until tears start pouring from her eyes. Is it an act? An involuntary physical response? A confession from the most inaccessible parts of her soul? All or none of the above?

The screen tests dissect the mystery of self-presentation only to reveal more mysteries. They hint that stardom is a scam, that a person is finally unknowable, while at the same time they assert the rich beauty of surfaces and the pleasure of getting lost in them. They prove everything and nothing—that we use movie stars as vessels for our own fierce, egotistical yearnings and that those yearnings will never be realized, not in any way that truly matters. At the same time, the screen tests look forward to our current era of webcams and Facebook pages. You make a Warhol screen test whenever you sit down for a video chat. They are the Rosetta Stone of modern populist celebrity.

Warhol and Dylan came at stardom from opposite directions but with the same intent, each man deconstructing the concept until it lay in beautiful, inscrutable pieces at his feet. This lesson—that star persona is infinitely mutable and ultimately meaningless—was picked up and carried forward by pop musicians like David Bowie and Madonna before pushing into the hip-hop age of Sean Combs (aka Puff Daddy, aka P. Diddy, aka Diddy, the persona shifting with each needless new name) and exploding as a daily fact of consumer life in the Internet age. Ironically, the one place the business of radical reinvention didn't make much of a dent was in Hollywood movies, the temple at which the rebels and their young audiences still worshipped even as they tried to tear it down.

13.

Free at Last: The Long Voyage of the African American Star

What none of this addresses is the assimilation of black culture and black stars into the white mainstream in the 1960s. In short, Elvis was ultimately overthrown by a thirst for the real thing. There were forerunners, important black artists acknowledged as such, as far back as Bert Williams, the beloved stage star of the pre–World War I era, but he was kept in such a small cultural box that the only way he could express his blackness was by wearing blackface, the then-accepted signifier of race to white audiences. Little Richard, Chuck Berry, Fats Domino, and other first-generation rockers had begun to pull down the wall in the 1950s with assistance from the likes of Elvis, Sam Phillips, and Alan Freed.

Sam Cooke had moved from gospel to blissful pop as early as 1957, when "You Send Me" went to number 1 on the white charts. They were all building on inroads made by jazz musicians from Louis Armstrong and Duke Ellington to Dizzy Gillespie and Miles Davis, as well as crossover figures like Nat King Cole, who not only was scoring pop hits in the late 1940s but in 1956 became the first African American to host his own TV show.

The process of cultural integration picked up speed in the early 1960s, fueled by the civil rights movement but also by producers like Phil Spector and labels like Motown that placed African American artists right there in the Top Ten. You couldn't get away from Smokey Robinson or the Marvelettes or Little Stevie Wonder if you tried, and there was James Brown crashing over from the R&B charts with "Papa's Got a Brand New Bag" and "I Got You (I Feel Good)." The success of Berry Gordy's stable of Motown stars—groomed, MGM style, with lessons in diction and comportment—was proof that African American singers could play the white pop game while retaining an aura of committed, progressive, unthreatening blackness.

Motown had stars, in other words, but it mostly lacked genuine personalities. Instead, Gordy played the impresario, retooling the Supremes so that the prettiest member, Diana Ross, was placed front and center, while the best singer, Florence Ballard, was edged back, out, and into obscurity. Marvin Gaye and Stevie Wonder both struggled to express themselves as artists, succeeding only in the early 1970s with Gaye's "What's Going On" and Wonder's run of classic albums beginning with *Music of My Mind.* In both cases, they had to overcome Gordy's specific and forceful objections about messing with a profitable thing. Wonder had to turn twenty-one, quit the label, then come back with a good lawyer and a 120-page contract that gave him creative control.

Atlantic Records, founded in 1947 by Ahmet Ertegun and Herb Abramson, had a more open-minded policy toward its recording acts, and in fact producers like Jerry Wexler encouraged artists like Ray Charles and Aretha Franklin to find a distinctive sound that functioned *as* their star persona. Franklin's second single for Atlantic,

1967's "Respect," established her as the voice of the new black American woman: soulful, loving, nobody's victim. Otis Redding, whose recordings on the Stax/Volt label were distributed by Atlantic, wrote and first recorded "Respect," and he served as the male analogue to Franklin, masculine yet sensitive, informing his listeners that they *got*-to *got*-to *got*-to try a little tenderness if they want to be happy in love. After Redding's 1967 death in a plane crash, his mantle would be picked up by, among others, Al Green, whose cuddly voice was pure aural intimacy: sex in your ear.

Few of these new African American artists behaved transgressively. For various reasons—upbringing, fear, corporate control, an awareness that they were "representing the race"—they reined in their behavior in ways that white musicians didn't feel pressured to. A scandal such as Sam Cooke's 1964 murder at a Los Angeles motel was both tragic and cruelly embarrassing, the gospel angel turned crossover pop prince revealed in the most tawdry light imaginable. (Fans quickly chose the nobler Cooke of his posthumous protest hit, "A Change Is Gonna Come.") A black Jim Morrison in 1967, the year of "Light My Fire" and "The End" ("Father? I want to kill you. Mother? I want to . . . YARGHHH!") is unthinkable.

What black artists did flaunt was pride, founded on the rock of the civil rights movement and patterned on the example of the movement's chief "star," Martin Luther King Jr. Even this generally didn't find expression in song until after King's slaying in April 1968, with James Brown's "Say It Loud—I'm Black and I'm Proud" coming out the following August. King represented one possible way for the descendants of slaves to participate in America: We shall overcome some day. Malcolm X represented another: By any means necessary. The journey of many black stars in the 1960s was from the first concept to the second, with King's assassination acting as a particularly vicious spur. In general, though, African American stardom at this time served the racial and social dilemma rather than personal self-expression. There was simply too much at stake to navel gaze. So while white counterculture artists drifted into self-absorbed hippie idealism or plugged in and blasted the kids' eardrums out, black artists either played nice or spoke to the issues.

In many cases, there just wasn't room to maneuver. Sidney Poitier was for all intents and purposes the only lead actor of color that Hollywood and white middle-American audiences were willing to consider from his 1950 breakthrough performance in *No Way Out* (as a black slum doctor dealing with a racist Richard Widmark) through his 1963 Best Actor Oscar win for *Lilies of the Field* to 1967, when he starred in *Guess Who's Coming to Dinner?*, *In the Heat of the Night*, and *To Sir, With Love* and was the year's top box office star. The components of Poitier's appeal were poise, intelligence, dignity, and a righteousness that never tipped into self-righteousness, and these were aspects that Poitier conveyed with natural warmth and, when called upon, appropriate anger. He was the civil rights argument distilled into a movie star.

What he was not allowed to do until the 1970s, even if he had wanted to, was play idiosyncratic or oddball or villainous or a thousand other things for which an actor might yearn. Poitier had one role, and it was assigned to him outside of the movies. There were plenty of other successful black actors—Ossie Davis, Harry Belafonte, Moses Gunn, James Earl Jones, Brock Peters—but as far as the film industry and the larger society were concerned there was only one acceptable African American movie hero.

Bill Cosby found himself in a similar situation when *I Spy* debuted in 1965 and he became the first African American to costar in a TV drama. The show, in which he joined Robert Culp as a secret agent team traveling around the world, was a hit in part because of Cosby's easygoing, nonconfrontational charm. He had already established his persona on the comedy circuit—a black guy whose material was not about race—and transferred it to the small-screen espionage genre without trouble. Ironically, as the series rolled into the late 1960s, Cosby came in for criticism that he wasn't addressing black cultural issues enough. Because he was the only African American in a prime-time leading role, he was expected to stand in for an entire people. Only in his onstage comedy act, in a hugely popular ad campaign for Jell-O, and with the massive success of *The Cosby Show* in the 1980s was he able to settle into his "real" persona of a lovable curmudgeon who could embody race, often forthrightly, without being defined by it.

If there was to be a confrontational 1960s black superstar, then, he had to come from a field outside movies and music, which were too deeply leveraged by white corporate power structures and distribution channels. So he did: Cassius Clay, aka Muhammad Ali, aka the Greatest. It is still astonishing to consider not just Ali's accomplishments in the boxing ring (an Olympic gold medal at eighteen, a 19–0 record by the age of twenty-one, three heavyweight championships overall) but also the defiance with which the boxer coolly, almost cruelly, stared down American society. He was not gracious or humble but absolute in his confidence. He boasted, vowing what he would do to opponents and in which round, and then doing it. He was playful and prankish, bursting into rhymes in the middle of the ring: "Some got mad and some lost money / when I ripped home that right as sweet as honey," he said after beating Archie Moore in four. Even Ali's approach to the sport was unconventional, a dancing and bending away from opponents' punches—the celebrated "floating like a butterfly"—rather than blocking them with his gloves.

And he followed Malcolm X rather than Dr. King; in anyone but a professional fighter, this would have been career suicide. Clay joined the Nation of Islam on the eve of his 1964 title fight with Sonny Liston, delaying the announcement of his conversion until after the match only at the request of his (white) promoters. He was renamed first Cassius X, then Muhammad Ali; most sportswriters refused for years to call him anything but Cassius Clay.

In accordance with the Nation, he advocated segregation for the sake of black Americans. In 1967, he was drafted to go to Vietnam and refused to serve, citing his religious beliefs and adding, in a widely reported comment, "I ain't got no quarrel with them Viet Cong. No Viet Cong ever called me nigger." He was stripped of his heavyweight title and found guilty of refusing induction into the armed services, whereupon he took his case to the Supreme Court, which exonerated him in 1971 and allowed him to fight professionally once more. As a matter of principle, then, he sat out three years of his professional peak.

The nerve of the man. The sheer, unyielding nerve. Did Ali know or care in 1967 that the country was moving more and more toward disgust with the Vietnam War, that his resistance would eventually dovetail with the majority? Probably not. But he probably did understand that a boxer, unlike a movie star or a musician, is a man alone in the ring with an opponent, and that the machinery that put him there—white promoters, white money—has no effect on what happens once the bell rings. That you throw your own punches and take them, too, and that the only way to do that is to be the author of your accomplishments wherever and however you go. The idea Ali acted out was the charm and power of total obedience to the self.

14.

Dig the New Breed: Mensches, Hippies, and Fame in New Hollywood

During the quarter century between the end of World War II and the peak of the counterculture, there were many figures who established personas outside of movies and music—who were rooted in politics, sports, and other "real life" arenas. John F. Kennedy, obviously, was the first U.S. president with the charisma of a movie idol, overcoming his Republican opponent in televised debate through the projection of absolute confidence and an upper lip that, unlike Richard Nixon's, didn't sweat. Now that TV had been in the home for more than a decade, star power and visual appeal on a mass scale became critical elements of electoral success, and Kennedy's attributes—ease, attractiveness, above all youth—made him a figure in which the rising tide of baby boomers could emotionally invest. This, in turn, set the stage for the tragedy of his assassination, an event that instantly turned JFK's public narrative from hope to martyrdom and served as the primal trauma of the counterculture: childhood's end for a generation.

Once set, star roles in politics prove difficult to sway. Kennedy was and still is a cultural hero even given his missteps in office and since-revealed sins. Nixon was a villain with perpetual five o'clock shadow no matter what his actual accomplishments were. Politics always periodically rises up into sustained drama, but the home broadcasting medium had the potential to turn it into live theater. The Watergate crisis of the early 1970s played out as a daily soap opera on TV and in the newspapers, with Saturday Night Massacres and wily old senators and creepy bad guys and mysteriously missing tapes. Each player had an assigned role, from conscience-stricken turncoat John Dean to anonymous source "Deep Throat," the latter's name taken from the hit porn film.

That was a token of how sleazy Watergate seemed, and the greatest mystery was what secrets the drama would ultimately disclose about the president himself. Because Nixon's persona was already set in the media's public eye (and, in any case, underscored once the White House tapes were made public and we heard the shadow Nixon, the "real" Nixon, foul-mouthed and paranoid), disgrace seemed preordained. The mystery of identity we had once sought to solve in movie stars we now plumbed in the highest of public servants.

Television made such shorthand possible and, in a sense, necessary, giving each figure in the news a narrative meaning and weight for as long as he or she was on the stage. An upper-class intellectual like Charles Van Doren could rise and fall as a game show winner on *21*, becoming in 1957 the embodiment of America's monied, educated elite and two years later the mortified face of a callow upper-class cheat forced to confess before a congressional subcommittee. An Abbie Hoffman could become the grandstanding Puck of the late-'60s antiwar movement, while a Charles Manson could stand for all of a culture's nightmares of unhinged hippies coming down from the hills with knives.

Real-life dramas unfolded like flowers blooming in slow motion. Starting in February 1974, Patty Hearst traced a year-and-a-half-long journey from kidnapped newspaper heiress to radical terrorist to bank robber back to brainwashed victim. Each phase was an adjustment from the one before, promising an answer to the secret—who was she *really*?—and a knowledge that was always denied. Hearst was a character in her own drama rather than its author, and after two years in prison she returned to semi-notorious obscurity, married her bodyguard, raised a family, and occasionally appears in movies as a genial found object, an empty pop vessel by which we faintly recall the meaning of what it once held.

The modern culture of celebrity has its roots here—the star system that runs around the clock, feeds whole corporations, and restlessly searches for new meat. The primary mediator of reality has become the TV set and the primary grammar of engagement is made from the image and the sound bite. No longer are Hollywood movies the vehicles for "personality." Now fiction and real life intertwine. *People* magazine was launched in March 1974, a spin-off of the popular "People" column in *Time,* and its success reconfirmed that the individual person, rather than issues or ideas, was the governing filter through which consumers saw the world. From the start *People* offered a mix of celebrity and "real people" stories, distancing itself from traditional movie fan magazines and blurring even further the lines between the famous and the average. All the world's a stage, the magazine announced, and you are all players. Or you can be, if you're special enough, or talented enough, or criminal enough.

Still, there was a movie star right there on the cover of the first issue of *People*: Mia Farrow as Daisy Buchanan in the upcoming film version of *The Great Gatsby.* Of course screen idols still mattered. But as what? In the transitional turmoil that accompanied the aging of the Greatest Generation and the rise of the boomers, movie stars as the industry had long understood the concept were in the midst of a twenty-five-year cycle of decline, transformation, and rejuvenation. As the old gods lost their power, new figures came forward, altering the contract between mass idol and audience. The underlying dynamic was one in which glamour slowly turned suspect and earthiness became the new arbiter of value.

How "real" were the new stars? How did they affect and project that realness, and how did it in turn affect the people who paid to see them? In the populist appeal of the new wave of young actors during the 1960s, we see once again the desire that animated the arrival of the talkies decades before—an insistent need for stars to mirror the audience more clearly so the audience would more clearly know how to behave. From its first stirrings in the late 1950s, the New Hollywood set about reclaiming what stardom meant and bringing it home.

Not surprisingly, the roots of the new realism lay in the home screen. The rise of mid-1950s televised drama anthologies like *Playhouse 90* and *Kraft Theatre*—based in New York, using New York actors, dealing with *issues*—infused Hollywood movies with fresh faces and energy. Some of the most celebrated films of the era were big-screen remakes of hit TV plays: *Marty, 12 Angry Men, Requiem for a Heavyweight.* The emphasis was on kitchen-sink realism rather than glamour, and some of the new stars, homely and proletarian, would have been character actors before the war. Now they briefly became tokens of Oscar-winning authenticity—Ernest Borgnine a Best Actor as the homely butcher Marty (shot on location in the Bronx), Shirley Booth a Best Actress as a deluded lower-class housewife in *Come Back, Little Sheba.* These performances struck audiences and the industry as art, much as Hilary Swank's in *Million Dollar Baby* did in recent years. The difference is that Swank is a Hollywood looker playing proletarian, whereas Borgnine and Booth would never be mistaken for matinee idols. (In both their cases, Oscars and movie stardom gave way to profitable lead roles in TV comedy series, where they could be stars on their own unpretty terms.)

Otherwise, the actors of TV drama and the New York stage tended to be young, diligent, serious; together they stood for an honesty that contrasted sharply with the sagging studio machine. Here is where the coming stars of the 1960s and '70s got their starts. Jack Lemmon, Paul Newman, Joanne Woodward, Eva Marie Saint, Shirley MacLaine, Anthony Perkins, and Robert Redford are all getting work at this point, all pointing toward the future. Newman, in fact, is a quintessential transitional figure. Plucked from the ranks and groomed to be an old-style studio star, he rebelled and instead became one of the towering personas of the New Hollywood.

Newman fled Cleveland, Ohio, and his father's sporting-goods business and arrived in New York in 1952, picking up TV bit work on the strength of his looks. He studied at the Actors Studio, and got a break in the 1953 Broadway run of *Picnic,* rising from an understudy to play a leading part. Warner Bros. offered the young actor a five-year contract and got ready to sell him as the next Brando, committed, macho, and impulsive. But Newman's first film, 1954's *The Silver Chalice,* was a toga drama so unwatchable that when a Los Angeles TV station aired it in the late 1960s, the actor took out a newspaper ad to apologize. Few other stars would have done that, and that's a key to the unpretentious cynicism that ultimately made Newman so appealing.

His movies got better—some of them—and the actor, crucially, made sure to return to the New York stage periodically. With the 1956 boxing biopic *Somebody Up There Likes Me,* Newman finally clicked with the public, and he began to show his adventurous side in three 1958 films: a Faulkner adaptation, *The Long, Hot Summer*; as a Method-acting Billy the Kid in *The Left Handed Gun*; and as Brick in *Cat on a Hot Tin Roof,* sexy and shirtless and the only man in America who doesn't want to sleep with Elizabeth Taylor.

He had arrived, complete with a Best Actor nomination for *Cat,* but now Newman did a curious thing. He spent half a million dollars to buy out his Warners contract and consciously broke free of the star machine. The actor later acknowledged that the decision "kept me poor for several years. But I was free, at last, to make my own decisions. If I failed in anything, it would be my failure, no one else's. All things considered, it was the best financial transaction I ever made." By the mid-'60s, he was making $750,000 per film as a free agent and was starting to dabble in profit participation.

More than that, the break was the first step in the creation of a screen image that, in retrospect, looks far more consistent and entertaining than Brando's, if never as haphazardly penetrating. Freed from the studio yoke, Newman busied himself with a number of movies, some of them downright bad (*From the Terrace, The Outrage*) but enough of them so *right* that he became bigger than he ever would have under Warners' tutelage. *The Hustler* (1961), *Hud* (1963), *Harper* (1966), and above all *Cool Hand Luke* (1967) established him as a glamorous and very male rebel, with a crazy twinkle that added to his appeal. Audiences loved the persona and were willing to overlook some of the characters' nastier traits, often to the actor's frustration. (Hud, in particular, is a creep.) The independent streak that kept Newman and his wife Joanne Woodward rooted on the East Coast rather than in Hollywood carried over to the star's roles and his growing legend. He seemed the perfect post-factory movie star: smart, centered, and ahead of the game.

(Interestingly, Woodward turned out to be one of the few great actresses of her era almost completely lacking in a cohesive and sellable star persona. Her Oscar came for her chameleonic changes in 1957's *The Three Faces of Eve*—and her film career suffered as a result. Woodward could walk down the street without attracting a glance. Her husband, by contrast, was mobbed. It is the difference between a craftsperson and a star.)

Newman knew the studios were dying. Their back lots were being bought for TV production, the Motion Picture Production Code of decent, boring onscreen behavior was breaking down in the face of movies like 1953's *The Moon Is Blue,* which dared to use the word "virgin." By the turn of the decade, *Some Like It Hot* and *Psycho* were both released and became hits without the Code's seal of approval, and in 1964, the Holocaust drama *The Pawnbroker,* after much back-and-forth, became the first film with a shot of bare breasts to receive Code approval. It was downhill from there. By 1968, new MPAA chief Jack Valenti had junked the Code and installed the ratings system of Gs and Rs we still live with, for better and for worse. No longer did the film industry treat audiences as one large age group. Now it treated audiences as four smaller age groups.

Even more problematic from the studios' viewpoint, the star factory as an idea no longer made much sense. Audiences increasingly favored performers who expressed the idiosyncrasy of an unmanufactured personality, or, to be precise, the illusion of same. Again, they wanted actors who looked like them, but their looks and behavior were changing. It didn't help that the limited and aging Hollywood phenotypes were being challenged by a wave of foreign-born talent who by their very foreignness were granted more leeway in moral matters. Europeans could have extramarital sex onscreen—even enjoy it—and not be killed off. On the contrary, their lusts and libidos and tragedies were expected to be bigger.

These stars arrived in the 1950s and '60s in imported films and then in Hollywood movies that struggled to package them in American terms. Italy's earth mother Anna Magnani appeared opposite Burt Lancaster in *The Rose Tattoo* (1955), which at least was written expressly for her by Tennessee Williams. By contrast, her countrywoman, the bounteous sex symbol Gina Lollobrigida, was signed by Howard Hughes, who then refused to put her in a film. She finally appeared in the turgid *Trapeze* (1956), Lollo and Lancaster and Tony Curtis all in circus tights. In the end, she never was done right by the American film industry; today, an actress like Penelope Cruz has the modest but impactful career Lollobrigida might have had.

Sophia Loren, guided by her lover-impresario Carlo Ponti, worked her way in from the margins. After establishing herself in Italian comedies, she appeared in a few Hollywood pictures shooting in Europe, then came to Hollywood for four Paramount films that each improved on the one before. She stayed in town long enough to star with—who else—Cary Grant (*Houseboat*) and Clark Gable (*It Started in Naples*), then departed for the career of a world star, stateless and alluring. Nor was she alone. Catherine Deneuve, Simone Signoret, Yves Montand, Harriet Andersson, Max von Sydow, Marcello Mastroianni, Melina Mercouri, Jeanne Moreau, Jean-Paul Belmondo, Monica Vitti—these were the faces of the new offshore chic. Some of them made films for the aging studios, others didn't bother, but all had an influence on hipper audiences and directors, not to mention on fashion and pop style and morals.

The easiest foreign stars to sell were the ones who spoke the Queen's

English—angry young charmers like Albert Finney and Richard Harris, dollybirds like Julie Christie, Sean Connery as a cruel stud of a James Bond, enigmatic Peter O'Toole. After the Beatles happened, anything British seemed hip, sexy. *Tom Jones,* a cheeky period romp starring Finney, won the Best Picture Oscar less than two months after the Fab Four landed at JFK. Also easy to sell, for obvious reasons, was Brigitte Bardot. Blank-eyed and sullenly carnal, she had been working in French films for four years when 1956's *And God Created Woman,* directed by her then husband, Roger Vadim, took off like a tumescent rocket in Europe and then the United States. An erotic trifle that made much of the star's derriere and the Saint-Tropez coastline, it fed into every red-blooded American male's fantasy of French licentiousness. Bardot kept the promise of Marilyn Monroe's calendar shot—or seemed to keep it better. She was a Marilyn who'd actually take her clothes off in a movie. Who needed Hollywood?

All these figures provided new models and meanings and uses for stardom, broadening the concept far beyond the classical studio model. The young barbarians from Broadway, the earnest TV drama actors, youthful rebels like James Dean and Natalie Wood, new global performers, Sidney Poitier, the sharp infusions of energy from the pop music sphere both in America and abroad—they all helped to create a shifting world where Warhol, working far underground, was creating and reflecting the new rules. These said: If you can stake the claim, if you can convince us through your very demand to be accepted as a star, then you are one. No factory necessary.

How else to explain Barbra Streisand? Even her own mother said, No, honey, stick to the typing. Streisand had already found growing success acting and recording—she won two Grammys for her 1963 debut album—and she arrived for good in *Funny Girl* on the stage (1964) and then the screen (1968), playing an ugly-duckling star of a previous era, comedienne Fanny Brice. Streisand asked more of us, though—she wanted to be a sex symbol. How could that be? This honking Brooklynite, the pride of Erasmus High, with the misshapen schnoz and crossed eyes, and the voice, Jesus, the *voice*—in the end, that was what opened the door. The voice was so undeniable that Streisand was undenied.

She was disappointed the movie cameras didn't miraculously turn her into Ava Gardner. Streisand told an interviewer, "I thought they'd make me gorgeous. I always wanted to be pretty," and what does that say about the star we carry in our heads, our secret selves made perfect? The consolation prize was a Best Actress Oscar, split, in a historic first, with Katharine Hepburn for *The Lion in Winter*. The Academy itself couldn't choose between what stardom had meant and what it was becoming.

As in the 1950s, there were Status Quo '60s stars, beacons of studied decency like Julie Andrews (*The Sound of Music,* both the most profitable film of 1965 and the most mocked); the boyishly dreamy Ryan O'Neal; his *Peyton Place* TV soul mate Mia Farrow, a fragile flower who acquired more dissonant pop meanings as the child bride of Frank Sinatra and, impregnated by Satan, the star of *Rosemary's Baby* (1968). Robert Redford falls hesitantly into this category at first, at least until *Butch Cassidy and the Sundance Kid* (1969) and *The Sting* (1973), where new pal Paul Newman mussed up Redford's staid WASP beauty. If Streisand couldn't be gorgeous onscreen, she could at least have gorgeous leading men like Redford, with whom she made 1973's *The Way We Were*. (And there, perhaps, is the crippled fantasy that got Clara Bow out of Brooklyn made whole and acceptable in this democratic new celebrity age.)

Players like Steve McQueen and Ali McGraw both broke the classic Hollywood mold and kept the pieces more or less intact, he as a brooding man of action-drama—a more conventional Brando type, but with a unique cool of his own—and she as the standard free-spirit gamin with added hippie-chick hair. McQueen raced through the streets of San Francisco in *Bullitt* (1968), McGraw died glamorously of Movie Wasting Disease in *Love Story* (1970), and when they met on the set of *The Getaway* (1972), the earth moved and she left her husband, producer Robert Evans. It's as if the two actors belonged to the same species, half evolved from one stage of pop stardom to the next.

Also in this middle range between standard glamour and open

rebellion were figures like Warren Beatty and his *Bonnie and Clyde* costar Faye Dunaway. He was the pretty-boy movie star and she was the willowy model, but both of them were ambitious in ways that would have been unthinkable during the studio days. Beatty especially burned to prove he was a mini mogul and an artist, producing and writing and directing his way to, after many tries, an Oscar for *Reds* in 1981. Respect at last, since merely being a handsome face and a legendary lover no longer guaranteed immortality. You had to earn it, prove it—show you were made of deeper stuff. You had to be real.

Or you could just look like a schlub, in which case the deeper stuff was assumed. The most radical shift in what movie stardom meant—as a reflection of reality, as a template for imitation—came with the ascension of what might be called the *menschlichkeit* stars of the mid-'60s and onward. Leading men who looked like your cousin Melvin.

Dustin Hoffman in *The Graduate* (1967) was the breakthrough, lumpen yet oddly sexy and in his very averageness a stand-in for every young moviegoer trapped in a world of plastics. The initial candidate to play the drifting, dissatisfied Benjamin Braddock was Robert Redford, but director Mike Nichols found him too relaxed, too confident—too starlike. "How many times have you ever struck out with a woman?" he asked Redford, who looked mildly perplexed and said, "What do you mean?" Hoffman, by contrast, was a thirty-year-old New York actor who, along with his roommate Gene Hackman, took what he did seriously in part because he would never be a matinee idol. He was scrawny and nebbishy, with a beak of a nose and a half-open mouth beneath it, as if he were a village idiot or a baby bird. Even Hoffman knew he was no star, telling film historian Mark Harris, "I thought, I'll work off-Broadway for the rest of my life and I'll be very happy and I'll have a nice apartment, and I'm not going to screw it up by making a Hollywood movie and being miscast." Meaning that *any* Hollywood part would be miscasting.

The *Graduate* audition was a fiasco, Hoffman pinching his Elaine, Katharine Ross, on the ass during the audition and getting shut down hard, generally behaving like an awkward, desperate klutz. Even

Nichols thought it was a bust until he saw the footage, and it turned out the actor was one of those natural movie behaviorists, like Gary Cooper, who did tiny things that the camera magnified to perfect life size. Hoffman had to go back to director Mel Brooks and tell him he couldn't play the Nazi playwright in *The Producers* because he'd just got the lead in the movie costarring Brooks's wife.

For that role, *The Graduate*'s Mrs. Robinson, Nichols had been desperate to cast a Hollywood icon. Doris Day was one idea but her husband, agent Marty Melcher, wouldn't even show her the script. Harris's 2008 book *Pictures at a Revolution* has a stunning anecdote about 1950s sex symbol Ava Gardner summoning Nichols to her hotel room, swanning about like a diva, pretending to ask him about *The Graduate,* then informing him in a teary, conspiratorial whisper that she couldn't act—never could. This is the old-line Hollywood star in a landscape without signposts, and it might have been a casting coup of *Sunset Blvd.* dimensions, driving a final wedge between the youth audience and the gods of an earlier day. It also would have toppled *The Graduate* into something it's not: a movie about Mrs. Robinson. Anne Bancroft, a studio hireling as early as 1952 (the suits at Twentieth Century-Fox changed her name from Anna Maria Italiano) but with an independent streak even before winning an Oscar for 1962's *The Miracle Worker,* eventually signed on. She was a star, certainly, but not a legend.

Once *The Graduate* opened to rapturous audience response—literally, cheers—Hoffman was a star too, to the shock of many in Hollywood. Nichols had been approached by industry types after early screenings and told the picture was fine but "it's just a shame about the boy." The media struggled to cope with this aberration in the firmament. The New York *Daily News* said the actor looked like both Sonny *and* Cher and that he'd never threaten Rock Hudson's image. (Relish the ironies as you see fit.) There simply was no precedent, because movie heroes looked heroic, not neurasthenic. But this is what young moviegoers wanted to see: their own certainty about their parents' sellout turned inside out and personified.

Hoffman himself seemed uncertain, and his two 1969 follow-ups to *The Graduate* represented a fork in the road. In *Midnight Cowboy,* he took what was in theory the secondary role of a shabby Times Square pimp, while *John & Mary* cast him opposite Mia Farrow in a story calculated to appeal to youth audiences: a couple meet at a bar, sleep together, *then* get to know each other. ("It's not your mother's love story," nudged the ads in 1969; these days the same story is called *Knocked Up* and it's a comedy.) In effect, the two films asked moviegoers which Hoffman they wanted to see, the actor or the star.

It wasn't even a contest. The diffident, diffuse *John & Mary* sank without a trace while *Cowboy* won Best Picture, garnered Hoffman his second Oscar nomination, and gave him a chance to steal a movie playing a character rather than the conscience of his generation. This opened up a new and fertile dialectic in star culture—the artist as icon—and no one in coming years would synthesize so many elements of the two as Hoffman. For the time being, he just opened the door to a lot of short, dark, or unhandsome: Alan Arkin in *Popi* and *Catch-22,* Elliott Gould in *Bob & Carol & Ted & Alice* and *M*A*S*H,* Hoffman's roommate Gene Hackman rising from the idiot brother in *Bonnie and Clyde* to play the flawed hero cop in *The French Connection,* George Segal an engaging schnook who became a bona fide romantic lead opposite Streisand in *The Owl and the Pussycat,* Donald Sutherland the gawky neo-noir hero of *Klute,* Harpo-haired Gene Wilder moving easily between farce and romantic comedy.

Related to the *menschlichkeit* stars were the stoners and hippies and free radicals—actors like Dennis Hopper, Peter Fonda, and Jack Nicholson, the latter arriving full-born into stardom after a decade of toiling in B-movies and behind-the-scenes work (he had a hand in the creation of the Monkees, among other things). Hopper was a serious young actor—he's in *Rebel Without a Cause*—who'd gone off the rails during the 1960s through dope and disillusionment, his angry stare weaving in and out of focus. Fonda was a Hollywood prince who'd abdicated his throne for, again, a vague but furious rebellion. *Easy Rider,* the 1969 biker flick Hopper and Fonda put together, was a success beyond all measure and the final cruel proof for old Hollywood that something was happening here and they had no idea what it was.

That said, the movie was dated within five minutes of its release and is nearly unwatchable today, a mumbling time-capsule approximation of incoherent attitudes toward freedom, America, women, drugs, and dialogue.

And yet, that very formlessness gave a supporting actor his opening. Playing a boozy southern lawyer who hitches up with the heroes for a few scenes, Nicholson is the only aspect of the entire movie that feels focused. He has a grip on the character—a failed son of privilege, standing outside his small-town culture, possessed of the wisdom and self-pity of the still-young alcoholic—and he conveys it incisively in word and deed and stance. He's idiosyncratic: the football helmet he wears while riding on the back of the motorcycle takes the piss out of biker culture as much as the character's own. His energy and humor are electrifying, and after the endless, stoned heaviosities of Hopper and Fonda, Nicholson seems to cut to the heart of the matter with joy and drawling wit. And he gets off the one line of dialogue that resonates: "This used to be a helluva good country. I can't understand what's gone wrong with it." He *conveys*, instantly.

Nicholson accompanied Hopper and Fonda to Cannes, where the world press scoffed at the American hippies before the lights went down for the premiere. When they came back up, everything was different. "I had been around long enough to know while I was sitting in that audience, I had become a movie star," Nicholson said later. "Nobody's ever had that experience, I think." Maybe. What Nicholson actually did in *Easy Rider* was remind audiences of old-fashioned screen charisma and show up the Warholian ideal that anyone can be a star. If Nicholson—*Jaaack*—turned out to be analogous to anyone, it was prime early-'30s Jimmy Cagney, with much of the same restless energy and malicious wit. As Cagney's persona was linked to criminal rebellion in his first movies, the early Nicholson served as an embodiment—and, at his best, a critical analysis—of social rebellion, from the brilliant *Five Easy Pieces* (1970) and *Chinatown* (1974) to the Oscar apotheosis of *One Flew Over the Cuckoo's Nest* (1975), by which point Jack was the first of the New Old Stars.

A third strand of male performer that came up in the 1960s and burst into bloom during the 1970s was the Second-Generation Brando, combining brute antisocial force with a monk's devotion to art: Al Pacino in *The Godfather* (1972), *Serpico* (1974), and *Dog Day Afternoon* (1975), Robert De Niro in *Mean Streets* (1973) and *Taxi Driver* (1976), Jon Voight in *Midnight Cowboy* (1969) all the way through *Coming Home* (1977).

These were stars who wore their stardom like a hair shirt. They took as their cue Brando himself, gloriously resurgent in *The Godfather*—a character part but a magisterial one. (He then refused his Oscar, revealed his inner demons with the extraordinary *Last Tango in Paris*, and subsequently gave up taking acting seriously at all.) Looking at it another way, Pacino and his peers took Hoffman's distaste for Hollywood and the pop marketplace into hostile territory by preserving the mystery, refusing to discuss what they did and scorning anyone lightweight enough to try. After a while, this became an accepted posture: the artist above the pettiness of celebrity, valued all the more for spurning his fame while treating his body as the clay of truth.

Initially, Sylvester Stallone appeared to belong to this group. He was brooding, Italian, and he wrote and produced his little Philly movie, *Rocky* (1976), all the way to an Academy Award, the ultimate home-brewed rebuke to the studios. Stallone desperately wanted to be a movie star, though, and he turned out to be less interested in probing the enigmas of character than becoming a pop culture player; as such, he belongs with the recombinant movie icons of the next chapter.

There were utility stars, too, who in the studio years might have fallen through the cracks between above-the-title hero and character actor but who now prospered as pop ambassadors of experience and doubt. Michael Caine, James Caan, James Coburn, Gene Hackman, George C. Scott (another Oscar refuser for *Patton,* sick of the whole "meat parade" and thus establishing an alternative glamour), Robert Duvall, Roy Scheider—all these men got leading roles, all were given critical respect, and each staked out a specific and personal turf between movie star charisma on one hand and hardworking New Hollywood realism on the other.

In the process, these actors often questioned and reinvented genres that had sustained the business for decades. The private-eye film, for instance, got several makeovers during the early, post-hippie 1970s, in which the corruption of the world extended into the political and the hero could be flawed or murderous or an abject failure. Elliott Gould in *The Long Goodbye* (1973), Jack Nicholson in *Chinatown* (1974), Gene Hackman in *Night Moves* (1975) were all unable to do what Bogart had done (save the girl, find the killer, expose the rot) because the fashionable cynicism of the times said the big boys always won. The revolution had failed: forget it, Jake, it's Chinatown. Even the prettier stars played this game—Warren Beatty in *The Parallax View* (1974), Robert Redford in *Three Days of the Condor* (1975). Downer drama was the only honorable, even possible resolution, because anything else was an old Hollywood lie about how the world worked. And the New Hollywood was, above all, about telling the truth—or its version of the truth—even if the audience eventually turned out to prefer the lies.

If you needed comfort—and people did—you could always turn to the real Bogart. One of the more unusual turns of the pop culture wheel at this time was the classic movie revival movement, which got its start in the late 1950s, when the Brattle Theatre in Cambridge, Massachusetts, began showing *Casablanca* during Harvard's exam week. A cult of Bogart was born—and W. C. Fields, and the Marx Brothers, and Greta Garbo, and Astaire and Rogers, and the directors who had filmed them all—finding expression in dorm-room posters and, by the early 1970s, at hip urban movie houses. Suddenly you could take a date to see not new stars but old ones, in a double bill of, say, *Sylvia Scarlett* and *Duck Soup,* both movies scorned in their day and both now hailed for their free-spirited energy. Even as young audiences rejected their parents' culture, they embraced their grandparents'. Dead stars were exhumed and turned into new points of light, even models of behavior and dress, while old movies like *Bringing Up Baby* provided the mulch for fond homages like *What's Up, Doc?* (1972), with Streisand and Ryan O'Neal doing their very best to sample the lunatic finesse of Kate Hepburn and Cary Grant.

This proves how durable the factory-made stars were but also that *menschlichkeit* has its limits. Old-school Hollywood glamour was the dirty secret young audiences kept tucked in the pockets of their faded jeans. More than that, the nostalgia fad introduced the novel concept that modern style could be rooted in the elegant safe house of the past—that, indeed, the stars of the 1930s and '40s were purer, less tarnished, than our own. In this you can see the urge for simplicity and certainty that animates so much of star worship—the need, once again, for a movie icon to embody a comforting ideal rather than a complex reality.

The actresses of the era, by contrast, had a challenging time of it. Notions of youthful female beauty and decorum held on through the late 1960s, with Streisand a notable outlier. There were a lot of passive hippie chicks with long straight hair and few intentions of upstaging the male leads: Barbara Hershey, Katharine Ross, Leigh Taylor-Young. Jane Fonda, with her classic Hollywood bloodlines, was one of the few new female stars whose persona had any real power, and if part of her appeal was sexual (at least in 1968's semi-scandalous *Barbarella*), most of it was through an impatient, even angry, force of intelligence that dovetailed with the larger social ideals of a counterculture for which she found herself a controversial sometimes spokeswoman. In *They Shoot Horses, Don't They?* (1969), Fonda brought a harsh modern despair to the Depression setting, and in *Klute* (1971) she played a call girl with a then-startling lack of romanticization. "Working in Hollywood does give one a certain expertise in the field of prostitution," she was famously quoted as saying, presumably loud enough for her father, Henry, to hear.

The only other powerful female roles for most of the 1960s, until the values of the women's movement began to be reflected in popular culture, went to Hollywood survivors like Liz Taylor and Katharine Hepburn, the latter winning back-to-back Oscars in 1968 and 1969 (splitting the second with Streisand). Faye Dunaway had a good run as Bonnie Parker in *Bonnie and Clyde* (1967), the doomed Evelyn Mulwray in *Chinatown* (1974), and the ball-busting TV executive of *Network* (1976), but here again is the difference between a celebrated star and a lasting one: Dunaway was beautiful, popular, talented, and unbearably chic, but there was no idea behind what "Faye Dunaway" meant other than looks and a certain cold and high-strung ferocity. Her fame built to and ended with her playing Joan Crawford in *Mommie Dearest* (1981). She could have been Mildred Pierce's long-lost daughter.

There were strong-minded women coming over from newly hip England, though, like Glenda Jackson in *Women in Love* (1969) and *Sunday Bloody Sunday* (1971) and the Redgraves, Vanessa (1969's *Isadora*) and Lynn (1966's *Georgy Girl*). And of course there were the sexualized heroines of the B-movies and the drive-in circuit. Anyone who has seen Russ Meyer's delirious *Faster, Pussycat, Kill! Kill!* (1965) knows that Tura Satana is a force of nature somewhere between appealing and appalling. Meyer's films are where the cultural breast fetish begun by Marilyn and *Playboy* turned playful, violent, and surreal—the celluloid sex fantasy in the last stages of repression before porn burst free.

By and large, though, the outrageous energy of the Meyer woman, a frank acknowledgment of female power sexual and otherwise, was kept off mainstream screens for the first half of the counterculture era. The breakthroughs extended to men only—if Streisand was the female Dustin Hoffman, she was offered a fraction of his range of roles—and only in the mid-1970s did defined parts for young American actresses begin to appear and cohere. Ellen Burstyn in *Alice Doesn't Live Here Anymore* (1974), Jill Clayburgh in *An Unmarried Woman* (1978), Marsha Mason in *The Goodbye Girl* (1977), Sissy Spacek in *Badlands* (1973) through *Carrie* (1976), Sally Field in *Norma Rae* (1979), a young Meryl Streep in *The Deer Hunter* (1978): these were all various faces of a new "real woman," confronting the same melodramatic situations as Barbara Stanwyck and Lana Turner but bringing a stressed, believable ordinariness to the playing. Diane Keaton was close to emblematic, the audience's representative shiksa in both the cloistered macho world of *The Godfather* and the antic imagination of Woody Allen. For the latter, Keaton finally bloomed in 1977 as the incomparable *Annie Hall*: the modern woman in vintage clothes, the movie star who talked, lah di dah, like we do.

That does indicate, though, that many of the strongest female performances of the era were guided to the screen by strong male directors—filmmakers who were often recognizable stars on their own. Keaton meant radically different things to Francis Ford Coppola and Woody Allen; for the first she's a moral intruder amid the Corleone men, naive but persevering, while for the second she's an alien playmate, tall and WASPy and unironic but still able to caper through nineteenth-century Russia or the Upper West Side. Allen's Keaton ultimately won out in the public mind, for when we think of her even now, we think of adorable stammering and the downcast look—we think of Annie Hall, a role that was cut from the cloth of the actress's real life. But how many other Diane Keatons are there, or could have been? It sometimes seems as arbitrary as Chaplin going into that costume room and emerging as the Tramp rather than the Professor.

Just coming into view at this point, in tandem with the new counterculture freedoms it initially made vague claims to being part of, was mainstream pornography. Rising from a subterranean history that goes back to the first decades of the film industry—to the beginning of artistic representation itself—movies like *Deep Throat* (1972), *Behind the Green Door* (1972), and *The Devil in Miss Jones* (1973) established the lopsided rules of the newly permissible genre. It was the actresses in porn who became stars rather than the men, subjects of fame for being objects of desire. Linda Lovelace of *Deep Throat* was a household name in part because she broke social taboos about women talking openly about sex and (more critically) enjoying it. The idea that she was liberated by porn gained enough pop currency for the star's eventual rebirth as a vocal antiporn crusader in the early 1980s to challenge counterculture orthodoxy and introduce a new feminist meme: porn as exploitation, as victimization, as cultural and literal rape.

For a while, though, porn chic roiled the culture in interesting ways. When it was revealed that *Behind the Green Door* star Marilyn Chambers had previously modeled as the face of Ivory Snow detergent ("99 and 44/100% pure"), the media convulsed happily from the contradiction between the bland homilies of the advertising industry and the fleshly "honesty" of porn. Aside from John Holmes, Ron Jeremy, and a handful of other actors, men in straight porn were largely interchangeable and continue to be. This most purely functional of movie genres exists primarily to satisfy its male audience's physical desires, and since that audience wants to imagine itself in the male actor's position, whatever detracts from the projection of self—character, star charisma, anything except dimensions and stamina—gets in the way. Even noticing the men in hardcore straight porn is suspect.

Female porn stars, by contrast, were allowed personas and character types within the limits of fantasy role-playing. As porn mutated and adapted and industrialized over the following decades, an alternate star hierarchy took shape that ran parallel to "real" movie stardom and occasionally overlapped it with a frisson of notoriety. In the 1970s and early '80s, for instance, Kay Parker was the genre's representative Older Woman, Vanessa Del Rio the Latina man-eater, Seka the chilly, elegant Euro-blonde, and so forth.

There was even a porno ingénue: Ginger Lynn, the "Vivid Girl" of the early 1980s (shades of the Biograph Girl), who, upon her return to hardcore in 1999, was quoted as saying "Let's be realistic here: If Hollywood would have given me Meg Ryan roles, I wouldn't be doing porno again." Beyond its function as utilitarian short-term fantasy, pornography offers a parodic mirror of mainstream celebrity, one in which star power is reduced to the mimicking of sexual excitement. It is, at long last, stardom with no secrets whatsoever, and as such is surprisingly useless for answering deeper audience needs of desire and identification. You can take a porn star to bed, but will she mean anything to you in the morning?

Another innovation of the counterculture era: director as star. The auteur theory, advanced by French critics during the 1950s, claimed the filmmaker as the bearer of a movie's sensibility and personality, its view of the world. A John Ford movie is different from, say, a Howard Hawks movie in everything from shot language to the moral universe that language conveys. This outlook was popularized in America by influential 1960s film critics such as Andrew Sarris, but a certain amount of readjustment had to happen before older directors like Alfred Hitchcock and Douglas Sirk could be defined as "artists" rather than "popular filmmakers." Even the filmmakers themselves found the process slightly bizarre. Hitchcock had been selling himself as a star for years—easy enough with that pear-shaped body and the voice of an amused undertaker—but in his 1967 interviews with François Truffaut you can hear him struggle to meet a new definition of himself in which every camera angle carries metaphysical weight. Hawks, talking with bright young scholars, clearly found the whole thing absurd: making movies was just a job—a great job, but still. Which in a way proves the auteurists' point. Intended or not, Hawks's witty, no-nonsense outlook percolates through almost every one of his films.

The filmmakers of the New Hollywood, by contrast, leapt at the chance to be self-conscious artists—stars of an aesthetic unbounded by the past. Coppola, Martin Scorsese, Robert Altman, Peter Bogdanovich, William Friedkin, and many others took advantage of their new stature—and of the utter confusion studio executives had over what would or wouldn't sell—to craft personal films in which artistic expression was paramount, no matter how many feet of film were exposed. They ached to be celluloid versions of singer-songwriters, little filmic Dylans. Some had the discipline to make it work; others—Coppola with 1979's *Apocalypse Now,* most ruinously Michael Cimino with 1980's *Heaven's Gate*—found that without the backbone of story their films evaporated into chaos.

Freedom of artistic movement did not, it turned out, mean freedom from form and narrative structure. Before the pendulum swung the other way, with the arrival of Steven Spielberg and George Lucas and other commercially minded kid titans, a druggy self-indulgence ruled the box office, and, yes, some remarkable films got made. Still, these men were public personalities, tamers of the moving image, and especially in Coppola, Altman, and Roman Polanski they established larger-than-life personas of Rabelaisian mavericks presiding over the creation of mysteries. For the first time, it became hip to want to tell the stories as well as star in them.

Two of the era's hardest to pigeonhole figures were both directors *and* stars, and they would each loom over the coming decades. Woody Allen and Clint Eastwood had, on the surface, diametrically opposed star personas, yet both are irreducible. When we say "Woody" or "Clint," everyone understands who we mean. Allen, you could argue, was *menschlichkeit* unbound, the Jewish schlump-hero taken to surrealist, self-lacerating extremes. He began as a gag writer for Broadway columnists and TV shows at the dawn of the 1960s, and only at the urging of his agent did he move into stand-up comedy. "I never set out to create any image at all," Allen maintained in 1964, yet he did manufacture a persona—a prickly, intellectual, perpetually neurotic, perpetually horny Manhattanite—that only partially overlapped with Allen's actual personality. By the time he began writing and directing his own movies—*Take the Money and Run* in 1969, *Bananas* in 1971—he was a well-established figure on TV talk shows and the counterculture's answer to Bob Hope, a perennially wisecracking coward.

His biggest early commercial success, though, was *Play It Again, Sam* (1972), directed by Herbert Ross from Allen's stage play and establishing the comedian as a genuine romantic figure guided, no less, by the spirit of Bogart (played by Jerry Lacy) in *Casablanca*. This was a brilliant stroke, using the iconography of the classic Hollywood star system to give credibility and depth to a shaggy modern antihero—an actor the old studios would have used as a sight gag, if at all.

In the films that followed (*Sleeper* in 1973, *Love and Death* in 1975), Allen consolidated his gains and pushed forward into both manically cross-referencing modern comedy and appealing everyman romance. *Annie Hall* (1977) was the Oscar-winning apotheosis, the moment at which Allen really did seem to represent everything rich and free and wise and good in New Hollywood and the surrounding culture. That included the filmmaker blowing off the Academy Awards to play clarinet at Michael's Pub in New York—another token of his perceived power, since *real* stars don't need awards.

Annie Hall was seen as an organic work of genius; that the film may actually have been salvaged by editor Ralph Rosenblum after disastrous test screenings didn't fit the auteurist formula. In fact, so fully did "Woody" embody for critics and cultivated audiences the idea of what a natural American filmmaker should be that the persona held steady for years despite Allen's immediate dismantling of it. His follow-up to *Annie Hall* was the morbidly serious *Interiors* (1978), hardly well received but understood as something Woody had to "get out of his system." *Manhattan* (1979) found him back in good graces, despite a romantic subplot about a very young woman (Mariel Hemingway) that foreshadowed a crucial and controversial element of Allen's later persona.

With *Stardust Memories* (1980), he pulled a Chaplin, insisting that "funny Woody" was dead, that drama had more intrinsic value than comedy, and that anyone who felt otherwise was a freak. This was a star spitting on his audience for buying the persona he had sold them, a monumental act of redefinition in the guise of artistic expression. Still, many fans held on, because Allen had come to stand for a critical aspect of the maturing counterculture's self-image. He was smart, engaged, insecure, funny; he was distrustful of authority and he was his own worst enemy. Love kept messing him up but, to quote *Annie Hall,* he needed the eggs. He was one of us.

Clint Eastwood, by contrast, was one of *them.* If Allen was a sock puppet for the popular culture's progressive left, Eastwood was a hero of the middle-American right. Both views, of course, would eventually be revealed as drastic oversimplifications. Eastwood had already reinvented himself once, from a second-banana TV cowboy (six years as Rowdy Yates on *Rawhide*) to the silent, cheroot-smoking Man with No Name in Sergio Leone's spaghetti-western trilogy: *A Fistful of Dollars* (1964), *For a Few Dollars More* (1965), and *The Good, the Bad and the Ugly* (1966). These were brilliantly made films—the last, especially—that reworked the Hollywood western for an age of irony, and they're much funnier than anyone credited at the time. That extends to Eastwood's performances and new persona. Because the Man with No Name didn't smile and because he resorted to guns, cultural commentators dismissed Leone's movies as junk, hip pop art at best, while consigning the star to the status of a B player catching a lucky break. Whatever Eastwood was doing, it wasn't really seen as acting. More like posturing.

The star consolidated his gains with Hollywood westerns and war films throughout the rest of the decade and then, in 1971, redefined himself in two radically different directions. What initially seemed the lesser change consisted of directing his first film, a tight little suspense shocker called *Play Misty for Me,* about a radio DJ (Eastwood) stalked by a psychotic fan (Jessica Walter). The second shift, which deeply polarized audiences and gave Eastwood's star persona a sudden political dimension, was *Dirty Harry.* Even the title announced that the gloves were off. The character of San Francisco police detective Harry Callahan, stepping far outside due process to bring a serial killer to justice, was a turning point—the moment at which the freedoms of the 1960s became excesses in the popular culture.

Gene Hackman's Popeye Doyle in the same year's *The French Connection* trod a similar rebellious line but without the social disgust Callahan put into every sneer and taunt. A commercial smash, *Dirty Harry* articulated the disenchantment of anyone who felt America was spinning out of control, that glamorizing criminals while calling police "pig bastards" was an inversion of the correct order of things, that enough was enough. The movie's resort to violence served as an emotional catharsis for this audience, as did the wave of early-'70s vigilante action movies that starred Charles Bronson, Bo Svenson, and Tom "Billy Jack" Laughlin, all glowering non–sex symbols. Just as usefully, *Dirty Harry* horrified critics and other pundits who lionized the New Hollywood. *New Yorker* critic Pauline Kael famously called the film "fascist medievalism" and a "right-wing fantasy." Roger Ebert described Eastwood's new persona as "the savage forced to follow the rules of society."

Actually, *Dirty Harry* was supposed to be a Frank Sinatra movie, but a broken wrist sustained during *The Manchurian Candidate* eight years earlier meant that Old Blue Eyes couldn't hold the heavy Magnum pistol comfortably. Steve McQueen and Paul Newman each turned the role down; clearly, it threatened the images they'd built of easygoing rebels. There's nothing easygoing about Harry—he's pissed off. Eastwood had less to lose, had worked with director Don Siegel three times before, agreed enough with the film's politics. Perhaps most crucially, he didn't care about alienating the critical community and the youth audience, sensing correctly that there was another, neglected audience that would respond. Or maybe he was just an actor intrigued by the drama of an unyielding man in a corrupt world.

In any event, Clint Eastwood spent the 1970s as a box office sensation who was reviled by mainstream pundits and tastemakers, whose action films and ramshackle comedies were derided as yahoo fodder even as he directed more and better movies, including one western, *The Outlaw Josey Wales* (1976), that's nearly the equal of the Leone films. He learned his trade and he kept his own counsel, and eventually the culture came around to him in the Reagan '80s, not because his superficial vigilante character was now acceptable but because Eastwood himself was revealed as a much more complete person than his persona had allowed. He was a jazz fanatic who made a Charlie Parker biopic (*Bird*, 1988); his views on crime and punishment came to be acknowledged as complex in the ways of novelists rather than rednecks. By the time the revisionist western *Unforgiven* (1992) won four Oscars—two to Eastwood for directing and producing—he had become something even his fans in 1971 would have found inconceivable. Clint Eastwood was an auteur.

It has to be noted that Eastwood still lost his *Unforgiven* acting Oscar to Al Pacino in *Scent of a Woman*—a towering slice of ham from a man perceived to be a *real* thespian. The wheel took a long time to turn, but it turned in the direction of resuscitated glamour, a *new* New Hollywood much more like the original one in its pursuit of beauty and the shallow, irresistible slaking of desire. The ragged stars of the 1960s became the confident superstars of the 1970s: Redford and Newman in *The Sting*, Jack Nicholson bestriding the world with his manic grin, second-generation Hollywood royalty like Jane Fonda and Michael Douglas saving the planet in *The China Syndrome* (1979). A culture of celebrity was poised to go nuclear in the coming decades, and the reality principle turned out to be a passing fancy. Marlon Brando found out the hard way. Long before he turned from his own stardom in contempt, he told a friend, "I've learned that no matter what I say or do, people mythologize me."

Well, yes. Of course. This is why we raise people to fame, to give us a mythology by which to explain the world; to establish gods we can aspire to, collect, desire, resent. To provide identities we can then take as our own. Yet every generation's deities are overthrown by the next, and as the baby boomers had rejected the factory-turned icons of their parents for more flawed models, so their own children turned once more to the manufacture of perfection. We said we wanted stars just like us. It turns out we just wanted them prettier.

15.

The Glamour Backlash: The 1980s

It isn't often that you get to witness one cultural epoch become another right before your eyes. On an evening in mid-1978 I was privileged to see the 1960s decisively turn into the 1980s, the 1970s being understood as one tortuously long transitional era punctuated by double knit and disco. The place was Dartmouth College, in Hanover, New Hampshire. The occasion was the release of *National Lampoon's Animal House.*

It was something of a homecoming. One of the film's screenwriters, Chris Miller, had gone to Dartmouth in the early '60s and had based a few of the film's characters and incidents on his experiences in the college's notorious Alpha Delta Phi fraternity. Now he was back in Hanover with a print of the movie, as part of a promotional tour or maybe just because he wanted to pay homage. That night *Animal House* screened in the little town cinema, and you could feel the collective mood swing like a compass needle toward a new north.

There's a famous scene where John Belushi's Bluto, upon hearing a wimpy collegiate folksinger serenade a group of girls, calmly takes the kid's acoustic guitar and smashes it to pieces. The Dartmouth students roared in approval, their impatience toward the unceasing sensitivity of their older siblings' counterculture finding an outlet at last. (The scene was shot in a University of Oregon frat house, and the hole Belushi put in the wall was subsequently framed and turned into a makeshift shrine.)

After the screening, the mood was exuberant to the point of a near riot. Miller answered a few questions at the theater and then was literally carried several blocks to Fraternity Row on the shoulders of dozens of cheering students, their faces flushed with joy. The street was crowded with kids celebrating—but celebrating what? Nothing less than the sudden finding of their generational voice. The country was still a year away from President Jimmy Carter's "malaise" speech ("a crisis of confidence . . . that strikes at the very heart and soul and spirit of our national will"), but the sense that America had lost its way was acute. More particularly, the progressive liberalism that had sustained the counterculture from before the Civil Rights era to the climactic vanquishing of Richard Nixon in 1974 had started to feel like oppressive doctrine. Still, if you were young and in college, you automatically had to subscribe to it, didn't you?

Animal House said, no, man, you didn't. You didn't have to Mean It at all. Wasn't it so much more honest, even revolutionary, to party your ass off, admit your sexism, cater to your impulses, get what you could for yourself? The movie fed into and articulated a growing frustration with the culture's overbearing political correctness—the fear that you couldn't say what you wanted to without stepping on someone's toes. Which, of course, made a lot of people want to step on someone's—anyone's—toes. Thus punk rock and thus smutty youth comedies in the movies, two pop developments that looked vaguely similar but that ultimately pointed in opposite directions, the first anarchic, the second reactionary.

In fact, if you were the right age in 1978—it helped to be male—this one film seemed to destroy a reigning timidity in the public discourse and replace it with a raucous, hip, funny stance that felt like the cold wind of Truth. That sensibility—we can offend people and *it's okay*—exploded like Bluto's mashed-potato zit into the zeitgeist and rearranged the rules, setting the stage for hormone-drenched teen farces like *Porky's* and its endless spawn, the suburban angst of the Brat Pack movies, even ascendant action heroes of the 1980s like Sylvester Stallone and Arnold Schwarzenegger. *Animal House* declared it was time to cut the crap.

It's no coincidence that the movie was set in 1962, before Kennedy was shot, the Beatles arrived, and the 1960s actually got started. By dialing back to a perceived pre-assassination Eden, *Animal House* returned audiences to a time when things (it was thought) were less complicated. In a sense, the film was a more comically aggressive variant on the pop nostalgia that had produced the 1950s revival in the mid-'70s: *Grease* on Broadway, *American Graffiti* on the big screen, *Happy Days* on TV, Sha Na Na on your radio. And that cultural conservatism (things were easier then, so let's go back) merged with a growing political conservatism that was struggling to find its voice. The left, some felt, had been guilting us for years with the insistence that we should always be better than ourselves, that we should join forces to help those less fortunate. But what was *wrong* with us? And, really, who cared about *them*?

No, I'm not saying that *Animal House* led directly to the election of Ronald Reagan two years later. But I am saying the movie empowered a generation of twentysomethings to aspire to a new hedonism—call it, at best, enlightened selfishness—that spilled over into the political sphere and helped crystallize the tenor of the times. Would my fellow students in the class of 1980 who founded the *Dartmouth Review*—the first major neoconservative college newspaper in the country—and who went on to write speeches for Reagan and the first George Bush have come together with such gleeful underdog purpose without *Animal House*? The way they saw it, *they* were the Deltas, detested by authority yet stubbornly true to the principles of personal interest; it was the liberals who were the cruel, powerful Omegas to be resisted. One of the *Review* crew, Peter Robinson, in his 2003 memoir *How Ronald Reagan Changed My Life,* describes seeing the movie "at least half a dozen times" in Hanover and admits, "Bluto seemed natural. Bluto was our man. We wanted to be just like him ourselves." Of course we did. In a time of lockstep Superego, Bluto was unchecked Id.

To his credit, Robinson goes on to discuss the inherent problems with that approach—you'd flunk out, for one thing—which, to nobody's surprise, Belushi personally demonstrated by dying of a drug overdose in 1982. "The trick," Robinson wrote, "lay in striking a balance," and in the wake of *Animal House,* everyone teetered back and forth on a fulcrum of celebratory apathy. The weekend before the screening, the frat parties at Dartmouth had all featured the usual kegs, tepid rock and roll, upstairs bongs, and a general sense of drift. A weekend later, everyone—I mean *everyone*—was wearing a toga, the new uniform for a stance of ironic and profoundly relieved decadence.

When a culture changes, obviously, the faces that embody it change. So: What kind of a star did this new mind-set produce? What did people desire in the 1980s, when desire and the willingness to satisfy it became paramount? Who did we see when we looked in the mirror, only better, sharper, sexier?

Well, Tom Cruise, for one. Cruise united all the disparate elements that transformed stardom in the new post-counterculture era—the catering to adolescence, a yearning for uncomplicated heroism, the rebirth of glamour, and, most of all, the return of confidence expressed as graceful, aggressive entitlement. The Tom Cruise hero wanted the world and he took it, and because he took it, he deserved it. No questions, and no bummer ending like in the 1970s. Not much below the surface, though—no enduring mystery, but it seemed like a fair trade at the time.

That's the short answer. The long answer is more complicated, and it involves much more than actors. It took eighteen years to get from Dustin Hoffman in *The Graduate* to Cruise in *Top Gun,* from Mensch Triumphant to Aryan Resurgent, each man the preferred movie stand-in for his generation. What had changed? The culture, clearly, and audiences. More to the point, the kind of audiences had changed. With television having replaced the cinema as the culture's primary media diversion over the course of two decades, moviegoers no longer represented the totality of America but a highly profitable segment. The cultural revolutions of the 1960s, the success of *The Graduate* and *Easy Rider*, and the trendy unease of the New Hollywood had brought the youth audience back to movie theaters while their parents tended to stay home to watch TV. By the 1970s, according to one analyst, three-quarters of all moviegoers were under thirty.

It was an impressionable mass audience with disposable income and a taste for the faddish. With *Jaws* in 1975, Hollywood discovered the pop phenomenon of the blockbuster, a property that could do insane amounts of business on the strengths of a simple hook and relentless marketing. (Delivering a great movie in the bargain was helpful but not, it eventually turned out, essential.) With *Star Wars* in 1977, the film industry learned that selling to kids, teens, and twentysomethings could be even more profitable—that a movie, in fact, could be just the first iteration in a franchise that straddled the entire consumer culture.

But the stars of *Jaws* were, in order, the shark, boy-genius director Steven Spielberg, and the likably flawed triumvirate of Richard Dreyfuss, Roy Scheider, and Robert Shaw, all appealing non-idols. And the star of *Star Wars* was the experience itself—the notion that movies could be grand, uncomplicated fun once more. Beyond that, what did you have? A pair of robots, an overgrown teddy bear, an aging British knight who thought the whole thing was ridiculous, and three nobodies.

It's in one of those nobodies, though, that the seeds for the new stardom of the 1980s reside. Not Mark Hamill, who played the film's nominal hero, Luke Skywalker. Adolescent and earnest, Hamill fit perfectly into George Lucas's teen space fantasy but had little resonance outside it. He was a star of *this* movie without being a movie star. Carrie Fisher had a royal Hollywood bloodline and an engaging snap to her performance, but you can't launch a serious career with a hairdo like that, and it turned out that the actress was too ironic and troubled and unfocused to try.

No, it was the guy in the supporting role who brought it, another actor so out of sync with prevailing winds that he had already thrown in the towel and become a carpenter. It's in the rise-fall-rise of Harrison Ford's career that we most plainly see the 1970s star morph into the 1980s superstar, the counterculture once more giving way to a mainstream pop discourse predicated on simpler pleasures and prettier faces. That Ford was deeply ambivalent—and still is—about his newfound super-celebrity is both to the point and beside it.

The most sensible way to think about Ford is as a '70's mensch who had the misfortune to look like a hunk and who, moreover, landed in Hollywood, where they thought they knew what to do with hunks. The New York theater orbit might have allowed the young Ford to explore his offbeat impulses, but when he arrived in Los Angeles from the Midwest in 1964, he encountered the death twitches of the classic star system. A contract at Columbia meant $150 a week, wearing a jacket and tie to the studio commissary, beefcake photo ops, and deportment classes. "It was 1964–65 and Columbia was still playing 1920–30," Ford later said. "Horrible, worse than any factory."

A bred-in-the-bone iconoclast, the actor gritted his teeth and went along with it—sort of. Told to change his name ("Harrison Ford" had also been the name of a silent-film star), he caustically suggested "Kurt Affair." At auditions he was a glowering, remote figure in jeans and work shirt. There were small roles in movies and on TV shows, but Ford alienated more executives and casting directors than he won over. The problem, said his sympathetic acting coach at Columbia, was that Ford's "type was out of style. Harrison was a young leading man; while the guys who were coming up like Dustin and Pacino, Hopper and Fonda, were the antiheroes. The problem was that he was not off the wall. And he was not short and homely."

There were chances Ford willingly passed up, like the role of Mike "Meathead" Stivic on TV's *All in the Family,* a show whose bigoted dialogue the actor couldn't countenance. Finally, he caught a break through his friendship with Fred Roos, the maverick casting director who'd be responsible for so much of the star map of the 1970s thanks to his work on *Five Easy Pieces, The Godfather, Apocalypse Now,* and other films. No one expected the second feature by a nerdy USC graduate named George Lucas to be much of anything, so Roos was able to get Ford in the door and into a key part. *American Graffiti* was a huge 1973 hit, but it was an ensemble piece that failed to establish the actor. Anyway, by this point Ford had more or less quit the business to become carpenter to the stars, a craftsman able to lavish his perfectionism on inanimate wood rather than an insensate movie industry. He was just one more failed actor in Hollywood. He was the norm.

This prompts the obvious question: Why didn't anyone *see* Harrison Ford? By the early 1970s, the actor had acquired the physical heft and moral weight audiences respond to on the screen. He was extremely handsome in a centered and comfortable way, with a scar on his chin that hinted at a rough-and-tumble history. (A minor auto accident, actually, but no matter.) Yet there still was no place for him in the culture, because Ford's specific persona—which combined elements of Redford's sex appeal, Nicholson's rebelliousness, and a cynical gravitas that went all the way back to Bogart—had yet to exist onscreen. Harrison Ford had to create the pop space within which he was necessary.

Or have others create it for him. Again, we have to credit Roos, and through him acknowledge the unheralded role that casting directors have played across movie history in creating actors who now seem inevitable and who were anything but before someone risked putting them in a movie. Roos knew that Lucas was casting for his proposed space opera *The Star Wars* (potentially the first film in a trilogy called *The Adventures of Luke Starkiller*) and in fact allowed the young director to hold cattle calls in the Zoetrope offices that Roos shared with Francis Ford Coppola. Not coincidentally, the casting director hired Ford at this time to build a new door for his office—a very complex door, necessitating several weeks of work.

Lucas auditioned hundreds of actors for the part of Han Solo—not the movie's lead role, but something much more important: the dashing, wisecracking comic relief. Han Solo is the attitude that makes

Star Wars a hip commentary on old *Flash Gordon* serials rather than a mere imitation of them; he gives the audience the necessary space to laugh with the film rather than at it. If an actor can be likable and sexy doing that, there really is no choice but to call him a star.

Lucas was stuck on the other main characters as well, and after a while he asked Ford to read opposite some of the actors trying out for Luke and Leia. He put some of the auditions on film, too, and finally he saw Harrison Ford. "He was by far the best," Lucas said later. "Within a minute or two of him being on the screen you got a whole sense of a lot of backstory with him. Part of it is just his physical ruggedness, but part of it is also the sly intelligence he keeps projecting."

Insert shot of Fred Roos innocently whistling.

In retrospect, Ford's Han Solo is a watershed creation, another one of those pivots, like the release of *Animal House* the following year, upon which pop eras turn. The character is a conscious throwback to classic star types in bearing and attitude—you can see Errol Flynn's lightness there, Bogart's world-weariness, John Wayne's swagger, Cary Grant's way with a quip. There are modern elements as well, specifically a refusal to be cornered into self-seriousness that smacks of Jack Nicholson.

Unlike many characters played by '70s movie actors, though, Han has no sociopolitical meaning, no message, because the movie in which he figures has none beyond giving us a mythic ride. He's not sleeping with Mrs. Robinson. He's not motorcycling across a fallen America. He exists only within Lucas's make-believe world and in relation to the classic "lowbrow" pop culture that helped create that world.

Ford—actor, not role—is the bridge that allows a hip '70s audience to enter Lucas's fairy tale, because his grounded, unflappable cool invites us in. This isn't a meta-thing; Ford doesn't overtly wink at us, because that would be unprofessional. Instead, his very counterculture distrust of happy endings and popcorn moralizing comes through in Han's impatience. Tellingly, Ford improvised many of his best-known lines, including the biggest and best laugh in the sequel, *The Empire Strikes Back*. When Fisher's Leia says "I love you" as Han is about to be frozen solid by the villains, the script had him responding "I love you, too." Ford rewrote the line to "I know," fought for it, and got it in—and not only does it fit the character, but it's the critical window through which anyone older than a child can enter *Star Wars*'s fundamentally naive fantasy world.

So Ford was a quintessential 1970s actor who provided the template for the 1980s franchise star. Post–*Star Wars,* the actor initially struggled in films that didn't take advantage of his gift for playing it straight while simultaneously seeming to comment sardonically on his own dialogue. There was a wartime romance (*Hanover Street*), a wartime action film (*Force 10 from Navarone*), a comic western (*The Frisco Kid*), and only the latter let Ford grin through his character. He was being molded into a classic male leading man, but it was his distance from the type while simultaneously honoring it that made him interesting.

Again, Lucas came to the rescue, and Steven Spielberg, too—the new toymakers for a mass audience predisposed to play. *Raiders of the Lost Ark* (1981) was Lucas's idea and Spielberg's baby, and both men put every bit of their love for old Hollywood action clichés into each frame. Indiana Jones, the academic adventurer, seemed created specifically for Ford, and after a brief, weird casting courtship with Tom Selleck, star of TV's *Magnum, P.I.,* Spielberg finally acknowledged the obvious.

Actually, it's a good question. What *does* Harrison Ford bring to a movie that Tom Selleck doesn't? Both men are handsome, both can do stunts, both can handle comedy. Selleck's persona is predicated on being lightly likeable, though, and Ford is one of the few actors who can make grumpiness seem sexy. In the words of Roos, "He's prickly but not a prick." This is a key to Ford's lasting star power, as opposed to his immediate impact—we trust him because he doesn't beg for our attention. On the contrary, he seems a whole and complete man without us.

There's also a bit of business Ford does in both *Star Wars* and *Raiders* that illustrates the difference between the two actors and that helps define why Ford is different from anyone who came before—why he resonated so strongly with a post-hippie audience. In *Star Wars,* the moment comes when Han gets frustrated at a cockpit communications device and blasts it into dust; the sudden *un*heroicness of the gesture gets a big laugh. The far more celebrated scene in *Raiders* is when Indy is confronted in a dusty Arab street by a scimitar-wielding assassin spoiling for a fight. Spielberg had a big battle scene planned and was getting ready to block it out, but the morning was hot and Ford was suffering from dysentery. "Why don't we just shoot the fucker?" he casually suggested.

There you have it: Harrison Ford shoots first. That scene in the film—the swarthy villain whirling his sword in intricate patterns, Indy sighing in exasperation, pulling his gun, and dropping him with one bullet—caused cheers and standing ovations in U.S. movie theaters six months after the Iranian hostage crisis had finally ended and Ronald Reagan had ascended to the presidency. No other star of the time—not Hoffman or Nicholson or Pacino, certainly not Paul Newman or Robert Redford—would have thought up the bit, let alone filmed it. Eastwood didn't have the light touch required; if he'd done it, the scene would have been freighted with more political meaning than it could handle. In truth, the gesture descends directly from Bluto putting the folksinger's guitar through the wall in *Animal House,* and it carries the same message: Screw your sensitivity.

In *Raiders,* that message is so buried that neither star nor director need to or even are able to articulate it. It's just a surprise twist on a classic movie showdown—but funny and cathartic because it mirrors the audience's impatience with ethnic baddies trying to bend us to their will. Just shoot the fucker. Yeah, that's it. The scene is sobering if you stop to consider it—can you imagine Gary Cooper's Marshal Will Kane in *High Noon* "cheating" like this?—and hilarious and liberating if you don't, and in its own small way it represented a major advance in the culture of Not Thinking About It that came to dominate late-twentieth-century media.

And in its insouciance and exasperation and punch, it depends on this particular star even as it defines him. Ford isn't a reactionary pop figure the way Eastwood was in the 1970s and Sylvester Stallone and Arnold Schwarzenegger were in the 1980s. He *was* the most appealing face of a reactionary trend in pop culture, films, and stardom—the retreat of narrative from meaning (or even the pretense of meaning) back into entertainment.

More critically, Ford can be considered the first star "brand" in a modern sense. As with Cagney or Bogart or Garbo, audiences bought tickets for a Harrison Ford movie with specific expectations of what the star would be and do. Unlike the earlier stars, the actor was now the foundation for a towering edifice of marketing that extended past the films to tie-in toys, TV appearances, magazine covers, sequels, and other aftermarket iterations. Properly presented, Harrison Ford was the gift that kept on giving. He is among the top box office moneymakers of all time and the anchor of two of the biggest movie franchises ever, and for the studios he reestablished the bankability of glamour.

Ford set the mold for the male star that would come to dominate the 1980s and '90s: the action figure with attitude. At first, though, audiences came out of the 1970s needing to laugh. A few flawed counterculture types—William Hurt, Jeff Bridges—hung around and did good work in worthy films, but the real money in the first half of the 1980s was made by comedians, and the pipeline ran directly from television to the movie theater. Seven of the top ten movies in 1980 were comedies, and while some of them featured actors most people thought of as movie stars—Jane Fonda in *Nine to Five,* Burt Reynolds in *Smokey and the Bandit II,* Gene Wilder and Richard Pryor in *Stir Crazy*—others featured personalities whose roots were in TV. That included Goldie Hawn, who revitalized her movie career that year with *Private Benjamin,* the first in a string of hits for the onetime bubblehead comedienne of NBC's *Laugh-In.* More tellingly, it also included refugees from *Saturday Night Live*—John Belushi and Dan Aykroyd in *The Blues Brothers* and (number 12 on the 1980 list) *Caddyshack,* starring Chevy Chase and the man who replaced him on the show, Bill Murray.

SNL had debuted in 1975 and made instant celebrities of its cast. Named the "Not Ready for Prime Time Players," they effectively created a new cultural prime time that was cooler than the old one because you stayed up for it and your parents didn't. You also got the humor, which was aggressive, anarchic, surreal—skit comedy with a druggy edge. This is where the '60s counterculture had finally and decisively landed on television, or so it seemed.

Chase, an ironic prankster beneath his bland preppie exterior, was the first major figure to leap from *SNL* to the movies. The film was *Foul Play* (1978), which paired him with Hawn and only proved how awkwardly Chase's stance of mockery chafed against the constraints of the romantic action-comedy genre. His deadpan did give new life to the detective movie in *Fletch* (1985), and his paterfamilias Clark Griswold in *National Lampoon's Vacation* (1983) was an archly subversive spin on TV's *Father Knows Best.*

Those films worked because Chase was able to play both sides of the net for a while. He looked like a conventional leading man but something was off, and that provided the tension and the comedy of his performance. Ultimately, that was all there was. Raised and defined in the ethos of improvisational skit comedy, Chase never was able to make his persona mean anything beyond one amusingly disconnected one-liner after another, a short-term pleasure that quickly ran the risk of seeming smug. Movie stars invite sustained interest; Chase deflected it. When he tried headlining an early-'90s late-night talk show—a medium where sincerity, or the faking of it, is critical to audience interest—the meltdown was public and disastrous, and Chase never recovered. The lesson: Being a smartass and only a smartass is not a viable career plan, because what seems at first like laughing at *them* very quickly comes to look like laughing at *us.*

What we needed, once more, were comedians who seemed like us, our representatives from the unwashed masses. *Animal House,* released the same year as *Foul Play,* was a revolutionary dismantling of the Hollywood mainstream. As mentioned, Belushi functioned for a while as the national Id, the entertainment equivalent of a charismatic stage crasher who commandeers the microphone. (Actually, wasn't that what the Blues Brothers were all about, the white frat boys from *Animal House* finally getting to play at being Otis Day and the Knights?) Belushi's insecurities and drug intake doomed him, though, and the cultural spin after his 1982 overdose was that, like a comic James Dean, he was too wild (meaning too pure) for lasting stardom. The question facing the *SNL* comics became how to sell out while retaining their hipster credibility.

Only Bill Murray was able to stake out a middle position between Chase's conceptual arrogance and Belushi's instinctive schpritz. (In passing, let us relish the memory of their rare triangulation: a legendary backstage fistfight between Chase and Murray when the former returned in 1977 to guest-host *SNL*. Belushi, trying to break it up, caught a punch in the face.) As with many of the rising stars of this transitional era, there's an ironic space between Murray and his characters that is precisely the source of the laughs. He'll play a dimwitted groundskeeper in *Caddyshack* (1980) or a reprobate army recruit in *Stripes* (1981), but the enjoyment—for both himself and the audience—is in the way he goofs on his own characters as well as the various authority figures they torment. Not Meaning It is what Bill Murray is all about, yet because he invites us into the relaxed silliness of his way of seeing things (instead of pushing us away as Chase does), we get to play along.

In other words, if Belushi was the Id of early *SNL*-derived stardom, and Chase was the smarmy Superego, then you'd have to argue that Murray served as the functioning Ego, harnessing wildness without neutering himself. How else would you describe his performance in *Ghostbusters,* the 1984 smash in which demons and Babylonian elder gods rampage through New York's Upper West Side and it's just another day at work for Murray's Peter Venkman? The star's persona is so uninterested in the machinations of plot and character and big-studio special effects that he can discover the gate of Hell in Sigourney Weaver's refrigerator and arch his eyebrow with an unimpressed but game *Well, hey now.*

Crucially, there's no cynicism to Murray's hipster laziness, just amusement that the rest of us take things so seriously. This isn't so much persona as philosophy in action (or, more properly, inaction), a commitment to the moment that has turned increasingly and overtly Zen as the actor has slowly moved into the art-house phase of his career, first with *Groundhog Day* (1993)—only the most metaphysically profound slapstick comedy ever made—and then, more seriously, with *Lost in Translation* (2003) and *Broken Flowers* (2005). Yet he can still turn up in a gleefully gory genre movie like *Zombieland* (2009), playing a movie star named Bill Murray who calmly survives a zombie takeover of Hollywood (well, *hey* now) and who, asked if he has any regrets, pauses and names *Garfield,* the worst film of his career.

Murray is the rare star, in other words, to share his self-awareness with the audience and to neutralize an actor's natural inclination to go where the money is (or to sell out, as you will) by commenting on it. In the twenty-first century, Murray has practically become the Laughing Buddha of the film industry, working without an agent, living far off the celebrity grid, and reappearing in whatever small or large projects he chooses. Furthermore, because he appears to be one of the very few movie stars to have opted out of the business of being a celebrity, he has become something unheard of—the movie star as urban legend. Google "Bill Murray" plus the phrase "They'll never believe you" and you'll be led to countless online anecdotes about the actor popping up in mundane, real-world situations over the years, doing something bizarre, and disappearing into the night after saying these words to startled witnesses. They can't all be true, but are any of them? Even Murray, when asked about it by interviewers, playfully refuses to confirm or deny, possibly because he knows the legend says nothing about the real Bill Murray and everything about the pop culture trickster who goes by that name.

This sort of grace is unique, and Hollywood is at a loss to imitate and package it. What the studios can do, and did do starting in the 1980s, is build a brand. If Bill Murray embodied the initial promise of *Saturday Night Live*—mockery as way of life—Eddie Murphy represented what the show became: a rigidly formulaic source of new stars and fresh (or not so fresh) catchphrases for the mainstream pop culture.

On *SNL*, Murphy had been the wild card and a racial breakthrough, fusing Richard Pryor's politically tinged comic rage with the profane ease of a younger generation that knew how much and how little had been gained by the 1960s. He played rudely funny variations on Gumby and Buckwheat—the latter both a criticism of Hollywood's minstrel tradition and an invitation to find it funny in a new way—and he helped revitalize what had become a moribund TV show. But what kind of a movie star would he be?

An action star, as it turned out, comfortable with chase scenes, tough talk, and gunplay but distanced —as Bill Murray and, to a lesser extent, Harrison Ford were with the genre films they appeared in—from the seriousness of the plot by his ability to comment from a superior position he shared with the audience. Like Murray, Murphy was a trickster, but one with a built-in racial edge. The fun in *48 HRS* (1982) and *Beverly Hills Cop* (1984) isn't just in watching Murphy take on straight America, but in watching him take on straight white America—a bar full of rednecks in *48 HRS*, an uptight maître d' in *Beverly Hills Cop*—in a way that made white audiences feel hip and progressive.

Unlike Murray, Murphy took being a star very seriously indeed, and the first half of his film career saw him veering between action sequels and attempts to establish himself as a comedic but genuine leading man in *The Golden Child* (1986), *Harlem Nights* (1989), *Boomerang* (1992), and *The Distinguished Gentleman* (1992). Some of these films worked and others didn't, but the larger problem was the lack of a cohesive persona that integrated the onscreen Eddie Murphy with some sense of who he was, or wanted to be, offscreen. Movie Eddie could be manic or rudely inspired; "real" Eddie was aloof and composed. The two sides didn't seem to square. He released R&B albums, too, and made stand-up comedy movies and cable TV specials. Which one of these entertainers was he, and why didn't "all of the above" seem to suffice? When does star persona get stretched too thin?

With his career in decline by the mid-1990s—a 1997 arrest for dallying with a transsexual prostitute didn't help—Murphy pioneered an image switch. He became a family entertainer with films like *The Nutty Professor* (1996), *Dr. Dolittle* (1998), and his voicing of the donkey in the *Shrek* films. This ultimately turned into an accepted blueprint for comic actors in the first decade of the new millennium, but it arguably boxed Murphy into a corner. When the performance that genuinely stood to revitalize his career came around—the Marvin Gaye–inspired pop star in *Dreamgirls* (2006), a part exquisitely acted and sung—the actor reacted to his Golden Globe win and Oscar nomination with a poise that was read by many commentators as cold, even ungrateful. And then Murphy went back to making splattery, critically reviled family comedies like *Norbit* (2007), which came out a few weeks before the Academy Awards and possibly squandered his newfound respect with voters.

He refused to play by the cultural script, in other words, and while that's fine and even fascinating, the alternative reading Murphy offered provided little insight. We want stars to be thankful for their second chances, maybe even to grovel a little—it reasserts the audience's power. So what was this star saying by his refusal to do so?

The mystery of Eddie Murphy's stardom and what he wants it to be remains unsolved. Perhaps the prospect of tailing off into character parts wasn't in his game plan. Maybe the way any African American actor responds to the expectations of the white entertainment machinery is his or her business rather than ours. Possibly he really is "doing it for the kids." His career arc, though, reflects the difficulty of branding a celebrity persona as one singular thing, especially if you come from a sketch-comedy tradition of putting on different masks. This is a lesson that Mike Myers, Dana Carvey, and other *SNL* escapees have discovered to their dismay. To really respond to a star, on not just a commercial level but also a cultural one, audiences have to sense that the persona is rooted in an actual personality—a core of perceived genuineness that may or may not actually be there. Who is Eddie Murphy? Because we'll never know, we ultimately don't care. Whereas Bill Murray, whose wise, funny detachment seems intrinsic to "who he is," is beloved.

Let's backtrack a bit. As the 1980s settle in and Hollywood moviemaking formulas are revived, we can see the leading men and women of the 1960s and '70s deciding how to re-establish themselves—critical if you didn't want to be become as passé as a tie-dyed T-shirt. In its way, the transition was no less wrenching than the shift to talking pictures had been a half century earlier, only the impetus was sociological and cultural rather than technological. Stars still had to adapt if they wanted to survive.

It was much harder for actresses, because pop culture in the 1980s was a man's, man's, man's world. Every year since 1932, the Quigley Publishing Company has polled theater owners to come up with a list of the top ten moneymaking stars; the rankings, released in the *International Motion Picture Almanac* and recently made available online, offer an instructive portrait of the shifting sands of gender popularity. In the early 1930s, female stars routinely held down six of the ten spots, but by the end of the decade, the average was down to five—then four women in the 1940s and two in the 1950s, until the dread year 1957, when no female stars were listed in the top ten at all.

The early 1960s saw Doris Day and Elizabeth Taylor—the virgin and the whore of post-Eisenhower popular culture—regularly make the list, and the latter half of the decade marked the ascension of Streisand, who held down spots even when no other women did. By the end of the 1970s, she had been joined by the women of the New Hollywood: Jane Fonda, Diane Keaton, Jill Clayburgh, Sissy Spacek, Sally Field. Four actresses made the list in 1980—the highest number of women since the 1940s—and again in 1981. But look at the difference between those two years. In 1980, the four most popular women at the box office were Fonda, Streisand, Field, and Spacek, the latter two offering gritty and sympathetic portraits of working-class women in *Norma Rae* and *Coal Miner's Daughter.* In 1981, the four were Fonda, Dolly Parton (a much-loved, big-busted country-and-western crossover star), Bo Derek (a sex goddess with no discernible acting talent), and Goldie Hawn (a gifted comedienne skilled at playing ditzes). The men on the list that year told the real story—they included easygoing Burt Reynolds in his ninth year on the list and fourth in the top spot, Clint Eastwood, and two newcomers to the top ten: Harrison Ford and Bill Murray, the rebel hunk and the class clown.

In 1983, there were no actresses on the list for the first time since

1957. The female stars who appeared later in the decade were comic actresses who got their starts outside the movies (singer Bette Midler, comedian Whoopi Goldberg) or throwback noir sirens like Kathleen Turner. The lone specialist in drama was the young Meryl Streep, who made the list in 1984 and 1985, and who proved to be highly suspect in an era predicated on uncomplicated good times.

Initially, Streep filled a role remarkably similar to the young Katharine Hepburn a half century earlier: the WASP artiste. There were the odd names—"Katharine" with its willful second "a"; "Streep" more a sound effect than a name—and the Ivy League/Seven Sisters pedigrees that marked them both as inhabiting a more refined plane of existence than the rest of us. Most of Streep's peers hadn't gone to Yale Drama, and even if they had, it wasn't part of the mythology.

Like Hepburn, Streep was honored early, Oscar nominated for her second film (1978's *The Deer Hunter*) and a Supporting Actress winner for her fifth (1979's *Kramer vs. Kramer*). Unlike the young "Katharine of Arrogance," she was well liked by her fellow actors and the industry, praised for her technique where Hepburn had bulled ahead blindly. And Streep was a changeling, tackling accents and altering her looks to serve the role rather than refashioning the role to serve a star persona. Craft *was* Streep's persona—the craft of transformation, the burnishing of specific actors' skills—and not in the style of a grand diva but akin to those super-serious movie men, like Pacino and De Niro, who martyred their celebrity to art. In her commitment to the performed moment, Streep was nearly a female Brando, but one who lacked the conflicts and the agony and the sex appeal that made Saint Marlon a star in spite of himself. Offscreen, she seemed rather happily dull, which on some level was another betrayal of why we go to the movies.

So her performances in 1982's *Sophie's Choice* (for which she won Best Actress), *The French Lieutenant's Woman* (1981), *Silkwood* (1983), and *Out of Africa* (1985) were considered brilliant, grueling works of impersonation that, to the greater public, increasingly tasted like medicine. The moment Streep appeared to overreach, with 1988's *A Cry in the Dark,* the culture pounced to mock her character's impassioned outburst, "The dingo's got my baby!"—because it was silly, because she didn't seem to realize it was silly even as she nailed the accent, because such expertise can seem hermetic and self-absorbed—and in so doing made it perfectly clear that craft is fine but stardom is necessary. You couldn't project your desires onto Streep, and you certainly didn't want to project them onto her tormented characters. This much apparently occurred to the actress herself, as she embarked upon a decade and a half of fiddling with roles, trying on parts as if they were personas, and emerging in the mid-2000s as something wholly unexpected: a beloved cross-generational movie star.

In the 1980s, though, Streep represented the state of the art to a culture not particularly interested in it. That's not to say there weren't plenty of other talented actresses during this period. Some rose from the status of sequel babes and remake cuties to be considered serious thespians, or as serious as the public and tastemakers allowed: Jessica Lange arriving in 1976's *King Kong,* Michelle Pfeiffer in 1982's *Grease 2*. Some, like throaty Debra Winger (*An Officer and a Gentleman,* 1982) and the more mercurial Sean Young (*No Way Out,* 1987), were marginalized when they started behaving out of their assigned boxes onscreen and off. Cher, like Bette Midler an interloper from pop music, was a longtime trouper who for a brief spell had the serious roles and the solid performances to win her an Oscar (for *Moonstruck* in 1987) before sliding back into a larger, shallower pool of showbiz glitz.

Female newcomers tended to be introduced in highly sexualized roles to which they brought striking personalities or unexpected wit, like Kathleen Turner smoldering like Veronica Lake reborn in *Body Heat* (1981) or Melanie Griffith making like a sex-bomb Judy Holliday in 1984's *Body Double* (and in those two titles you see exactly what the culture and Hollywood expected of '80s actresses). Turner bounced back and forth between the adventure heroine of *Romancing the Stone* (1984)—her character saved by Michael Douglas in a sharp Harrison Ford impression—and hot-to-trot stuff like the lugubrious *Crimes of Passion* (1984), never quite resolving the conundrum (for the period, anyway) of a woman both smart and sexual. What a waste, for Turner had the savvy and the killer purr of a new Stanwyck. Griffith's persona seemed even more limited—a helium-voiced bimbo with unexpected brains—but she showed range in the sharp-edged indie adventure *Something Wild* (1986) and the romantic-comedy throwback *Working Girl* (1988) before running aground in labored melodramas in the 1990s.

The love object in *Working Girl* was a docile Harrison Ford, and the villainess—the WASPy executrix to Griffith's soft-focus outer-borough secretary—was Sigourney Weaver, further proof of the trouble the era's movies had with women. Even more than Streep, her Yale Drama classmate, Weaver came from patrician entitlement (her father was TV programming legend Pat Weaver), but unlike most of her peers she excelled at playing with the boys in genres like science fiction (the *Alien* series, the second of which features perhaps the greatest action performance by an actress in the history of the cinema) and the splattery comedy of *Ghostbusters*. Put her in a movie with an impressionable male lead, like Mel Gibson in *The Year of Living Dangerously* (1982), and Weaver could come close to the iconic power of classic studio-era stars. Stand her on her own and she could anchor a complex biopic like *Gorillas in the Mist* (1988). But put her in a film with a more conventionally sexual woman—like Griffith—and she's desexualized, dangerous, a "bony-assed" threat for the kittenish heroine to overcome.

What was missing for all these actresses was a support system of sympathetic directors, producers, and especially screenwriters, the sort who in earlier decades had provided rich and rewarding roles. If Streep was the era's Hepburn, Glenn Close may have been its Bette Davis, and all you need to know about the 1980s and how times had changed for portrayals of women in popular culture is to look at the two versions of *Fatal Attraction*, the 1987 thriller that made Close a fraught household name. The ending as originally scripted had Alex Forest, the unbalanced stalker played by Close, kill herself with a sword carrying the fingerprints of Dan, Michael Douglas's cheating-husband character—a brilliant bummer with a twist and a resolution eminently worthy of Davis at her take-no-prisoners peak.

Test audiences hated it. The producers conferred and hastily shot an ending in which Alex comes back from the dead—boo!—and is gunned down by Dan's wife (Anne Archer). While Davis and her peers acted out the moral complexities of love, sex, and rejection for the women of the 1930s and '40s, any sympathetic aspect of Close's character was obliterated by the commercial need for punishment and closure. In the '80s, the moral was: Just shoot the fucker.

By contrast, those male counterculture stars with the smarts and flexibility to do so stepped into 1980s genre pieces, classing up entertainments with their talents while giving their personas a commercial polish. *Tootsie* (1982) let Dustin Hoffman play to a tradition of comic cross-dressing as old as the Greeks while poking fun at the star's own reputation as a persnickety Method diva—the laughs are deeper because it's this star rather than, say, Robert Redford or Richard Dreyfuss. *The Shining* (1980) let Jack Nicholson walk the tightrope between Stephen King lowbrow horror and Stanley Kubrick highbrow direction; it's the iconic weight Nicholson brings to the movie that gives his character (another *Jack,* interestingly enough) both unsettling menace and manic here's-Johnny humor. By the end of the decade, though, the mainstreaming and neutering of Nicholson's rebelliousness would be complete. His Joker is a cartoon rebel and Tim Burton's 1989 *Batman* is a big-budget extravaganza that may be the final triumph of the *new* New Hollywood over the counterculture, a movie that's hip as hell and means absolutely nothing.

Older stars were warier of playing with new toys. Paul Newman allowed himself to age and deepen in *The Verdict* (1982)—it's the Best Actor award he should have won—and Robert Redford turned to directing and did win an Oscar for the careful parsing of middle-American dysfunction in *Ordinary People* (1980). These were both respected dramas that missed the sea change in pop culture by hewing to old-fashioned verities of character and meaning. They Meant It, which turned out to be the last thing anyone really wanted from the movies.

At the dawn of the 1980s, Clint Eastwood was still doing redneck comedy (*Any Which Way You Can,* the comparatively thoughtful *Bronco Billy*), but, ironically, he chose to meet the changing landscape halfway with smarter, more soulful films that critics were predisposed to like (1982's *Honkytonk Man,* the psychologically complex 1984 thriller *Tightrope*). Even the Dirty Harry sequel *Sudden Impact* (1983) found favor, in part because the character's politics were in vogue during the Reagan era (to the point where the president himself appropriated the film's catchphrase, "Go ahead, make my day"), but also because the star had successfully begun to distance himself from the character through the diligence and intelligence of his directing. Clint *wasn't* Harry Callahan, after all—in the early 1980s, this was a novel concept.

Who was he, then? By the end of the decade, after 1985's allegorical western *Pale Rider* and the jazz biopic *Bird* (1988)—the first time since 1973's *Breezy* that he had directed a movie without acting in it—Eastwood had successfully created a more complex image for himself that stood outside the movies and (once again) seemed closer to the person he actually was. The transformation from sullen action-movie archetype to committed Hollywood craftsman would lead to 1992's *Unforgiven,* the culmination of a rare wholesale renegotiation with public and industry as to what persona means and how much control an actor has over that meaning. If you think it's easy, look at how hard it has been for Mel Gibson to repeat the trick.

On the other hand, look at the ease with which Jane Fonda surfed atop concurrent waves of persona for two decades, from second-generation Hollywood starlet in the early 1960s to the fist-clenched political activist of the late 1960s—the country split between interpreting her new identity, "Hanoi Jane," as a hero or a traitor—to the Oscar-winning powerhouse A-level star of the 1970s. Fonda's reinvention in the 1980s can alternately be read as entrepreneurial genius and wholesale surrender. After the sentimental family reunion of *On Golden Pond* and the gooey high-finance thriller *Rollover,* both in 1981, she leveraged her stardom and the new medium of home video for *Jane Fonda's Workout,* the first in a series of exercise tapes that made her a millionaire many times over. The new revolution was called *personal fitness*—a fusing of Me Decade self-empowerment with Reagan-era self-discipline—and it was so much easier to achieve than overthrowing the state. The narrative of Fonda's new image was that dedication and repetition can build a better you, and that a better you (as opposed to a better anyone else) was what it was all about. Firm your ass and your mind shall follow.

Across the board the time was right for selling out, as long as you promised easy answers and asked no unpleasant questions. Reagan himself had refashioned himself and his beliefs—which had the beguiling simplicity of Louis B. Mayer's beloved Andy Hardy movies—into a presidency and a worldview, an idealized lost America that represented the triumph of Hollywood artifice over messy reality. A newly born star like Sylvester Stallone could translate those new simplicities into a new persona, one in which aggrieved victimization—the repeated, increasingly politicized humiliations of Rocky Balboa, or John Rambo's sense that the Vietnam War was a tragedy that America suffered rather than made (or, to be precise, both)—became the pretext for violent fantasies of revenge and resolution.

Stallone's breakthrough, *Rocky*, had been heartwarming as much for its sloppy Philly realism as for its triumphant underdog story: the title character was halfway between *Marty* and a mensch. As the vogue for warts-and-all storytelling gave way to a preference in the new decade for old-fashioned genre thrills, Stallone—always a smarter man than either his characters or his persona allowed—followed the tide. The Rocky of the sequels is a simpler, more maudlin creation than the original, and where *First Blood* (1982) sees the character of rampaging Vietnam vet Rambo with a measure of critical distance, the 1986 follow-up is one big pity party of oiled biceps and endless ammo—and a massive hit for that very reason.

Stallone's non-franchise projects like *Cobra* (1986) and *Tango & Cash* (1989) were successful but intentionally thin exercises in macho cop theatrics—*Dirty Harry* without the cultural punch. The star kept putting these movies out because there was an audience for them, and it suddenly wasn't in the theaters. With the rise of home video and national pay-cable movie channels, the platform for films and stars started to fragment along fault lines of age, class, geography, and release date.

Before home video and pay TV, there had never been a coherent aftermarket. A movie came out and you saw it in theaters; once it left that brick-and-mortar exhibition circuit, it vanished for a few years and then resurfaced on TV as the "movie of the week," shown a handful of times in censored versions interrupted by commercials. Television did represent a critical means for viewers to reconnect with older movies and stars—if you wanted to see Bogart in 1971, you had to live in a city with a revival movie house or a college film society, or wait until *The Big Sleep* came on the UHF channel at one a.m.—but the luster of modern stars was still dependent on a big screen, and it was something you, as a paying customer, did not own. Instead, you leased your favorite actors in two-hour increments and had to go to the temple to see them.

In the late 1970s and early '80s, the temple came to us. In the process, stars became unmoored from the films in which they appeared and were relocated to the larger pop culture, increasingly as brands with multimedia portfolios. The entertainment industry ceded, or appeared to cede, ownership of films and actors to the audience. Eventually you could take possession of every Cary Grant classic or Clint Eastwood western available to the public and watch them when and where you chose—an assumption of control over exhibition that would have given Adolph Zukor fits. It's no coincidence that the first serious copyright battles over entertainment product erupted around the videotape recorder in the early 1980s. Before then, the notion of who owned a movie had never seriously been questioned. But if Harrison Ford was in your house and at your disposal, wasn't he in some sense yours for keeps?

16.

Machines and Macho Men: Cable, VHS, and Arnold Rewrite the Rules

Video and cable changed the rules and gave consumers power in different ways. Specifically, home video gave viewers active agency over their entertainment choices, while cable TV provided greater passive choice. Sony introduced its Betamax machine in 1975, JVC its VHS technology in early 1977. Both devices were sold as extensions of the network-television schedule, allowing consumers to record their favorite shows and "time-shift" viewing at their convenience.

But consumers, as well as entrepreneurs, followed their own dictates. In October 1977 a company called Magnetic Video cut a deal with Twentieth Century-Fox and released the first studio films on tape, star vehicles of the previous decade like *Butch Cassidy and the Sundance Kid; Hello, Dolly!; The Sound of Music;* and *Patton*. The cost per tape was a steep $50, meaning you really had to love Paul Newman, Barbra Streisand, Julie Andrews, or George C. Scott. Many did, but not enough to sustain a business. Within months, though, two businessmen working separately, one in Los Angeles and one in New York, had opened up the first videocassette rental stores, signing up members and charging a fee per rental "turn." Despite the initial resistance of the studios, the idea caught on, and within six years there were ten thousand video stores across the country. By 1986, there were more video stores in America than movie theaters.

Of course, it wasn't just Julie Andrews selling the new technology—it was porn. Explicit sex tapes were the early home video industry's dirty little profit center, the source of half of all prerecorded-tape sales through the end of the 1970s. Delivery medium and content were made for each other; *Deep Throat* and other 1970s breakthrough hits aside, few people really wanted to go to a movie theater to see onscreen sex in the presence of other paying customers. Voyeurism is as much a private act as sex—no one likes to be watched watching—and the introduction of a technology that allowed consumers to view it in private preserved the compact between each audience member and his or her fantasies.

Taking porn into a retail sphere, though, meant the creation of a proactive audience that had to buy a VCR, go to the video store, and shuffle through the cassette boxes seeking one's particular kink. A coherent big-business aftermarket for porn slowly replaced the limited theatrical market, based on the privatization of the viewing experience and increasingly dependent on name stars like Seka and Veronica Hart to move units and preserve the one-on-one "relationship" between viewer and viewed. These weren't just stars whose desires we seemed to know; when we chose their films, they seemed to know *our* desires.

Upon this base would ultimately be built the porn ziggurat of the modern Internet. The lessons learned in the early days of home video would be applied tenfold to new technologies, but the essential shift in behavior—a closed-off, self-willed arena in which to experience people on film who seemed to have no secrets to their personas whatsoever—was already complete. You could even argue that the shadow world of porn satisfied a primal need for *knowing* that allowed mainstream movie stars to reacquire the glamour of mystery. Open sexuality, especially among female stars, became increasingly stigmatized in the 1980s—think of Glenn Close in *Fatal Attraction*—in part because depictions of lust had been roped off to a seamy sideshow that garnered huge profits and no respect. Bad girls in the movies did porn. Good girls in movies didn't do much of anything.

Hollywood came around to home video soon enough, with studios launching their own in-house tape divisions and selling their films to the rental market. As more titles became available and the cost of the players came down, VCR ownership soared, from 18 percent of all homes with TVs in 1984 to 52 percent a mere three years later. By that point, tape rentals and sales were actually outpacing theatrical box office grosses—and it was new money, not a cannibalization of the existing market. People were going to the movies *and* they were watching them at home. Two different needs were being fed: going out and staying in. And as the rental market slowly evolved into a sell-through market—as studios lowered their price points and consumers got used to the idea of owning a movie experience and even of collecting all the iterations of their favorite stars—a theatrical release became only the first step in a chain of transactions, sometimes even a loss leader that would reap profits further down the line.

The first movie to play Home Box Office, on November 8, 1972, was *Sometimes a Great Notion,* starring Paul Newman and Henry Fonda—little-known film, big names—and the audience consisted of under twenty thousand subscribers in Manhattan. Over the course of the decade HBO rolled out to a national audience via satellite distribution, and in 1981 the service switched to a twenty-four-hour schedule. By that point, cable TV had already upended the three-channel monopoly of the networks while changing the way we consumed entertainment and celebrities. Instead of buying a ticket and watching a single movie, customers paid a monthly fee and gained access to many movies. As HBO gained strength and financial clout, the studios gladly made their product available for a price, and soon the pay-cable schedules began to resemble a bazaar of entertainment offerings, with Home Box Office getting the major and minor Hollywood movies and its sister service Cinemax filling various niches: classics, drive-in B flicks, softcore porn, made-for-TV fare, an ascendant breed of independent films, and a smattering of foreign-language cinema.

What this meant was that choosing a movie to watch was no longer necessarily an active choice—hey, let's go see that new Burt Reynolds movie tonight—but passive consumption, easily accessed from a prone position on the couch. The cinema and its stars had become a utility, like electricity, gas, or sewage treatment. You turned on the tap to get a glass of water. You turned on HBO to get a movie.

This changed things. As with videotape, it allowed for multiple viewings of a single title, an activity that prompts obsessiveness toward stars you may like as well as a chance to appreciate those you've never noticed before. Second, cable, because it was just *there,* let audiences privately sample different kinds of movies and stars, especially those heretofore deemed culturally disreputable. The HBO/Cinemax schedule was a cultural leveler that placed A-level elegance next to Z-level swill, or, to put it a slightly different way, Meryl Streep next to Pia Zadora. And because you were in the privacy of your own home, no one knew you watched a lot more Pia Zadora than Meryl Streep. Well, no one except HBO's in-house audience research department—of which the author of this book was a fresh-out-of-college employee in 1982—which tabulated the Nielsen viewing diaries and saw how many people actually did watch the elfin trash-queen Zadora in *The Lonely Lady* at two a.m.

What I and my fellow cable programmers quickly noticed was that subscribers used the services both broadly—sampling many different movies across a spectrum of types—and deeply, drilling down into favored niches. Each of those niches had favored faces as well. Action fans turned to a raft of variations on the Ass-Kicking He-Man, many of whom sported martial arts training to make up for their acting deficiencies: Steven Seagal the Zen meathead, speaking softly and breaking bones; Chuck Norris, the gruff, down-home kickboxer; Jean-Claude Van Damme, the histrionic "Muscles from Brussels"; and so on, all the way down to such interlopers from the world of legitimate movies as Patrick Swayze, who played a philosophy-major/bouncer in 1989's deathless *Road House*.

The difference between these actors—and less-remembered macho players of the 1980s like Fred Dryer, Sasha Mitchell, Dolph Lundgren, et al.—and B stars of the studio age was that the new breed had a following that could be programmed and marketed to an audience that went out of its way to find these gentlemen and their movies instead of merely encountering them on the bottom half of a double bill. The market for the new he-men had been primed by a number of key developments: the stardom and early death of Bruce Lee, whose genuine martial arts skills raised the bar for everyone else; a legacy of '70s vigilante flicks like *Death Wish, Walking Tall,* and *Billy Jack,* all critically panned and commercially successful; the '80s cultural swing to the right and ensuing revival of classic American male types. And the final, crucial variable: *Ah*-nuld.

Arnold Schwarzenegger was possibly the most emblematic '80s star—even more so than Tom Cruise—because he embodied the revived American dream in a manner both time-tested and of the moment. As an Austrian immigrant who had patiently climbed the rungs of success since his arrival in the late 1960s, Schwarzenegger was a classic capitalist success story. His transformation from Teutonic teen weakling to four-time Mr. Universe to action-movie hunk to A-list star—and, ultimately, to the governorship of the nation's most populous state—is the kind of self-motivated makeover crucial to this country's sense of itself (as is, oddly, the scandal that always seems to follow, bringing the aspirant thudding back to our level). In the 1980s, he brought critical respect and mass audiences to the culturally derided genre of rip-snorting male action films while demonstrating the new commercial muscle of home video and cable TV, aftermarkets that he dominated and used as a bridge to mainstream celebrity. There is a 1984 photo of a beaming Schwarzenegger shaking hands with President Reagan that says it all: Made it, Ma—top of the world. And not through traditional channels but by first building a body and then, on top of that body, a brand. Other immigrants opened businesses. Schwarzenegger was savvy enough to see himself as the business.

That said, without *The Terminator* and director James Cameron, the brand might have never crossed over. Before that 1984 sci-fi action film, Schwarzenegger was a pop culture punchline, the musclebound star of *Conan* movies and the ingratiating found object of the 1976 semi-documentary *Stay Hungry*. In the latter, he seemed too disproportionate and unnatural to belong in the same league as "real" stars Jeff Bridges and Sally Field. Arnold didn't play by the counterculture rules that distrusted makeovers and put a premium on physical imperfection. Someone who would do *that* to his body must want fame too much to get it. You can't trust a star who needs us, can you?

Then the ground rules changed. Macho came back into vogue with the country's cultural shift and the election of Reagan, and the new venues of cable and home video brought Schwarzenegger and his ilk to audiences that might not have seen them in theaters. But the final difference was that the star showed with *The Terminator* that he had the self-knowledge and sense of humor to be ironic about himself. In this film and with the help of writer-director Cameron, Arnold Schwarzenegger winked, and the surprise was that this slab of Black Forest ham *could* wink. It meant there was a brain in there, and a sense of self-mockery. "Ah'll be beck," says the unstoppable cyborg from the future, and the joke is in the gulf between the flat, metallic cadences of the line and the overkill firepower you know is coming. The further delight is that you realize Arnold gets the joke and in so doing is suddenly more than the steroid robot we mistook him for.

The Wink quickly became a critical component of male movie stardom in the 1980s—the space between a celebrity and his roles in which he could engage the audience and reassure them that nothing was meant to be taken seriously. Heroes were still necessary, perhaps more than ever after the upheavals of the 1960s, but uninflected heroism played as corny and unhip. If you could save the world and toss a wink to the audience, you were fusing classic modes of behavior with post-'60s self-awareness. And you flattered the audience into feeling hip, too. The James Bond films had pioneered the approach, but that series had quickly run aground on camp—the wink taken too far—and the lean, sadistic elegance of Sean Connery had little to do with the musclebound stars of the new era. A more proper antecedent was Harrison Ford, whose sarcastic asides kept *Star Wars* and *Raiders of the Lost Ark* from fatal earnestness.

Some stars were better at it than others. Stallone tried, but his flip catchphrases ("You're the disease and I'm the cure," from 1986's *Cobra*) were obvious and clunky. Bruce Willis would turn up at the end of the decade as a purveyor of nothing *but* winkery, first on TV's *Moonlighting* and then in the *Die Hard* films, in which the action is never complete without the glib bon mot to cap the scene.

Mel Gibson, by comparison, took a while to learn. The U.S.-born, Australia-raised actor made an international splash as the silent action hero of *Mad Max 2: The Road Warrior* (1981)—a repotting of Clint Eastwood's Man with No Name into a Looney Tunes postapocalyptic setting—and was immediately snapped up by Hollywood as the latest brooding stud, a Dangerous Man à la Clark Gable. The studios paired Gibson with established actresses and marketed him to female audiences and fans of glossy drama: between *Road Warrior* and its sequel, 1985's *Mad Max Beyond Thunderdome,* he played a dashing journalist wooing Sigourney Weaver in *The Year of Living Dangerously,* a prison escapee wooing the warden's wife (Diane Keaton) in *Mrs. Soffel,* a struggling heartland farmer married to Sissy Spacek in *The River,* and a bare-chested Fletcher Christian in a remake of *The Bounty*—one of Gable's most iconic roles, incidentally.

It worked. Not only was Gibson the first star to be named "The Sexiest Man Alive" by *People* magazine, but legend has it that he was responsible for the branding of the phrase itself when a female editor at the magazine responded to a story pitch on the actor with "My God, he's the sexiest man alive!" From that unscripted swoon came an annual beefcake crown bestowed on whichever star fits a given year's prevailing cultural needs—himbo, rogue, sweetheart, pal.

Yet Gibson was incomplete as a boy-toy star. He was connecting with female audiences, but the *Mad Max* films hinted that there were other Mels to be tapped. The antic cop thriller *Lethal Weapon* (1987) changed the script and let him be the wild card, with Danny Glover playing exasperated straight man to Gibson's partner; they're like an action-comedy variation on the classic screwball dynamic of dizzy heiress and stuffed shirt. The role of Detective Martin Riggs, manic and suicidal, was both a dramatic reach and unexpected entertainment for moviegoers, and the wink had everything to do with it. When Gibson drops a Curly Howard *nyuk-nyuk-nyuk* into the action, he's bonding with the audience over their mutual enjoyment of lowbrow comedy—the kind that Mom said we shouldn't watch—and acknowledging that he's one of us. Gable only shared the screen with the Three Stooges (in 1933's *Dancing Lady*); Gibson shared our love for them. In the long run, Riggs's gonzo intensity proved to be more an integral part of Mel Gibson, real and imagined, than anyone suspected.

Schwarzenegger turned out to be surprisingly good at the wink, too—able in movies like 1987's *Predator* and 1990's *Total Recall* to deliver action-movie testosterone to core genre fans while flattering mainstream audiences with wit, or at least its semblance. He was also savvy enough to branch into straight comedy. A movie like 1988's *Twins*, which paired the towering Teuton with the diminutive Danny DeVito, didn't need to be any funnier than its concept to establish Schwarzenegger's pop mastery. (And it wasn't.) It did, however, create a channel through which future musclemen like Dwayne "the Rock" Johnson could themselves conquer Hollywood.

Eventually, Schwarzenegger's movies became formula affairs of slam-bang action stunts and jokey one-liners; *Last Action Hero* (1993) and *Eraser* (1996) provided noisy entertainment with no surprises. A wink that lacks humility becomes smug, and the cockiness of action stars like Schwarzenegger and Willis began to pall. The ascendant alt-cinema of the coming decade and the stars it introduced represented as far a move away from meathead cinema as possible, even as mainstream actors once more began to play it straight as well. It turns out we do want our stars to want us—a little.

17.

The Kids Are All Right: Brat Packers and the New Teen Idols

In the 1980s, as the kinds of available movies narrowed but the venues in which you could see them broadened, the audience separated into discrete demographic camps. Schwarzenegger and Stallone may have been crossover stars, but beneath them was an army of un-ironic action figures like Seagal and Norris, who sold mostly to men. Beneath *them* was an entirely new universe of professional wrestlers, real-life cartoon characters about whom nothing was real—not the names or the bouts or the chemicals in their muscles—and who sold like crazy to kids and young men who adored their bellowing lack of subtlety.

On a business level, the pro wrestling boom of the 1980s was a stroke of genius through which World Wrestling Federation head

Vince McMahon recognized the power of cable TV to destroy the old, established regional networks of the "sport." On a cultural level, such early WWF celebrities as Hulk Hogan and Andre the Giant were half-way to the reality stars of the present day, pretend-nonfiction athletes played by actor-entertainers. The fake narrative that fans followed—a sort of hoarse he-man soap opera—was strung between the actual fights, which only summed up and resolved the rivalries with a flying turnbuckle or a chair over the head. If you were very young or very naive, that "reality" was the draw. If you knew better, you could still have fun, just with an added ironic appreciation of the stunts.

If you were in the middle—old enough to be jaded and young enough to still want to believe in something—then you were a teen-ager and you were in luck, because the entertainment industry was newly dedicated to feeding you around the clock. This wasn't a matter of providing an alternate political and social message in the form of youth films and pop music, as in the 1960s and '70s. By now the alternate *was* the mainstream, teen culture was the primary source of industry profits, and the tone of films and TV shows that were aimed at kids shifted from questioning the adult world to flattering their youthful audiences, relocating the grown-up melodramas of earlier decades to high school, where they seemed newly hatched.

Writer-director John Hughes was the most self-conscious practitioner of the 1980s teen movie, building a stable of actors that was dubbed "the Brat Pack" and revisiting character types and themes until, in the consistency of his work, he came to resemble a miniature studio. If you were young and white and suburban in the mid-1980s, you recognized yourself in movies like *Sixteen Candles* and *The Breakfast Club* (and if you weren't young and white and suburban, the 1980s weren't really about you). Hughes's key stars fulfilled both eternal teen archetypes and classic Hollywood personalities. What was Molly Ringwald if not an update on Judy Garland's wistful Esther Smith in *Meet Me in St. Louis,* pining for the Boy Next Door while her family looks at her without truly seeing her? Matthew Broderick in *Ferris Bueller's Day Off* was the privileged son of Andy Hardy, Judd Nelson in *Breakfast Club* a crude caricature of Brando by way of Dean, Anthony

Michael Hall and Ally Sheedy the equivalent of studio-era character actors—Donald Meek and Zasu Pitts, respectively—given generous time in the spotlight.

Hughes extended the ultimate compliment to middle-American teenage moviegoers, re-creating Hollywood as a younger, hipper, more self-absorbed version of itself. Because his scripts were so sympathetic and his casting instincts so savvy, the stars of Hughes's movies seemed closer, more real, than other actors. The "Brat Pack" label that was initially applied to his output soon extended to this entire generation of stars. As with other sealed-off consumer niches created by the new distribution technologies of video and cable—the most obvious example is porn, but it's applicable to everything from pro wrestling to the Disney Channel—the larger Hollywood star system was replicated here on a smaller scale, with assigned leading men, good girls, vamps, and comedians.

Francis Ford Coppola held down the art-house wing of the '80s teen movie with his 1983 adaptations of two S. E. Hinton novels, *The Outsiders* and *Rumble Fish*. More self-consciously poetic—*Rumble Fish* was shot in black-and-white—and almost fetishistically worshipping at the altar of the '50s juvenile delinquent movie, the films introduced a host of actors who would become major stars in the 1990s and early 2000s. Here is Nicolas Cage when he had hair and baby fat; here, too, are Mickey Rourke, Diane Lane, Matt Dillon, Ralph Macchio, Rob Lowe, Patrick Swayze, and lonesome Tom Cruise, all captured before their respective cultural meanings had coalesced. Hughes served his stars, and so we know Emilio Estevez as the misunderstood jock of *Breakfast Club*. It's a performance, yes, but the bluff, aggressive earnestness of the character is part of who we think the actor is. Coppola's stars, by contrast, served the director and his vision, so Estevez's Two-Bit Matthews in *The Outsiders* is not critical to our understanding of what, if anything, the actor represents in the pop cosmology of his times.

On a much simpler level, the teen sex comedy arose from the combined DNA of *American Graffiti* and *Animal House*. *Porky's* (1982) was the breakthrough and immediately afterward came endless variations of the young, the raucous, and the horny: *The Last American Virgin* (1982), *Losin' It* (1983), *Spring Break* (1983), *Hardbodies* (1984), *Hot Dog: The Movie* (1984), and so on up to smarter versions like *Fast Times at Ridgemont High* (1982) and the underrated sub-Hughes comedies of "Savage" Steve Holland, *Better Off Dead* (1985) and *One Crazy Summer* (1986). Teen product by designation, the sex comedies of the 1980s were exclusively aimed at boys, but what the titles promised—nookie—the story lines almost always denied except for a few obligatory topless shots.

Who were the stars of these movies? Who cared? Such films provided a way for young actors to test out their screen appeal while audiences went trolling for future stars (and still do, unto 1999's *American Pie,* 2007's *Superbad,* 2012's *Project X,* and beyond). You could find the young John Cusack already working the kinks out of his lovable-mensch persona in the corners of Hughes's comedies, in *Better Off Dead,* or in Rob Reiner's *The Sure Thing* (1985). There was Sean Penn as the stoner dude of *Fast Times* and the wonderful one-two punch of James Spader and Robert Downey Jr. in 1985's *Tuff Turf,* a *Rebel Without a Cause* update with bigger hair and smaller stakes. Back then, they all seemed as ephemeral as the actors we don't remember, like David Knell in *Spring Break* or Lawrence Monoson in *Last American Virgin.* And forget about actresses like Diane Franklin, Kim Richards, Betsy Russell, and Deborah Foreman, the latter delightful and wholly lost to pop memory while her *Valley Girl* costar Nicolas Cage is one of the most unlikely of all twenty-first-century movie idols.

The stars of the '80s youth-movie boomlet were cost-effective and interchangeable and, like the original stars of the silent era, slightly more archetypal and attractive stand-ins for the audience that paid to see them. Spader started out doing misunderstood heroes but his natural air of superiority—he was a prep school dropout—made him interestingly arrogant and steered him toward shiftier roles in *Pretty in Pink* (1986), *Less Than Zero* (1987), and beyond. Cusack worked his way up from geek comic relief to romantic leads on the strength of his rueful intelligence—he came on like Jimmy Stewart's sharp-tongued grandson—until he found his defining role in 1989's *Say Anything.* That performance captures Cusack's appeal so precisely that we recall not just a scene but a single image: Lloyd Dobler outside his lost love's bedroom window, hoisting the boombox that plays their song.

If you were a young middle-class American male when that movie came out, it spoke to you because Cusack seemed a better, more interestingly flawed version of you. He was who you were; Broderick's Ferris Bueller was who you wished you could be (or maybe were glad you weren't). If you were a girl, Molly Ringwald in *Sixteen Candles* could mirror your hopes and anxieties as cleanly as Joan Crawford did for the young, striving women of 1933. Not all of it was identification, though—there had to be an almost alchemical aspect on the part of the actor that made the characters' small dilemmas seem exactly as momentous as you felt yours to be. The female lead in *Say Anything* was equally complex—a high school beauty isolated by her brains—and Ione Skye gave the part poise and depth, but she didn't have the quickness, the immediacy, of onscreen presentation that makes a moviegoer sit up and recognize something that feels real and right. Cusack had it. An actor like Judge Reinhold may be the most sympathetic figure in an ensemble high school comedy like *Fast Times,* but we still gravitate toward those, like Penn, with the gift of charisma—who make the lightning impression that catches us off guard and leaves us craving more.

The stellar example, of course, is Tom Cruise, the boy who came out of the pack to swallow Hollywood and the greater pop culture. What makes Cruise especially interesting is that he exudes maximum charisma with minimum depth—he's dazzling without being especially interesting. As such, he is the purest '80s star of them all.

I could go into the usual biographical detail here, but really, it's just not that fascinating. A childhood neither terribly hard nor terribly easy, it was marked more than anything else by a series of challenges young Tommy Mapother had to overcome. His engineer father moved the family around a lot, then divorced his mother when the boy was eleven. Tom was seriously dyslexic; he used athletics to meet new people and paper over the uncertainties in his life. During high school, he tore some ligaments in his leg and could no longer wrestle, so he tried out for *Guys and Dolls* and was cast as Nathan Detroit. The bug bit; "I felt like I had a way to express myself," he later told *People*. He moved to New York to wait tables and audition. His first role was a small speaking part in *Endless Love* (1981). And here we are.

That's the official version, anyway. The unofficial version is probably much the same but without the inevitability of hindsight. In a decision that may be unique in the history of ambitious young movie stars, Cruise chose to give no interviews during the three most concentrated years of his ascent to fame, from 1983's *Risky Business* to 1986's *Top Gun*. That hints at a need for privacy, and certainly since becoming a massive global superstar who, since the late 1980s, has also practiced a controversial religion that places a premium on secrecy, Cruise has kept his "real self" behind a wall. But there's also the sense that Cruise's "real self" isn't all that important even to him and that, really, the telling of who he was in the past has nothing to do with who he is at the moment. That who he is right now *is* the only thing that matters. Analysis and introspection are foreign to the Cruise persona. He's the star who exists most completely in the nanosecond of filmed presence.

It took a while to figure that out. Cruise lucked out with his early roles, including a showy bit as a psycho military cadet in *Taps* (1981), and he was there in the crowd of Coppola's Lost Boys in *The Outsiders* (1983). He later pooh-poohed his first teen sex comedy, 1983's *Losin' It*, but it introduced him to the cable TV hordes and Cruise is endearingly awkward in the film. The same year's *Risky Business* was a teen sex comedy too, but one with a smart script and unexpectedly soulful direction by Paul Brickman, and it rose to the level of a John Hughes comedy—beyond, even. Could any ambitious young actor have played Joel Goodsen, the kid who ends up hosting a bordello in his suburban home while his parents are away on vacation? Honestly, yes, except for that one scene where Cruise slides into his empty living room in his tighty-whities and mimes along to Bob Seger's "Old Time Rock and Roll." That took confidence and the ability to jump into the moment without looking back, but it also comes as a delightful shock given what a straight arrow Joel has seemed up to that point. His best friend, played by the *echt* '80s-movie best friend Curtis Armstrong, is the one who urges all the Joels of the world (which would be us) to lighten up and live a little: "Sometimes you've just gotta say *What the fuck* . . ." Joel, the good son, has to be coaxed into repeating the words. Other actors might have winked to let us know *they* weren't such stiffs. Cruise didn't wink.

The movie was a hit, but what "Tom Cruise" meant was hardly clear. He played a high school football player in *All the Right Moves* (1983) and an elf (or something) in *Legend* (1985) and only *Top Gun* (1986) came along to save his skin. Again, it should be asked: Could any young actor have played the role of the cocky jet fighter pilot Maverick to such commercial pop impact? Many could have played it better—Sean Penn, for one—but better was not the point. The plot of *Top Gun* is older than Hollywood and, in fact, goes all the way back to Greek myth and the overconfident flyboy getting too close to the sun. Except that *Top Gun* and director Tony Scott knew that Reagan-era audiences didn't want tragedy but the shallower, more immediate rewards of triumph and noise. It was morning in Hollywood, and we wanted to uncomplicatedly believe in American military destiny again and in the heroes who, as the movies used to tell us, fulfilled it. Cruise's performance is as thin as the movie's poster and exactly what is called for, since weighty dramatics would have dragged the thing down. *Top Gun* was made up almost entirely of the twinkling eye, the confident strut, the adorable karaoke sequence ("You've Lost That Loving Feeling," in this case), the brooding plot downturn, and—more than anything else—the killer smile.

The value of a smile in the movies is underestimated. It can be abused: Gene Kelly's Pepsodent grin is infectious but he turns it on and leaves it on like a klieg light. A smile can also complete and individuate a star personality. Julia Roberts blooms and appears to become a real person, not an actress, when she smiles in a film; she breaks the spell of narrative in an intensely pleasing way. Cruise's smile is something different. It's a can-do manifesto, erupting in an almost ferocious baring of teeth that crinkles the actor's eyes up toward his forehead. The smile isn't accompanied by a thumbs-up gesture and doesn't need to be. It says *I'm here, I've got it covered, and I have never been more sure of myself.* The smile is almost arrogant but stops short; Cruise isn't smiling at us but *for* us, and with us. We're just the lesser mortals who get to come along for the ride.

In some of the movies that followed, Cruise repeated his *Top Gun* performance to substantial box office and diminishing critical returns. You didn't really need to see *Cocktail* (1988) or *Days of Thunder* (1990) to have seen them. At the same time, and fascinatingly, he also set out to prove he was a Great Actor. He went about the process intelligently, allying himself with top-rank directors and the acting titans of preceding generations. *The Color of Money* (1986) was a *Hustler* sequel costarring Paul Newman and directed by Martin Scorsese. *Rain Man* (1988) was directed by Barry Levinson and put Cruise up against Dustin Hoffman as his autistic savant half brother. On what planet do Cruise and Dustin Hoffman even share the same gene pool? But the younger man wanted awards and the respect that comes with them, and he wanted the challenge and the mentorship of working with the greats. He wanted to win.

What happened was unexpected. Despite his giving excellent performances in both movies, audiences refused to believe in Cruise as an actor rather than a star. His older costars won Oscars—Newman finally bagging an acting award after seven previous nominations—while Cruise went un-nominated. Fine, then; in 1989, he dispensed with mentors and played the real-life paraplegic Vietnam vet Ron Kovic in Oliver Stone's *Born on the Fourth of July,* about as far from the recruitment-poster fantasies of *Top Gun* as you can get in three short years. It is a painstaking, deeply felt job of acting and surefire Oscar bait on countless levels, from the wheelchair to the epic time span that allowed the star to age with the aid of makeup to the raw emotional scenes in which the character finally uncorks his demons in the face of his small-minded parents.

He got nominated, at least. Stone won the directing Oscar that year, but Cruise lost to Daniel Day-Lewis in *My Left Foot*—two fit, gorgeous movie stars battling to see who could more realistically portray the greater infirmity. You've lost the use of your legs? Ha—I can only move my toes. Of course Day-Lewis won; he was British, so therefore he was the better actor. And of course Cruise lost, since he wasn't an actor at all but a huge global superstar.

This gets to the heart of the matter, for no modern figure illustrates the central dialectic of movie stardom—the push-pull between acting and celebrity, between craft and presence, between becoming and being—more than Tom Cruise. He must have felt deeply frustrated by the 1989 Oscar loss, because he had played the game and played it well. Both his and Day-Lewis's performances are heartbreakingly good and to consider one "better" than the other is ridiculous. On the other hand, do we want heartbreakingly good performances from Tom Cruise? Or do we want the thousand-watt smile and the sense that he's not acting at all—that offscreen he is much like he is on? Not long after he played the lead in 1996's *Mission: Impossible,* Cruise was involved in several real-life rescues, stopping to help a hit-and-run victim to the hospital (and pay her bills) and saving two young boys from getting crushed by a crowd. This is his version of the Bill Murray magic trick mentioned earlier, but it fits the Cruise persona—of the late 1990s, anyway—with an absurdly satisfying *snap.* Why shouldn't his entire life be one big Mission Possible?

And yet he kept trying for respect. The film before *Mission: Impossible* was *Interview with the Vampire,* in which America's sweetheart Tom Cruise played a bisexual bloodsucker, and 1996 also saw him Oscar nominated for *Jerry Maguire,* a revision of his can-do comeuppance formula that made both audiences and critics happy. It's not a coincidence that he plays a Hollywood sports agent in the film, since Cruise always seemed to have more in common with the suits upstairs than the plebes on the set. In Paul Thomas Anderson's *Magnolia* (1999), he bites his own hand even harder, playing a frighteningly profane self-help guru who represents the darkest side of the American dream. It's a scarifying, very aware performance and he was nominated again, but he didn't win.

He'll never win. They'll give Cruise a plaque at the end of his career like they did with Cary Grant and Fred Astaire, two other stars who were judged, wrongly, as locked into performing helpless variations on themselves. I'm not saying Cruise is on a par with Grant, but I am saying that both men impersonated the person they each wanted to be with a diligence and craft and shifting nuance that doesn't get half the credit it might. Anyway, why struggle to reframe Cruise as a master thespian when he's more entertaining as a celebrity, especially after he seemed to undergo a complete persona meltdown in the new century? (More later in the "When Stars Go Bananas" section.) The rule seems to be: If you play "yourself," it's not acting, so we can't give you respect, but we do love (and hate) you more, since the magnetism of a functioning personality strikes deeper than the art of always being someone else. We want desperately to believe that person you play is real, because if he is, we can try to be like him or at least believe that it's possible. But we also wait, a little too hard, for the moment that you can't play him anymore.

18.

MTV and Its Discontents: Michael Jackson, Madonna, and the Rise of the Meta-Star

Tom Cruise's rise to fame was enabled, in part, by the changes roiling pop music. This was the era in which rock and roll ceased to be the sound of youth and fragmented instead into many musics of many different kinds of youth, a process that has only increased with the ensuing decades. In the new landscape, Cruise was a comforting figure: the classic rock of young movie stars, lip-synching to Bob Segar and the Righteous Brothers on film and firing up music videos from the hit *Top Gun* soundtrack on TV.

By the late 1970s, the twin wedges of disco and punk had split rock's past off from itself—you were either for or against the new sounds with every fiber of your being—but U.S. radio, by now a corporate force for conservatism, hadn't kept up. If you loved the Ramones, you couldn't hear them on the mainstream airwaves but had to experience them via college radio or in the club medium. The words "classic rock" would have seemed nonsensical a decade earlier; now they represented a last stand against the mohawked Huns and effeminate disco queens. Not surprisingly, record sales and radio station shares began dropping as kids pursued the new sounds elsewhere.

The innovation that turned the business around in the early 1980s—an upstart cable channel called MTV—was not aural but visual, and it enabled consumers to think about musicians in ways that were both new and framed by notions of presentation established by the movies. It allowed pop musicians to think and dress and pose like film stars. At the same time, MTV destroyed the way people used television and, even further, the way they thought about visual entertainment. To watch a series of music videos for an hour or two—or all day, as some early MTV addicts did—was more than just listening to the radio with your eyeballs. It mashed everything together, imposing the need for narrative form onto the three-minute pop song while at the same time disconnecting long-term narrative from the television medium. For over three decades, visual storytelling had been bounded roughly by the two-hour movie and the half-hour TV show. Now each pop video was bite-sized and instantaneous, unrelated to the videos preceding and following it, and making its impression right here in the present.

Taken as a whole, the channel was really one single feed—a pop IV drip—of sound and color and peacock finery and rebellion, consciously structured that way because MTV head Robert Pittman understood that his target audience—ages twelve through thirty-four—had grown up with TV and used it differently from their parents. In interviews, he'd talk about how kids accessed pop culture in a nonlinear and concurrent fashion while grown-ups still did one thing at a time. MTV was short-attention-span theater, the foundational rock upon which the average twenty-first-century consumer's media experience is founded. The Internet would accelerate the phenomenon—let's call it simultaneous multiple-point consumption—beyond previously conceivable boundaries. Still, Warner Amex's little music video channel is where our modern world of media aphasia begins. You could watch it for hours and come away hungrier than when you sat down.

So what did you see? You saw Rod Stewart and you got your hair cut like his, or so a midwestern barber told MTV executive Tom Freston. You saw Cindy Lauper singing "Girls Just Want to Have Fun" and were won over by her neo–Betty Boop effervescence. You watched videos by Duran Duran and Flock of Seagulls and a-ha and other bands you'd never heard of and wanted to dress like a New Romantic. Radio's stonewalling of new music and new groups was end-run by the visual novelty of these bands. A threesome like the Stray Cats was just another rockabilly revival outfit on the airwaves; once seen, they became a statement of rebel nostalgia. As movie stars did in the studio era and rock stars during the heyday of the counterculture, the stars of '80s music videos deeply affected the look of its generation—what you wore, how you cut your hair, the rhythms with which you walked down the street.

Everybody won. Advertisers finally had regular access to the wary teen market; record labels could give a band a flashy look and a hip director and sell the hell out of them; pop fans could now see and be freshly entertained by their idols. Movie studios raided the ranks of video directors for their feature films while established filmmakers jockeyed to heat up their reputations by directing music videos. The mutual marketing relationship between movies and the music industry metastasized, with pop songs piled onto the soundtracks of the '80s box office hits *Flashdance, Footloose,* and *Top Gun,* while music videos for the songs included footage from the movies so consumers were getting it from both ends, pop stars and movie stars in one big orgy of cross-promotion. No one complained; everyone made money.

Well, yes, if you were a singer-songwriter who just sat there with a guitar, it wasn't your time. Even so, there was value and credibility in swimming against the tide. The scrappy, beloved Minneapolis hardcore band the Replacements had already written their song "Seen Your Video" (" . . . that phony rock and roll . . .") when they caved in to label pressure for their new album. The first video, for "Bastards of

Young," was a single shot of a stereo speaker, a work that functioned as both an acceptable music video and a refutation of everything the form stood for. And if you were a visually inclined old-guard rocker, like David Bowie or Peter Gabriel or even a wheezy boogie outfit like ZZ Top or a reformed folkie like Kenny Loggins, you could make yourself over and be given new meaning and new credibility in the pop marketplace.

Bowie extended his creative and commercial shelf life for at least another five years because video let him bring his abiding theatricality to a new sphere (while simultaneously allowing him to become the one kind of pop idol he had never been—the bland Top 40 superstar of 1983's *Let's Dance*). Ever the chameleon, he had long since mastered the Warholian trick of constantly reinventing himself and passing each stage off as the "real" David Bowie. It was a tactic supremely well suited to the new medium of music video, which wasn't music or TV or a movie but utilized aspects of all three to create, if you wished, a convincing illusion of authenticity. There were young people in the audience taking notes.

What you didn't see a lot of on MTV, especially in the beginning, was black people. Nobody really noticed, because you didn't see them anywhere else in mainstream culture either.

I'm exaggerating, but not by much. The 1980s were about the retrenching and recovering of older American values after the upheavals of the previous two decades, and while you couldn't exactly pretend the Civil Rights era had never happened, you could shift your attention elsewhere. African American popular culture seemed to disengage from the white mainstream in this period, too, burned by years of cultural theft and (sometimes) well-intentioned liberal co-opting of black social and artistic struggle. The nation's crack epidemic, which ravaged inner-city neighborhoods and effectively crippled a generation, didn't help, diverting and destroying youthful energies that could have developed more positively. Nor did the new president's policies, which gutted social programs with what seemed like punitive determination.

But white America didn't want to hear from angry black America. Audiences wanted to watch *The Cosby Show,* in which Bill Cosby's character, the upper-middle-class Brooklyn obstetrician Cliff Huxtable, presented a warm, engaged model of hard-won African American assimilation that neither threatened nor sold out anybody. The comedian had always been loved, but now he was necessary; the top-rated TV show from 1985 to 1989, *Cosby* was an indication of how critical the star had become to the country's sense of itself as a progressive society whose racial problems were tucked safely in the past.

Otherwise you had MTV, which pretended rock and roll was a white invention, and you had the emergence of hip-hop, the latest African American musical revolution that, unlike minstrel songs and jazz and the blues and R&B and rock and disco, seemed specifically built to keep the white kids off the porch. It didn't work, obviously, but at first the sheer vibrancy of this new culture ran parallel to the Reagan-era mainstream. Hip-hop was rooted in beat and bricolage (which necessitated new words like "sampling" and "turntablism"), and it expanded to affect clothing and dance and street art and slang—an entire alternate world of experience.

It was there if anyone cared to look—and plenty did—in occasional Hollywood cash-ins like *Breakin'* and *Beat Street,* both from 1984, and erupting from clubs and street radios and twelve-inch records. The scene very quickly formed its own stars, like Grandmaster Flash and LL Cool J and—a welcome dose of sociopolitical defiance—Public Enemy, whose music formed the spine for Spike Lee's *Do the Right Thing* (1989). As the 1990s loomed, the new scene was already "safe" for white artists both credible (the Beastie Boys) and ridiculous (Vanilla Ice), as well as black artists even parents could understand (the young Will Smith, who soon had a hit TV sitcom). For the bulk of the decade, though, hip-hop and rap weren't underground—they were widely covered, if often misconstrued, in the mainstream press—but they were largely ignored by middle America and the pop media industries that served it.

There was still plenty of soul and funk and dance music, parlayed by acts like the Commodores and Rick James, who complained loudly that MTV wouldn't play his records. There was an upstart kid named Prince, who seemed to fuse every aspect of black popular music into one psychosexual all-night dance party. But he sang about getting head (or was it giving head?) and having sex with his sister—no way that was going to get played on cable TV.

And there was Michael, who blew everything wide open. Michael Jackson was, in the mid-1980s, that very rare phenomenon, the consensus figure: a public personality that everyone of every age and class and gender and even nation suddenly agrees is essential. Chaplin had been one, as had the Beatles. Mickey Mouse was one. Elvis wasn't; essential and influential, obviously, but many older listeners and elitists couldn't abide him, and that was his importance—he drew the line and made you take sides. Sinatra was arguably a consensus figure in the 1950s, when he was the Chairman of the Board, even if the heat of his initial landing amid the 1940s bobby-soxers had worn off.

Jackson, in fact, is arguably the last consensus figure of modern popular culture (what's the competition? Will Smith? Julia Roberts? Beyoncé?), and he may remain so until someone strides forward to reunite what seems like geometrically subdividing demographics of taste and belonging. Part of the consensus was the recognition of the grown-up Jackson's immense talents as a singer and a dancer, and part of the thrill was that that recognition could be pinpointed for millions of people to the exact moment he went into the moonwalk on Motown's twenty-fifth anniversary special when it aired on May 16, 1983. But the pleasure so many listeners took in his first mature albums, *Off the Wall* (1979) and *Thriller* (1982), was rooted in a much deeper satisfaction, that of being able to witness the boy becoming the man—and what seemed at first a beautifully whole man.

Growing up in public is the hardest act of all to pull off successfully—and by successfully, I mean for the artist and for everyone watching. For every Elizabeth Taylor, morphing from eerie innocent to willful sex goddess, there are five Margaret O'Briens who just grow older and are probably glad of it. The roadsides of fame in America are littered with the bodies of gifted children who lost the freak-prodigy spark that drew us in the first place, or who spun out of control, or who simply became ordinary. Macaulay Culkin and Lindsay Lohan would probably be the first to tell you that it looked so easy and then it wasn't.

Yet Jackson made it look more than easy: in him, it seemed preordained. The meaning he conveyed—the story with which he soothed us—was that true talent, the real thing, will come through the fire intact. His message was that artistic maturity is the just reward of the brilliant child. In early 1983, when *Thriller* hit MTV and the larger global culture like a nuclear bomb, we didn't know about the beatings Joe Jackson regularly gave his young sons when they didn't rehearse to his demanding specifications. We hadn't thought about the childhood denied, as, from the age of five, Michael plied the chitlin' circuit and then the American Top 40 with determination and what appeared to be joy. (And there's this, too: the preternaturally talented black child, buck-and-winging his way into the master culture's heart, is an image that goes back to the earliest days of slavery. Not that that has anything to do with the happiness a white listener feels when listening to eleven-year-old Michael and the rest of the Jackson 5 singing "I Got You Back"—does it?)

What we saw, instead, was assurance and a young man taking control of his destiny. The obvious role model was Stevie Wonder, who in the early 1970s had emancipated himself from his "Little Stevie" persona and from Motown head Berry Gordy's narrow-minded ideas about how his stars should sing and dress and behave. Wonder came of age with songs like "Superstition" and "Living' for the City"—hits that fused pop with engaged social awareness—and when the Jacksons left Motown for Epic in 1975, Michael may have looked toward these as possible roads to adulthood.

He met producer-arranger Quincy Jones during the production of the movie *The Wiz,* and the older man's mentorship and taste—no beatings this time—led to their collaboration on *Off the Wall,* an album that keeps every promise Jackson's early work made. "Rock with You" sounds cuddly-sexy in the most appealingly confident way imaginable; the up-tempo "Don't Stop 'Til You Get Enough" is an eruption of cross-rhythms atop which the singer rides with ease and mastery. Even the cover photo, Jackson at his leisure in a white tuxedo in front of a brick wall, is relaxed and secure—a candid snapshot at the biggest senior prom ever.

Three years later, *Thriller* raised the stakes and intensified the emotions. Suddenly the lyrics were full of doubt and uncertainty. They're out to get you, better leave while you can, don't want to be a boy, you wanna be a man. Or: They're out to get you, there's demons closing in on every side. Or: The kid is not my son. But the music and the moves denied what the words implied; we believed the former and discounted the latter because the illusion Jackson was offering was so psychologically meaningful to his listeners. Watching him on the Motown special, surrounded by the aging stars of Gordy's stable, you felt Jackson had not only survived the machinations of the star factory but had conquered them and come out whole, improved, in possession of himself. The illusion he offered from the late 1970s to about 1985 was that you could grow up hugely famous and still not be screwed up, and that felt *wonderful*. Celebrity, or the drive to achieve it, doesn't destroy one's soul, he seemed to say. Properly managed and kept in perspective, you could even benefit by becoming the better man and the greater artist.

That was the lie, and audiences bought it because they wanted to believe it and because Jackson was a brilliant and entertaining liar—and because no one had ever done what he did, appearing on MTV twenty times a day to sing and dance with beautiful abandon. He was the first pop music superstar whose impact was equally balanced between sound and vision. (Yes, more than Sinatra, Elvis, or the Beatles, none of whom were dancers.) The songs were astoundingly good but you had to see the videos to be fully transported, so impulsively watchable was the way he moved. Jackson forced the medium of music video into an early artistic maturity on the quality of the music but also through the ambition of the productions, with "Billie Jean" a dance number worthy of (and approved by) Fred Astaire followed by the choreographed psychodrama of "Beat It" followed by "Thriller," a miniature horror dance musical complete with a Hollywood director (John Landis) and a cameo by Vincent Price, the living signifier of '50s camp screamers. Jackson knit wildly disparate eras of showbiz together with a serenity that implied he knew exactly what he was doing.

Maybe he did, or thought he did. But dissonances began to show between the sort of star people wanted Michael Jackson to be—a perfect star, nothing less—and the damaged talent he actually was. Media coverage of his eccentricities began in the mid-1980s: the pet chimp, the whitening skin, the plastic surgeries, the urge to buy the bones of the Elephant Man. Jackson's psychological needs increasingly appeared to shape the public presentation of his private life. There was the declaration that he was the "King of Pop" (true until he insisted on it); the marriage to rock princess Lisa Marie Presley, as though two royal houses were being united; a mysterious second marriage and children with a nurse who may have been a lover, a friend, a petri dish. The retreat called Neverland for lost boys like him, and the things he may or may not have done to them there (and for which, in any event, he was fully exonerated in a 2005 trial). Did he love them too much? Or did he just love his missing childhood too much?

Such pop psychology banalities were what we came to talk about when we talked about Michael. The melodrama of his weirdness quickly overtook the image of his pop triumph and became his primary narrative and meaning. How you felt about Jackson defined how you felt about stardom and famous people, whether they were deserving of adulation or scorn. To those who saw him as "Wacko Jacko," he was a nutcase and a predator and an embarrassment, not least because he had once fooled us into loving him, and you never, ever forgive the people who've fooled you. To those who still believed in him, he was a martyr to the cruelties of prosecutors, the media, and public opinion, innocent and crucified for the sin of being too sensitive for this world.

Most observers were stuck in the middle, unsure what to believe, remembering how whole and complete songs like "Rock with You" and "Wanna Be Startin' Something" had once made them feel while looking at photos of Jackson in the papers and thinking *Freak*. That is the position he put us in and no other star has done the same. His unexpected death in 2009 changed nothing, other than to rev up the dichotomy again and ensure that it runs in perpetuity. When it comes to Michael Jackson, we're all members of both the defense team and the mob, and what we're really arguing about is why we need him to matter so badly.

Not all kid prodigies lose control of their meanings as they grow up. While Jackson's behavior was becoming stranger throughout the 1980s, the former child actress Jodie Foster was staking her claim for sanity. She, not he, best represents the successful passage of the brilliant child into adulthood, and part of her point is that the process is often a painstaking one that depends on separating the double helix of public persona and private personality. Foster early on experienced the diseased perspective that the two are one and the same, when John Hinckley shot Ronald Reagan in March 1981 because he believed the actress actually was the tough, threatened child prostitute she had played in *Taxi Driver* (1976). Hinckley called his act "the greatest love offering in the history of the world," and Foster intuitively understood that even to engage with such madness is to endorse it. She has spoken of him only very rarely, and why should she speak of him at all? Who she is and what "Jodie Foster" meant to John Hinckley have nothing in common. Since then, Foster has scrupulously maintained an image as an actress rather than a public figure.

This is a tricky and fairly disingenuous position to take. It requires nuance and diligence, in both managing one's career and managing the expectations of those who are watching. If Foster weren't such a skilled performer—honest, unshowy, earning an audience's respect through the respect she extends to her characters—she might not have successfully diverted our attention away from who she "really is." But because of the silence she maintained around the subject of her stalker, because she tackles difficult roles with a minimum of fuss, and because she has scrupulously avoided being seen as a sex object or even a romantic object on film and in public, Foster has carved out a niche as a perceived class act. She's the master craftsman of actresses, not serving art à la Streep but simply the role and the woman embodied in the role.

Her choices as a child actress were risky—*Taxi Driver,* yes, but also the eerily grown-up title character of *The Little Girl Who Lives Down the Lane* (1976) and the wild-child daughter of a hooker in Scorsese's *Alice Doesn't Live Here Anymore* (1974). If it makes you feel better, she was in Disney movies (the original *Freaky Friday*), played Becky Thatcher in a 1973 version of *Tom Sawyer,* and had years of TV work under her belt. Like Jackson, she was a seasoned professional at an early age.

Her adolescence straddles the 1980s, and you can see the young Foster trying out different personas as though they were masks: the good bad-girl of *Foxes* (1980), a circus brat in *Carny* (1980), the incestuous object of Rob Lowe's desires in the playfully odd *The Hotel New Hampshire* (1984), a World War II resistance fighter in *The Blood of Others* (1984), a neighborhood girl plagued by a stalker in *Five Corners* (1987)—the closest she came to confronting Hinckley onscreen—and so forth. Off camera she attended Yale and kept a low profile. It wasn't clear whether she actually wanted to be a star, or if she did, what kind.

Actually, she may have wanted to be a star in the worst way, but on her own terms. *The Accused* (1988) was Foster's graduation to adult actress, a harrowing, fully realized portrait of a rape victim that toys with audience sympathies to establish a greater sympathy that, in turn, is the film's moral imperative. The message is that no woman is "asking for it"—ever—but the performance subsumes that message beneath raw observed detail. There is nothing preachy about the character of Sarah Tobias. Foster won a Best Actress Oscar and then, three years later, a second for the role of Clarice Starling in *The Silence of the Lambs,* another beleaguered heroine summoning up the courage to deal with the violence of men.

Again, there's nothing doctrinaire in Foster's playing—she's genuinely interested in women under pressure—and that dedication to craft at a time when audiences were wearying of actors who lectured them endeared her to the public. She's one of the very few major movie stars who maintain the respect of a public that doesn't know much about her and, moreover, rejects even the desire to know. Her "classiness" is her ticket to privacy. This is remarkable when you consider that Foster's sexual orientation is common knowledge within the film industry and to anyone outside nosy enough to dig for it, that it has been reported in the tabloid press, that she even partially came out of the closet to praise her then partner, producer Cydney Bernard, at a 2007 industry event—and all this at a time of unceasing celebrity gotcha journalism and the online pandering of stars' dirty laundry.

No one cares. That is the bargain Jodie Foster struck with fame and with us: I will give you solid, interesting performances, I will not play the diva, and you will let me live my life in peace. In the process, the actress has done a remarkable and subtle end run around sexuality. There are precious few romances in her movies; they're simply not what the films are about. We accept this because we've perceived Foster as an independent mind since she was a child, and because, unlike so many child stars, she came of age as privately as she possibly could.

An actress can do that, though—hide behind her roles—and if she wants to be taken as an actress rather than a star, she will vary the roles enough while still stringing them along a commonality of persona. A musician, by contrast, is stuck playing him- or herself, unless he's David Bowie and he wants to mess with the audience's head.

Or Madonna. Let us leave the 1980s by pausing to consider the willful artistry—or is it crass manipulation?—of Madonna Louise Ciccone, who controlled her destiny as surely as Foster controlled hers but who put the issue of who she was and how sexual she could be right out front as the main order of business. In a sense, she had to. Ever since the 1960s and the rise of the singer-songwriter movement, pop stars were supposed to represent honest, direct expressions of themselves. If they didn't, how could anyone believe their lyrics? Madonna had been watching Bowie's mind games, though, and she certainly was empowered by the mix-and-match remainder bin of style and image in post-punk Manhattan, especially Deborah Harry's "Blondie" persona, an ironic retro goof to those in the know and a straight-up sex symbol to everyone else. And she came out of the dance club scene, where everyone could be somebody different from night to night.

The persona Madonna patched together, then, was a pastiche of

Marilyn and Harlow and Dietrich and other predecessors—a collage of sex symbols, like something a teenage girl might put on her wall—that was offered with confident enthusiasm at first and then a gathering of steely will. Her first hits, in early 1983, were baubles—"Holiday," "Lucky Star"—so inanely catchy it almost didn't matter that the voice was pinched and thin. The songs and the persona were an effortless encapsulation of the nightclub penchant for living in the moment; by all rights, Madonna should have been forgotten by 1984.

Instead, she released her second album, *Like a Virgin,* and its attendant title single, as an act of conscious provocation. Madonna understood music videos to be a key component—in fact, *the* key component—in her campaign to dominate pop culture, so in "Like a Virgin" she flounced on a bed in a wedding dress and ate up the controversy that followed. The song, she said, was about being so loved by someone that you felt brand-new, *like* a virgin. Which meant of course that she wasn't. Which threw a monkey wrench into the prevailing madonna/whore complex governing pop culture's view of women. It was right there in her name.

Madonna was the first postmodern female celebrity—Bob Dylan had been the first male one—in that she considered "authenticity" to be just one more mask to put on in a grand game of celebrity dress-up. She didn't "mean it," or, rather, she didn't mean just one thing. In fact, to wonder who Madonna "really is," which many fans did and still do, is to miss the point. Instead, she engaged audiences in an ongoing debate over how we prefer women to behave in pop culture. As brazen hussy, demure lover, sexual initiator, emotional victim? What happens when you start mixing and matching the categories? Can you be a sex object without an audience of gazing men, and how does it make you feel? Powerful? Dirty? Powerful *and* dirty? Are the two inextricably linked or only if you were raised Catholic? How much sex is too much? How much *Sex* (her vacuous 1992 coffee-table nudie book) was too much?

So many bothersome questions, posed by Madonna on levels both conscious and intuitive. When she appeared in the early 1980s, she appalled feminists (of both genders) who couldn't wrap their minds around a "Boy Toy" belt buckle as a subversive token of female power. Her tours were infamous riots of costumes and choreography—really, the birth of the modern Live Nation extravaganza, as impromptu as catechism—and while she put on a great show, the point was not to convince us of her sincerity (other than the plaintively banal emotions of her songs, she had none) but to propose personal emancipation in the form of endless possible personas. This was her gift to you: because she could be anybody, so could you. Did you have the nerve? And did that mean there was nothing truly fixed about who you were, or thought you were?

Here are the beginnings of the identity games with which we live in the new century, the endless sheddings and adoptings of personas that adults stumble into with shame and delight and that our children navigate with the ease of birthright. Madonna was ahead of her time because she saw that image was mutable and that audiences were ready to accept that notion (as they were not when Marilyn had clumsily tried to change who we thought she was). Moreover, Madonna had the tools: a recording contract and a studio, a music video team and a distribution network in the form of MTV. Consumers—the people who bought the records and stood in line for tickets—didn't have any of those things.

For the time being.

19.

The Corporate Star: The 1990s and Beyond

The 1980s reset the needs and ambitions of popular culture after the turmoil of the counterculture years. Simply put, people wanted to be entertained rather than to change the world.

The 1990s, by contrast, are kind of a drag. Not because nothing happened—plenty happened—but because it's clear in hindsight that the decade was a transitional period between the 1980s and the first years of the new century. At the end of the Reagan era, stardom was still a matter of Them—the beautiful people on the hill brought to you by their handlers in Hollywood—and Us, the passive, obedient, envious consumers. Twenty years later, the World Wide Web and radical changes in content programming and delivery have made us all stars in ways both real and illusory. Traditional stars exist more than ever at our sufferance, their unscripted moments able to be exposed to a global audience. In the process, the notion of celebrity has been devalued by our new ability to celebrate ourselves, whoever those selves may be at any given moment. We're just starting to ask what part of us may be getting devalued in the bargain.

So stardom in the 1990s was a slow-motion battle between the opposing forces of consolidation and fragmentation, each cued to specific developments that affected the kinds of people audiences wanted to watch and emulate. The first and most critical development was the rise of the corporate entertainment oligarchy that seeks to control and profit from every aspect of what consumers put into their brains: movies, TV shows, music, news, books, and then a secondary tier of information *about* the entertainment industry that ensures that we never have to wake from the dream. A second development was the reactive push-back on the part of a subsection of consumers: a codification and constant redefining of a noncorporate underground culture—*alt* culture—as a more "authentic" channel for artistic role models and the experiences they provide.

The third development was the Internet revolution and its related technological advances. The fourth was "reality," which bears only a tenuous relationship to that which actually is reality.

But you don't want to read about this. You want to read about Julia Roberts.

And, yes, of course Julia Roberts matters, not least as proof that the classic star system still worked in the early 1990s, and could still serve up a fresh young discovery to our massed delight. Along with Tom Hanks, Roberts was the closest the decade got to a consensus figure on the order of a Chaplin or a Michael Jackson, and to the parasite industries of fan magazines and entertainment news she was that godsend, a beautiful young woman who was a predictable source of secondary profits. At magazines like *Entertainment Weekly* and *People,* it was common knowledge that Roberts's face on the cover could boost newsstand sales by a double-digit percentage, so onto the cover she would go as often as editors thought they could get away with it. It was the same dance that had been going on since *Photoplay* began publishing in 1911 and for the same reason: Roberts possessed an ability to seem at ease—to seem *herself*—in front of a camera. For most of 1990 and 1991, she was a cultural intoxicant, proof that youthful star energy still existed and could be brought to our notice.

It's worth pointing out that her fans were mostly women. Men liked Roberts, sometimes a lot—she was a reliably entertaining presence—but not necessarily *that way*. She could be beautiful and even sexy, but her appeal wasn't predicated on sex, and the reason her 1990 breakthrough *Pretty Woman* works as a boneheaded Cinderella story is that Roberts's fundamental innocence remains intact. The pieces of that appeal were obvious—the adorably out-of-balance facial features that somehow combine, the transformative smile, the lusty laugh—and they were oversold in previews for her movies because they were brand identifiers. That's how studio marketing departments thought of stars by the 1990s: as brands with differing demographic appeals, like cars.

After *Mary Reilly* and *Michael Collins,* both in 1996, she rarely tried to act. I don't mean that as an insult—quite the opposite. The women Roberts plays in *Erin Brockovich* (her 2000 Oscar winner) and the first two *Oceans* caper films and *Eat Pray Love* (2010) all have differences of costume and accent and class, but they're all recognizably Julia Roberts in nerve and playfulness, which is what audiences pay to see. She is, in celebrity terms, the best kind of professional. She understands what we want and she gives it to us.

This is the very model of a modern Hollywood star, and Roberts has stayed popular, with fadings in and out of fashion, for two decades now. For her and for a select group of actors, the factory still functions as it used to. But to understand why there are far fewer relevant movie stars now than there were at the dawn of the 1990s—why they simply seem to exert less primal pull on our imaginations—we have to look at the nature of the machine and where it has mutated and evolved over time.

A basic question: Who creates stars? Roberts represents the rare fluke for which everybody wants to take credit, especially the moviegoers who "discovered" her after three years and five previous films.

And, yes, audiences have always had the final say in star-making, as studio executives like Samuel Goldwyn (whose 1930s protégé Anna Sten was dubbed "Anna Stench" by theater owners) have learned to their chagrin. But in the company town that is Hollywood, the true stars—the people the town actively worships—are traditionally the men who have the power to get movies and careers made. That power is sex appeal *and* charisma *and* money *and* desire all wrapped up in the person of a production executive who might be porcine, stupid, or cruel, who can claim to gauge a film's quality by the itching of his ass (as did Columbia chief Harry Cohn), but who nevertheless has the throne and the thunderbolt that goes with it, and who can hurl that bolt at whichever day player or pliant starlet he wishes.

What was changing was who in Hollywood had that power. It was no longer the studio heads. By the early 1960s, the men who had built the dream factories were dead (Cohn, Louis B. Mayer) or in decline (Goldywn, David O. Selznick), and while Jack Warner at Warner Bros. and Darryl Zanuck at Twentieth Century-Fox still had fiefdoms, they no longer had the stables of actors from which to pluck and groom a new sensation. Zanuck, who was forced out of Fox in 1956 and returned in 1962 for nine increasingly unpleasant years at the studio he had built, tried to create stars out of his various European girlfriends—Bella Darvi, singer Juliette Gréco, Irina Demick, Geneviève Gilles—but the casting couch is not the place to make business decisions. Zanuck, to his discredit, forgot that just because a mogul sleeps with an actress doesn't mean the rest of us want to.

Not only were the men who created the studios losing power, the studios themselves were dwindling in stature. In the two decades from the 1960s through the 1980s, the original production houses that had ruled from the teens onward were bought by outsiders, the first stage in their gradual absorption into the immense corporate media powers we know today. Few of the new owners had backgrounds in film or even entertainment. In 1969, for example, Warner Bros. was bought by the Kinney Corporation, which had started as a parking lot/car rental/funeral parlor business with vague mob ties. MGM was picked up in 1970 by Las Vegas businessman Kirk Kerkorian, who promptly sold off the legendary sets and props at a fire-sale price of $1.5 million. The auction house Kerkorian hired made a profit of $12 million; the ruby slippers from *The Wizard of Oz* alone went for $15,000. Right there is the problem with buying a dream factory, for how do you put fair valuation on fantasy?

The one studio that, in the long view, seemed to have the right idea was Universal. It got involved with the talent agents. In 1958, the studio's back lot was bought as a facility for TV production by MCA Inc., the powerful agency (nicknamed "the Octopus") run by Jules Stein and Lew Wasserman. Almost all of Universal's major stars—James Stewart, Doris Day, Lana Turner, director Alfred Hitchcock—were MCA clients by this point anyway.

In 1962, MCA bought the studio outright but was forced by Robert F. Kennedy's Justice Department to sell off the talent agency. In a sense, that didn't matter, because one of the strategies Wasserman had pioneered in TV production was the practice that would come to be known as "packaging." MCA would put together a screenwriter, a director, and stars—all of whom the company represented—and offer it to the networks as a done deal, a useful approach to the business that gave Wasserman and his agents power over who audiences saw and who they didn't.

By the late 1960s, Wasserman was probably the most powerful figure in Hollywood—his nickname was "the Pope"—and his influence was everywhere. His mentorship of Jack Valenti, hired from President Lyndon Johnson's administration to run the MPAA ratings board on Wasserman's say-so, greatly affected the content of movies from 1968 onward. And Jules Stein's early sponsorship of Ronald Reagan, the actor who wanted to become a politician, would come to affect the country and the world. You could argue that here was the company that repackaged Hollywood stardom—the smile that sells, the confidence that makes us feel better about ourselves—for the corridors of political power.

As far as moviemaking and the immediate business of celebrity went, Wasserman's packaging concept turned out to be the model that would dominate the film production and star manufacturing industries of the 1990s and beyond. Why not earlier? First the major movie companies had to be sold once more, this time to multinational media conglomerates that needed a studio as the first machine in the factory—the one that spits out the widget all the other machines need to make money.

Here's how the dominos fall. In 1985, four years after buying Twentieth Century-Fox, oilman Marvin Davis sells the studio to Australian news baron Rupert Murdoch, who makes it the content hub of his media empire. Time Inc. acquires Warner Bros. in 1989, the same year that Sony buys Columbia from Coca-Cola. Sumner Redstone's Viacom gains control of Paramount in 1994. Universal—are you sitting down?—is bought in 1990 by Japanese electronics manufacturer Matsushita, which sells it to Canadian liquor distributor Seagrams in 1995, which is bought out by French water utility Vivendi in 2000, which sells the studio and its theme parks to General Electric, parent company of NBC, in 2004. (The resulting subsidiary, NBCUniversal, gets taken over by cable giant Comcast in 2011.) Don't even ask about MGM, which Ted Turner buys in 1986 only to promptly sell off everything but the film library; Louis B. Mayer's pride and joy is the only major film studio to fail spectacularly at the media-conglomerate game and has become a prostrate corpse at the mercy of its debt holders.

The others have spectacularly succeeded. In 1996, in the biggest deal of them all, Disney gained control of Capital Cities/ABC for $19 billion; the buyout brought with it ten TV stations, twenty-one radio stations, seven daily newspapers, and majority stakes in cable channels A&E, Lifetime, and ESPN.

Overall, that makes six hydra-headed behemoths that among them exert ownership and control of by far the majority of entertainment and information in the U.S. and around the globe. They need constant product to stoke the profits. Franchises and series are especially welcome, since you can print money off them vertically and horizontally for years. The conglomerates don't own stars outright, but stars remain the primary unit of exchange between them and the consumer, able to be sold across platforms and regardless of project. You could argue that certain properties—comic book heroes, old TV shows refurbished for the screen, CGI family films—have become, in effect, a new kind of star, but the fact remains that the original bargain holds. We still go to movies to see the people in them.

So how do those people get there? In the late 1980s and '90s, the agents took over Hollywood and put Wasserman's packaging concept on steroids. The new Creative Arts Agency amassed power by amassing stars and using them as chips to forge (or force) deals with the studios. It was the studios' old shell game of block booking, applied to people—I'll give you Jack Nicholson but you have to take C. Thomas Howell—and they got away with it. In 1992, CAA represented Warren Beatty, Steven Spielberg, Paul Newman, Bill Murray, Jane Fonda, Dustin Hoffman, Robert De Niro, Tom Cruise, Robin Williams, Michael Douglas, Sean Connery, Barbra Streisand, Sylvester Stallone, Madonna, Michael Jackson, and Martin Scorsese. You do not make a move in Hollywood without being very aware of what this company is doing. Even the agency's head, Michael Ovitz, established his own industry star persona as a sort of legendary Zen Machiavelli, speaking softly while his minions carried the sticks.

The new system worked. Stars are who we want to see, thus stars are power. Tom Cruise, the long-range missile of the 1980s, paired with Dustin Hoffman, the fussy actorly conscience of the 1970s? Hell, yes, I'll pay to see that. To the agents, stars are a means to power, so CAA comes across Barry Morrow's script for *Rain Man,* written with Hoffman and Jack Nicholson in mind, and uses it as a come-on to keep director Martin Brest hooked after another Hoffman project, *My New Partner,* has fallen apart. They sweeten the deal by offering Cruise in the Nicholson role—who cares if there's a twenty-four-year age difference between the two actors, figure it out in rewrite—and when Brest leaves and Steven Spielberg flirts without committing, they bring in director and CAA client Barry Levinson. The movie gets Best Picture and $172 million in grosses, Hoffman wins an Oscar, Cruise gets (some) respect, the agents make a killing, and *it's a good movie.* Why are you complaining?

Because more often the agents put together a package that makes no sense even if the ducks line up perfectly. *Family Business* (1989) was a heist comedy that cast CAA clients Hoffman, Matthew Broderick, and Sean Connery as father, son, and grandpa, a notion that defies basic genetic logic. The film tanked—$12 million at the box office—but the agents still made their commission, the disconnect between deal and denouement completely beside the point. With the agencies running the show, the primary business of Hollywood became closing the sale and getting the client the biggest payday. The actual making of movies was what you did after the contracts had been signed and the champagne poured.

As a result, movie stars got bigger and blander, safe bets that guaranteed maximum returns and justified the deal—and, more important, the deal after that. It's no coincidence that around this time movie grosses became an obsession both within the industry and in the consumer press. A company called EDI had started reporting weekend box office figures in 1976, but the town's competitive streak was brought out by the go-go '80s mind-set, the agencies' rise to power, and magazines like *Premiere* (launched by Rupert Murdoch in 1987) and *Entertainment Weekly* (launched by Time Warner in 1990), as well as syndicated shows like *Entertainment Tonight* (around since 1981). Where films used to take weeks, even months, to roll across the country, opening in a complex hierarchy of theaters, now the first weekend became the primary mark of worth and, crucially, the worth of the star in it. How you opened was who you were.

To protect that opening weekend and the larger investment, the business needed stars to be inclusive rather than divisive, one reason why there was a gradual move away from bulging '80s cartoons like Stallone and Schwarzenegger toward more believable Everyman action heroes like Bruce Willis in the *Die Hard* films, Keanu Reeves in *Speed,* and the Will Smith of *Independence Day*. Appealing to men and women, teens and grandparents, Republicans and Democrats, the new nice guys were typified by Kevin Costner and Tom Hanks, each of whom was explicitly viewed as the descendant of a classic Hollywood icon and each of whom it's worth spending a little time thinking about.

According to the magazines, Costner was Gary Cooper all over again, from his predilection for westerns (1985's *Silverado*, 1994's *Wyatt Earp*) and baseball films (the one-two punch of *Bull Durham* and *Field of Dreams* in the late 1980s) to his lean poise and laconic terseness. Costner had more spunk, though, and audiences went nuts for him starting with his Eliot Ness in *The Untouchables* (1987). In the time-honored formulation, women wanted him and men wanted to be him, and the momentum built until it crested around his big statement, 1990's *Dances with Wolves*, a three-hour, fiercely partisan, pro–Native American western that Costner produced, starred in, and directed. He was aiming for the same transformation of persona that Warren Beatty had pulled off with 1981's *Reds*—from a pretty-boy actor to a respected auteur—and with twelve Oscar nominations and seven wins (including Best Director and, unlike *Reds*, Best Picture), Costner actually outdid his model.

Yet he fell out of fashion with surprising speed. The backlash began with the next year's *Robin Hood: Prince of Thieves*, a package movie (CAA kicking in Costner and Morgan Freeman, the latter playing an unlikely Moorish sidekick) in which the star's flat California tones seemed drastically out of place. The same year's *JFK* was controversial, with Costner coming across as a pawn of director Oliver Stone's "assassination counter-myth" games. In the mid-1990s, hoping to repeat the epic impact of *Dances*, Costner made two apocalyptic sci-fi fantasies that were roundly mocked in the media. *Waterworld* (1995) was one of those troubled productions that become much-reported train wrecks in their own right, and while the film actually made money it was considered a critical disaster. *The Postman* (1997) was just a bust.

What went wrong? For one thing, Costner and the entertainment media had developed an antagonistic relationship, with critics and pundits declaring that his ego was out of control and the star bristling at reviews and tabloid coverage of his 1994 divorce. The sly wit that had marked Costner's performances prior to *Dances with Wolves* seemed to have disappeared, and he appeared to be taking himself very seriously with his period pieces and end-of-the-world epics. An

Everyman star can't afford to behave like an Olympian star; it creates dissonance and discomfort. There really does seem to be a parallel between Costner's travails in the 1990s and the failure of silent star Charles Ray, whose baseball dramas were wildly popular in small towns across the country, to be granted the artistic respect he sought with 1923's *The Courtship of Miles Standish.*

The issue goes deeper, though, and to the heart of what we look for when we look at movie stars. Costner had developed not one persona but two, and each spoke to different constituencies. The sexy sharpie of *Bull Durham* (1988), of the twisty diplomacy thriller *No Way Out* (1987), with its hot limousine seduction scene, and even of *Field of Dreams* (1989), in which the star's cynicism beautifully melts away over the course of the film—that Kevin Costner had sarcasm and style, and he appealed to moviegoers who like their heroes a little smartass and a little dangerous: urbanites, the young, media pundits, the rising alt-crowd who had to have irony sprinkled on everything or they wouldn't eat it.

The other Kevin Costner spoke directly to middle America, and he talked of honor and sacrifice and doing the right thing, even if you're the last mailman on a post-nuclear Earth. The first Costner went away after *Dances with Wolves,* and some people (including most reviewers) never forgave him for losing his edge. The second has tempered his message with age. Costner has wandered all over the map in the new millennium, playing serial killers (*Mr. Brooks*), Coast Guard rescue swimmers (*The Guardian*), and *The Graduate*'s Ben Braddock all grown up (the amazingly wrongheaded *Rumor Has It,* no fault of his). He directed one honey of a mature western, *Open Range,* in 2003. But lately he is playing men who had it all and blew it and who are grateful to get a little back (*The Upside of Anger, Swing Vote*). This is a unique niche, and a worthy one for an actor no longer young to pursue.

By contrast, consider the other regular fella who came to stardom in the same period. Everybody called Tom Hanks the new Jimmy Stewart, and he played right along, to the point of posing with the older actor in a *Life* photo spread and remaking Stewart's 1940 film *The Shop Around the Corner* as 1998's *You've Got Mail.* Like Costner,

Hanks had sass and sex appeal in his early roles—*Splash* and *Bachelor Party* in 1984—but he was more overtly comic and while, like most funny men, he ached to be taken seriously, he appears to have held on to the conviction that great drama is not without absurdity and great comedy is not without grief. Unlike Costner, Hanks slowly evolved a whole and complete persona that allowed people to laugh at him and feel for him as necessary.

That implies self-knowledge, and one of the reasons audiences respond to Hanks is that his persona projects a healthy perspective about himself and his stardom that reinforces his commonality. He doesn't behave like a star, even when he does. In public or on talk shows he has the gift of telling funny tales on himself and laughing uproariously—Can you *believe* it? Wasn't I *ridiculous*?—with such crack timing and evident delight that it's impossible not to be charmed. Hanks avoids movies in which he has to save the world, because swaggering is not what he does—in fact, he's built to undercut swagger and reveal its hollowness. In 2006's *The Da Vinci Code* and its sequel, the rare movies that do call on him to save the world, he's stiff and unconvincing, well outside his comfort zone.

That said, you could argue that *Philadephia* (1993), for which he won his first Best Actor Oscar, was exactly the sort of role for which Hanks is least suited—not just dramatic but actorly, a disappearance into character when the star is who we instinctively want to see. The movie proved he had the goods to transform himself and it gave him a new respect; for one thing, he was playing a gay lawyer dying of AIDS when no other straight actor of his stature would likely have touched the role. (Remember, at that point there were no out gay movie stars in Hollywood.) (Oh, wait, there still aren't.) The accolades were as much for Hanks's daring as for the performance. But in the context of his stardom, his favored meaning to audiences, it is an anomaly.

Forrest Gump, the following year, was more like it. An acting stretch that was both nominally daring (he played a man of limited mental faculties) and genuinely funny (Forrest has more horse sense than most "smart" people, and he turns up everywhere), it sealed the public's love affair with Hanks even as the movie reassured audiences that the counterculture years had all been a dreadful mistake. There was a second Oscar, after which Hanks embarked on a period in which he was the country's best idea of itself, holding down the NASA fort in *Apollo 13* (1995) and sacrificing himself for American motherhood and honor in *Saving Private Ryan* (1998). So he won over the heartland and the "greatest generation" as he had won over women with the sweet, funny Mr. Rights of *Sleepless in Seattle* (1993) and *You've Got Mail* (1998), as he won over kids and parents as the voice of *Toy Story*'s Woody, as he won over hipsters by writing and directing the rock-and-roll fable *That Thing You Do!* (1996). Hanks wasn't an Everyman star, he was everyone's star.

There were other breakthroughs as the agencies and studios sought broad-appeal new personalities at the turn of the 1990s, including the first genuine post-Poitier African American leading men in Denzel Washington and Will Smith. By "post-Poitier," I don't mean "post-racial"—there is no such thing in America—but simply that a star like Washington was now able to give performances that included blackness without necessarily being about it, unless it was called for and, say, Spike Lee was directing him as Malcolm X. No longer was an African American lead role in an otherwise white movie a de facto progressive political statement; no longer was a film that was set primarily among people of color, like *Mississippi Masala* (1991), in which Washington woos Sarita Choudhury, aimed only *at* people of color.

By the mid-1990s, Smith had become a superstar in *Independence Day* and *Men in Black* in roles that could easily have been cast white, just as Washington had his pick of dramatic parts regardless of color. Neither man sold out who he was—and race was clearly part of who they were—but the white mainstream was able to relax and enjoy both actors in the comfortable knowledge that race was not all of who they were and that no one was going to put them on the spot. Once that bridge had been crossed, actors like Jamie Foxx and Don Cheadle were able to rise unchallenged, their skin color an issue in their roles only when they wanted it to be.

Morgan Freeman, by contrast, had a great career in this era without achieving post-Poitier status for himself until very late in the game; arguably, he went farther down the road paved by Danny Glover, a much-loved character star whose greatest mainstream commercial impact was the stolid African American family man opposite crazy Mel Gibson in the *Lethal Weapon* series. Freeman's own breakthrough was as the vicious pimp in 1987's *Street Smart*, and although he quickly switched to noble, altruistic characters like the long-suffering chauffeur of *Driving Miss Daisy* (1989) and the kindly convict of *The Shawshank Redemption* (1994), Freeman's color remained part of his casting even when—especially when—he was playing God (*Bruce Almighty*, 2003), the president (*Deep Impact*, 1998), or Nelson Mandela (*Invictus*, 2009). It's less an issue in genre thrillers like *Se7en* (1995) and *Kiss the Girls* (1997), and, anyway, by now his persona as a gentle, firm, benevolent man is so established that it's a moot point: he's not black, he's Morgan Freeman. That said, look for the little-known *10 Items or Less* (2006), in which the actor plays a prickly has-been movie star researching a role in a supermarket. It's the rare film that gives you a fuller and wittier sense of who the actor we know as Morgan Freeman may actually be.

Not coincidentally, the new decade was also a terrific time for actresses, especially coming after the testosterone-heavy Reagan era. The reasons were twofold: the studios needed bankable female stars to play opposite their new Everymen, and, more important, a busy and prosperous female-oriented fan industry was springing up. In the decades following World War II, the fan magazines had been considered increasingly déclassé, but now they returned to the middle class with a vengeance in the wake of *Entertainment Weekly*, *Entertainment Tonight*, *InStyle*, *Premiere*, the increasingly powerful *People*, and the resurgent *Us Weekly*, which *Rolling Stone* publisher Jann Wenner bought from the *New York Times* in 1986.

The content mixes of these outlets varied, but all combined industry news, reviews, celebrity gossip, style commentary, glamour shots, and red carpet photo spreads, and they revitalized an interest in the triangulation of women, fame, and personal style that would only gather strength in the coming years. They offered the same promise as the classic movie magazines of the silent era—that by showing you a star's life offscreen, the magazine could bring you closer to what they liked and what they wore and who they were and who you could become. The magazines confirmed personas, created public narratives, represented public judgment in times of scandal, and dispelled the primal movie mystery by replacing it with an illusion of access and knowledge.

But you needed female stars to tell the narrative. Because the gossip magazine audience was primarily female, male stars were mere events, obstacles, and prizes. And those female stars had to seem closer than Meryl Streep or Glenn Close to the average reader of *People,* a magazine that had always included human-interest stories—tales that celebrated you and me—along with its star coverage. Glamour was important but, increasingly, so was approachability.

This is why a star like Meg Ryan comes to the fore. She's the new Girl Next Door, like you but sweeter, sassier, funnier—or as sweet, sassy, and funny as you felt on the inside. She popped up in '80s movies—that's her as the best friend's rowdy wife in *Top Gun,* more down-to-earth than Tom Cruise could handle—but she comes into her own as a matched saltshaker to the pepper of attractively schlubby normal guys like Billy Crystal in *When Harry Met Sally* (1989) and Hanks in *Sleepless in Seattle* and *You've Got Mail.*

In truth, those movies were the only three to fully fit the script, and Ryan busied herself throughout the 1990s playing an alcoholic (*When a Man Loves a Woman*), a Desert Storm helicopter commander (*Courage Under Fire*), Albert Einstein's niece (*IQ*), a neo-noir femme fatale (*Flesh and Bone*), Mrs. Jim Morrison (*The Doors*), an inmate in a seventeenth-century British madhouse (*Restoration*), and three different women opposite Hanks in the fascinating 1990 bomb *Joe Versus the Volcano.* Didn't matter. None of them stuck. Ryan shared America's Sweetheart duties with Julia Roberts (and seemed even more clearly to evoke the distant memory of Mary Pickford), but she was locked in by the expectations of the persona, despite faking a perfectly good orgasm in Katz's Deli in *When Harry Met Sally.*

Her 2000 tabloid scandal is illustrative. When Ryan left her husband Dennis Quaid for costar Russell Crowe during the Ecuador shoot of the action drama *Proof of Life,* the three stars' preestablished images determined how it would play out in the public mediasphere. Quaid (manly, raffish, a stand-up guy) was perceived as wronged, while Crowe (boorish, mercurial, *foreign*) was the talented cad who does what cads do. Because Meg Ryan did not behave according to the public laws of Meg Ryan (hopeful fusspot who always ends up making the right choice), her behavior was deemed inexplicable and she was punished with tabloid headlines accusing her of being an unfit mother. (Quaid came to her defense, which did accord with the laws of Dennis Quaid.)

Imagine if Ryan were Elizabeth Taylor. It would have been, in every sense, a different story, one in which a sex goddess gives in to a passion we mere mortals will never understand. (Hapless Eddie Fisher was no Quaid, although Crowe is an acceptable stand-in for Richard Burton.) To bring it closer to the present day, if Ryan were Angelina Jolie, this would be a tale of an imperious Amazon taking what she deems her due, with Jennifer Aniston cast as the wronged wife and Brad Pitt the dazed stud they're fighting over.

All three versions of the story sell papers and get ratings because they seem to be a better movie than the movies we often get and because they're real, or sold to us that way. But the *Proof of Life* affair was the rare instance where the adulterous female star was punished for not acting in agreement with her accepted persona, and Ryan's career never fully bounced back. Three years later, she starred in the lugubrious psycho-feminist thriller *In the Cut,* directed by Australia's much-admired Jane Campion (*The Piano*), as if saying to the world *Yes, I can get naked and perform fellatio and that's what acting is sometimes about.* And the world recoiled in disgust. One particularly cruel reviewer observed, "If there ever was an era when America wanted to see Meg Ryan naked—and this is doubtful—it surely ended 10 years ago." As ever, stardom could be a prison.

Anyway, if Ryan didn't want to play the game and Julia Roberts was still hashing out what her persona actually was (before realizing it was simply "Julia Roberts"), there were enough subsidiary sweethearts to go around. Sandra Bullock was the tomboy variant, able to keep up with the hero amid the speed of *Speed* (1994) and hold down the romantic-comedy center of *While You Were Sleeping* (1995). She was cute, klutzy, resilient, a little sardonic, a little heartsore—very much how many of the women who bought the tickets thought of themselves and not too distantly descended from silent archetypes like Colleen Moore and sassy '40s gals like Ann Sothern. The trouble was how to bottle that persona within the genres available to Bullock, a process that failed with thrillers (*The Net*), period pieces (*In Love and War*), and topical dramas (*A Time to Kill*), until she gave up and just started producing her own lightweight comedies and dramas (*Miss Congeniality, Hope Floats*) that, for all we know, are still playing as in-flight entertainment somewhere.

Suddenly, there seemed to be infinite variants on the new '90s movie heroine, some of them sharper and more complex, others perfectly nice. Susan Sarandon: political, sexual, plus she'd been around the counterculture block. Emma Thompson: wise and British, so much more civilized than you or I. Kate Winslet: Thompson's willful little sister (literally, in 1995's *Sense and Sensibility*), building critical and audience credibility until she's ready for the big one. Feisty down-home version: Holly Hunter. Moody teen variant: Winona Ryder. There still was room for a ruthless vamp, although Sharon Stone seemed the only actress interested in the job, and the panty-free shock of *Basic Instinct* (1992) quickly gave way to the empty heavy breathing of *Sliver* (1993). As ever, audiences felt uncomfortable about actresses who felt comfortable about sex. And Australia slowly colonized Hollywood. Nicole Kidman had a hit in 1989's yacht thriller *Dead Calm*, was cast opposite Tom Cruise in 1990's *Days of Thunder*, and married him to become instant Hollywood royalty. By the late '90s, Cate Blanchett had appeared in *Elizabeth* and shortly thereafter Naomi Watts broke through in David Lynch's *Mulholland Dr.*

An interesting thing about the Australian stars, though: aside from the quality of their performances, which is uniformly high, they're almost completely unknowable. Blanchett is exclusively about the work and appears to transform into a different person from role to role—the pop marketplace finds no place to get traction. Watts has talent but, again, no discernible personality beyond her films. Kidman's persona is increasingly blurry; she spent eleven years in the black box of marriage to Cruise—maybe light gets in, but none escapes—and since then has been the subject of gossip and derision concerning her rumored cosmetic procedures. This is more than just a star's lot in the age of Internet vultures, for the buzzing fills the space where Kidman's image might be. Faced with a persona vacuum, the public will gladly make one up. It's people's way of spinning folktales about the gods and their sins.

Some of these women and a lot of the men were coming from a new source of movie stars: independent cinema. Which wasn't supposed to be about stars at all but about ideas and experiences and fresh moviemaking blood. But, look, here we are eight decades out from Carl Laemmle's invention of Florence Lawrence, and the American concept of celluloid fame has long since conquered the world. Unless you're an animator or lonesome Stan Brakhage gluing moth wings onto film strips (*Mothlight*, 1963; see it), people will access your movie through the human beings in it.

Alternatives to established systems of commercial filmmaking existed from the dawn of movies—Universal, Paramount, Fox, and others all started as independents. Art films by directors like Maya Deren and Kenneth Anger flourished in the cracks of the Hollywood factory in the 1940s. With the post–World War II breakdown of the studio system and the rise of counterculture audiences, underground cinema was born: Warhol's downtown experiments, the cheap camp epics of the Kuchar brothers, John Cassavetes's off-Hollywood angst, the transgressive kink of John Waters's early films. Warhol tried to broker a whole stable of DIY stars, but Waters arguably did him one better with his three-hundred-pound drag queen, Divine (aka Harris Glenn Milstead), featured player of such outrages as 1971's *Pink Flamingos*, in which the lady stoops to eat doggie poo. Top that, Joan

Crawford. Divine replaced the blank stare of the Warhol superstars with an outsider's defiance; she was a hilariously grotesque parody of Hollywood glamour that demanded to be appreciated fully or not at all.

By the 1980s, a circuit had coalesced of established art houses, distribution companies, and video labels that were willing to take a chance on independently produced movies. Directors tended to be the focus—John Sayles, Spike Lee, the young Coen brothers, Allison Anders, Alex Cox of *Repo Man* and *Sid and Nancy*—which dovetailed with the more serious concerns of the movement. You could have fun at an indie film, but it was always about more than just fun; at the very least your patronage struck a blow against the whole rotten system, man. By the end of the decade, indie cinema was poised to go wide thanks to a handful of powerful producer/distributors—Miramax chief among them—and the establishment of several important film festivals, primarily Robert Redford's Sundance.

The watershed came in 1989, when Steven Soderbergh's *sex, lies, and videotape* stormed through Sundance, Cannes, Hollywood, and the sensibilities of adventurous moviegoers while in several important ways taking the "indie" out of independent cinema. For one thing, the movie had movie stars, or at least actors who had already carved a space for themselves in the entertainment industry. Andie MacDowell had a successful modeling career, Peter Gallagher had done movies and TV, and James Spader was well known as the love him/hate him snob of '80s teen movies. Yet the film, which despite the title was mostly talk, allowed all these people to be different from who we had assumed them to be. Spader especially impressed as a perv philosopher who turns out to be a closet romantic. These actors reignited their careers but also announced that persona was suddenly negotiable outside the confines of major studio product.

That is what indie film meant to the 1990s and early 2000s: a second chance, a route back to authenticity—the selling of the romance of who you "really were" and the idealism you had once valued before you sold out. This applied equally to the actors in the movies and the audiences watching them. Because authenticity is a desired commodity in an increasingly plastic media world, the indie concept became valuable to both hipsters and the mainstream, to art-house studios and majors like Disney, which bought Miramax in 1993.

In addition—and perhaps more importantly—indie cinema developed into a farm team for young stars and directors and screenwriters, a proving ground for the studios that, at its best, was a major arena of its own, both in terms of quality product and a means by which an audience could define itself as "other." And here we come to a critical development in popular culture: the rise of alt.

There has always been a subsection of consumers—they don't think of themselves as consumers at all, but as connoisseurs—who've sought out nonmainstream books and music and other media. Such people were traditionally defined and self-defined by their marginalization from the over-culture. Bohemians, beatniks, longhairs (in the prewar classical music sense)—whatever you want to call them. The counterculture established this as a mass phenomenon, but after a brief struggle known as the 1960s, the counterculture *became* the culture. Popular music meant rock and roll, which was why the Ramones invented punk and the Sex Pistols immediately picked up on it: there will always be people who look at what everyone else is doing and head in the other direction. If you have to specify the difference, you could say that alt necessitates irony—an attitudinal stance outside—while the mainstream can't handle irony. Sarcasm, yes, flip jokes, the posturing of hipness, and the occasional pun, but not irony. (Ironically, this may be why Alanis Morissette's 1996 song "Ironic," which tries to describe irony and fails, was a Top Ten hit.)

In the 1990s, for arguably the first time, this split became formalized in popular culture, as audiences began to define themselves by whether they felt comfortable in the mainstream (*Titanic,* Shania Twain, John Grisham) or its alternative (*The Big Lebowski,* Neutral Milk Hotel, Nick Hornby). I just picked 1998 products out of the air, but any year will do. Furthermore, the alt is not one alt but many different alts, so your own 1998 parenthetical might include *The Miseducation of Lauryn Hill* or *Metal Gear Solid* or *300* (the original graphic novel, not the 2006 movie) or even Michael Tilson Thomas and the San Francisco Symphony's landmark recording of Berlioz's *Symphonie fantastique.* The important aspect was that the choice established your own distance from the big top and thus helped to illustrate, in a very real sense, your public and private identities. Your cultural choices were becoming both signifiers of and advertisements for your personality; they served as mating plumage, too, and territorial marking. None of this had been possible when everyone appeared to agree.

Coined either by the music industry or the pioneering Internet bulletin board Usenet (which shunted off-topic conversations into an "alt" hierarchy), alt came to function as an all-purpose modifier by the turn of the millennium. Let's apply it to movie stars. Your choice of who intrigues/amuses/obsesses you now announces who you are and, importantly, who you are not. We saw this back in the 1960s when the hippies rejected John Wayne in favor of Peter Fonda, but now the options are wide-ranging and surprisingly fluid. Perhaps your personal pantheon includes Leonardo DiCaprio and Kate Winslet. Fine, but which era are you talking about? The period during 1993 and 1994 when DiCaprio played the mentally challenged Arnie in the small-town drama *What's Eating Gilbert Grape* and Winslet debuted as a murderous schoolgirl in *Heavenly Creatures*? Or 1997, when the two conquered the planet in *Titanic*? Or 2008, when they reunited in *Revolutionary Road,* an upmarket literary adaptation about marital strife? Each era is a new thing, with different meanings to different audiences.

In other words, the rise of alt as an idea and a market niche liberated the film industry's creative community and allowed its actors to define themselves on a project-by-project basis—to balance the financial rewards of mainstream studio fare with the critical plaudits and cultural respect of more challenging work. Some stars don't play the game. Catherine Zeta-Jones seems to relish being an old-school movie diva and will probably never dowdy down and take a pay cut. But many do.

In the early 2000s, both Halle Berry and Charlize Theron played against their glam personas (note the titles: *Monster's Ball* and *Mon-*

ster), and won Oscars for their perceived guts. Yes, Adam Sandler makes his living from idiot comedies, but there he is in P. T. Anderson's *Punch-Drunk Love* (2002) as a touching art-house variant of his traditional stumblebum. Anderson's films, in fact, have served as a reclamation ward for some of Hollywood's most generic personalities, like Burt Reynolds in *Boogie Nights* (1997) and Tom Cruise in *Magnolia* (1999). Surround a bland box office star with hip character actors like Philip Seymour Hoffman and William Macy, and the cool rubs off on them. Mark Wahlberg went into *Boogie Nights* as a ridiculed acting wannabe and came out a lionized young talent with a brilliant career ahead of him. Alt works.

John Travolta and Bruce Willis in *Pulp Fiction* (1994), the former saving his career from the has-been bin, the latter reminding us that he has a weary authority that, when it all clicks (which it too rarely does), gets him within view of Bogart on the distant mountaintop. Julia Roberts yoking herself to Soderbergh's career plan, big (*Oceans Eleven, Erin Brockovich*) and minuscule (*Full Frontal*). George Clooney and Brad Pitt shuttling between box office fluff and the Coen brothers. This is how stardom functions now, and there's crossover the other way as well, with respected non-glam actors like Philip Seymour Hoffman, Paul Giamatti, Laura Linney, John C. Reilly, Marisa Tomei, Toni Collette, and John Malkovich livening up studio films in character parts while starring in odder, harder, more rewarding movies for the specialty market.

Indeed, *Being John Malkovich* (1999) is almost a metaphor for the new order, with mainstream performers John Cusack and Cameron Diaz (the latter unrecognizably frumpy) traipsing through a portal in the title actor's head. Tilda Swinton, pale and unforgiving, equally haunts art-house films and big-budget epics, winning an Oscar opposite George Clooney in *Michael Clayton* (2007) while drawing small, appreciative audiences to a film like *Julia* (2009), a withering portrait of an alcoholic. You can even retire into alt-land as Bill Murray has done, enraging *Caddyshack* fans who wander into the brilliant Buddhist drift of *Lost in Translation* (2003) and *Broken Flowers* (2005).

The movie star has become a cultural free agent, and the new watchword is reinvention. Because an actor in the modern media age has almost always come from somewhere else—a TV sitcom (DiCaprio in *Growing Pains*), an hourlong drama (George Clooney in *ER*), a teen soap (Katie Holmes and Michelle Williams in *Dawson's Creek*), a horror movie (Johnny Depp in *A Nightmare on Elm Street*), *SNL* (too many to count)—the ones who cross over to success, who we want to see more of, have pasts they've already moved beyond. They're already version 2.0, which brokers the notion that there are further upgrades to be discovered.

This is Warhol's theory of postmodern celebrity as a matter of daily business, and it spills over into the actual financial and creative business of stardom, as the more powerful movie actors extend their control into production companies *and* screenwriting. There may be no other choice, since the constant renegotiation of image promised by the rise of alt is the ambitious star's only way to avoid becoming corporate product. Reinvention is proof in a world of six major media behemoths that stars are independent and that we in the audience retain freedom of choice, even if they aren't and we don't.

In the new millennium, young stars arrive and define themselves in public, improvising as they go. Think of Joseph Gordon-Levitt graduating from TV's *Third Rock from the Sun* and patiently experimenting with high school noir (*Brick*), action drama (*The Lookout*), romantic comedy (*[500] Days of Summer*). Who will he be? We don't know, but audiences respond to the attempt. When *Inception* opened in 2010, supporting actor Gordon-Levitt, not lead Leonardo DiCaprio, sat atop the Internet Movie Database's "STARmeter," a fickle but key popularity index, for weeks.

This template may first have been hammered out by Keanu Reeves. A seeming found object in '80s indie films like *River's Edge* (1986) and earnest studio fare (*Permanent Record*, 1988), he has since been a teen goofball (*Bill & Ted's Excellent Adventure*), a vampire fighter (*Dracula*), a French chevalier (*Dangerous Liaisons*), a surfing cop (*Point Break*), an action star (*Speed*), Buddha (*Little Buddha*), a gay hustler (*My Own Private Idaho*), and the messiah of the enslaved human race (*The Matrix*). There's no through-line there, and yet we can say with assurance that we know who Keanu Reeves is, at least onscreen—an oddly elegant space cadet of a leading man. The black lab of movie stars. Gregory Peck reincarnated as a dude.

This sense of open-ended options is the hope of younger stars. Think of all those yearning kid celebrities from Nickelodeon and Disney TV—tweener factories that replicate the classic studio system for the only gullible audience left—who are desperate to graduate to "real" stardom, even if that means a scandal or two. Shia LeBeouf has worked like crazy to reposition himself from Disney's *Even Stevens* to a nerdy teen action hero to a young heartthrob to a serious thespian, yet the jury's still out, as it is for Miley Cyrus, Zac Efron, Brenda Song, and Nickelodeon's currently reigning Good Girl, Miranda Cosgrove, who in 2011 landed on the cover of the *New York Times* Sunday magazine in an article wishfully titled "Big Girl Now." The tweener stars are adolescent parodies of iconic Hollywood personas and character types, but to break out of the hermetic world of kid TV, they have to mean more. But what does that mean?

As mentioned earlier, reinvention can reposition a manic comedian like Robin Williams, Jim Carrey, or Adam Sandler as a dramatic actor. It can come to the aid of stars who are cautious and bored, like Johnny Depp, so wary of the Hollywood game that he moved to France, was coaxed back for a megabudget action film based on a Disney ride, treated the role like the joke it was—only with wit and craft—and became bigger and more beloved than ever.

Meryl Streep—this is my favorite. Streep, the queen of suffering '80s cinema, whose movies are good for you whether you like it or not, effectively says the hell with it in the 1990s and tries *anything*. The body-morphing satire of *Death Becomes Her* (1992) and the action-heroine strenuousness of *The River Wild* (1994). The autumnal romance of *The Bridges of Madison County* (1995)—opposite *Clint Eastwood*, has the world gone mad? No: reinvention. By the early 2000s, Streep appears to have completely lost her marbles, but she's definitely having fun. The undone *New Yorker* writer of *Adaptation* (2002), hooked on lust and orchid powder. A dithery aunt in *Lemony*

Snicket's A Series of Unfortunate Events (2004). The loosey-goosey half of a sister act in *A Prairie Home Companion* (2006), playing mother to Lindsay Lohan the way a duchess might give birth to a mall rat.

And then comes *The Devil Wears Prada* (2006), and I can still see the expression on my eleven-year-old daughter's face as she turns to me in the darkened theater and whispers, "*That's* Meryl Streep? She's *amazing*." All the actress's technique and all her insights were brought to bear on the pop character of Miranda Priestley, a monster she turned human against the expectations of a young audience that really *didn't* know from great acting based on what they'd seen on the Disney Channel. The hordes of young girls came to the movie for Anne Hathaway and left gobsmacked by their conflicted feelings toward Streep as the movie's villainess, eviscerating underlings without ever raising her voice—and there was a new idea, that you can kill people quietly. Good acting forces you to consider fresh notions of human behavior, and suddenly the actress was bringing the news to everyone.

The result, after *Prada,* and the joyous Eurotrash cheese of *Mamma Mia!* (2008), and the equally delightful culinary impersonation of *Julie and Julia* (2009), is that Meryl Streep is possibly my daughters' generation's best-loved movie star, a statement of fact that would have floored a moviegoer in 1986. Joy, in fact, has much to do with it, the perceptible pleasure a gifted actress has toward the art she once treated as a higher calling. There's freedom there, too. If Meryl Streep can invent herself as she goes, can't anyone?

Well, no. Because she was established as an actress rather than a star, mutability was always expected of Streep. When persona is limited and locked in, as with Meg Ryan, there's only so far you can reinvent yourself before the public pushes back. By contrast, if you make playing with your persona part of your act, it's hard to get the audience to invest in just one face. That's why Madonna, for all her commercial success, has never been a movie star. Her image as a pop deconstructionist is so entrenched—she's always Madonna before she's anyone else—that we can't indulge the fantasy of her being another person for even the two hours required of a movie. We're not watching Evita but Madonna playing Evita as an essay in star ambition, onscreen and off. Her most convincing performance is still in *Desperately Seeking Susan* (1985), where she plays the young, cheeky Manhattan wild child she seems to have been at that point. Suspension of disbelief, the first step in buying into a movie star, is simply not an option with this woman. Madonna is far more interesting to not take on faith, which may be frustrating for her—she really wanted that Oscar—but is unimportant to audiences playing by the rules she herself established.

So, no, some stars can't reinvent themselves. And sometimes reinvention can go wrong, an increasingly frequent occurrence in a media culture where every mistake is instantly amplified, commented upon, tweeted, and blogged. The admired actress Melissa Leo ran into a field of angry pop static when she attempted to tweak her persona from tough mama to glamour queen during the 2011 Oscar race. Nominated for Best Supporting Actress for her role as the fearsome manager mother in *The Fighter*—a part well within her accepted range of working-class characters—Leo took out trade ads featuring her in an evening gown with full hair and makeup. Atop the ads was a single word: "Consider."

Consider what? Rather brilliantly, Leo left it up to us. Consider her as something more than a character actress, a postmillennial Thelma Ritter? Consider a fortysomething woman who hasn't had any work done as a sex symbol? Consider the ways we assign value to performers based on their looks, and consider how that might limit an actor of ambition? Consider Melissa Leo not as an actress at all but as a star?

To her misfortune, the lines between categories are not so easily blurred when we think we know who someone is. Leo was heavily criticized for her affront to taste—because in Hollywood it's all right to want an Academy Award but not okay to appear to want one—and she lost some pop standing and cultural cachet. But who's to blame here? The actress for thinking outside her persona or the public for refusing to let her? It's Little Mary's Dilemma for an age of postmodern celebrity. The flexibility we allow some stars we refuse to countenance in others, depending on what we've seen of them and what we're willing to entertain. A tough mama in an evening gown is too dissonant to withstand scrutiny in the daily marketplace of pop ideas.

At least Leo had an established star persona with which to play. The catastrophic miscalculation of actor Joaquin Phoenix in 2009, with his "decision" to leave the profession, grow a beard, and concentrate on a rap career, was that he thought we knew or cared who he was. The public response was immediate and confused. Had Phoenix lost his mind? Was it a conceptual prank? With the 2010 appearance of the mockumentary *I'm Still Here*—the title blissfully name-checking the 2007 cinematic Bob Dylan deconstruction *I'm Not There* while calling into question who, exactly, "I" was in this case—it was clear that it *was* a prank, and a conceptually daring one. After some initial perplexity on the part of the nation's movie critics, director Casey Affleck went on talk shows and confessed all.

It was also clear that most audiences didn't find the joke very funny or even enlightening. Would a different actor, one whose initial movie star persona was less awkward or more alluringly mysterious—one who had a coherent star persona from which to deviate—have invited audiences into the head games rather than pushing them away? We'll never know, but having thrust the meaninglessness of a star's "reality" into audiences' faces, Phoenix broke his compact with the public. Don't expect him to be forgiven anytime soon, either. No one likes to be told they're dupes.

Sometimes reality intercedes to reinvent a star against his or her will. Mel Gibson—you knew we had to get back to him sooner or later—successfully pulled a Kevin Costner in the mid-1990s, winning Best Picture and Director Oscars (but, again, not Best Actor) for his medieval Scottish epic *Braveheart* (1995). In the process, he established himself as a multitalented artist. Note that this was at least Mel version 3.5, following his arrival in *The Road Warrior,* the early romantic-stud films, the action hijinks of the *Lethal Weapon* series, and even a credible 1990 *Hamlet*. The major upgrade came in 2004, though, when a born-again Gibson—Mel 4.0—released his self-financed life of Jesus, *The Passion of the Christ,* to the outrage of the chattering classes and the rapture of masses of Christian moviegoers. At this point, his meaning split in two: either Gibson was a gifted filmmaker doing God's work and getting crucified by the heathen media or he was a violence-obsessed, anti-Semitic, homophobic nutjob still living in the Dark Ages. Which Mel you believed in, and argued for, said less about him than about you.

Interestingly, there was a third Mel Gibson at the time—the one the movie industry saw. This Mel was a solid filmmaker, a stand-up guy to his casts and crews, and a reliable center of profits. Maybe a little weird about his religion, but it's L.A., everyone has a guru one way or another, and besides, did you see the money *Passion* made? Success in Hollywood answers all doubts, at least until the Malibu police pull you over for driving drunk and you start ranting about the Jews. Introducing Mel Gibson 5.0—Crazy Mel.

But, again, this is public narrative—a filtering of received media images and response—rather than anything you or I will ever truly know about the actual Mel Gibson. Following that 2006 DUI bust, he did the contrition media roadshow (pioneered by actor Hugh Grant in 1995 after he was arrested with a prostitute) and was, rather surprisingly, forgiven by the industry and by Jewish leaders, if not by the non-evangelical section of the public. His next movie, *Apocalypto* (2006), a Mayan action film in which Gibson doesn't appear and whose dialogue is entirely in the extinct Yucatec dialect, opened to mostly positive reviews and ticket sales while furthering the notion that the star might be seriously unhinged.

By the time the revenge thriller *Edge of Darkness* came out in early 2010, violence and weirdness had become folded into Gibson's persona, yet it seemed aestheticized and under control. He was in production on *The Beaver,* a comedy drama about a delusional man who believes that the beaver puppet on his hand speaks to him. At this point, it sounded like typecasting. Jodie Foster was directing, and if the immensely admired Foster could get behind an accused bigot, why shouldn't we? The sense was that Gibson might be a lunatic, but he was *our* lunatic.

The release of the "Gibson tapes" onto the Internet in the summer of 2010 changed the drama yet again. This was not just another upgrade to the persona but rather a major version change; it didn't report on but allowed us to seemingly personally confirm that the star could spin violently out of control. In that confirmation, the choice of how to respond came down to each individual member of the public in a way unprecedented in the modern history of fame. To listen to the recorded conversations of Gibson, hoarsely raging at his girlfriend in the most savage language imaginable—to hear him threaten her with murder—is not something one is inclined to let Jodie Foster or the Anti-Defamation League explain away, let alone Gibson by going on *Late Night with Jimmy Fallon*.

He didn't, of course; he lay low, knowing the evidence had gone viral. His agency dropped him; *The Beaver* was in the can but unreleasable for the time being; his defenders grew defensive and ugly. We'll talk further on about how the Internet has allowed the masses to fully and finally penetrate the secrets they believe are at the heart of stardom by enabling global distribution of those secrets—the police reports, the sex tapes, the cell phone rants, the nudie shots. Supposedly we're getting at the real celebrity, when in fact we're just getting his or her most damning moments. Listening to Gibson, though, is like peering behind the smiling showbiz mask into a black hole of self-pity and rage—the screaming big-baby Id that's at the core of not just stardom and its discontents but of the disappointment inherent in human experience itself; the anger that my life is not what I thought it would be, that *it's not about me and it's not fair.* This is the secret beyond secrets, the infant's will to attention that turns into the scream for fame. Aren't you sorry you asked?

It's not fair, but that's how it goes. We dig our own graves and make our own images in the public sphere, whether that sphere is our school, our workplace, our Facebook page, or the world's movie and TV screens. Mel Gibson's narrative—his meaning as a famous person—has now moved out of the theaters and into the spaces between movies, where we debate what people do rather than how they playact. As such, he's rather more useful to discussions of racism, domestic abuse, homophobia, and alcoholism, because when a star says these things—"Fucking

Jews," "Do I *sound* like a homosexual?," "If you get raped by a pack of niggers, it will be your fault"—we rightly question why we should cut him a break just because he made *The Road Warrior* or *Passion of the Christ.*

Can Gibson be reinvented yet again? Anything is possible. In the short-attention-span theater of modern pop culture, all it takes is one hit movie (in his case, maybe three) and the wheels of public forgiveness start turning. If you had said in 1999 that Gibson's good friend Robert Downey Jr.—then spending a year in California state prison for possession of heroin, cocaine, and a Magnum handgun while speeding down Sunset Blvd.—would in a decade be not only a bigger star than ever but a dearly beloved public personality, you would have drawn horselaughs. Downey's public flameout as a result of his substance addictions included multiple arrests, getting fired from the cast of TV's *Ally McBeal,* and a bizarre interlude in which he wandered into a neighbor's bedroom and fell asleep. The prevailing attitude toward him was more pity than censure, though, because his established persona of a quick-witted bon vivant allowed room for a tragic reading: the *doomed* quick-witted bon vivant.

Because Downey was liked—because he was likeable—the public backed his ultimately sincere attempts to clean himself up. Critical to his return to the screen was Gibson (see? it's complicated), who personally backed the insurance bond for his friend's starring role in 2003's *The Singing Detective.* Over the next few years Downey built up a persona similar to but deeper than his pre-prison image. He was now the bon vivant who has been through the fire and come out the other side, wit intact but knowing things you're lucky you don't. When *Iron Man* came along in 2008, Downey gave the stock comic-book-hero archetype both moral weight and a subversive humor that made the film an unexpectedly broad-appeal hit. That same year, *Tropic Thunder* cast him as a pompous white actor wearing blackface, and the general consensus was that in all of Hollywood only Downey had the intelligence and quickness to negotiate the political and racial nuances of a dangerously tricky role. Imagine the firestorm if Gibson had tried.

There are, of course, a few movie actors who resist reinvention, and they are the true heirs of the Hollywood factory system—performers whose charismatic consistency of persona renders them old-school stars, with the power and allure that implies. George Clooney is always George Clooney, regardless of the size of the movie or the nature of the role. Like the matinee idols from whom he's descended, he understands that infinite shades of human psychology can be conveyed within an apparently limited set of behaviors and attitudes. (This is known as Cary Grant's Law.) Angelina Jolie cannot *not* be the matriarchal Amazon warrior queen, onscreen or on the cover of *People,* nor do moviegoers want her to be otherwise, whether they like or dislike her.

Her consort, Brad Pitt, is a curious case, though. *Fight Club* (1999) aside, he's a superstar with little persona other than a sort of earnest dude-ishness, except when he takes on a character part, as in *Twelve Monkeys* (1995) or *Burn After Reading* (2008), at which point he suddenly becomes engaged, inventive, watchable. Pitt is a binary star, part classic screen icon, part reinventive character actor, and only recently, with 2011's *Moneyball* and *The Tree of Life*, has he come into focus. Meanwhile, Pitt's former wife, Jennifer Aniston, had a coherent and appealing TV persona on *Friends* that she has never been able to expand into a convincing big-screen personality. You could spend all week leaping from one modern star to the next, charting how each has or has not managed the balancing act of consistency and reinvention necessary to seem constantly relevant. To seem irrelevant, of course, is celebrity death.

It's most fascinating to watch a new generation of actors dive into this game and learn the rules as they go. You sense them asking: Who am I? Who should I want to be? What the public wants? What my agent wants? There are actors like Anne Hathaway and Michael Cera who arrive with fully formed images, hers classically elegant, his postmodern and reactive. Will they stay as they are or will they—can they—start rethinking themselves? Hathaway is trying hard, broadening her palette with accents and nudity in *Love and Other Drugs* (2010) and bad-girl demons in *Rachel Getting Married* (2008). Cera seems hardly to be trying at all, and the danger is that modern audiences will tire of too much repetition. Can he be someone appreciably different while still being Michael Cera? Or can the right part focus that persona while giving it fresh appeal, as happened with Jesse Eisenberg and *The Social Network* (2010)?

Keira Knightley arrives as the latest lovely from England in *Pirates of the Caribbean* (2003) and *Pride and Prejudice* (2005) and immediately varies her hand as the violent bounty hunter of *Domino* (2005)—it doesn't work, but it's the attempt that matters. Ellen Page comes in from the other direction, as the smart-mouthed pregnant teen of the Sundance hit *Juno* (2007), then essays the multileveled blockbuster character action of *Inception* (2010). Who will she be next? She may have the acting range, but does her image—sardonic woman-child with heart of flame—have the elasticity?

As always since the very invention of movie stars, these actors and their peers each embody an idea, a narrative whose potential energy is shaped by aspects of physical appearance, attitude, talent, and luck. Hathaway: grace. Kristen Stewart: grace wrapped in sullenness. Dakota Fanning: the new brilliant child, a baby Streep. Cera: nerd irony. Ryan Reynolds: snark. The difference is that the possibilities for reinvention are endless in the push-pull of the multiplex, art-house, and gossip universe. As of this writing, Reynolds is trying to make himself over from a frat-house wiseass to the superhero of *Green Lantern* and the tough guy of *Safe House,* to the point of fitting his body with the latest biceps and abs. Good luck to him, but will the old persona work in the new body? And if he tries a new persona, will anyone be interested? The cold evolutionary fact is that if a baby star cannot make that first impression, that sense of a functioning personality we want to know better, they may prosper on their looks for a while but sooner or later they'll cease to matter. Some of us are still trying to figure out what, if anything, "stars" like Amanda Seyfried or Katherine Heigl or Paul Walker mean. But most of us don't really care. We just watch them until they're no longer beautiful.

20.

Pixel Persona: Stardom in the Internet Age

It may be that the games of reinvention played by famous people in the first decades of the twenty-first century are simply a reflection of where the greater society has been heading in the last two decades. All of us now have the ability to transform ourselves over and over in ways that extend and blur our "real" identities, empowering and depersonalizing us at the same time. I'm speaking, of course, of the Internet, the most transformative of the technological and cultural tidal waves that have washed over us since the rise of motion pictures. This is where the flow of fame's history in the last century has been leading, where the waters fan out into a delta of infinite tributaries leading to a vast, undifferentiated sea of celebrity. Here is where we, the audience, get it back: the personal stardom everything in our culture says we deserve. Here, too, is our revenge on those presumptuous enough to be stars in the old style. And here, finally, is the flowering of our fully enabled culture of the self.

It has been an inexorable process, this creeping democracy of celebritude. Each mechanical advance over the course of the past media century has brought the gift of fire closer while diminishing the gods offering it. The silent cinema projected human actors into giant, iconic phantasms of desire, but talkies brought those icons down a peg by letting us hear what they sounded like. Television brought the politics of stardom into the living room and celebrated the ordinary; cable and home video offered control over what and when we watched. The digital revolution let audience members become their own film and recording studios; the Internet has provided a means of instant global distribution and exhibition.

We have drifted far from movie stars by now, but that's the point: so has the culture. The current landscape is a minefield in which old values of celebrity have lost their meaning and new ones are continually being hashed out. The fan press that was bolstered by the arrival of *People* in the 1970s and by the expansion of the print and broadcast gossip universe in the '80s and '90s has now metamorphosed into an online killing field, with upstart Web sites delivering the awful secrets to our browser doors: celeb photos with the cellulite and wrinkles circled in digital highlighter, photocopied police reports and mug shots, sound files of cell phone tirades and on-set tantrums, career-crippling videos that the old studio bosses would have buried six feet under.

A side effect of this infinite expansion of stardom is that the mainstream gossip press treats anyone and everyone as a celebrity. Jon and Kate Gosselin, stars of the fertility-reality show *Jon & Kate Plus 8*, were able to up their cover appeal by getting a divorce. Kim Kardashian, with her sisters Khloe and Kourtney, represents a new breed of star famous for nothing much apart from being famous. It starts with a sex tape; you can't get anywhere without having a sex tape, and if it isn't leaked by someone else, you can always sell it yourself, as did former *Saved by the Bell* castmate Dustin Diamond. If you're lucky, you then move on to a cable reality show, a line of perfume—however far your ambition and hustle take you. This is Warhol's legacy, no-cal fame divorced from reason or even meaning and sustained only by the will to be seen.

This modern mirror has many faces, from TV and laptop screens to the magazines that beckon with both promises of reinvention and tragedies about those who fall short. *THE TRUTH ABOUT MY NEW BODY—Kate Gosselin: Botox? Breast implants? The reality star reveals what she's done to look this good. Plus! The gossip about her bodyguard? "It's absurd."*

To figure out what's going on here—in this case, the cover of a national celebrity gossip magazine on a typical week in September 2010—you have to parse the language. The word "truth" wars with "Botox" and "breast implants" before all three fall before the imperative of "looking good," a notion underscored by the selling point—the words "MY NEW BODY" popping off the cover in big, bold yellow font. (You can't really *get* a new body, though, can you? You're stuck with the one you've got until you die. The magazine promises otherwise.) Then there's the oxymoron of "reality star," two words that didn't exist together before the year 2000—they would have struck most twentieth-century consumers as nonsense—and that now signify a less predictable, more accidentally entertaining alternative to the staid clotheshorses of Hollywood.

The titillation of "gossip" balances against the hedging of "It's absurd," offering scandal yet withholding it, baiting and chiding the reader simultaneously. Wouldn't you like to be this person, the magazine asks—the housewife-mom who was just like you before she became a star and got a new body and a new life? And aren't you both vaguely embarrassed and glad to be yourself?

But, wait, Kate Gosselin isn't a movie star. She's pop flotsam, a woman who had eight kids, got a TV show and a divorce, and who now floats between mediums as an all-purpose, downmarket household name. She's just . . . famous. Movie stars, by contrast, still inhabit an exalted sphere in the twenty-first century, don't they? Or does the culture now use them in radically different ways than back in the days of Bogie, Kate, and Bette?

The Internet existed well before popular culture got a hold of it, obviously. Still, its cold war roots as a combined Defense Department/academia initiative took a radical turn with British computer scientist Tim Berners-Lee's creation and 1990 launching of the World Wide Web, a method of viewing hypertext documents linked across wired networks. Suddenly, the Internet had both a delivery method for audiovisual material and a way for information itself to become a vehicle of discovery.

Before the Web, you read a book and in it was the name "Charlie Chaplin" and if you wanted to know more you had to go get another book, probably an encyclopedia, or go to the video store and rent the films. Today the words "Charlie Chaplin" in blue type on a Web page are an invitation to dive into a rabbit hole of online facts and factoids. Click those words in your browser and you can watch Chaplin's movies, hear his voice, learn about his life, argue about his meaning. You can access Chaplin's page on the Internet Movie Database—on the Web by 1992, the site began life as "Those Eyes," a list of actresses with "beautiful eyes" kept by a member of the Usenet newsgroup rec.arts.movies—and from Chaplin you can follow the flow of links anywhere you wish, through his movies, his collaborators, their works, and so on. And this is only the beginning.

It's also perhaps the shallowest use of this staggering cultural breakthrough. Since going global in the mid-1990s, the Web has become an instrument for the empowerment of humanity, allowing lifesaving information and connections to circle the planet while enabling the extragovernmental communication that is a necessary component of political freedom. As has been pointed out by many others, the Net is the most radically democratizing technological advancement since the invention of the printing press, a cheap, universally accessible means of expression for every person on the planet who can get to a computer or a cell phone.

So what happens when you introduce a medium this revolutionary into a popular culture predicated upon entertainment, celebrity, self-gratification, and corporatized mass consumption?

For starters, you get the Baleheads.

No one seems to know what the very first movie star fan site may have been or to whom it was dedicated, but by 1996 Web sites and chat groups devoted to the actor Christian Bale, then a brooding, lesser-known movie actor with few lead roles to his credit, had grown so numerous that the mainstream media started picking up on the trend. What caught the attention of magazines like *Entertainment Weekly* wasn't that fans would use the tools of the Web to build digital shrines to their idols but that the Internet apparently allowed for *different* stars to be celebrated. In the real world of theatrical box office and *People* covers, the reigning gods were Mel Gibson and Will Smith. Online, Bale had a fan site that got 76,000 hits in one week—not bad for 1996—a chat group, and twelve MovieTalk folders devoted to him on the Internet service America Online. Gibson had only three. Interviewed in *EW,* Harrison Cheung, the head of the online Christian Bale Fan Club, said, "When we saw the range of Christian's talents and how little coverage he's been getting, we, as a fan network, saw the gap between hype and reality."

Now, this is interesting. It's no longer a fan club but a fan network, the grammar of celebrity worship already reflecting the structure of the new host medium. The implication is that this isn't just a collection of vaguely awkward fans wielding glue sticks and scrapbooks in a basement but a semiprofessional global army united by purpose. That strength allows them not only to celebrate their chosen idol but also to try to affect the official media organs of star reportage and even the Hollywood casting process itself. The magazines and news shows, after all, only report the "hype." The fans, according to Cheung, know the "reality."

In the gulf between those two words is the unarticulated resentment of a captive audience toward its captors. The movie studios took it seriously enough that the site's Webmaster was invited to Bale's next movie premiere. Cheung eventually became Bale's personal assistant but had quit by the late 2000s, after which he dished to gossip magazines about his former employer. Right there is the modern arc of star worship, from reverent distance to active engagement to disillusioned abandonment to the attempts to take stardom for oneself.

Why did Bale attract such online attention? Because he was cute and talented, but mostly because he was underappreciated. The new medium represented unclaimed pop culture real estate, a vacuum that savvy fans sought to land-grab for their chosen favorites. Nor was Bale the only beneficiary of the Internet's penchant for celebrating the uncelebrated. In the mid-1990s, thousands of fan sites bloomed, all built upon similar junk edifices of jpegs and .wav files and breathless information cobbled together from multiple unverified sources. This was the initial spasm of discovery in the online pop boom, the realization that one's idolization of a famous person could be shared not just with friends and wary family members but with like-minded souls the world over—that one's love for Bale or Christina Ricci or Katharine Hepburn or Peter Lorre was not a thing to be nurtured in silence but could find the validation of numbers. (Even if only imagined numbers. Just because no one visits your Lupe Velez site doesn't mean it doesn't exist.)

As fan sites proliferated, building their rafts out of non-copyright-approved photos and other materials, the studios, agents, and stars themselves took notice and began to create official star sites—points of dissemination for allowed information and a method by which to further massage a public persona. This could take on major proportions and, in some cases, serve as a vehicle for entire alter-identities. Launched in the late 1990s, Melanie Griffith's "Melanie Online" (www.melaniegriffith.com) was envisioned as not just a compendium of facts and multimedia for fans but also an immersive, full-blown faerie environment that served as a portal to the "real" Melanie, which was different from the "movie" Melanie but still a construct far removed from the actuality of the person who bears that name.

Visitors to the site clicked through doors in a faux–Maxfield Parrish landscape to access information on the star's charity work. There were "private" musings on fame, painkiller addictions, and plastic surgery;

inspirational meditation techniques; a "Goddess Book Club"; and a "Magic Door" to live chats and bulletin board postings. Not every early star site was this ornate or unintentionally hilarious, but in her desire to give fans an authentic Melanie Griffith, the actress created a simulacrum that unintentionally reads as New Age Norma Desmond. Particularly telling is the photo/diary section titled "In 2 Me C" (i.e., Intimacy); not only is it subtitled "A Glimpse into My Life," but on clicking into the page a visitor hears a sound file of Griffith murmuring those very words, an eerily truncated token of fake realism. The genuine Griffith is coming to us via a Web presence far more artificial than anything in her movies.

Although Melanie Online was accessible until very recently, it hadn't been updated since 2005; it was a dead site that said more about its subject's career than it intended. It reflected, too, the initial misunderstanding by mainstream stars and their minders as to what the Internet was about. Griffith (or whoever talked her into creating the site) saw it as another wing of the movie temple—a persona add-on and, to be sure, a locus for fascinating image games. As the online world has evolved and new technologies have emerged, and as the audience has become more empowered, those stars who choose to participate in the digital slipstream have done so more directly. The official movie star Web site eventually gave way to the MySpace page which gave way to the Facebook page which has, for the time being, given way to Twitter. Each new wrinkle in social media posits more "immediacy" and "authenticity"—more apparent closeness to the star—than the one before it.

Twitter lets users send out brief blasts of text describing what they're doing right now, or maybe it's their publicist's version of what the star's doing right now—it's never clear. The list of celebrities who tweet is long and varied. Actor Ashton Kutcher was an early outlier and, as of this writing, Lady Gaga has surpassed Britney Spears as the most followed tweeter on the planet. Tom Cruise, Tom Hanks, Oprah, Björk, Yoko Ono, Ice Cube, Ice-T, and Jay-Z all tweet. Lindsay Lohan tweets. The president of the United States tweets.

What do they tweet? Quotidian observations ("Turtles are amazing. Really." Actor Ben Stiller, 3:00 a.m., August 24, 2010), boilerplate inspiration ("Everybody has a talent, you just gotta find yours and work on it!!" Rapper Kanye West, 4:25 p.m., August 4, 2010), sociopolitical commentary ("WOW, bummed 9th Circuit put gay marriages on hold. loving families shouldn't have to wait for equality. stay strong." Comedian Kathy Griffin, 6:07 a.m., August 17, 2010), and self-promotion ("I will be on the @todayshow within the 8am hour discussing kitchen tips from the September issue of @MS_Living please tune in!" Lifestyle guru Martha Stewart, 7:50 a.m., August 23, 2010).

The concept undergirding Twitter is that it allows the great unwashed to peek firsthand into the lives of the famous *through* the eyes of the famous. Far more than Melanie Online, this represents an unheralded collusion, or the illusion of collusion, between the worshipped and the worshipper. If model/cookbook author Padma Lakshmi cares enough to let me into her life ("Small pinkberry mango perfect breakfast for fitting into Emmy dress!!"), then she must care about me, or about people like me, or about broadcasting her real self to a vast unknown audience of people like me. Whatever, it's a more authentic Padma Lakshmi than the one hosting *Top Chef*, isn't it?

Maybe. But even if it is, it still won't bring you as close as you may want to be—close enough to solve the mystery of the real Padma Lakshmi. Still, Twitter represents the nearest consumers have yet come to the unmediated thoughts of a star, whether those stars are genuinely expressing themselves in 140 typed characters or merely playing the role of the tech-savvy, charity-minded modern celebrity. It's certainly amusing to think what the studio heads of the golden age would have made of the technology. Can you imagine Jack Warner's ulcer twitching as he reads Bette Davis's latest tweet? ("Had enough of this dump. Sailing to England. Screw @JLW AND his contract." 12:10 a.m., April 22, 1936.)

In a weird way, Twitter really does let fans access a different star narrative from the ones they're given by official releases and the news media. To follow the tweets of Lindsay Lohan is to veer schizophrenically between impersonal celebrity charity-speak ("thank you from lindsay lohan's team for being a part of working w/children in need today #makeadifference") and blurts that reveal the yawning gap between celebrity and reality ("the only 'bookings' that i'm familiar with are Disney Films, never thought that i'd be 'booking' into Jail . . . eeeks"). Yet in the hands of a smart artist-provocateur, Twitter can itself be part of the creative process of persona building: "Nothin like watchin Maiden videos with a Jameson diet in my paw. Is it considered studio rehab if it involves inspirational hairmoves+booze?" (Lady Gaga, 10:45 p.m., August 26, 2010).

What changes the dynamic, of course, is that stars aren't the only ones tweeting, or blogging, or chatting, or otherwise engaging in the public cybersphere that for many now constitutes the waking world. We all are, and in the doing of it we are taking part in a profound conceptual cultural shift—the large-scale broadcasting and fictionalization of the self. If the counterculture years saw the rise of mass bohemianism (everyone wanting to be different from the grown-ups) and the Gen-X years the codification of alt (everyone wanting to be different from everyone else), the Internet era has provided the tools to finally realize the urge to be different—and, most important, to be seen and recognized while being different. The desperate 1914 cry of Florence Lawrence's admirer—"the very soul in me seems to cry out for the chance to express what it has concealed for years"—has found its answer in the protocols and packet switching of the World Wide Web.

The invention of the Web browser solved a critical problem of do-it-yourself celebrity: the need for a stage. The personal computer itself does something more revolutionary, since it combines the traditional Holy Trinity of mass media commerce—production, distribution, exhibition—into one small box that can be carried to the nearest coffee shop. Inexpensive digital video cameras and cellphones, editing software that allows for ambitious special effects, laptop mixing boards to enable sophisticated musical scores—the average American teenager has at his or her disposal the fundamental moviemaking facilities of a Hollywood studio in the 1930s.

As for distribution, you have only to put your video on your blog or YouTube, push the button, and you've sent it to the world. Exhibition? Everyone with a computer is an audience member with a movie screen. Everyone with a computer is also, potentially, a movie studio, and that movie studio has one star. We have arrived at an unprecedented and absolute leveling of the field, a cultural moment that can only be read as the triumph of celebrity socialism. The means of the production of stardom are at last in the hands of the people.

Thus we can celebrate ourselves and our creativity in ways often more unexpected, entertaining, and subversive than the dull sameness of the corporate mainstream, where every film is a sequel or a remake and every singer uses Auto-Tune. (One of the main reasons thirteen-year-old Rebecca Black was roundly mocked for her 2011 YouTube video "Friday" was the voice-filtering technology that made her sound like a "real" pop star while unintentionally proving her vocal inadequacies.) Since much of it is free, online content undermines both the advertising and pay-for-play revenue models, and that constitutes another revolution.

To see how these new channels of self-promotion and accidental stardom are being absorbed by consumers, follow a group of middle schoolers through a day. They will listen to Top 40 or their chosen alt music in the car, watch Nickelodeon or MTV or a rerun of *That '70s Show* on TV after homework, then huddle with their friends and surf the latest viral videos on YouTube, passing them along via links in e-mails, on Facebook pages, or on Tumblr. Often they'll do all these things at once, a digital din in which they embrace in breadth what they're unable or unwilling to negotiate in depth.

It's the viral videos that get the biggest laughs and most surprised responses; because they come from outside the corporate machine, they're recognizably human and thus retain the ability to surprise. The homemade crudity of production is part of the charm of an erratic series like *Harry Potter Puppet Pals* (www.potterpuppetpals.com), a creation of Kingston, Massachusetts, filmmaker Neil Cicierega that's an exemplar of a new field of endeavor that might be called "parasite entertainment" and that encompasses fan fiction, song parodies, and much more.

Parasite entertainment attaches itself to a corporate host object—in this case the *Harry Potter* literary-filmic franchise—and engages with its content in a complex dance of celebration and sabotage. The value to consumers is in the noncompromised authenticity of the response and the notion that a "real person" has gone to all the trouble. The *Star Wars* universe is one of almost constant parasite co-opting, rewiring, and re-presenting, from the 1999 short *George Lucas in Love* to the 2002 Internet cartoon *How the Sith Stole Christmas* and beyond. There's even an annual *Star Wars* Fan Film Awards that since the early 2000s has been sanctioned by George Lucas, the rare executive to understand the needs of the new digital cargo cult.

But *Harry Potter Puppet Pals* is only an indirect celebration of Neil Cicierega, since most visitors to his site don't even know who he is. Other regular online productions are designed expressly to spotlight their creators and to serve as stages for the parading of their various identities. In late 2006, a Brockton, Massachusetts, actress-singer named Jodie Rivera dubbed herself VenetianPrincess and began posting a homemade series—shot in her bedroom closet—called *The Princess Chronicles*. By mid-2007, she was the subject of mainstream media stories and had embarked on a series of celebrity music video parodies in which she commented on and imitated Angelina Jolie, Britney Spears, Lady Gaga, the Jonas Brothers—whoever was popular at the moment. The parasite entertainer par excellence, she returns the favor by posting fan videos on her site (www.vprincess.com) that re-create her own efforts—parasite upon parasite upon parasite, each receiving its moment of fame. She plays the game in the opposite direction as well, having legally incorporated the "VenetianPrincess" persona and offering branding opportunities within her videos.

This is the modern will to celebrity made manifest, using the tools at hand to reach the maximum number of people while accessing the maximum levels of media attention. Rivera is less interested in expressing herself than in showcasing her creativity—she doesn't seem particularly interested in coming out from behind her VP alter ego—but other up-from-the-Web stars are more frank in their need to be seen and named. Shane Dawson, a twenty-one-year-old from Long Beach,

California, started posting his videos to YouTube in 2009 and quickly found a mass audience. He plays a likeably comic version of himself, narrating his tales of woe from his bedroom and illustrating them in skits where he plays all the parts, usually with bright red lipstick, wigs, and naughty language.

And he's a hit, at least for the next pop spin cycle, winner of the Choice Web Star award at the 2010 Teen Choice Awards and proprietor of, at the moment, three YouTube channels: ShaneDawsonTV, ShaneDawsonTV2, and Shane, the latter reserved for videos made on his cell phone. He's working on a thirty-minute pilot that will air on YouTube but that is aimed, obviously, at an audience of TV executives. You're still not really famous until you crash the corporate entertainment barricades and cut a deal.

Some of these people may become "genuine" stars recognized by the masses, although to do so they'll have to create original personas rather than riff on established ones. They'll probably have to have broader talents than, say, Lucas Cruikshank, a seventeen-year-old Nebraska kid whose YouTube alter ego, Fred Figglehorn, is a helium-voiced toddler forever on the verge of a tantrum. Yet Nickelodeon quickly signed up "Fred" for a TV movie, and Cruikshank appeared on tweener shows like *iCarly* and *Hannah Montana*. His alternate YouTube channel, named after himself, lets us glimpse the real Cruikshank as himself, playing music and video-blogging without the obnoxious voice. Clearly Cruikshank understands the basics of modern reinvention and is positioning himself to do so when and as necessary.

These are only some of the intentional new Web celebrities, and even if you don't know who they are, your children do, which is all that matters. These people *want* to be famous. Yet because its content tributaries come from so many directions and with such vastly different intentions, the Internet can't help but deliver accidental celebrities as well—people who don't know they're entertaining because they're too young or they don't speak the language very well or because they're not in control of their image and are unaware of how entertainingly it plays. One's response is thus tinged with cruelty; in large part or little, this is where the old carnival freak show has moved. We're drawn to the accidental Net stars because their oddness breaks through the wall of sameness.

Mahir Cagri was probably the first to go viral, picking up mainstream mention in magazines and *Letterman Show* sketches as early as 1999. All that the native of Izmir, Turkey, had done was put up a personal Web page that featured photos of him enjoying his hobbies and whose text expressed a willingness to make new friends. Since Cagri wrote in fractured English ("I kiss you!") and since the photos included one of him playing the accordion, he fit into the "Wild and Crazy Guy" stereotype as established by Dan Aykroyd and Steve Martin in their 1970s *Saturday Night Live* skits.

Cagri quickly became a snarky found object of the new Web irony, with attendant viral links, copycat sites, and T-shirts. As a character in pop culture (as opposed to a living human being with feelings and sensibilities), Mahir seemed to predate and influence British comedian Sacha Baron Cohen's character Borat, although a 1998 Borat TV sketch indicates that Borat actually may have predated Mahir. It doesn't matter. The meme is the same—a clueless but adorable foreigner for us to make fun of.

In fact, the attitude toward Mahir balanced between elitism and fondness because his innocence was unfeigned—genuine rather than played. He had the last laugh, too. Cagri got a brief British ad gig out of his initial burst of fame, and his current home page (www.ikissyou.org) features him posing with fans during his travels and posts news about humanitarian issues and organizations. Without too much of a fuss, he has managed to ride the long tail of accidental celebrity while reclaiming his image so that we see the real person as well as the pop culture goof.

Antoine Dodson wrestled with the same issues in a different fashion. A native of Huntsville, Alabama, Dodson appeared in a July 28, 2010, news story on local TV, interviewed by reporters after he had scared off a late-night intruder who had tried to sexually assault his sister. The loose, sashaying cadences of Dodson's outrage as he stared into the camera and warned at-home viewers that "y'all better *hide* your kids, *hide* your wife, and *hide* your husband, 'cause they rapin' *every-*

body out here" made the video a viral sensation. A Brooklyn-based comedy-music group called the Gregory Brothers saw the news segment, edited it into a music video with the help of Auto-Tune software, and soon "The Bed Intruder Song" was available on iTunes, where it got more downloads than the new Lady Gaga single.

The by-now-standard media rinse cycle kicked in—mainstream news interviews, T-shirts, heated discussions of whether Dodson represented black America embarrassingly or honestly. Yet accidental celebrity as a social phenomenon was so established by this point that Dodson knew precisely how to respond. Within days he had a Facebook page, a Twitter account, a YouTube channel, a lawyer, and a manager. The Gregory Brothers split their iTunes profits with him, and Dodson announced that he would use his windfall to move his family out of the projects. He was interviewed by NBC and CBS, and a *Washington Post* article proclaimed that "in this age of fake reality TV, [Dodson] puts the real in reality."

His newfound fame, however long it lasts, raises questions. Is Dodson still "real" now that he knows we're watching? Are we interested in him now that we know he knows we're watching? How much of our response has to do with old cultural stereotypes, and what does it mean when those clichés intersect with actual observed behavior? Does the discovery of Dodson, which was predicated on laughing at his eccentric body language and speech patterns, differ from our continued interest in him (or not) as an actual person? In other words, does an actual person—in this case, a working-class African American of a type the mainstream either pigeonholes or prefers not to see, other than to laugh at—"deserve" to be famous? Or do we just want to be diverted and move on?

Such questions don't arise when the accidental celebrities are very young, like William Nilsson the famous Laughing Baby, or Harry and Charlie Davies-Carr, the stars of the 2007 YouTube video called "Charlie Bit My Finger." The latter is a simple little thing, a British dad's videotape of his two sons, 1 and 3; the younger bites the older on the finger, the older cries a bit, and then they both bust out laughing. Cute. And for a time the most-viewed video in the history of You-

Tube, eventually surpassed by Justin Bieber and Lady Gaga music videos but still amassing 420 million individual views as of February 2012. The boys' parents now maintain a blog and video series, regularly uploading new videos of Harry and Charlie; there are fan clubs and T-shirts and limited-edition calendars, but no mugs or key rings, since their father insists he will "deliberately not commercialize the children." The original video remains the draw, though, because it so delightfully illustrates the innocent savagery and emotional fickleness of children while demonstrating the strength of brotherly love.

Are such people stars in the sense that we have been discussing throughout this book? No and yes. We don't look to any of the accidental celebrities to feed deeper needs of identification and desire. They don't prompt a search for the real person behind the celebrity. They *are* the real person, and that is their value as entertainment and as cultural objects of potency. They're funny or weird or attractive without working at it, and in so doing they imply that the accident of fame could just as easily land on us, for better and for worse. In addition, they act out the drama of ground-level stardom, and we watch very closely. These are the canaries in the coal mine of modern fame, object lessons at a time when everyone is a public figure waiting to happen.

Some people try to fake being accidental stars. Suspicions were raised early on about lonelygirl15, an alleged adolescent girl whose video diaries turned up on YouTube in 2006. Within months, thousands of online surfers joined forces to prove she was actually a nineteen-year-old actress named Jessica Rose performing in a scripted Web series whose makers were represented by the powerful Creative Arts Agency. Wired fame and the authenticity it represented had become so powerful that the corporate over-culture was now attempting to infiltrate and control it, desperate to leverage profits off all that realness.

By the end of the decade, the urge to fame was everywhere on the Web. Was Chris Crocker acting in his tearfully melodramatic "Leave Britney Alone" video, a parasite entertainment (or accidental Web car wreck) that received 4 million views over two days in 2007? Did Rebecca Black's "Friday" get 60 million views in 2011 because it was good or so hilariously bad? Does it matter? When a Filipino singer named Charice Pempengco can cross over from YouTube to the cast of TV's *Glee,* or when Justin Bieber can be discovered in homemade videos and ascend to the pinnacle of teen-idol superstardom, what's real and what is manufactured becomes immaterial. The underlying assumption is not just that we all want fame but that we each deserve it, and that to ignore the Internet's power as a staging area is a dereliction of our duty to the spotlight.

Right about here is where we have to peer into the dank and bottomless shadow world of Internet porn, where Web sites charge men money to watch "actual" college girls (or moms or simply women supposedly picked up on the street) have sex in hotel rooms or in the backs of vans. The pretense is that this is really happening, that no money has passed between producers and performers, and the videos maintain a scrupulously amateur vibe that's the exact opposite of the plush celluloid productions of porn's 1970s heyday. Where recorded explicit sex once aspired to Hollywood production values, it now fakes the do-it-yourself aesthetic of the Web, where anyone and everyone's a star, clothed or not.

As for intimacy, it doesn't exist online. Actual intimacy requires actual physical presence, remember? But the mainstreaming of online pornography offers young men in particular a drastically unrealistic picture of what women want, and it represents the most extreme evidence of a chasm that has widened between boy culture and girl culture in the past decade. What women *and* men want, of course, is all over the map, and it depends upon the individual. Internet porn doesn't sell individuals, it sells the scripted catechism of fantasy. It's the new lie that knows audiences are really turned on by authenticity, and it knows they don't care if that authenticity is fake.

How else do you explain reality TV? There's precedent here, since the use of nonprofessionals as entertainment had been a programming staple since the rise of radio in the 1920s and '30s. *Queen for a Day* (but only a day), *Candid Camera* (originally *Candid Microphone*), and Art Linkletter's *People Are Funny* all moved from radio to TV in the 1950s, and the PBS series *An American Family*—high-toned documentary voyeurism—was a media sensation in the early 1970s. As always, changes in technology brought the audience closer to the screen and vice versa. The rise of affordable consumer video cameras in the 1980s sparked the hit TV show *America's Funniest Home Videos,* the ancestor of accidental YouTube celebrities like Harry and Charlie. The year 1992 saw the launch of the MTV reality series *The Real World,* which put a group of young adults in an apartment and let the personalities clash.

This, it turned out, was the template for almost everything that followed. The producers of *The Real World,* Mary-Ellis Bunim and Jonathan Murray, understood three things: that everyone today considers him- or herself a star; that there's conflict in that; and that schadenfreude—bad things happening to other people—makes for marketable entertainment. All that was missing was the element of actual competition, which British TV producer Charlie Parsons pioneered with the 1997 Swedish series *Expedition Robinson.* In an inauspicious start, the first person ever "voted off the island" in a reality show, a man named Sinisa Savija, committed suicide shortly thereafter. The rules of engagement between noncelebrities and their entertainment-world handlers—not to mention an understanding of what reality fame meant—were not yet established.

Survivor and *Big Brother* both appeared on U.S. TV in 2000, the former smoothing out the wrinkles of the *Expedition Robinson* formula, the latter upping the ante on *Real World* by locking the participants in the house for three months. The emerging reality genre shared with the growing online world a sense of enabled excitement—the realization that average people were not only as interesting and entertaining as established performers but in fact could be more so. Average people were unscripted and thus unpredictable, and therein lay the suspense. The insistence of Richard Hatch, winner of the first *Survivor,* on going nude during the show was a much-discussed example of "real people" thinking outside the box of entertainment character roles, and yet the careful presentation of *Survivor* gave us traditional heroes and villains, turncoats and crybabies, and, in the immortal words of contestant Susan Hawk, "snakes and rats."

It's the editing that makes reality TV so riveting while robbing it of genuine realism. Indeed, the case has been made that the genre was unworkable before the advent of digital editing systems such as Avid, which allows large amounts of footage to be shaped quickly and cohesively. Reality producers manipulate wherever they can, casting antagonistic personality types in preproduction, encouraging conflicts and alliances during filming, and using editing in postproduction to carve narrative arcs and build suspense. The goal is to assign real people classic dramatic archetypes to which the audience will respond—roles that may or may not have anything to do with who they are in actuality but which the player will accept as the price of fame.

Were Kelly Wiglesworth of the first *Survivor* and Omarosa Manigault-Stallworth on *The Apprentice* genuine backstabbers? Was Jennifer Hudson the done-wrong martyr of *American Idol*'s third season? Is Nicole "Snooki" Polizzi really the trashy found object *Jersey Shore* presents her as? It doesn't matter, since the shows' shaping of their on-camera personas (augmented by coverage in the media and online) is as all-encompassing as any old-school studio grooming. If an action doesn't fit the script, it ends up on the digital cutting-room floor, and if the reality star departs from the assigned persona too often, it's not considered good TV. *Survivor* producer Mark Burnett freely admitted to a reporter in 2003 that the show is "storytelling enveloped in a great concept, great vicarious travel experience and really good casting. I tell good stories. It really is not reality TV. It really is unscripted drama."

The most interesting aspect of these programs is the place where "real people" and "celebrities" intersect, creating a pop culture collision in which the lines get redrawn over and over again. Hoboken pastry chef Buddy Valastro, the reality star of the Learning Channel show *Cake Boss,* is a real person with the natural charisma of a classic Warner Brothers character actor, and he's enjoyable because he can't be anything but his irrepressible self, or so the show's editing and structure implies. In fact, Valastro is clearly playing a version of himself—the savvy but excitable Italian American craftsman—with the finesse and at least partial self-awareness of a born ham. But the audience response is similar to the mid-1940s playgoer who couldn't understand what the young Marlon Brando was doing: "This guy, he's not acting." The difference is that the entertainment business has learned how to package and sell the uncertainty.

When Susan Boyle took the stage in April 2009 on *Britain's Got Talent* to sing "I Dreamed a Dream," the contrast between her look (dowdy, middle-aged, *real*) and her voice (strong, impassioned, *real* in an entirely different way) became a moment of high public drama. The video was played hundreds of millions of times on YouTube in the ensuing weeks, as if repeated scrutiny might solve the mystery of how the voice of a star could reside in a non-star body. For media pundits, it was an occasion to chew over the divisions separating amateurs and professionals and to wax philosophical on the illusory importance of physical beauty in modern stardom. For audiences, it was worth it just to see the eyebrows on Simon Cowell—the love him/hate him judge of *American Idol* whose own persona is that of an unforgiving arbiter of professional quality—shoot up in astonishment. Here she was: the Secret Star, the woman who had yearned for so long for a chance to express what she had concealed for years. And Simon saw it. We all saw it.

Boyle was validated and became a celebrity, and the first thing she did after not finishing first on *Britain's Got Talent* was have a nervous breakdown and disappear into a clinic. Think of it as an air lock between her old and new selves. She subsequently released her first album, *I Dreamed a Dream,* which broke sales records in most countries and still stands as Amazon's fastest-selling pre-sales release—meaning that people wanted to order the CD almost more than they wanted to hear it, to extend the happy glow around Boyle's triumph. It is extraordinary: out of all the "success stories" of reality competitions, Boyle's is the one that most directly addresses the ache to be seen—or, in her case, to be heard—that fuels the genre and the audience's hopes and resentments alike.

Why, then, do already established celebrities feel the need to go on reality shows? What explains ABC's *Dancing with the Stars,* which pairs famous people with professional dancers, thus turning stars into temporary "real people" who we just happen to know? Why do skater Scott Hamilton, former basketball pro Dennis Rodman, country singer Clint Black, and comedian Joan Rivers and her daughter Melissa compete against each other to win *Celebrity Apprentice* and the approval of Donald Trump? What on God's green earth would induce actors Lou Diamond Phillips and Stephen Baldwin, *American Idol* castoff Sanjaya Malakar, and disgraced politician's wife Patricia Blagojevich, among others, to battle each other in the jungles of Costa Rica for the marvelously titled *I'm a Celebrity . . . Get Me Out of Here*?

One obvious reason is that these people barely are celebrities anymore—once riding high, most of them are currently hanging on to the bottom of the C-list—and they hope that reinventing themselves as "real" will keep people watching. Among their other putative entertainment aspects, the celeb reality shows testify to the addictive qualities of modern fame and to the endless humiliations a star will endure to extend it, the thinking being that if these stars want to mortify themselves for our viewing pleasure, we'll happily take them up on it. We are now approaching the death throes of the old order of stardom—famous people flinging themselves willingly into the pit.

The only genre of reality programming more conceptually repellent and socially astute is what might be referred to as the Cautionary Trash Comedy: TV shows that document real people who have no idea they're appalling. This is not a value judgment but the conceptual hook itself, and it depends for its impact on the audience's built-in assumptions about class, consumerism, and perceived social merit. Celebrities can play, as attested to by the ratings success of *The Simple Life* (2003–07), with the much-mocked Paris Hilton and Nicole Richie, or the slow-motion exploitation of *The Anna Nicole Show* (2002–03), starring the doomed model Anna Nicole Smith. More often, though, it's the unknowns on shows like the *Real Housewives* series, *My Super Sweet 16,* and the notorious *Jersey Shore* who attract viewers and who, ironically, become pop culture celebrities in their own right.

The position of the audience to these players is unique. We are meant to look down on them and be entertained by the distance—the exact opposite of the traditional star/consumer dynamic. They behave horribly to each other, dress in bad taste, shriek, plow through life with the self-centered entitlement of the proudly unconscious, and audiences reward them with derisive attention. There are object lessons, too. Young girls can watch the spoiled brats of *My Super Sweet 16* railing at their parents for not throwing a bigger party, and understand the message: Laugh at these people, but do not be like them.

These shows both celebrate consumption and warn against its perils—much as a Gloria Swanson silent melodrama did—and at their heart is a callous and uneven bargain that their stars accept even while understanding its inequity. Is fame worth the mockery of a nation of viewers? Most of the reality stars would say it is, and that's a challenge to us as well, asking us to consider whether we would go that far to be noticed. On *Jersey Shore,* where the "entertainment" lies in watching inarticulate meatheads fight, mate, and split up—this is how the show is structured, like a window onto a zoo exhibit from which we choose our favorite meerkat—the responses to fame vary. Early on, Mike "the Situation" Sorrentino used his celebrity to make $5 million in product endorsements, a clear and even admirable execution of striking while the iron was hot.

By contrast, his castmate Snooki—the unstoppable, risible, indefensible Snooki, who claims to have read two books in her entire life, who is adored and detested because she's so purely herself—struggles with the meaning of her fame. Polizzi tried to trademark her nickname but was turned down by the U.S. Patent Office. In a new marketing wrinkle quickly dubbed "unbranding," fashion houses sent Snooki their competitors' handbags, hoping she'd be photographed with them and thus taint them with her toxic celebrity. Even her father, in a 2010 *New York Times* article, professed to having no idea what draws people to her: "She don't sing. She don't dance. I don't want to say she don't have talent . . ." The writer of the *Times* article likens talking with Snooki to "getting down on your hands and knees with a child." Snooki herself can only say people respond to her because "I'm a nutjob. And I don't care."

Why is this woman famous? Because she both assumes she deserves to be and isn't self-conscious enough to be anyone other than herself. Snooki is the ultimate reality star and a surreal mirror to her audience's own unexpressed desire for stardom. To be a functioning professional celebrity, you have to know yourself—to understand the image you're projecting and adjust as necessary. To be a pure celebrity, which is what Snooki is, self-knowledge is counterproductive. She is, in fact, probably the purest star in this book—the Extra Girl triumphant—and the one closest to the desired marriage of fame and authenticity. Be careful what you wish for.

Not surprisingly, it's a hard time to be a conventional movie star. Witness Sandra Bullock, who had the career comeback of a lifetime in 2009 with three movies, two hits, and one Best Actress Oscar, yet who only became *People*'s 2010 multiple-cover girl when she adopted a child at around the same time it was revealed that her husband had been serially cheating on her. In other words, Bullock no longer functioned in the public fan sphere as a movie star but as a reality star, and her assigned persona morphed from plucky girl-next-door to wronged wife and mother, a sympathetic and familiar pose from which the gossip universe has profited for decades.

What we're seeing in the new millennium, in fact, is a marked devaluation of the traditional movie star, a shrinking in power and pop value directly attributable to the Internet and related technological advances. For one thing, we don't see the stars on theatrical movie screens that much anymore. Because they're available on TV, computer screens, and handhelds, these people just aren't as visually and psychically big. Content piracy enabled by such downloading strategies as LimeWire and BitTorrent has further robbed stars of meaning, because how much is someone worth when you can get them for free?

More critically, the Internet and the multichannel, multiscreen media Omniverse conspires to strip movie stars of their mystique by distributing their secrets—the realness we think we want to know—to the world at large. This is the new arena for scandal, and it has replaced the films and fan magazines as the primary locus of star narrative for a number of well-known actors. Mel Gibson sees his DUI police report and recordings of his raging phone calls posted to the Web. Alec Baldwin screams at his teenage daughter on a recorded phone message and briefly becomes a media pariah before successfully reinventing himself as a beloved sitcom character actor instead of a fading matinee idol. Christian Bale throws a tantrum on the movie set of *Terminator: Salvation* and the audiotape goes viral, quickly getting repurposed into a music video by online cargo-cult artists and thus serving more frankly as entertainment. In the process, Bale's persona is temporarily recalibrated from "intensely serious actor" to "egotistical control freak."

The ubiquity of cell phone cameras means that everyone's now a paparazzo, an empowering of the audience in ways that can cripple celebrity image. When you can snap a picture of Lindsay Lohan passed out in a parked car and post it instantly to the world, Lohan no longer has control of her public meaning. Just the opposite: *you* have the means of revealing the secret reality that the star factory has worked so long and so hard—and, for decades, so successfully—to conceal. If the Internet had been around in the 1920s, someone at Fatty Arbuckle's fatal Labor Day party would have uploaded a video showing what happened to Virginia Rappe. Douglas Fairbanks and Mary Pickford wouldn't have been able to carry on an adulterous affair without incriminating photos circling the planet. The secrets would be out, and then why would we need movie stars?

To gauge the effects of this new world on the traditional movie star, look no further than Tom Cruise, whose seemingly impermeable image went bizarrely off message in the middle of the new millennium's first decade. In part, this was due to his choice of projects. Films like *Mission: Impossible 2* (2000), *Minority Report* (2002), *The Last Samurai* (2003), and *War of the Worlds* (2005) were all sizable commercial hits that nevertheless revealed a stalled persona; in comparison to the challenging roles of the 1990s (*Jerry Maguire, Magnolia,*

Eyes Wide Shut), Cruise seemed content to play shallow mass market heroes. The exception, 2004's *Collateral*, in which he played a manipulative hit man, proved the rule, getting decent reviews and box office receipts and barely making a dent in how the actor was perceived.

The same year, Cruise took the radical—and, in retrospect, foolish—step of firing his longtime publicist Pat Kingsley and replacing her with his sister. Kingsley was much more than a celebrity handler. She was a powerful shadow figure who set the standards for celebrity access in the 1990s: raising her clients' value and mystery by refusing all but the most high-profile cover shoots, demanding that journalists give her final approval over their articles, and scrupulously managing her stars' public identities. Kingsley and her approach to celebrity image maintenance is the reason that Tom Cruise was, in the words of a 2004 *Slate* article, "the world's most famous movie star and the one about whom the least is known or understood." Which meant that when Cruise fired her, he suddenly had to redefine himself in the public sphere or have the audience do it for him.

Both happened, and it wasn't pretty. In 2005, Cruise fell in love with actress Katie Holmes and decided to tell the world about it on *The Oprah Winfrey Show*. It made sense, since Winfrey and Cruise had an established media relationship and the host served as both a conduit to the women of America and their cultural arbiter of value. The star's appearance on her daytime talk show confirmed Winfrey's status as a power broker while asserting Cruise's accessibility and a new willingness to be "just like us."

That was how it was supposed to play out, but without Kingsley's guidance Cruise radically misjudged the tenor and tone of "just like us." The result was the infamous "couch-jumping" incident in which the actor acted out his love for Holmes as if he were a hyperactive cartoon character. He raced around the set, hopped up and down on Oprah's divan, moaned and swooned in a parody of smitten inarticulateness. In retrospect, Cruise clearly thought this was how a man in love was supposed to behave. He was trying to reconnect with his audience by being human, emotional, "real," but in the process he forgot what people actually want from a traditional movie star, which is the cultivated poise of Olympian distance. Tom Cruise no longer understood what "Tom Cruise" meant—and if he didn't know, why on earth should we tell him?

If the couch-jumping incident had happened before the advent of YouTube, Cruise would have been the butt of a week of late-night talk show jokes and the culture would have moved on. But because the video immediately went up on the Web, it became the instant property of the public and was forthwith recut, repurposed, and re-mulched into endless iterations of parasite entertainment, the wired masses playing with the corpse of Cruise's persona like vultures picking at roadkill. He was no longer a reliable source of entertainment. By turning unreliable, he had become entertainment.

Cruise's relationship with the Church of Scientology—a religion to its faithful and a cult with powerful media proponents to its detractors—was next to come into focus. When Kingsley was steering Cruise's career, Scientology had always been a reportorial no-fly zone, but shortly after appearing on Winfrey's show, Cruise used the church's proscription on psychiatry to attack actress Brooke Shields in the press for her comments on postpartum depression therapy. Suddenly, there he was lecturing *Today* host Matt Lauer on the dangers of Ritalin and calling psychiatry a "Nazi science" in the pages of *Entertainment Weekly*. Cruise apologized to Shields and the matter cooled down, but in 2008, footage of the actor waxing passionate about his beliefs for an in-house church video was leaked onto the Internet, and the debate about who Tom Cruise was or was supposed to be flared anew.

Movie stars, of course, are not supposed to profess religious beliefs other than safely mainstream ones; if they follow different spiritual drummers, they can't talk about it without compromising their broad appeal. (The only church we worship as a culture, really, is the church of celebrity.) Cruise obeyed this rule—the extreme secrecy of his church demanded it—but the fully wired, 24/7 Omniverse refused to play along. Why should it? If a moment of reality has been captured in digital form, like water flowing to the sea it will always find its way to the greatest audience possible. The threat of law (copyright, libel—whatever works) is the only potential impedance to this flow, and often not even then. YouTube took down the Scientology video under threat from Cruise's lawyers, but the gossip Web site Gawker.com continues to make it available.

Privacy, in other words, is no longer an option of fame. Reality TV stars and online celebrities understand this and welcome it, but it is a body shock to the established system of stardom as it has been understood for the better part of a century. To not be subject to the constant stare and the threatened gamesmanship of the Omniverse, a celebrity has to behave (no tantrums), keep invisible (move to Europe), or otherwise remain so dull that the millions at their keyboards no longer care. At which point, is that person even a star anymore? When we know all their secrets, or seem to—when we read their Twitter feeds and hear their unscripted comments and watch their sex tapes—we're still no closer to the actual person behind the fame and yet we've seen all we want. The stars are no longer bigger than life itself. As we hold them in our cell phones and laptops, they are finally much smaller than we are.

Obviously, immensely potent movie stars still walk among us. We continue to pay to see visions on a giant wall, and there are people who seem to fit on that wall and nowhere else, figures who call up complicated crosscurrents of desire and envy and emulation. Any list of bona fide movie stars currently working would have to include Johnny Depp, Meryl Streep, George Clooney, Julia Roberts, Leonardo DiCaprio, Angelina Jolie, Brad Pitt, Tom Hanks, Tom Cruise, Will Smith, Robert Downey Jr., Denzel Washington, Clint Eastwood, Harrison Ford. If you're under a certain age, you look at Emma Stone and Keira Knightley and Joseph Gordon-Levitt and, God help us, Taylor Lautner, and say, yes, those are movie stars too. The mystique still holds, but it serves at our sufferance, and no amount of 3D digital cinema will restore it to its former glory. There are simply too many competing screens and celebrities. A movie star looks good in a gown or a tuxedo on the red carpet and he or she still draws us into the dark to gaze up at the promise of a secret that we know now is terribly easy to break. But then we go home and engage in the more important business of celebrating ourselves.

The machinations of identity manufacture and remanufacture are ours for the keeping now—the tools at our fingertips when we log on at the beginning of each day. Who do we want to be? How many of me can there possibly be? As many screen names and online alter egos as I can dream up? On Facebook we are each the stars of our own page and that page is our major production, a movie and a scrolling soap opera that positions each of us at the center of the universe, as indeed all of us are certain we are. To access other universes from which our own can be glimpsed, click on a friend. If you don't like who you are on Facebook, you can be another person on your blog, or on share sites like Tumblr or 8tracks, or in the comment field under a newspaper article, or in the user reviews at Yelp or the Internet Movie Database. All is mutable: gender, age, outlook, persona.

This is not news and hasn't been for some time. But what does it do to our need for larger fixed personas who might act out our dramas—the gods of myth or the movie stars of the past century? And what does it do to us to live from childhood in this warm and enveloping culture of Narcissus, one in which the real world—the one you can walk out into and smell and taste and touch—becomes less important than the endless self-images we invent in the effort to locate our actual selves?

What, in fact, becomes of identity? The ease and addictiveness of personal celebration as empowered by the democratizing technological Eden in which we now live ultimately seems to prompt two end-stage stances: mania or catatonic self-regard. The first is everywhere in our culture but captured most tellingly in the 2010 documentary *Catfish*, about a midwestern woman who manufactured dozens of online personalities to convince a Facebook acquaintance in Manhattan that she was not, in fact, who she was but someone younger, prettier, hipper. The woman co-opted the online photo albums of a stranger—an actress-model living in Canada—and created a new self via identity theft. Why go to such lengths? The movie offers an easy but alluring answer: a former dancer (or, really, a girl who dreamed of dancing), she was now stuck in a small town caring for her husband's mentally challenged sons and desperate for a persona that was closer to what she once wished for.

Seventy years ago, this woman would have gone to the movies and looked up at Bette Davis fighting off the world to be herself—would have gone to all of Davis's and Crawford's and Stanwyck's films to test out and fantasize about the many different women she might be. She might even have gone home and written a fan letter into which she poured her ache to express what she has kept hidden for years. Or she might have written a novel with all those characters she carries inside her. With Facebook, she can simply make an imitation of life. If other people believe in it, doesn't that make it real?

The other response—the stupor of a society that can't tear itself away from the mirror—can be seen in the fascinating 2006 YouTube video titled "everyday," in which, as advertised, Brooklyn-based photographer Noah Kalina takes a photo of himself every day for six years, then strings them together to a thunderous piano score in a five-minute-forty-six-second montage of time passing. The short film is elapsed life as high drama, and isn't that the promise of every movie, the promise we want to take home from the theater—that anyone's mundane days can be epic if they're only seen in the right light? Kalina's pose in each photo is the classic modern "selfie," arms outstretched toward the digital camera turned to face him. It's a stance that can be found by the millions on Facebook and elsewhere, and it serves notice that we are, at last, our own cameramen. The "selfie" is how we see ourselves and how we reposition ourselves to be seen by others.

It's also a perfect representation of the everyday self-indulgence at the end of the road of modern celebrity, a road that began with the dirt ruts of anonymous silent movie actors and slowly became a glamorous high-speed highway on which Hollywood, the nation, and the world traveled. The great stars were signposts, promising defined destinations and ways to get there and, at the end of the road, the reward of being someone different while at the same time becoming more like oneself. In Kalina's "everyday," self *is* content, time is the plot, and the gaze never, ever moves. Ten years after he started, the filmmaker is still posting each day's selfie on his Web site (www.everyday.noahkalina.com), expression somber and fixed, as though expressiveness itself were a control variable. What is he looking at? What is he looking *for*? What are *we* looking for?

That's easy: the answer to the question of who we are—really, truly, finally. For centuries, identity was not an issue that mattered much to anyone but philosophers. Consciousness was directed outward toward matters of survival, and answers to any larger mysteries were to be found in religion. With the rise of the Enlightenment, Romanticism, leisure time, psychoanalysis, and the consumer revolution, the gaze turned inward toward the mystery of self—of who it is that experiences what "I" perceive, thinks what "I" think, and owns what "I" own. Movie stars, among the other pleasures they offer, have served a crucial and psychologically necessary function as role models for trying on different identities and projecting alternate ways of being. They are the greatest dress-up dolls yet invented, or they were until the advent of the Internet freed our own identities from the bonds of body and name. Until then, the stars' primary function was to convince us that an immutable inner identity—a central organizing reality for each person—existed in the first place.

That still begs the question, though, of where one's true self actually is. We are closer to the heart of the matter now, yet deeper in the dark. The unhooking of persona from identity in the digital age represents an ultimate Warholization, with our various manufactured online selves just a piece of the mirror into which we peek. Each is the face of a star that cannibalizes the larger identity into which we have traditionally put meaning and value. But who's to say the woman in *Catfish* isn't that younger, prettier, hipper person she feels she is inside? Who are we to say she isn't by looking at her from the outside?

The new mutability of persona does more than free people up to engage in wonderful online lies and fantasies, or to engage in functional multiple personality disorder. It calls into question that singular root-file identity itself. The names that parents gave their children at birth are ultimately as arbitrary as the screen names we choose for chat rooms; ask your mother what she almost called you and think hard about how much of your sense of self hangs on the sound of your name. Perhaps we're so fascinated with the stars' gift for changing roles yet retaining core personas because we know in our hearts that we ourselves are constantly changing and desperate to grasp what lasts. The person we are at fifty is barely recognizable as the person we were at fifteen, as though a cloud had changed shape from an elephant to an airplane when we weren't looking.

What endures is fame, or so we dare to think; fame and the spiritual realm that is only indirectly the subject of this book. The power of celebrities—and movie stars were for a century the most mythically potent variation on the concept of celebrity—is that they combine the evanescence of glamorous reinvention with a seeming eternity of self. They prove, or seem to prove, that identity matters. Clark Gable was always Clark Gable, Julia Roberts will always be Julia Roberts; their filmographies sustain them, stringing the different faces of their roles into a cohesive line united by strength of purpose. The sameness of Cary Grant soothes us, invites us to be like him and maybe share that cohesiveness, too. But Grant understood the awful truth, which is that neither Cary Grant *nor* Archie Leach really existed.

Anyway, Grant betrayed us and his own Olympian unity by aging and dying, and so will the modern gods. So will we, and with us will wink out all our endless invented selves. Even the promise of immortality embodied in movie stardom is an illusion, for it's very probable that less than 5 percent of college students in 2010 know who Clark Gable is, just as you had never heard of Florence Lawrence a few hundred pages ago, no matter that both actors had in their time been for millions proof of something bigger, brighter, and forever.

What draws us to other people's fame is the hope of discovering a self that is and that never dies—in the stars and, by extension, in ourselves. What keeps us there, obsessively digging at the roots of celebrity, is the urge to prove it. That is why we yearn for the authenticity we're sure is at the center of each star we love, why we need to know their hobbies, who they sleep with, what they do and who they really are when no one's watching. Because what if they're not there at all—not the Gable or Roberts or Depp or Chaplin we're sure we think we know? What if it's all made up, a trick of the light?

Here, in the end, is the revelation that all of stardom works to deny, the dirtiest and most unfathomable secret—the one that, if we are to be honest with ourselves, most people suspect whenever they sit down at their computers and greet the day. It's that identity itself is the grandest illusion of all. What if the sum of who we are is not a magical inner seed that only fame or self-actualization can cause to bloom? What if we're not all the things we wish for or blog or project, but simply the actions we take for ourselves and for others—our marks upon the waking world? What if we are what we do, not the other way around? Stardom is the best dream we've yet invented, a luxurious fantasy of the fixed self. The question we need to ask ourselves is how long we want to keep sleeping, and what we'll dare to do when we finally wake up.

Postscript: Star Death

Whenever I visit Los Angeles, I make a point of dropping into Westwood Village Memorial Park Cemetery, just to see how everyone's doing. It's tucked behind Wilshire Boulevard three-quarters of the way along that street's long march from downtown L.A. to the sea, a pocket-sized burial ground in a lot that could be the footprint of a good-sized office building. Backing onto the cemetery are a branch of the city's public library, a Presbyterian church, an English-language school, a movie theater. The place doesn't announce itself as does, say, Grauman's Chinese Theater seven and a half miles to the northeast. Grauman's has the handprints and footprints of the stars preserved in concrete—proof they once walked among us. Westwood Village just has the bones, remnants of people who have stopped being stars. I visit anyway, as do others. At any given time, there are four or five of us silently walking around.

Jack Lemmon and Walter Matthau are both here, though not bickering side by side as the ten movies in which they costarred would make one hope. Lemmon lies near his great director Billy Wilder, though, and right next to Carroll O'Connor, whose TV character, bigoted Archie Bunker, lives on even as the politically left-wing actor who portrayed him molders. Pop Caruso Roy Orbison is buried here, close to the unmarked grave of rock polymath Frank Zappa. Fox head Darryl F. Zanuck lies too far from Natalie Wood to make a pass.

The cemetery, in fact, represents a final collapsing of the hierarchy of fame, with murdered actress-model Dorothy Stratten buried near Beach Boy Carl Wilson, whose remains are near strapping movie idol Burt Lancaster, who's not far from tart character actress Eve Arden, who's catty-corner from historians Will and Ariel Durant. In a corner by the entrance, maverick actor-director John Cassavetes, author Truman Capote, chicken-necked comedian Don Knotts, industrialist Armand Hammer, *Green Acres* star Eva Gabor, child actress Heather "They're *heeere*" O'Rourke, and singer Mel "the Velvet Fog" Torme all cluster together, as if they were comparing notes during a coffee break from celebrity.

No, that's a pointless metaphor. They're just dead. So is Marilyn Monroe, who's in Crypt 24 in the Corridor of Memories, second vault up in the corner of a wall of interment slots in the northeast section. When her ex-husband Joe DiMaggio was alive, he arranged for flowers to be delivered weekly to the gravesite, and every time I come to Westwood Memorial there are fresh roses left by one admirer or another. *Playboy* publisher Hugh Hefner has bought the crypt next to Monroe, as if knowing that even when he's no longer in a position to care about fame, her presence will help keep his memory alive a little longer. In 2009, the widow of the man in the crypt above Monroe announced she planned to exhume her husband and sell the property on eBay to pay the mortgage on her Beverly Hills mansion. The top bid, $4.6 million, went to a Japanese Monroe fan who later reneged on the offer. Perhaps he couldn't convince himself that he'd be famous by lying atop a star's corpse.

Monroe's death and the industry surrounding it spill over to the Internet. Her page on the "Find a Grave" Web site has fourteen thousand digital "flowers" and notes posted by fans. By contrast, Will and Ariel Durant have a combined seventy-eight. Unlike Marilyn, they never let the wind from a subway grating blow their skirts up, or slept with a president, or died young and beautiful, which is the only way to ensure that fame lasts forever, or what we want to believe is forever.

Star death represents a functional paradox. It immortalizes figures we have already assumed are bigger than life, and it does so by proving without a shred of doubt that the people in question are, in fact, mortal. But isn't that how it should work in the metaphysics of fame, since the human being, the thing that can die, is always secondary to the image he or she projects? When the persona is what we cling to, the person who created it becomes dispensable.

This is especially true for stars who have naturally aged past their most potent popular image—who have, in essence, retired behind the public scrim of themselves. When James Stewart died in 1997 at the age of eighty-nine, or Katharine Hepburn in 2003 at ninety-six, the mourning was genteel and accompanied by clips from *Mr. Smith Goes to Washington* and *Adam's Rib,* freezing the icons at their peak moment of accessibility. This was the Jimmy Stewart we all agreed upon, rather than the harsh western loners of the Anthony Mann films or the sad, twisted detective of Hitchcock's *Vertigo.* The remembered Kate was shown on TV paired with Spencer Tracy or Cary Grant or Humphrey Bogart, rarely on her own as the gauche social climber of *Alice Adams* or the cruel matriarch of *Suddenly Last Summer.* The obituaries and related public conversations surrounding timely movie-star deaths work as summings-up, final assessments of worth before the dirt hits the cultural coffin lid.

Sometimes a performer outlives not only his or her image but the pop context that held it. When Lillian Gish died at ninety-nine in 1993, the silent era in which she had functioned as the Virgin Queen of Art was so far in the past, lost from sight beneath so many layers of technological advances and accumulated pop strata, that commentators had to dig Gish's meaning out and decode her for the modern reader. As someone whose day job includes the regular writing of movie star obituaries, I have to admit there's a conceptual pleasure in knowing that a life story has been completed and that its full shape can not only now be glimpsed but also measured, weighed, tested for endurance, and sifted for surprise.

Sometimes I even look forward to the process. Not that I wish him ill, but part of me has been waiting for Mickey Rooney to shuffle off the stage just so I can trace his daft, nearly century-long funhouse ride through fame, from silent-era child star to Number One status at the box office to has-been ignominy and back, through multiple marriages, a Tony award, religious conversions—it's all there, as if he were the cynosure of stardom itself, the peephole through which every aspect of celebrity can be glimpsed. But not yet. At this writing, at ninety-one, Rooney has four movies in the pipeline. His story's not done. It may not *ever* be done.

Stars who outlive their glamour but are still working when disease or accident or a bad heart takes them off prompt a different sort of public mourning, one that acknowledges the whims and cruelties of fate. A long battle with cancer—Sammy Davis Jr., Frank Zappa, Dennis Hopper—gilds a persona with the tragic nobility of suffering and the honor of fighting a good fight. Conversely, what the British so piquantly call "death by misadventure" can taint a star's image in perpetuity. William Holden drunkenly hitting his head on a coffee table and bleeding to death, David Carradine dying in a Bangkok hotel closet of autoerotic asphyxiation, 1960s sitcom star Bob Crane murdered in mysterious sexual circumstances, Sam Cooke shot dead with no pants on by a motel manager, and so on up the chain of escalating misfortune—these deaths alter who we think these stars are by introducing a note of unfiltered reality, the secret no one really wanted to know. Because they couldn't control that secret, the stars' images are subsequently revised to include personal weakness, but in truth we downgrade them for letting the mask slip and giving the game away—by reminding us they're flawed and human. Crane's redefining was so drastic that in death he became an altogether different kind of star, one doomed by his sex addiction, and so served as a cautionary tale in the 2002 biopic *Auto Focus*.

The death of certain stars comes as a shock even when it shouldn't. Marlon Brando was eighty when he died in 2004, yet the two faces of his public persona—the charismatic wild man of the earliest films and the weathered master of *The Godfather*—were still so relevant to the cultural discourse that the actual Brando receded behind them. In his final decades he appeared in movies good (*The Freshman,* trading on his fame as Don Corleone), bad (*Christopher Columbus*), and weird (*The Island of Dr. Moreau*), and he was propelled back into the news in 1990, when son Christian Brando shot his half-sister's boyfriend. The public image of Brando in the final years of his life was one of sad profligacy and ego bloat—the star who could not control his weight, his children, his meaning.

Yet because he ventured so rarely into public and didn't play the role of retired star (as did, say, James Stewart), Brando remained young in the culture, even as his secondary image—and probably the more important one—was to illustrate what happens to youthful insolence when it grows old and loses its way.

But we don't want to know about entropy. It's a turn-off and it's not why we look to stars in the first place. By their very existence, movie stars insist that entropy cannot exist, that glamour and youth never fade or, if they do, get resculpted into something of harder, better value. Katharine Hepburn's 1991 autobiography, *Me,* dovetailed with the aging actress's starchy noblesse oblige, whereas Brando's own 1994 book, *Songs My Mother Taught Me,* only added to a sense of unfocused narcissism that we never wanted from him. Better to believe in the immediacies of Brando the young ape-god and Marlon the middle-aged craftsman, and, yes, his death was a surprising reminder that a real Marlon Brando still walked the earth.

Paul Newman, too, should never have been allowed to get old, predicated as the idea of "Paul Newman" was upon wry, unquenchable virility. The actor addressed aging in several very fine late-career movies—*Nobody's Fool* (1994), *Twilight* (1998)—and in fact briefly seemed to have triumphed over old age by making it seem sexy and wise.

After a few character parts and a voiceover role in the Pixar movie *Cars,* Newman's final decade saw him step away from the indignity of being seen; in line with his public image, he insisted on declining in private. Yet he still remained quite literally in the marketplace, an ever-youthful face on a bottle of salad dressing or a bag of potato chips. By the turn of the millennium Newman had become a food industry brand whose raffish trademarked smile carried only the faintest afterglow of movie glamour. This is what kept the star young in the culture, and this is why we felt stunned when he died in 2008. Hadn't we eaten one of his fig bars just yesterday?

The dead stars who matter most, of course, are the interrupted. Those who die in youth by their own devices or at the hand of cruel, uncaring fate we solemnize only in hindsight. James Dean racing his career into a head-on collision at the age of twenty-four. Rudolph Valentino succumbing at thirty-one to appendicitis and gastric ulcers and peritonitis and an infected lung, the public mania around his funeral attempting to make up for the dull medical catastrophe of his death. Marilyn Monroe, at thirty-six, ending her love-hate relationship with fame by swallowing pills—or was it murder, and was it the CIA?

The roll call of pop martyrdom carries into the counterculture era, with the holy trinity of rock-god casualties, Jimi Hendrix (1970, age twenty-seven, asphyxiated on his own vomit after too much red wine and sleeping pills), Janis Joplin (1970, twenty-seven, heroin overdose), and Jim Morrison (1971, twenty-seven, heroin overdose or heart attack, depends on who's talking). It leaps into derangement with the 1980 shooting of John Lennon by an insane fan who thought he could kill what the singer meant to him. It acquires an air of international tragedy with the car crash of Princess Diana, inevitability with the suicide of Nirvana's Kurt Cobain, the status of preordained vendetta with the street murders of rappers Tupac Shakur and Biggie Smalls. It claims talent cresting with Heath Ledger's accidental overdose of prescription medicine. With the death of Michael Jackson, it claims the brilliant child himself.

These are stars whose lives seem gilded with doom and whose deaths now seem foretold only because we quickly reorganized their meaning *around* their deaths. It's important to remember who these performers were in the months and weeks leading up to their unexpected exits. Joplin was struggling with drugs and alcohol; Hendrix's career was in disarray after a botched European tour; Morrison had fled to Paris an overweight burnout. All three had quit the bands in which they had first made their names and were considered stars in flux if not active trouble.

Monroe had been fired from her last film, *Something's Got to Give,* although Fox later renewed her contract and there were plans to start reshooting. The media catcalls concerning Valentino's masculinity were at their peak in the months before his death, and money problems forced him into a sequel to *The Sheik,* a movie and a role he hated. Diana, Princess of Wales, had seriously risked her popularity with the British people and the press by dating Egyptian playboy/film producer Dodi Al-Fayed.

Only in the instances of Cobain, Shakur, and Smalls (aka the Notorious B.I.G. aka Christopher Wallace) did the possibility of violent death seem likely, if not obvious, before the event. Cobain had spiraled through several suicide attempts and was clearly in severe mental and emotional distress; Shakur had survived one shooting and was an active participant in gangsta rap's coastal rivalry. All three men, moreover, had built personas that were towering edifices of martyrdom and imminent demise. Their songs and albums reflected postures of nihilism in their very titles, from B.I.G.'s "Ready to Die" and Tupac's "Death Around the Corner" to "I Hate Myself and I Want to Die," the semi-joking original name for the final Nirvana album, *In Utero.*

There was no surprise, in other words; just a sense of awful fulfillment (and, in the case of Cobain, anger that no one in his circle got him help). Because there was no surprise, the mythification of all three began the instant they were dead—indeed, had begun before they were dead, as their own doom-mongering had been a primary source of appeal for fans disaffected from the mainstream and finding truths and emotional sustenance in gangsta or grunge.

By contrast, the deaths of James Dean and Heath Ledger—both young actors whose careers were peaking at the time of their deaths—were interpreted as the fates robbing the audience of powerful new icons. In both cases, the next product out of the pipeline became a touchstone for consumer grief and industry acknowledgment: an Oscar nomination for Dean (*Giant*), an Oscar win for Ledger (*The Dark Knight*), and an intensely focused pop grief in which the actors acquired a larger meaning, not to mention a greater popularity, that had eluded them in life.

Actually, the commercial benefits of dying unexpectedly are well established, especially when the posthumous release has the appropriate tone of farewell. Otis Redding's wistful "(Sittin' On) the Dock of the Bay" in 1967, Joplin's "Me and Bobby McGee" in 1970, Jim Croce's "Time in a Bottle" in 1973—all number 1 hits by recently deceased pop stars. The seven months that passed between Ledger's death and the July 2008 release of *The Dark Knight* was, uniquely, a period of escalating hype and mourning, as though the actor could not be laid to rest until this final performance had been processed in the public sphere. The character's traumas were conjoined with the actor's, and what little we knew of Ledger's private troubles (he had recently divorced and was by all accounts going through a stressful period) was recast in the manic creative glow of his performance as the Joker.

Would *Dark Knight* and Ledger's performance have been as celebrated had the actor lived? Possibly; there was already excited advance word about the film and his work in it before he died. Yet death made the film a memorial and immemorial, as if containing Ledger's final complete work rendered it a done deal—"the best movie of all time" in the words of a generation who had never experienced one of their own dying young. To think the film might be anything less was, if you were the right age, speaking ill of the dead.

Star death saves careers by immobilizing them, preventing an actor from aging out of his or her primary persona. Whether or not they would have moved on to more interesting work once they were free of bondage to our expectations becomes a moot point. If James Dean had lived, would he have kept following Brando into self-pity and bloat? Or would he still be lithe and crazy and creative—just an older version, without the dreams of millions of kids propping him up? Would the drugs have gotten him as they did his *Rebel Without a Cause* costar Dennis Hopper, and would he have come out the other side? Would he be a grand old man of indie movies or just another Celebrity Apprentice? It's immaterial. Death spared Dean the "problem" of turning ordinary, froze the persona in mid-stride, and gave us someone to worship forever.

What would Monroe have made of the cultural and cinematic freedoms of the late 1960s? Would she have flowered or fled? One can see her working happily with the Scorseses and Coppolas of the New Hollywood, and one can just as easily imagine her holed up out of sight like a latter-day Mary Pickford.

One thing is certain: Marilyn's role as the premiere Dead Star of the twentieth century made her more commercially and culturally successful than ever. In life, she was mocked: journalists looked down on her, women sharpened their claws, men leered. Death not only ennobled Monroe but also exposed and codified the culture's mistake in not seeing the sensitive, unhappy woman behind the pneumatic facade. The current pop attitude is that we all wronged her by perceiving her wrongly, so it is up to us to atone for our sin by renting her movies and growing misty when Elton John sings "Candle in the Wind" (so powerful a work of public keening that it was later reworked for Princess Diana). If you direct your Web browser to marilynmonroe.com, you will find that it is the site of the late actress's licensing resource center. In 2004, according to *Forbes* magazine, Monroe's estate made $8 million.

Which, honestly, is a pittance compared with what a dead star *can* earn. Per *Forbes,* the Elvis Presley estate made $55 million in 2009; during the same period, the still-living Britney Spears made only $35 million. And when a star's death hits every major cultural pressure point on the spectrum, the response can be as profitable as it is emotional. Michael Jackson made $90 million in the four months following his death in June 2009. Early the following year, Sony paid the singer's estate $250 million for the right to distribute his music until 2017, the highest contracted amount in history for a single artist alive or dead.

Ironically, Jackson had spent the better part of the previous decade plagued by financial problems, but he had settled his debts and was gearing up for a concert tour that had already broken sales records. After two and a half decades of ongoing public eccentricity, Jackson seemed poised for a grand reinvention—a major comeback and full-scale reassessment of his cultural worth.

Instead, he died. His personal physician gave the singer the wrong cocktail of medications, Jackson had a heart attack, and he died. Because his passing combined more than the usual number of prerequisites necessary for a major pop event, what ensued was amplified beyond any previous scale. For one thing, Jackson had been an artistic prodigy, and that prodigy had matured into an artist of unparalleled commercial and cultural impact; *Thriller* is still the best-selling album of all time. Public adoration had been followed by public confusion and hostility as the singer's strangeness overtook his persona, and while he had his defenders, Jackson was for many years a figure of ridicule. So there was plenty to atone for if you wanted to feel guilty.

He died young(ish); he died unexpectedly (but not entirely); he died on the verge of reclaiming his crown (unless, of course, the concerts turned out to be less than expected, which we'll never know). All these fueled the flames of public grief because, taken together, they implied that Michael Jackson died unfairly. If he hadn't been mounting a comeback—or hadn't sold out all fifty shows—the death might have been the passing of an oddball recluse who once meant something very big.

The most decisive shift of all was the public reassertion of Michael Jackson as a victim: the brilliant child who'd been wronged by his father, by Berry Gordy, by Billie Jean, by the Santa Barbara county prosecutors who failed to understand that sleepovers with adolescents might be nonsexual in nature. Anyone who'd thought of Jackson as a victimizer—which, face it, was almost everyone—suddenly seemed to have wronged him as well. To properly repent, you just had to listen to *Off the Wall* or *Thriller* again and recapture the moment before weirdness (his) and doubt (ours) took over. If you didn't own the CDs, then you had to go download them. Purchasing the evidence was the consumer version of filing past the casket.

Jackson's death turned into mass theater. As the first major celebrity to die unexpectedly in the age of social media, he almost literally ground the Internet to a halt. Twitter and Wikipedia both crashed the day he died. Google executives were convinced that the tidal wave of searches under the singer's name meant the site was under attack. Gossip sites like TMZ.com and perezhilton.com went dark, their servers overwhelmed; mainstream news Web sites slowed to a crawl under the traffic. Presidents of countries around the world released statements of national mourning. The memorial service at L.A.'s Staples Center a week after Jackson's death was broadcast live and watched by an estimated global audience of one billion.

Here's a heretical question: Why? Who or what are we grieving for when a famous person dies? Why did people who a day earlier would have been making Michael Jackson pedophilia jokes suddenly listen to "Wanna Be Startin' Something" with tears of nostalgia?

A number of reasons present themselves. A star's death allows us to gather communally around his or her best moments and around what those moments mean to us, as a culture and as people. It lets us create a final narrative of his or her life in which the suspense of not knowing what's coming next—comeback or nosedive—is resolved. We like emotional catharsis and don't much care where it comes from. Or we're mourning a part of ourselves that once believed in the innocence of a pop song or a movie—their power to elevate and define our lives.

Whichever or all of the above, when we grieve for dead stars, we're doing it for us more than for them. As a public and as individuals, we engage in a complicated process in which persona is reinvented one final time, without the star's consent but with several factors crucial to sustaining it (and us) over the long haul: narrative closure, assigned meaning, a tragic dimension, the self-flagellation of the audience. All the resentful ill-will that surrounded dead stars while they lived—and sneers were directed at Michael Jackson, Marilyn Monroe, John

Lennon, and the rest for various perceived sins against their paying customers—dissolves in a bath of sentiment and licensed consumerism.

Is it possible to genuinely mourn a person we never personally knew? Of course not. But it's possible to feel good about feeling sad, and to use a star's death as a way to remind ourselves we're still alive. In public mourning and remembrance, there is always the power of the survivor, whether it's expressed by watching with the rest of the planet as a pop singer is laid to rest, by signing a digital memory book on a Web site, or by walking through a quiet Hollywood cemetery while the star factory hums on in office buildings and bungalows a few blocks away. We're still here. The gods lost. We won.

Acknowledgments

This book would not have been conceived and cajoled into shape without the long-suffering patience, sharp insights, and gracious good humor of my agent, Sarah Burnes of the Gernert Company. It was her enthusiasm for my idea of a history of movie stardom—as both a good read and a way to deal with a growing cultural issue—that got me from idle talk to formal pitch and beyond. Zack Wagman, my initial editor at Random House, brought an intelligent postmillennial perspective that was sorely needed and called me on matters of focus, overlength, and rampant semicolons. Andrew Carlson, under the aegis of Marty Asher, took over for Zack with grace and a sharp eye.

Closer to home, I owe a debt of gratitude to the Boston Public Library, the Newton Free Library, and the greater Minuteman Library System of suburban Boston for making DVDs, research material, and writing space so readily available. Thanks, too, to Paul Schneider and Roy Grundmann of Boston University's Film and TV department for allowing me to organize much of the material in this book into an undergraduate course, and many thanks to the students of FT 553 for helping me develop and refine so many of the ideas here.

My editors at *The Boston Globe*—Martin Baron, Doug Most, Rebecca Ostriker, and Janice Page—were extremely understanding in allowing me to take on a project of this scope in addition to my weekly duties as film critic. *Globe* arts editor Scott Heller, now at *The New York Times,* was an early and enthusiastic supporter of the ideas here and allowed me to explore many of them in the pages of the *Globe.* Mark Feeney was—is—editor, colleague, and friend, and his thoughts on the subject of stardom and experience in the business of writing cultural histories proved invaluable, on the micro level of grammar and phrasing and the macro level of themes. My fellow critic, Wesley Morris, kept my spirits up and perspective intact as we trudged ever on through the trenches of *Transformers 2* and *The Last Airbender.*

A genuflection in the direction of the Berkshire Boys, Bob Svikhart, Ed Goldfinger, and Matt Kenslea, who either read this manuscript in its various stages of gestation or endured the author endlessly hashing out the notions contained herein only to ask the one relevant question that would either puncture or justify the blather. Fred Dalzell read the first chapters with the eye of a professional historian and a good friend. And a special, extra-deep bow goes to the head Berkshire Boy, Jon Abbott, and his wife, Shari Malyn, plus their friends Chris Plaut and Nancy Winkelstein, for allowing their mountain home to be used as a writer's retreat over the course of several extremely necessary weeks. For the peace, quiet, and head space, I thank you.

My daughters, Eliza and Natalie, kept me alive to insights into stars both classic and up-to-the-moment. From both of them came my understanding of how an icon like Bette Davis or James Cagney can speak to a modern teenager; from them, too, came my introduction to people like Antoine Dodson and Rebecca Black.

My wife, Lori Yarvis, has been as involved in this book as I have, dealing with two and a half years of weekend absences and the occasional weeks of full-on disappearance. Throughout it all, she has kept her enthusiasm and sense of humor even when my own has flagged, and her editorial insights have always been dead on (even on the occasions when it took me a while to see it). She is this book's first and best reader, from conception to execution, and she is this writer's best and only companion in the ongoing adventure. Without her, none of it happens.

Notes

FRONTISPIECE

epigraph **"It's all—nothing! It's all a joke":** *The New Yorker,* May 23, 1925, p. 9.

INTRODUCTION

xxiii **"Bogart's a helluva nice guy":** *Movie Talk: Who Said What About Whom in the Movies,* David Shipman, St. Martin's Press, 1988, p. 18.

1. THE STAR IS BORN

4 **"Will you please answer this letter, a postal will do":** *Picture Personalities: The Emergence of the Star System in America,* Richard deCordova, University of Illinois Press, 1990, p. 57.

5 **"In order to have some kind of name for you":** *Movie Crazy: Fans, Stars, and the Cult of the Celebrity,* Samantha Barris, Palgrave, 2001, p. 18.

5 **"She is all right":** *Florence Lawrence, the Biograph Girl: America's First Movie Star,* Kelly R. Brown, McFarland and Co., 1999, p. 48.

7 **"A buzzing and roaring were heard":** *The New York Times,* April 24, 1896.

10 **an estimated 9,000 small theaters:** *Movie Time: A Chronology of Hollywood and the Movie Industry from Its Beginnings to the Present,* Gene Brown, Macmillan, 1995, p. 9.

10 **Between 1907 and 1908, narrative movies:** *Picture Personalities,* p. 27.

11 **"The repertoire actor has discovered":** Ibid., p. 35.

15 **"Miss Eliza Proctor Otis as Nancy Sykes":** Ibid., p. 41.

15 **"Miss Lawrence has a one hundred percent health certificate":** *Florence Lawrence, the Biograph Girl,* p. 50.

16 **"You've Seen Them On The 'Screen' ":** Ibid., p. 57.

16 **"there were enthusiastic shouts from female voices":** Ibid., p. 56.

16 **"tearing the buttons from her dress":** Ibid., p. 55.

17 **"I had no idea that so many people":** Ibid., p. 56.

17 **"We do not know the lady's name":** Ibid., p. 31.

18 **"That those who pose for the Silent Drama":** *Picture Personalities,* p. 66.

18 **America was no longer an agrarian society:** *Starstruck: Celebrity Performers and the American Public,* Jib Fowles, Smithsonian, 1992, p. 22.

19 **Average household spending:** *Movie Crazy,* p. 53.

19 **The number of theaters in New York City:** Ibid., p. 39.

20 **"If anyone had told me two years ago":** *Working-Class Hollywood: Silent Film and the Shaping of Class in America,* Steven J. Ross, Princeton University Press, 1999, p. 32.

21 **"We pay for the whole actor, Mr. Griffith":** *The Movies, Mr. Griffith, and Me,* Lillian Gish with Ann Pinchot, Prentice-Hall, 1969, p. 60.

21 **"Good screen acting":** *Screen Acting,* Mae Marsh, Frederick A. Stokes Co., 1921, pp. 81, 79.

21 **"I knew Mary Pickford had had picture experience":** *The Movies in Our Midst,* Gerald Mast, University of Chicago Press, 1983, pp. 117–18.

2. THE FIRST GODDESSES

25 **"an artiste of the highest rank":** *Picture Personalities: The Emergence of the Star System in America,* Richard deCordova, University of Illinois Press, 1990, p. 70.

25 **"It seems as though she was not acting at all":** *Movie Crazy: Fans, Stars, and the Cult of the Celebrity,* Samantha Barris, Palgrave, 2001, p. 44.

26 **"Mr. Griffith always wanted":** *The Movies in the Age of Innocence,* Edward Wagenknecht, Limelight Editions, 1997, p. 161.

26 **" 'The screen public will choose its favorites' ":** *The Public Is Never Wrong: The Autobiography of Adolph Zukor,* Adolph Zukor with Dale Kramer, Putnam, 1953, p. 98.

26 **"I did not quibble":** Ibid.

27 **"Little Mary Pickford comes into her own":** *Variety,* December 31, 1913.

27 **"the best-known girl in America":** *Ladies' Home Journal,* January 1915, p. 9.

27 **"If I could grow up to be one hundredth part":** *Movie Crazy,* p. 46.

28 **"[T]o reject this girl in haste":** *Stars of the Silents,* Edward Wagenknecht, Scarecrow Press, 1987, p. 11.

28 **"I became, in a sense, my own baby":** *The Stars Appear,* Richard Dyer MacCann, Scarecrow Press, 1992, p. 105.

28 **"It is ironical, I suppose":** *The Public Is Never Wrong,* pp. 191, 174.

29 **"Don't worry, I die before it's over":** *Movie Star: A Look at the Women Who Made Hollywood,* Ethan Mordden, St. Martin's, 1983, p. 43.

32 **"that skunk":** *Silent Stars,* Jeanine Basinger, Alfred A. Knopf, 2000, p. 138.

33 **"an outstanding example of the fascination that comes from power":** *The Talmadge Girls,* Anita Loos, Viking, 1978, p. 28.

36 **"You bring me a picture like this":** *The Movies, Mr. Griffith, and Me,* Lillian Gish with Ann Pinchot, Prentice-Hall, 1969, p. 221.

37 **"Tell the camera what you feel":** Ibid., p. 37.

38 **"But we weren't doing it for money":** Ibid., p. 234.

38 **"It could be worse. Suppose I'd been nominated and lost to Cher?":**

Movie Talk: Who Said What About Whom in the Movies, David Shipman, St. Martin's Press, 1988, p. 86.

38 **"Oh, I'd *love* to have played a vamp":** *The Stars Appear,* p. 85.

39 **"I was the spark that lit up flaming youth":** *Movie Star,* p. 25.

41 **"It, hell":** *Silent Stars,* p. 435.

42 **"Miss Lawrence, have you a protégé?":** *Movie Crazy,* p. 65.

43 **"Out of 100,000 persons who started at the bottom":** Ibid., p. 75.

43 **"Don't go to Hollywood!":** Ibid., p. 76.

44 **"I guess I know what that means":** Ibid., p. 74.

44 **"It wasn't ever like I thought it was going to be":** *Silent Stars,* p. 449.

3. THE MATINEE IDOLS

46 **"the screen's most perfect lover":** *Silent Stars,* Jeanine Basinger, Alfred A. Knopf, 2000, p. 399.

51 **"He is, I believe, the most widely known man in the world":** *New York Tribune,* December 30, 1917.

51 **"Charlie was a god, you forget":** Cherrill interview, *Unknown Chaplin,* DVD, Thames Television, 1983.

52 **"He does things":** *Stars of the Silents,* Edward Wagenknecht, Scarecrow Press, 1987, p. 101.

53 **"Is there a man named Chaffin":** *Charlie Chaplin and His Times,* Kenneth S. Lynn, Cooper Square Press, 2002, p. 106.

53 **"A year at that racket":** Ibid.

53 **"I had no idea what make-up to put on":** *My Autobiography,* Charles Chaplin, Simon and Schuster, 1964, p. 148.

56 **"People were standing at railroad junctions":** Ibid, p. 187.

57 **"Chaplin *is* vulgar":** *Stars of the Silents,* p. 97.

57 **"My clowning, as the world calls it":** *Charlie Chaplin: Interviews,* Kevin J. Hayes, ed., University Press of Mississippi, 2005, p. 46.

61 **a manual on the benefits of staying faithful to your spouse:** *The Talmadge Girls,* Anita Loos, Viking, 1978, p. 42.

62 **"every year might be my last in pictures":** *Stars of the Silents,* p. 11.

62 **"Fairbanks will survive":** *The Public Is Never Wrong: The Autobiography of Adolph Zukor,* Adolph Zukor with Dale Kramer, Putnam, 1953, p. 191.

62 **"scriptural":** *Stars of the Silents,* p. 13.

62 **"living proof of America's chronic belief in happy endings":** *The Stars Appear,* Richard Dyer MacCann, Scarecrow Press, 1992, p. 125.

63 **"[their idols] had materialized":** *Pickford: The Woman Who Made Hollywood,* Eileen Whitfield, University Press of Kentucky, 2007, p. 201.

63 **"I touched her dress!":** Ibid., p. 203.

66 **"the feeling that here was a young man":** *The Public Is Never Wrong,* p. 218.

67 **"The confusion was indescribable":** *The New York Times,* August 25, 1926.

67 **"Film producers, too":** *The New York Times,* August 31, 1926.

68 **"It seemed like an intrusion to yell 'cut!' ":** *Dark Star,* Leatrice Gilbert Fountain with John R. Maxim, St. Martin's Press, 1985, p. 125.

4. SODOM

73 **"At Hollywood is a colony":** *Picture Personalities: The Emergence of the Star System in America,* Richard deCordova, University of Illinois Press, 1990, p. 130.

73 **"a dictator of principles":** Ibid., p. 131.

73 **"nothing is wrong with moving pictures":** Ibid., p. 134.

74 **"this film star [who] has been entirely too closely connected":** *Picture Personalities,* p. 92.

75 **got a lifetime of guilt:** *Swanson on Swanson,* Gloria Swanson, Random House, 1980, p. 242.

77 **"I have spent the greater part of my life":** *Ladies' Home Journal,* February 1963.

77 **"one of the best natural actors":** *The New York Times,* May 15, 2005.

78 **"It is hard to feel that you have given the best of your life to motion pictures":** *Florence Lawrence, the Biograph Girl: America's First Movie Star,* Kelly R. Brown, McFarland and Co., 1999, p. 132.

5. JUDGMENT DAY

79 **"[The talkies] have 'gotten me' ":** *The Talkies: American Cinema's Transition to Sound, 1926–1931,* Donald Crafton, University of California Press, 1999, p. 487.

80 **"Who the hell wants to hear actors talk?":** *The Shattered Silents: How the Talkies Came to Stay,* Alexander Walker, William Morrow, 1978, p. 6.

82 **" 'Ladies and gentlemen,' he said":** Ibid., p. 56.

86 **"Eet is a fad, a curiosity":** Ibid., p. 76.

86 **"Did you ever hear any Swede talk like that?":** Ibid., p. 159.

87 **"Go away, you little bastards":** *The Speed of Sound: Hollywood and the Talkie Revolution, 1926–1930,* Scott Eyman, Johns Hopkins University Press, 1999, p. 379.

87 **"What [Chaplin has] really got is a gentleman complex":** *The Shattered Silents,* p. 132.

87 **"forever talking the dictionary":** *The New Biographical Dictionary of Film,* 4th ed., David Thomson, Knopf, 2004, p. 153.

89 **"I was an epidemic":** *The Shattered Silents,* p. 204.

89 **"We have been looking for Rudy's successor":** *The Talkies,* p. 494.

91 **"the sound of his voice puts something gritty":** *The Shattered Silents,* p. 156.

91 **"A few more talker productions like this":** *The Talkies,* p. 503.

92 **"I heard my first talking picture a few days ago":** Ibid., p. 490.

94 **Colleen Moore released a notarized affidavit:** Ibid., p. 512.

6. THE STARS WHO TALKED

96 **"For Miss West the change from the silks":** *Becoming Mae West,* Emily Wortis Leider, Farrar Straus Giroux, 1997, p. 167.

96 **"No one believed that the Mae West of the stage":** Ibid., p. 234.

96 **Paramount posted losses of $21 million in 1932:** Ibid., p. 236.

97 **"The street outside [the theater]":** Ibid., p. 283.

98 **"Mae West is the first real Waterloo":** Ibid., p. 256.

98 **"the greatest female impersonator of all time":** George Davis, *Vanity Fair,* May 1934, pp. 46, 82.

101 **"He was so gorgeous, so clean":** *Long Live the King: A Biography of Clark Gable,* Lyn Tornabene, Putnam, 1976, p. 27.

101 **"He was boyish, mannish, a brute":** Ibid., p. 194.

101 **"I don't believe any woman is telling the truth":** Ibid., p. 132.

102 **"There's this guy, my God":** Ibid., p. 155.

102 **"was the biggest man I ever knew":** Ibid., p. 128.

102 **"He was willing to be molded":** Ibid., p. 130.

102 **"The Great American Male Has Hit the Screen at Last":** Ibid., p. 137.

102 **"What a Man, Gable!":** Ibid.

103 **"We learned a lot from acting":** Ibid., p. 193.

103 **"You know, this king stuff is pure bullshit":** Ibid., p. 15.

103 **"Before I did this, I was shoveling":** Ibid., p. 154.

103 **"Clark would have given his right arm":** Ibid., p. 206.

104 **his movies brought in $500 million:** Ibid., p. 26.

105 **a mute girl in England saw 1934's *Bright Eyes*:** *Child Star: An Autobiography,* Shirley Temple Black, McGraw-Hill, 1988, p. 73.

105 **"During 1936, almost 90% of reported [Fox] corporate net profits":** Ibid., pp. 162–63.

106 **"I suddenly saw only a mosaic of arms and faces":** Ibid., p. 245.

106 **"A fundamental fact of life began to sink in":** Ibid., p. 247.

106 **"Now she's lovable":** Ibid., p. 221.

107 **"Tears came to my eyes":** Ibid., p. 301.

108 **"an explosive little broad with a sharp left":** *Dark Victory: The Life of Bette Davis,* Ed Sikov, Henry Holt and Co., 2007, p. 2.

109 **"often speaks too rapidly for the microphone":** *New York Times,* February 11, 1932.

109 **"It was always difficult for me to speak slowly":** *Mother Goddam: The Story of the Career of Bette Davis,* Whitney Stine and Bette Davis, Hawthorn Books, 1974, p. 32.

109 **"Our little Bette craves something with guts":** *Dark Victory,* p. 81.

110 **"He insisted no one would want to see a film":** *Mother Goddam,* p. 97.

113 **"It was as deliberate a projection as you'll ever see":** AP obituary, June 12, 1979.

113 **"I pretended to be somebody I wanted to be":** *Cary Grant,* Marc Eliot, Harmony, 2004, frontispiece.

114 **"personality, functioning":** *The Great Movie Stars: The Golden Years,* David Shipman, Little, Brown, 1995, p. 254.

7. THE FACTORY

120 **"MGM was a wonderful place":** *James Stewart,* Donald Dewey, Turner, 1996, p. 139.

120 **"[I] couldn't believe what I was watching":** Ibid., p. 274.

123 **the studio executives had a chart tracking the menstrual cycles:** *Long Live the King: A Biography of Clark Gable,* Lyn Tornabene, Putnam, 1976, p. 157.

123 **the studio might even pay off your wife to get a divorce:** *The MGM Stock Company: The Golden Era,* James Robert Parish and Ronald L. Bowers, Bonanza, 1977, p. 761.

8. MONSTERS, SCARLETT WOMEN, AND OTHER CHARACTERS

129 **"it was a bit shattering":** *Dear Boris: The Life of William Henry Pratt A.K.A. Boris Karloff,* Cynthia Lindsay, Knopf, 1975.

136 **"I personally will go home and weep":** *Frankly, My Dear: "Gone With the Wind" Revisited,* Molly Haskell, Yale University Press, 2009, p. 59–60.

137 **"from seductress to woman of action":** Ibid., p. 11.

138 **"It was insanity that I not be given Scarlett":** *Dark Victory: The Life of Bette Davis,* Ed Sikov, Henry Holt and Co., 2007, p. 108.

138 **"had too much dignity and not enough fire":** *Frankly, My Dear,* p. 173.

138 **"I think Hepburn has two strikes against her":** *Memo from David O. Selznick,* Rudy Behlmer, ed., Samuel French, 1989, p. 171.

138 **"I was too strong for it":** *Showman: The Life of David O. Selznick,* David Thomson, Alfred A. Knopf, 1992, p. 271.

138 **"completely inadequate":** *Memo from David O. Selznick,* p. 175.

139 **"I must see Mr. Cukor":** *Scarlett, Rhett, and a Cast of Thousands: The Filming of "Gone With the Wind,"* Roland Flamini, Macmillan, 1975, p. 77.

140 **"all we have to do is line up a complete cast":** *Memo from David O. Selznick,* p. 172.

140 **"Scarlett O'Goddard":** *Scarlett, Rhett, and a Cast of Thousands,* p. 127.

141 **As legends go, it's close enough to the truth:** Ibid., pp. 154–60.

141 **"Naturally, I am the only person in the world":** *Showman,* p. 285.

9. THE AFTERNOON SHIFT

144 **"Wake up Hollywood producers!":** *The Golden Girls of MGM,* Jane Ellen Wayne, Carroll and Graf Publishers, 2002, p. 147; *The Lost One: A Life of Peter Lorre,* Stephen D. Youngkin, University Press of Kentucky, 2005, p. 519.

146 **"seeing your mother drunk":** *Time,* December 22, 1941.

152 **"a magnificent specimen of the rampant male":** *Bring On the Empty Horses,* David Niven, Putnam, 1975, p. 124.

152 **"You know Flynn":** *People Will Talk,* John Kobal, Alfred A. Knopf, 1985, p. 566.

153 **By 1952, the FBI's files on Chaplin:** *Charlie Chaplin and His Times,* Kenneth S. Lynn, Cooper Square Press, 2002, p. 484.

153 **"cheap Cockney cad":** *City of Nets: A Portrait of Hollywood in the 1940s,* Otto Friedrich, Harper and Row, 1986, p. 192.

154 **"I suddenly stopped reading":** *Wilder Times: The Life of Billy Wilder,* Kevin Lally, Henry Holt and Co., 1996, p. 188.

155 **"Waxworks is right":** *Swanson on Swanson,* Gloria Swanson, Random House, 1980, p. 483.

155 **"a modern extension of Pirandello":** Ibid., p. 482.

155 **"You bastard!," "Fuck you," "Go shit in your hat":** *On Sunset Boulevard: The Life and Times of Billy Wilder,* Ed Sikov, Hyperion, 1998, p. 303.

156 **"It slowly dawned on me":** *Swanson on Swanson,* p. 259.

156 **"During my years of obscurity":** Ibid.

10. BARBARIAN AT THE GATES

160 **thinking that a young player was having a seizure:** *The New Yorker,* October 28, 1972, p. 133.

160 **"People suddenly started looking at him":** *Brando,* Peter Manso, Hyperion, 1994, p. 104.

160 **"The curtains went up":** Ibid., p. 146.

161 **"What you saw was the elements of truth":** Ibid., p. 174.

161 **"In fifty years in the business":** Ibid.

162 **"Hers seemed to be a performance":** *Elia Kazan: A Life,* Elia Kazan, Knopf, 1988, p. 343.

162 **"You've become a star tonight":** *Brando,* p. 232.

162 **"The theater to me is just a job":** Ibid., p. 234.

163 **"the fat one":** *Marlon Brando* (Penguin Lives), Patricia Bosworth, Viking, 2001, p. 82.

163 **"I'm not afraid of anything and I don't love money":** Ibid., p. 67.

163 **"wanted to get a pike at this kid Brando":** *Brando,* p. 296.

163 **"a blue-jeaned slobbermouth":** *Marlon Brando,* p. 89.

163 **"I was the antithesis of Stanley Kowalski":** *The New York Times,* July 23, 1950.

165 **"His eyes changed":** *Marlon Brando,* p. 134.

166 **"Mr. Dean appears to be wearing":** *Brando,* p. 390.

166 **"because I do it":** Ibid.

167 **"Marlon created these guys":** *Marlon Brando,* p. 175.

169 **"When we weren't making movies":** *Idol: Rock Hudson,* Jerry Oppenheimer and Jack Vitek, Villard Books, 1986, p. 29.

175 **"I had the radio on":** *Time,* May 14, 1956.

176 **"has a quite unconscious but basic resistance to acting":** *All the Available Light: A Marilyn Monroe Reader,* Yona Zeldis McDonough, ed., Touchstone, 2002, p. 159.

176 **"She had no techniques":** *Marilyn: Norma Jean,* Gloria Steinem, Signet, 1988, p. 123.

177 **"I have always had a talent for irritating women":** *All the Available Light,* p. 70.

177 **"That's the trouble, a sex symbol becomes a thing":** *Life,* August 7, 1964, p. 70.

11. THE NEW MACHINE

180 **Consumer spending on appliances and home furnishings increased 240 percent:** *The Columbia History of American Television,* Gary R. Edgerton, Columbia University Press, 2007, p. 102.

180 **By contrast, film attendance plummeted:** *The American Film Institute Desk Reference,* Melinda Corey and George Ochoa, Dorling Kindersley, 2002, p. xxxiii.

181 **It wasn't the 3.8 million people who tuned in to the games during October:** *The Columbia History of American Television,* p. 86.

181 **"It's not lappy enough":** *The Box: An Oral History of Television 1920–1961,* Jeff Kisselloff, Viking, 1995, p. 304.

182 **"Ed does nothing":** *The Columbia History of American Television,* p. 116.

187 **during the 1950s, women represented 55 to 60 percent of evening viewers:** *The Columbia History of American Television,* Gary R. Edgerton, Columbia University Press, 2007, p. 136.

188 **The four years from 1947 to 1951:** Ibid., p. 179.

188 **Walt Disney's new ABC show *Disneyland*:** Ibid., p. 182.

190 **the 13 million teenagers who in 1956 had a total spendable income of $7 billion a year:** Ibid., p. 188.

12. VINYL

192 **"What are you doing?":** *Last Train to Memphis: The Rise of Elvis Presley,* Peter Guralnick, Little, Brown, 1994, p. 95.

195 **"I guess it's just something God gave me":** Ibid., p. 260.

196 **"You did not have to love them all to love the group":** *The Rolling Stone Illustrated History of Rock & Roll,* Jim Miller, ed., Random House/Rolling Stone Press, 1976, p. 182.

13. FREE AT LAST

208 **"Some got mad and some lost money":** *Time,* November 23, 1962.

14. DIG THE NEW BREED

214 **"kept me poor for several years":** *Paul and Joanne: A Biography of Paul Newman and Joanne Woodward,* Joe Morella and Edward Z. Epstein, Delacorte Press, 1988, p. 81.

219 **"How many times have you ever struck out with a woman?":** *Pictures at a Revolution: Five Movies and the Birth of the New Hollywood,* Mark Harris, Penguin, 2008, p. 237.

219 **"I thought, I'll work off-Broadway for the rest of my life":** Ibid., p. 273.

220 **"it's just a shame about the boy":** Ibid., p. 364.

222 **"I had been around long enough":** *Five Easy Decades: How Jack Nicholson Became the Biggest Movie Star in Modern Times,* Dennis McDougal, John Wiley and Sons, 2008, p. 104.

228 **"Let's be realistic here":** www.vintage-porn.us/vintage_pornstars.htm.

230 **"I never set out to create any image at all":** *The Unruly Life of Woody Allen,* Marion Meade, Scribner, 2000, p. 53.

232 **"fascist medievalism":** *New Yorker,* January 15, 1972.

233 **"the savage forced to follow the rules of society":** *Chicago Sun Times,* December 29, 1971.

234 **"I've learned that no matter what I say or do":** *Brando: Songs My Mother Taught Me,* Marlon Brando with Robert Lindsey, Random House, 1994, p. 145.

15. THE GLAMOUR BACKLASH

238 **"Bluto seemed natural":** *How Ronald Reagan Changed My Life,* Peter Robinson, Regan Books, 2003, p. 137.

239 **By the 1970s, according to one analyst, three-quarters of all moviegoers were under thirty:** *American Cinema/American Culture,* John Belton, McGraw-Hill, 1994, p. 290.

240 **"It was 1964–65":** *Harrison Ford: Imperfect Hero,* Garry Jenkins, Carol Publishing Group, 1998, p. 77.

240 **"Kurt Affair":** Ibid., p. 76.

240 **"type was out of style":** Ibid., p. 82.

242 **"He was by far the best":** Ibid., p. 119.

243 **"He's prickly but not a prick":** Ibid., p. 99.

244 **"Why don't we just shoot the fucker?":** Ibid., p. 165.

247 **a legendary backstage fistfight:** *Live from New York: An Uncensored History of "Saturday Night Live,"* Tom Shales and James Andrew Miller, Little, Brown, 2002, pp. 119–21.

251 **Every year since 1932, the Quigley Publishing Company:** www.quigleypublishing.com/MPalmanac/Top10/Top10_lists.html.

16. MACHINES AND MACHO MEN

260 **within six years there were ten thousand video stores across the country:** *Veni Vidi Video: The Hollywood Empire and the VCR,* Frederick Wasser, University of Texas Press, 2002, pp. 100–01.

260 **the source of half of all prerecorded-tape sales through the end of the 1970s:** Ibid., p. 93.

261 **VCR ownership soared:** Ibid., p. 50.

17. THE KIDS ARE ALL RIGHT

272 **"I felt like I had a way to express myself":** *People,* September 5, 1983.

18. MTV AND ITS DISCONTENTS

278 **In interviews, he'd talk about how kids:** *MTV: The Making of a Revolution,* Tom McGrath, Running Press, 1996, p. 48.

279 **You saw Rod Stewart and you got your hair cut like his:** Ibid., p. 70.

19. THE CORPORATE STAR

305 **"If there ever was an era when America wanted to see Meg Ryan naked":** http://www.ericdsnider.com/movies/in-the-cut/.

313 **an article wishfully titled "Big Girl Now":** *The New York Times Magazine,* March 27, 2011.

318 **"Fucking Jews":** *The New York Times,* July 30, 2006.

319 **"Do I *sound* like a homosexual?":** *El País,* December 1, 1991.

319 **"If you get raped by a pack":** *Guardian,* July 2, 2010.

20. PIXEL PERSONA

324 ***"THE TRUTH ABOUT MY NEW BODY":*** *People,* September 15, 2010.

326 **"When we saw the range of Christian's talents":** *Entertainment Weekly,* October 11, 1996.

335 **"in this age of fake reality TV":** voices.washingtonpost.com/postpartisan/2010/08/antoine_dodson_is_for_real_yal.html, August 8, 2010.

336 **"deliberately not commercialize the children":** (London) *Sun,* July 30, 2010.

339 **"storytelling enveloped in a great concept":** (Melbourne) *Age,* November 13, 2003.

342 **"She don't sing. She don't dance":** *The New York Times,* July 23, 2010.

345 **"the world's most famous movie star":** www.slate.com/articles/arts/culturebox/2004/04/cruise_control.html.

346 **"Nazi science":** *Entertainment Weekly,* June 8, 2005.

POSTSCRIPT: STAR DEATH

361 **In 2004, according to *Forbes* magazine:** *Forbes,* October 24, 2004.

361 **Per *Forbes*, the Elvis Presley estate made $55 million:** *Forbes,* October 27, 2009.

361 **Britney Spears made only $35 million:** *Forbes,* June 3, 2009.

361 **Michael Jackson made $90 million:** *Forbes,* October 27, 2009.

Bibliography

Austin, Thomas, and Martin Barker, eds. *Contemporary Hollywood Stardom.* Arnold, 2003.

Bach, Steven. *Marlene Dietrich: Life and Legend.* William Morrow, 1992.

Balio, Tino. *Grand Design: Hollywood as a Modern Business Enterprise, 1930–1939.* University of California Press, 1996.

Barnouw, Erik. *The Golden Web: A History of Broadcasting in the United States.* Oxford University Press, 1966–70.

———. *Tube of Plenty: The Evolution of American Television.* Oxford University Press, 1990.

Barris, Samantha. *Movie Crazy: Fans, Stars, and the Cult of the Celebrity.* Palgrave, 2001.

Basinger, Jeanine. *Silent Stars.* Alfred A. Knopf, 2000.

———. *The Star Machine.* Alfred A. Knopf, 2007.

Behlmer, Rudy, ed. *Memo from David O. Selznick.* Rev. ed. Samuel French, 1989.

Belton, John. *American Cinema/American Culture.* McGraw-Hill, 1994.

Black, Shirley Temple. *Child Star: An Autobiography.* McGraw-Hill, 1988.

Bosworth, Patricia. *Marlon Brando* (Penguin Lives). Viking, 2001.

Bowser, Eileen. *The Transformation of Cinema, 1907–1915*. University of California Press, 1994.

Brando, Marlon, with Robert Lindsey. *Brando: Songs My Mother Taught Me*. Random House, 1994.

Britton, Andrew. *Katharine Hepburn: Star as Feminist*. Studio Vista, 1995.

Brown, Gene. *Movie Time: A Chronology of Hollywood and the Movie Industry from Its Beginnings to the Present*. Macmillan, 1995.

Brown, Kelly R. *Florence Lawrence, the Biograph Girl: America's First Movie Star*. McFarland and Co., 1999.

Brown, Kelly R., and Steven J. Ross. *Working-Class Hollywood: Silent Film and the Shaping of Class in America*. Princeton University Press, 1999.

Brown, Robert J. *Manipulating the Ether: The Power of Broadcast Radio in Thirties America*. McFarland and Co., 1998.

Brownlow, Kevin. *The Parade's Gone By*. Knopf, 1968.

Butsch, Richard. *The Making of American Audiences: From Stage to Television, 1750–1990*. Cambridge University Press, 2000.

Cagney, James. *Cagney by Cagney*. Doubleday, 1976.

Chaplin, Charles. *My Autobiography*. Simon and Schuster, 1964.

Clarens, Carlos. *Crime Movies*. Norton, 1980/Da Capo Press, 1997.

Corey, Melinda, and George Ochoa. *The American Film Institute Desk Reference*. Dorling Kindersley, 2002.

Crafton, Donald. *The Talkies: American Cinema's Transition to Sound, 1926–1931*. University of California Press, 1999.

Dardis, Tom. *Keaton: The Man Who Wouldn't Lie Down*. Andre Deutsch, 1979.

Davis, Ronald L. *The Glamour Factory: Inside Hollywood's Big Studio System*. Southern Methodist University Press, 1993.

deCordova, Richard. *Picture Personalities: The Emergence of the Star System in America*. University of Illinois Press, 1990.

Dewey, Donald. *James Stewart*. Turner Publishing, 1996.

DiBattista, Maria. *Fast-Talking Dames*. Yale University Press, 2001.

Doherty, Thomas. *Pre-Code Hollywood: Sex, Immorality, and Insurrection in American Cinema 1930–1934*. Columbia University Press, 1999.

———. *Teenagers and Teenpics: The Juvenilization of American Movies in the 1950s*. Temple University Press, 2002.

Douglas, Susan J. *Inventing American Broadcasting, 1899–1922*. Johns Hopkins University Press, 1987.

———. *Listening In: Radio and the American Imagination*. Times Books, 1999.

Dyer, Richard. *Heavenly Bodies: Film Stars and Society*. Routledge, 2004.

Edgerton, Gary R. *The Columbia History of American Television*. Columbia University Press, 2007.

Edwards, Anne. *Shirley Temple: American Princess*. William Morrow, 1988.

Eliot, Marc. *Cary Grant*. Harmony, 2004.

Everson, William K. *American Silent Film*. Oxford University Press, 1978/ Da Capo, 1998.

Eyman, Scott. *The Speed of Sound: Hollywood and the Talkie Revolution, 1926–1930*. Johns Hopkins University Press, 1999.

Flamini, Roland. *Scarlett, Rhett, and a Cast of Thousands: The Filming of "Gone With the Wind."* Macmillan, 1975.

Fountain, Leatrice Gilbert, with John R. Maxim. *Dark Star*. St. Martin's Press, 1985.

Fowles, Jib. *Starstruck: Celebrity Performers and the American Public*. Smithsonian, 1992.

Freedland, Michael. *Fred Astaire*. W. H. Allen, 1976.

Friedrich, Otto. *City of Nets: A Portrait of Hollywood in the 1940s*. Harper and Row, 1986.

Gabler, Neal. *An Empire of Their Own: How the Jews Invented Hollywood*. Crown, 1988.

Gish, Lillian, with Ann Pinchot. *The Movies, Mr. Griffith, and Me*. Prentice-Hall, 1969.

Guralnick, Peter. *Last Train to Memphis: The Rise of Elvis Presley*. Little, Brown, 1994.

Hadleigh, Boze. *Conversations with My Elders*. St. Martin's Press, 1986.

Hampton, Benjamin. *History of the American Film Industry: From Its Beginnings to 1931*. Dover, 1970.

Harris, Mark. *Pictures at a Revolution: Five Movies and the Birth of the New Hollywood*. Penguin, 2008.

Harvey, James. *Movie Love in the Fifties*. Alfred A. Knopf, 2001.

Haskell, Molly. *Frankly, My Dear: "Gone With the Wind" Revisited*. Yale University Press, 2009.

Hay, Peter. *MGM: When the Lion Roars.* Turner Publishing, 1991.

Hayes, Kevin J., ed. *Charlie Chaplin: Interviews.* University Press of Mississippi, 2005.

Higashi, Sumiko. *Cecil B. DeMille and American Culture: The Silent Era.* University of California Press, 1994.

Hilmes, Michele. *Radio Voices: American Broadcasting, 1922–1952.* University of Minnesota Press, 1997.

Hirsch, Foster. *Acting Hollywood Style.* AFI Press, 1991.

Hodges, Graham Russell Gao. *Anna May Wong.* Palgrave Macmillan, 2004.

Irwin, Will. *The House That Shadows Built: The Story of Adolph Zukor and His Circle.* Doubleday, Doran and Co., 1928.

Jacobs, Lea. *The Wages of Sin: Censorship and the Fallen Woman Film, 1928–1942.* University of Wisconsin Press, 1991.

Jenkins, Garry. *Harrison Ford: Imperfect Hero.* Carol Publishing Group, 1998.

Kazan, Elia. *Elia Kazan: A Life.* Knopf, 1988.

Kisselloff, Jeff. *The Box: An Oral History of Television 1920–1961.* Viking, 1995.

Kobal, John. *People Will Talk.* Alfred A. Knopf, 1985.

Kobel, Peter, and the Library of Congress. *Silent Movies: The Birth of Film and the Triumph of Movie Culture.* Little, Brown and Co., 2007.

Koppes, Clayton R., and Gregory D. Black. *Hollywood Goes to War: How Politics, Profits, and Propaganda Shaped World War II Movies.* Free Press, 1987.

Koszarski, Richard. *An Evening's Entertainment: The Age of the Silent Feature Picture, 1915–1928.* University of California Press, 1994.

Lally, Kevin. *Wilder Times: The Life of Billy Wilder.* Henry Holt and Co., 1996.

LaSalle, Mick. *Complicated Women: Sex and Power in Pre-Code Hollywood.* Thomas Dunne Books, 2000.

Lasky, Betty. *RKO: The Biggest Little Major of Them All.* Prentice-Hall, 1984.

Leaming, Barbara. *Katharine Hepburn.* Crown, 1995.

Leff, Leonard J., and Jerold L. Simmons. *The Dame in the Kimono: Hollywood, Censorship, and the Production Code from the 1920s to the 1960s.* Grove Weidenfeld, 1990.

Leider, Emily Wortis. *Becoming Mae West.* Farrar Straus Giroux, 1997.

Lindsay, Cynthia. *Dear Boris: The Life of William Henry Pratt A.K.A. Boris Karloff.* Knopf, 1975.

Loos, Anita. *The Talmadge Girls.* Viking, 1978.

Louvish, Simon. *Keystone: The Life and Clowns of Mack Sennett.* Faber and Faber, 2003.

———. *Mae West: It Ain't No Sin.* St. Martin's Press, 2006.

Lynn, Kenneth S. *Charlie Chaplin and His Times.* Cooper Square Press, 2002.

MacCann, Richard Dyer. *The First Tycoons.* Scarecrow Press, 1987.

———. *The Silent Screen.* Scarecrow Press, 1997.

———. *The Stars Appear.* Scarecrow Press, 1992.

MacDonald, J. Fred. *Don't Touch That Dial!: Radio Programming in American Life, 1920–1960.* Nelson-Hall, 1979.

Mailer, Norman. *Marilyn: A Biography.* Grosset and Dunlap, 1973.

Manso, Peter. *Brando.* Hyperion, 1994.

Marsh, Mae. *Screen Acting.* Frederick A. Stokes Co., 1921.

Mast, Gerald. *The Movies in Our Midst.* University of Chicago Press, 1983.

McCabe, John. *Cagney.* Alfred A. Knopf, 1997.

McDonough, Yona Zeldis, ed. *All the Available Light: A Marilyn Monroe Reader.* Touchstone, 2002.

McDougal, Dennis. *Five Easy Decades: How Jack Nicholson Became the Biggest Movie Star in Modern Times.* John Wiley and Sons, 2008.

McGilligan, Patrick. *George Cukor: A Double Life.* HarperCollins, 1991.

McGrath, Tom. *MTV: The Making of a Revolution.* Running Press, 1996.

Meade, Marion. *The Unruly Life of Woody Allen.* Scribner, 2000.

Miller, Jim, ed. *The Rolling Stone Illustrated History of Rock & Roll.* Random House/Rolling Stone Press, 1976.

Mordden, Ethan. *The Hollywood Studios: House Style in the Golden Age of the Movies.* Knopf, 1988.

———. *Movie Star: A Look at the Women Who Made Hollywood.* St. Martin's, 1983.

Morella, Joe, and Edward Z. Epstein. *Paul and Joanne: A Biography of Paul Newman and Joanne Woodward.* Delacorte Press, 1988.

Mosely, Leonard. *Zanuck: The Rise and Fall of Hollywood's Last Tycoon.* McGraw-Hill, 1984.

Musser, Charles. *The Emergence of Cinema: The American Screen to 1907*. University of California Press, 1994.

Nachman, Gerald. *Raised on Radio*. Pantheon, 1998.

Niven, David. *Bring On the Empty Horses*. Putnam, 1975.

Oppenheimer, Jerry, and Jack Vitek. *Idol: Rock Hudson*. Villard Books, 1986.

Parish, James Robert, and Ronald L. Bowers. *The MGM Stock Company: The Golden Era*. Bonanza, 1977.

Peary, Danny, ed. *Close-Ups: Intimate Profiles of Movie Stars by Their Costars, Directors, Screenwriters, and Friends*. Workman, 1978.

Ramsaye, Terry. *A Million and One Nights*. Simon and Schuster, 1964.

Redmond, Sean, and Su Holmes. *Stardom and Celebrity: A Reader*. Sage Publications, 2007.

Robinson, David. *Chaplin: His Life and Art*. McGraw Hill, 1985.

Robinson, Peter. *How Ronald Reagan Changed My Life*. Regan Books, 2003.

Ross, Steven J. *Working-Class Hollywood: Silent Film and the Shaping of Class in America*. Princeton University Press, 1999.

Schatz, Thomas. *Boom and Bust: American Cinema in the 1940s*. University of California Press, 1999.

———. *The Genius of the System: Hollywood Filmmaking in the Studio Era*. Pantheon, 1989.

Schickel, Richard, ed. *The Essential Chaplin: Perspectives on the Life and Art of the Great Comedian*. Ivan R. Dee, 2006.

Settel, Irving. *A Pictorial History of Radio*. Grosset and Dunlap, 1967.

Shales, Tom, and James Andrew Miller. *Live from New York: An Uncensored History of "Saturday Night Live."* Little, Brown, 2002.

Sharp, Kathleen. *Mr. & Mrs. Hollywood: Edie and Lew Wasserman and Their Entertainment Empire*. Carroll and Graf, 2003.

Shipman, David. *The Great Movie Stars: The Golden Years*. Little, Brown, 1995.

———. *The Great Movie Stars: The International Years*. Little, Brown, 1995.

———. *Movie Talk: Who Said What About Whom in the Movies*. St. Martin's Press, 1988.

Sikov, Ed. *Dark Victory: The Life of Bette Davis*. Henry Holt and Co., 2007.

———. *On Sunset Boulevard: The Life and Times of Billy Wilder.* Hyperion, 1998.

Sklar, Robert. *Movie-Made America: A Cultural History of American Movies.* Chappell and Co., 1978.

Sperling, Cass Warner, and Cork Millner, with Jack Warner Jr. *Hollywood Be Thy Name: The Warner Brothers Story.* Prima Publishing, 1994.

Steinem, Gloria. *Marilyn: Norma Jean.* Signet, 1988.

Stine, Whitney, and Bette Davis. *Mother Goddam: The Story of the Career of Bette Davis.* Hawthorn Books, 1974.

Swanson, Gloria. *Swanson on Swanson.* Random House, 1980.

Thomson, David. *The New Biographical Dictionary of Film.* 4th ed. Knopf, 2004.

———. *Showman: The Life of David O. Selznick.* Alfred A. Knopf, 1992.

———. *The Whole Equation: A History of Hollywood.* Alfred A. Knopf, 2005.

Tornabene, Lyn. *Long Live the King: A Biography of Clark Gable.* Putnam, 1976.

Vineberg, Steve. *High Comedy in American Movies: Class and Humor from the 1920s to the Present.* Rowman and Littlefield, 2005.

Wagenknecht, Edward. *The Movies in the Age of Innocence.* Limelight Editions, 1997.

———. *Stars of the Silents.* Scarecrow Press, 1987.

Walker, Alexander. *The Shattered Silents: How the Talkies Came to Stay.* William Morrow, 1978.

Wasser, Frederick. *Veni Vidi Video: The Hollywood Empire and the VCR.* University of Texas Press, 2002.

Wayne, Jane Ellen. *The Golden Girls of MGM.* Carroll and Graf Publishers, 2002.

Whitfield, Eileen. *Pickford: The Woman Who Made Hollywood.* University Press of Kentucky, 1997 and 2007.

Youngkin, Stephen D. *The Lost One: A Life of Peter Lorre.* University Press of Kentucky, 2005.

Zukor, Adolph, with Dale Kramer. *The Public Is Never Wrong: The Autobiography of Adolph Zukor.* Putnam, 1953.

Index

ABOUT THE AUTHOR

Ty Burr is the film critic for *The Boston Globe* and the author of *The Best Old Movies for Families: A Guide to Watching Together.* He has written about movies and popular culture for *Entertainment Weekly*, *The New York Times*, and many other publications. He estimates that, after forty years of serious movie watching, he has seen on the order of 14,600 films. On a good day, he remembers half of them.

A NOTE ON THE TYPE

This book was set in Caledonia, a Linotype face designed by W. A. Dwiggins (1880–1956). It belongs to the family of printing types called "modern face" by printers—a term used to mark the change in style of the type letters that occurred around 1800. Caledonia borders on the general design of Scotch Roman but it is more freely drawn than that letter.

Composed by North Market Street Graphics

Printed and bound by Berryville Graphics

Designed by Iris Weinstein